# Well-Being
## and Higher Education

Bringing
Theory to
Practice

1818 R Street NW, Washington, DC 20009

ISBN 978-0-9853088-6-5

# Well-Being
## and Higher Education

**A Strategy for Change
and the Realization of
Education's Greater Purposes**

Edited by Donald W. Harward
*Bringing Theory to Practice*
Washington D.C.

# TABLE OF CONTENTS

*Continued next page*

# Table of Contents

# TABLE OF CONTENTS

## PART 4   The Logic of Change: Why, What, and How?

# Acknowledgements

## *Donald W. Harward*

*Well-Being and Higher Education: A Strategy for Change and the Realization of Education's Greater Purposes* emphasizes the integration of the work of Bringing Theory to Practice (BTtoP) and the more than 500 campus grants, which over the last 15 years, have collaborated in accomplishing that work and advancing the greater and intertwined purposes of higher education: engaged learning, well-being, civic purpose, and preparation for living meaningfully in the world.

With the support of co-founder Sally Engelhard Pingree, the unflagging encouragement of Julie Johnson Kidd and the Endeavor Foundation, and the assistance of steadfast colleagues Jill Reich, Ashley Finley, Barry Checkoway, Lee Knefelkamp, Jennifer O'Brien, and Caitlin Salins, the BTtoP Project has supported—and benefitted from—scores of scholars, campus leaders, association and foundation leaders, public intellectuals, practitioners, and many others who participate in and support higher education. Those contributions have been captured in the integrated emphases of the project and the major publications that have been produced.

*Transforming Undergraduate Education* (2012) explored how an understanding and practice of engaged learning connected to civic engagement and to how that connection was essential to higher education's mission. The five volume *Civic Series* (2012–2014) developed that thesis with multiple essays focused on more specific consideration of analysis, implications, and practices. Campus grants and the provision of the essays in the *Series* as downloadable without charge enabled thousands of uses of the monographs by campuses and independent civic groups to provoke conversations and then actions—asserting why and how learning and the civic are essentially connected.

Inextricably linked, and demonstrable as a core dimension of the greater purposes of higher education, this volume, *Well-Being and Higher Education*, brings to fruition a greater depth and clarity regarding the necessary connections of learning and well-being. This volume makes the persuasive and compelling case that institutional changes that result from an attention to well-being are essential to fulfilling the promise of higher education.

The essays in the volume could each stand alone. They reflect multiple insights and serve intentionally to provoke further discussion, consideration, and evidentiary support. Even when inclusive and thorough, the essays are windows, not boundaries.

I am particularly grateful for the patient and insightful professional editing assistance of Caitlin Salins and Jennifer O'Brien; of Liz Clark's superb work of design and layout, greatly aided by her colleague Diane Buric; and of Angie Hartley, whose careful eye and skill with assuring consistency with Chicago Style added to the quality of the volume.

## About the Editor

Donald W. Harward is president emeritus of Bates College in Lewiston, Maine. Since 2002, when he cofounded the Bringing Theory to Practice Project, he has been its director.

# Sally Engelhard Pingree

*Well-Being and Higher Education* is the product of years of dedicated efforts on the part of Don Harward and our colleagues, all of whom believe as we do in the promise of higher education to advance its greater purposes, including affecting the lives of its participants—their well-being.

For the last fourteen years, Bringing Theory to Practice (BTtoP) has worked with generous and creative colleagues to allow the project to come alive—in word in publications and in deed in campus actions. The strategy has been to use institutional and academic strengths of engagement—opportunities and expectations— to gain positive and confirmable effects on the learning, behaviors, and lives of students.

Resources from the Charles Engelhard Foundation, from Julie J. Kidd and the Endeavor Foundation, and from many others have provided over the last decade multiple opportunities for research, campus projects, conferences, and workshops linking forms of intensive academic learning, civic development, and the well-being of students. Attending to the well-being of those involved—students, faculty, staff, and community—has not only raised the full and greater purposes of higher education to the fore, it has also signaled a strategy for helping institutions of all types make the changes, often transformative changes, that they determine necessary to fulfill their mission of learning and discovery and their commitment to the wholeness of the lives of their students.

That is what has inspired me. And as co-founder and a supporter of BTtoP, I want to thank all of those who have made our work possible and useful, and I want to especially congratulate the scholars and practitioners who have made such insightful contributions to this important volume. It will be among the most significant, comprehensive, and helpful resources for the many within and outside the academy who seek to support and extend higher education's full promise.

# FOREWORD

## *Julie Kidd*

When I first entered college in the fall of 1963, and for three but only three years thereafter, parietal hours still existed. The dormitories were single sex though the college was co-educational. Freshmen women were required to be in their dorms by nine o'clock except on Friday nights when ten o'clock was the curfew, and on Saturday nights when eleven o'clock was the curfew. Those restrictions were increased by one hour during each of the following years. Each of the women's dorms had a house mother, and she saw to it that the doors were locked at the time of curfew. While all of us found this limiting, there were times when each and every one of us was glad to fall back on these rules. Colleges in those days were in loco parentis. They felt that they were responsible for the well-being of each student, and they took this responsibility very seriously.

In that era, students were not considered adults the minute they entered college but rather were thought of more in terms of emerging adulthood. Educators and society at large did not think or act as if there was a magic cut-off age of eighteen at which a young person was fully formed and ready to assume the full mantle of adulthood. College was a time to pair one's emerging sense of identity and value system with what was being learned in the classroom: the intellectually broadening and enriching experience of studying within the liberal arts tradition. In this tradition the student learned what the great philosophers of the past and present had thought about the unanswerable questions of life; how the great

writers, artists and musicians had expressed the emotions of life along with their reactions to the milieu around them; how the study of history illuminated the politics of the current day and the pitfalls to be avoided; and what the scientists had so far learned about our world and how they had done so. It was well understood at that time that the emotional and intellectual development of students were inextricably intertwined and that it was the responsibility of the college to create a milieu in which the intellectual and personal development of its students were that to which attention was devoted. While the means to accomplish this objective may have been too restrictive and the connections between classroom and social life too vague and unexplored, nonetheless, the commitment was there.

In the fall of 1966 when I returned to campus for my senior year, all that had changed. There were no more parietal hours of any kind, no more house mothers, and the sheath dresses and heels that my roommate and I wore to the first play of the year were clearly yesterday's mode of dress. We were suddenly surrounded with jeans and sneakers. Yes, it was that stark. We were seniors, though, and accustomed to conducting ourselves in a certain manner and continued in that mode. The common lounges in the dorms remained elegantly furnished and so their quality remained respected. We also retained the sense of respect and refinement with which we had come to view our lives and our soon-to-come place in the adult world.

Of course, given the deeply disturbing spectacle of the Vietnam War and the gathering momentum of the Civil Rights Movement, students chafed at the neat little world that was the college of the late 1960s and demanded freedom from the perspectives of the generation that was sending them to a senseless war and suppressing and treating unjustly an entire race of people. Unfortunately, though, in response, the baby was thrown out with the bath water.

When I returned to my alma mater as a trustee in 1975, the elegant common lounges were gone. The rooms were still there but instead of the Persian rugs and antique furniture with which students had formerly lived, these spaces were occupied by battered and cheap furniture, sloppily arranged, with no rugs on the floor or artwork on the walls. Also gone was the commitment of the college to the well-being of the student as a whole person.

Today, I believe that we must reassert that commitment. By now the world has become ever so much more complex and challenging, and we all struggle to maintain our balance with an ever-shifting foundation beneath our feet. I do not regret the cultural progress that led to this complexity or advocate a return to parietal hours and single-sex dorms as a means of assisting young people to find a basic sense of well-being. I advocate instead for the principle of well-being as a core purpose of higher education— a principle that would seem intrinsic to this cultural progression and yet appears largely lost in the infrastructure of the academy. The modern world of higher education must find new ways to reclaim this mission and assert the iron

link between classroom learning and personal development if humankind is to become a positive form of life on this planet and if personal contentment and fulfillment are to become part of each individual's experience.

To this effort, Bringing Theory to Practice has been dedicated for the past fifteen years and has made significant contributions, against difficult odds, to restoring the link between learning and well-being. This volume contains much of the best thinking on this subject in the world today. The ideas, methods, and perspectives this volume conveys will be invaluable tools as our institutions of higher learning hopefully move together as one body with one voice to place in proper relief the power and beauty of an education meant for a more far-reaching and greater purpose than only the conveyance of skills and knowledge.

# Introduction

# Well-being Essays and Provocations: Significance and Implications for Higher Education

*Donald W. Harward*

*Welcome to this collection of essays.*

You have most likely encountered in recent print and in discourse numerous mentions of well-being, perhaps including some similar to the following quotes and contexts:

- "... we are studying the well-being of people around the world. Our research reinforces the fact that the ultimate outcome of an education is fundamentally about well-being."[1]
- "Gauging people's well-being is one of the central political issues of our time. It is time we admitted that there is more to life than money and it's time we focused not just on GDP but on GWB—general well-being."[2]
- A philosophical or historical tracing might reveal that the notion of well-being is not peripheral—rather it has been and continues to be a nuanced concept at the very core of Platonism, Aristotelianism, the work of Cicero, the explorations of its relation to pleasure in Stoicism, Bentham, the Utilitarian tradition and J.S. Mill, the heart of the Enlightenment and Humanism, the work of Dewey, contemporary pragmatism, and such recent moral and political Theorists as Nozick and Rawls.[3]
- Improving higher education means focusing on the quality of a student's relationships . . . [I]f the ultimate purpose is the individual wholeness, flourishing, sense of direction and agency [well-being], then the various practical applications of liberal learning are—or should be—woven together in the person of the student.[4]

In contrast to the frequency of multiple references to well-being, however, there has been only modest consideration given to its connection to higher education—what that connection means, what it suggests, and why it is important. This collection of essays offers to explicate and convince why attending to well-being and understanding its complexity is to realize a fundamental dimension of the purpose of higher education—a dimension so connected to learning and its associated outcomes as to be rooted in a shared analysis of their meaning.

Well-being and higher education are connected, and those connections matter. They matter for the individual lives of the student and those who teach; they matter for the institution; they matter for the promise of a democratic civic society; and they matter for whether or not the unique and full promise of higher education—its greater purposes—can be advanced and realized. Analyses of the meanings of well-being, their multiple expressions or manifestations that affect learning, and what institutions must do to facilitate greater connections among them point to the direction of changes that will make possible the recognition and the realization of well-being as a dimension of the greater purpose of higher education and to the wholeness of those participating.

That there has been scant attention given to an adequate theoretical foundation that connects learning and well-being has meant that well-being has often been dismissed as "not what we are about" within the college or university or has been set aside to the periphery—theoretically disconnected and thereby structurally disconnected to the core purposes of higher education. The essays in this volume offer redress, provide a theoretical basis with which to explore the essential connections of learning and well-being, and point to the evidence that confirms those connections.[5]

Initiating a more theoretical framework begins by finding reference to well-being nearly ubiquitous in those writings in which the authors consider the ultimate questions of a purpose for "the good life." Whether it is found in Aristotle's *Nicomachean Ethics, or the Journal of Personality and Social Psychology*—whether it is found in the Declaration of Independence, the UN Universal Declaration of Human Rights, or the parent extolling the core hope for her child—it is the pursuit, hopefully the gaining, of happiness and well-being found across time and across cultures that is the objective of the life well-lived. It is not wealth, or power, or superior gain in competition, but happiness—well-being!

## DEFINING WELL-BEING

If it is to be more than a frequent and easy figure of speech, what does well-being mean? Happiness, well-being, can be framed conceptually as a complex construct but one that is analyzable. It can be parsed, and a nuanced understanding of its complexity can be presented. Framing the examination of well-being as conceptual is important. Its full analysis reflects a necessary conceptual connection to learning, to the knowledge and discovery purposes of the college or university—regardless of the scope of the course or tutorial, regardless of whether the context is academic or student affairs, regardless of where it is expressed in the curriculum, in pedagogy, or in the institution's structure or priorities.

Like the construct *the weather* (which allows reference to multiple meanings—rain or shine, storm or calm), there is no specific, single designation or referent for *well-being*. Rather, there is a weave of meaning, a braid-like connection of uses with no one thread running throughout. Each thread (among them, for example, purposefulness, identity, flourishing, mindfulness, a sense of belonging, grit and persistence, which themselves are often complex and without a single common referent) in such a weave emphasizes dimensions of meaning—uses that fits a context—and provides an opportunity for analysis and understanding. The braid of well-being intersects with that of health, for health too is a complex construct.[6]

The braid of uses of the languages of health, physical or mental, is most often positive, not diagnostic. Health is not the absence of something, such as pain or suffering. *Health* and *illness* are not oppositional terms of a common category. *Illness* is the language of diagnosis, limitation, even foreboding. *Health* is characterized by flourishing, by wellness—beyond feelings or emotive states of pleasure—to being well, being aware of identity, of one's commitment to the integrity of others, to persisting, and to being resilient. Being well can characterize a person or a community, an economy (supplementing GNP), or social and political vitality, and it can be used as the criterion for determining public policy objectives (see the J. Bronsteen's essay).

Recognizing well-being as a construct—not as a concept with a single referent—is to understand that well-being has two major emphases or dimensions, each manifest in particular contexts or traditions of use. The *hedonic* tradition emphasizes well-being as *feelings*—non-cognitive expressions referring to an individual's (or a community's) special state, experience, or condition—all of which can be discerned and measured. In the hedonic tradition, well-being or happiness is real in the only sense that anything is real—it is an item of empirical study (see the J. Pawelski and S. Dahill-Brown & E. Jayawickreme essays). The *eudaemonic* is an alternative tradition that contends that well-being may be understood not as a feeling, or a mental act, or even a state of mind, but as a relational activity (a long term practice) of being well—even being fully well, or more fully human, as in a *life well-lived* (see the C. Ryff, E. Minnich, W. Sullivan, and C. Keyes essays).

Both of the traditions of analysis of the strands of meaning of well-being have direct bearing on higher education—their relevance to the campus culture, and the power of that culture to provide transforming opportunities for those participating. Seeing well-being as inextricably connected to learning is to see that both dimensions or emphases of well-being are relevant—the hedonic because it captures occasions for the stimulation and receptivity of feelings that reinforce participation in learning opportunities and the eudaemonic because it is at the core of what learning means.

It is this second dimension that is often overlooked but is essential. It is this connection of well-being to learning that is found in their sharing of a fundamental analytic feature of being *relational* and not simply descriptive. Learning, or coming to know, is essentially a relational concept. An agent (learner) stands in relation to an object of inquiry (for example, a fact, or a state of affairs, or an experience). The relation is not a description of special acts or feelings; rather it is the *occasion of engagement*. This engagement may or may not subsequently involve acts (such as memory or judgment, contemplation, or the repetition of a pattern of acts and behaviors—e.g., acquiring a skill), but it is not itself an act. It is the complex relation of being engaged with. It is learner in relation to object, learner being engaged, learner as agent in the midst of multiple learning opportunities that is at the core of the analysis. What and whether such engagement results in subsequent memories or behaviors (Did she remember the sequence of English kings? Did he learn how to serve in tennis?) can be assessed, but the relationship is distinct from those effects.

Whether it is learning something or learning how to do something, the analysis of learning involves a relationship—that of engagement—and the outcomes of those occasions of engagement may be acts or behaviors. Standing in relation to an object (what is *other*, some object independent of learner) brings with it self-awareness as well as the responsibility to honor and preserve the integrity of other, be it fact, person, community, or nature.

These features are what separate our being learners from the rat in the maze or the machine's software. We are self-aware of our learning, and we can make the judgment to honor the integrity of (i.e., value or respect and want to sustain) what it is that serves as object and our relationship to it.

Well-being and learning, each a complex construction, are both in part relational concepts—the nexus of their connection is in engagement—learner to object, learner to respect for the integrity of other. And standing in relation to other requires self-awareness—recognition that *I am engaged; it is I, an agent, so engaged*—that can link learning to self-identity, to being purposeful and whole. Learning, whether in the classroom, the lab, or the community,

> *Seeing well-being as inextricably connected to learning is to see that both dimensions or emphases of well-being are relevant— the hedonic because it captures occasions for the stimulation and receptivity of feelings that reinforce participation in learning opportunities and the eudaemonic because it is at the core of what learning means*

is an opportunity to be engaged, and it is equally an opportunity to support the learner's well-being. They are inextricably connected.[7]

There are occasions in which it is clear that well-being, in its hedonic dimension, describes feelings, and in doing so does reinforce, even make possible, profound learning experiences and the willingness, the disposition, of the learner to participate or engage. The student who has her contribution to the class discussion honored may have an immediate feeling of belonging—"I do belong here"—that is indeed a most important well-being *feeling* directly connected to engaged learning. Such a feeling has duration, intensity, and can be compared to other feelings (see T. Seifert's essay). Understanding some dimensions of well-being as feelings or states—because as feelings they have demonstrable, often immediate, effects—helps to understand why some students persist and others do not. Receiving commendation is connected to a feeling of acceptance, even self-efficacy. Those feelings (see J. Pawelski's essay) of belonging are identified by empirical positive psychology as a key to *grit* or a willingness to progress. They are well documented in the scientific literature (see the S. Dahill-Brown & E. Jayawickreme essay) and have become a part of popular culture as captured in the metaphoric musical lyric *walk on* (persist, keep going) *with hope in your heart* (feel hopeful) *and you are on a path to happiness* (well-being).

To sum up, the argument is that learning and well-being are complex constructs connected by an analysis of what they mean—not peripheral or accidental but core and essential. We go deeper in understanding them by considering their relational dimensions. Those connections, how to draw and sustain them in multiple and frequent opportunities, and how to encourage agency and participation in those opportunities can define a campus culture that attends to whole persons.

MAKING THE CASE FOR ATTENDING TO WELL-BEING IN HIGHER EDUCATION
Regardless of interpretations of the complexities of well-being or learning, critics may reply, "my well-being is my responsibility, not the college's" and "my learning is my responsibility, not the college's." If both are correct, what *is* the college's responsibility or role? What connects well-being and engaged forms of learning to higher educational institutions—their structure, their curricula, their practiced pedagogies? Where are they found? How is their importance promoted as essential, not accidental? What links individual, institutional, and community well-being?

If students choose to free themselves, emancipate themselves from ignorance, prejudice, or conventionality, the institution must create the context in which they can choose to learn, to engage, and to be well. The academy and the public at-large can champion the expectation that institutions make the changes needed to realize well-being as among their greater purposes, to understand the connections to the civic and to the preparation for meaningful life-choices (including but not limited to work), and to make explicit their direct connection to learning in any discipline, with any pedagogy. Clarifying purpose may be necessary, but it is not sufficient for making change. The hard part is hard! It requires re-directing resources and re-aligning priorities. But while hard, it is not mysterious. Attention to well-being and its multiple connections to learning and being fully whole can begin the campus conversations needed to initiate collective interest in change. And it is now—in this period of challenge regarding what the future of higher education must be—that it is timely to do so.

Attending to well-being is not a therapy for those who are ill. Attending to well-being is to realize a fundamental dimension of the purpose of higher education! And it is the unique responsibility of higher education to provide the multiple opportunities for the manifestation of greater purpose. Beyond schooling and acculturation, *higher* education is the context that most clearly reveals the interdependency of learning and the civic, the paths for realization of self and its dependency on other, as well as skills and values connected to work and service, leadership and meaningful life choices. It is the unique role, responsibility, of higher education—not the family, church, social club, or training—to serve that function.

*Attending to well-being is to realize a fundamental dimension of the purpose of higher education!*

Attending to the multiple strands of meaning of well-being for all students, privileged or underserved, regardless of how the opportunities are crafted in institutions of varying type, has documentable results. It directly connects to student persistence, the development of clearer senses of purpose for all constituencies, as well as emphases on feeling valued, and succeeding. Honoring the well-being of all of our students can be a core motivation to provide access to higher education (see the L. Schreiner essay). What facilitates well-being at De Anza Community College (see B. Murphy's essay) and generates for most of its first generation students a developing sense of agency and civic awareness may not be what facilitates the sense of purposefulness and resilience gained at a different institution which requires a senior thesis or expects that students participate in international study, but each is honoring and facilitating the well-being of its students.

THE OVERARCHING CHALLENGE OF PURPOSE

Many contend that higher education's purpose is essentially utilitarian—that if the purpose of higher education means anything at all in the 21st century, it means that institutions must emphasize forms of learning that can be efficiently expressed with uses of technology and information transfer modalities. Higher education must provide the information, skills, and credentials needed for success in the work place. In this view, disruptive forces (technological, social, economic, and demographic) will insist that higher education provide a *fix* for this societal need, or higher education as we know it should disappear.[8]

Others claim that the distressing evidence of the devolving weaknesses of higher education is to be found in its retreat from its unique purpose in an open society to be counter-normative—to be critical, if not contrarian, of convention. They contend that higher education has become mute on real social problems and is now the handmaiden of a corporate culture—considering students as customers, faculty as labor (service providers), and in which ultimately, individual gain is prized over any public good.[9]

Each of these firmly held contentions regarding purpose is partially on target—but only partially. A full response to the overarching challenge of "What ought the purpose of higher education be in the 21st century?" could be: a renaissance of attention to the whole—the full and greater purposes of higher education, the inextricable connections among them, and the identification of their sources in the opportunities and culture of engagement unique to and inherent in higher education. The outcomes of each core purpose are linked to learning; to civic development; to preparation for meaningful life choices and values, including work; and to self-realization, identity, purposefulness, and well-being (see Figure 1). Determining learning outcomes involves consideration of well-being and civic outcomes; they are linked in meaning and in practice.

Amidst the clamor is the need to recognize well-being as an inextricable, but not sole, dimension of higher education's greater purpose. We know that on any campus, a strategy of attending to well-being by participation in engaged forms of learning could be emphasized, opportunities made available, and expectations met (see the H. Elmendorf, J. Riley, and N. Lucas & P. Rogers essays; J. Wilson addresses a special institutional mission). The individual learner could be valued as a whole person. If the campus exhibits clear commitments to what is beyond it—to some notion of public good or social justice—then evidence confirms that a measurably greater expression of participants' learning, their civic development, and their preparation for making meaningful life choices, including purposeful work, can be realized.[10]

Colleges and universities can (and many do) take advantage of hard-earned achievements in curricula development, in deep-learning pedagogies, and in strengthening the complexity and diversity of their populations. As reflected in the hundreds of campuses that are recipients of small grants from Bringing Theory to Practice and that subsequently report the data of their initiatives and persisting work, if supported, faculty and staff want to broaden and deepen what it means to be engaged with persons and communities, ideas and discoveries, the crafted and the natural environment, in and out of classroom, directly and with the use of artifacts and technology. They want to provide multiple, intentional opportunities for engaged learning experiences and a campus culture that expects involvement, including opportunities for participants to realize a deeper understanding of the connection of learning to action. And if they are respected, valued for what they bring to the relationship, and encouraged and expected to engage, students will encounter their own individual identities and agencies, grasp their obligations beyond themselves to a greater good, take risks and have the resilience to try again, gain their own sense of purposefulness, and flourish (see T. Seifert's and C. Ryff's essays).

*If they are respected, valued for what they bring to the relationship, and encouraged and expected to engage, students will encounter their own individual identities and agencies, grasp their obligations beyond themselves to a greater good, take risks and have the resilience to try again, gain their own sense of purposefulness, and flourish*

Students can be told that this is the purpose, that this is what the mission and vision of the institution promise them. But for how many is the promise empty? Perhaps for reasons that they did not choose to or were not expected to engage, higher education could seem to many learners empty and hollow save for the acquisition of the credential. One can assume that many students conclude: *If that's all it is, I'll get it for the cheapest cost or effort. I'll find the least burdensome route to the credential.*[11]

Realizing and connecting purposes is not asking campuses to add on or to do more; it is asking them to *be* more. It is asking them to be intentional regarding a renaissance of full purpose—re-distributing resources, altering expectations, and realigning practices and priorities so that learning opportunities are maximized and engagement is expected and supported. A more meaningful understanding of costs would follow. Being respectful of the intensity of a need to lower costs does not require lowering quality. What is required is agreement to debunk the either-or mindset. A call to the renaissance of full purpose is

Figure 1.

THE GREATER PURPOSES OF HIGHER EDUCATION.

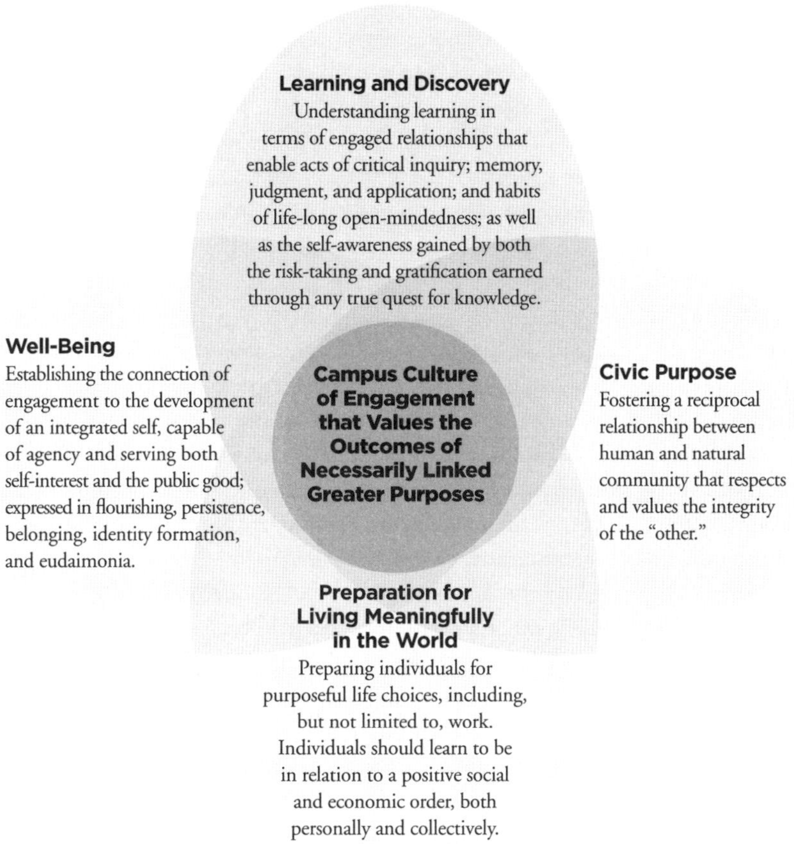

**Learning and Discovery**
Understanding learning in
terms of engaged relationships that
enable acts of critical inquiry; memory,
judgment, and application; and habits
of life-long open-mindedness; as well
as the self-awareness gained by both
the risk-taking and gratification earned
through any true quest for knowledge.

**Well-Being**
Establishing the connection of
engagement to the development
of an integrated self, capable
of agency and serving both
self-interest and the public good;
expressed in flourishing, persistence,
belonging, identity formation,
and eudaimonia.

**Campus Culture
of Engagement
that Values the
Outcomes of
Necessarily Linked
Greater Purposes**

**Civic Purpose**
Fostering a reciprocal
relationship between
human and natural
community that respects
and values the integrity
of the "other."

**Preparation for
Living Meaningfully
in the World**
Preparing individuals for
purposeful life choices, including,
but not limited to, work.
Individuals should learn to be
in relation to a positive social
and economic order, both
personally and collectively.

not an appeal to being irrelevant—it is a strategy for being more relevant.[12] The renewal or renaissance of purpose brings with it a radically different organizing metaphor—not one of sequestration (a retreat to the ivory tower in order to gain, i.e., receive knowledge), not a simple understanding of learning as information transfer, but a complex one of deep and guided critical inquiry, immersion in and off campus, sometimes *from* but more often *in* the world, that addresses connections as well as separations, knowing and discovering as relational concepts that link judgment to agency in behavior and future disposition.

Such a case and its promotion could begin to change conversations: those around the board table, those around campus seminar tables, those around the media editorial table, and those around the family kitchen table. Attitudes could be altered and expectations changed, then policies, practices, and priorities could be changed in light of those expectations. Real problems that affect the lives of students and communities could be addressed as central rather than peripheral topics (see the J. Riley & H. Elmendorf essay). Value could be placed on creating environments of *safeness* in which engagement, critical thinking, and academic risk-taking could thrive (see J. Metzl's essay). Retention could be affected positively as levels of reported student satisfaction are boosted. Admissions could be enhanced by the reality of the institution's cultivation of a context that is supportive of individual attention and that clearly indicates that commitment is beyond individuals to the public good—to a bolder view of agency (that one must act to make a difference) that affects a more just social order, the sustainability of the planet, and the real existential issues of living together. Institutional relationships with their local communities could grow and flourish as intentional and defined partnerships. Faculty and campus administration could feel a greater sense of purpose and meaning in their work—that they truly affect the lives of their students, create contexts for the manifestation of well-being of the campus, and imbue culture with the expectation of engagement (see the T. Wolf & A. Rodas and the W. Sullivan essays).

Given its history and culture, the demographic conditions of its audience, and the specific emphases of its particular mission, a campus may require re-thinking about what facilitates well-being—what manifestations of well-being are most important for its participants. For example, resiliency to the challenges of balancing work and study or supporting identity formation for many who are first generation may be among the higher-order issues for a campus as it examines and adjusts to how opportunities for engagement remain paramount—contextualized but necessary (see the M. Phillips, D. Scobey, and J. Wilson essays). In her Provocation, Phillips warns of compartmentalized judgment and implicit dismissal of who the students are and the intellectual traditions they are part of and expect. Scobey explores the relevance of self-authorship, its connection to underserved students' self-efficacy, and how they build capacity to transform the circumstances that impede their learning and well-being. Wilson provides an example of how community well-being that is developed in a sustained campus culture directly affects individual well-being and how students at historically Black colleges and universities understand the purpose of their participation.

Current discussion of the Black Lives Matter movement and related emphases on social justice underscore an emerging sociological analysis of well-being. Such a view explores, in part, the effect of hegemonic social conditions on an individual's sense of self-worth, identity, and purposefulness. Enduring conditions of racism, poverty, and political and social oppression reinforce the barriers to actualization and being well.[13]

THE PATHWAYS TO CHANGE

Even if greater purposes and their realization in ascertainable outcomes are theoretically clear, what are the manifestations and expressions of well-being that connect to strategic changes? How do they become more widely appreciated, evidence-based, and thereby capable of directing expectations from broad audiences of those involved or those who will be involved? And if well-being is an implicit dimension of higher education, what explains the expressed tension when those on campus are being asked to consider attending to the well-being of its constituents?

These matters are complex; however, the route to credibility, the path to change, has all to do with convincing those now within the academy—with a theoretical and compelling rationale that cuts across disciplines and is reinforced with established evidence of successes—that practices crafted on individual campuses by their engaged constituents are rewarded for being so engaged.

> ...higher education does more than give students the skills and capacities to be productive members of the workforce. It gives them the confidence, the self-esteem, and sense of purpose that will enable them to find meaning in their lives and careers. These outcomes can seem foreign to faculty until the idea of empowerment in the classroom, or the idea that students should take ownership of their learning is raised. We often disconnect the assessment of student learning from the very outcomes that could be the most predictive of student success: the confidence and perseverance to want to stay in school, to want to take on an internship, to stay the path of graduation. What if the connection of learning to student development in well-being wasn't just the purview of student affairs? What if how learning helps students feel about themselves and others is what matters most?"[14]

The essays in *Well-Being and Higher Education* collectively present an argument for change that gives priority to and support for those experiences that make learning and well-being connected objectives. The essays can be used at institutions of all types as the campuses shapes their own agendas and take positive, affordable, and purposeful steps on their own paths—their own arcs of change—connecting theory to practice and moving within their own histories and cultures to make and assess changes.[15]

Along those arcs of change, institutions, faculty, students, their families and communities will be examining what affects their thinking and steps of action. Some of those steps may result from addressing or debunking unsupported categorizations or assumptions (myths), some of which are found in prevailing narratives.

*Myth 1:* There is an irreducible and categorical distinction between the cognitive and the non-cognitive (thought and feelings) and the related sub-myth that the academic is wholly separated from the non-academic. Thus, faculty and academic affairs are structurally separated from student services and student affairs.

*Myth 2:* Learning takes place only or primarily in the class room, and engaged learning opportunities are constructed only, or primarily, by faculty,

*Myth 3:* Learning is deepened by developing only vertical content. Rather, the axes of learning are multiple. Vertical axes champion disciplines and authorities expressing, if not controlling, their boundaries. Horizontal axes champion relational interactions, interdependencies, and the inter-disciplinary. *Deepened learning* means exploring the conceptual landscape and discovering connections, rarely boundaries. It means that deepening by association and connection require collaboration—learning, finding, or seeing in relation to what others find or see.

*Myth 4:* Learning and action are independent. Rather, they are more often interdependent. Theory links to practice; knowing obliges learner to act. It is the ethical imperative of learning and part of why higher education connects the learner to acting in order to achieve a common good. For instance, it is why we, with Aristotle, Kant, John Dewey, Elizabeth Minnich, Derek Bok, and moral thinkers of many traditions argue that it reasonable to declare that to come to know the face of . . . . (e.g. desperate poverty) is to adopt the imperative to act to address it. Directly or indirectly, many of the essays in this volume suggest the importance of demythologizing these assumptions, questioning their veracity, weighing their implications, and then promoting the reduction of their influence.

*Well-Being and Higher Education* does not assemble or prescribe best practices—to do so would generalize the unique character of each institution of higher education and undermine our argument that learning, well-being, civic engagement, and preparation for living meaningfully in the world are relational and contextual. The essays do, however, by dealing with *how, why, what,* and *for (and by) whom* (see the K. Kruger & S. Gordon essay) present and discuss pedagogy, practices, and curricular design that help make manifest opportunities for campus-wide attention to the meaning, manifestations, and facilitation of well-being that opens pathways to change. Consider D. Scobey's presentation of a large category of underserved students whose well-being is rarely considered; or L. Schreiner's detailed account of the manifestation of well-being in thriving; or A. Seligsohn's consideration of whether well-being can be sought in contexts of pernicious inequalities; or C. Keyes' answer to the question "Why well-being?"

Actual campus discussions and actions that attend to well-being could be initiated by asking questions most relevant to one's own campus and institutional history. Those questions and the campus responses could help begin the change in the conversation on campus that can result in real consideration of and the taking of steps of action—even transformation.

- Is student well-being an explicit, core purpose *at this institution*? Are well-being objectives linked to learning objectives?
- Was well-being inadvertently (or perhaps intentionally) de-emphasized as a core objective or aim of higher education at this institution? What specific strategies will make it (or return it to) an expected and achieved objective?
- What do we *at this institution* think that a deeper and broad understanding of well-being should include? And in what contexts can it be realized—in the classroom, in relationships, in the community, through local and international engagement?
- How can we *at this institution* understand well-being as integrative of multiple dimensions of being unique as well as whole, contextually influenced, with some elements developmental and others not?
- What evidence supports changes in *our* curricula, pedagogy, structural and practiced collaboration between academic and student affairs as co-educators, policies and rewards that would maximize opportunities and their use for well-being? What would initial projects or changes look like (e.g., in advising, curricular infusion, participatory and action-oriented research)? What would more advanced projects or changes look like? How would any project or change be assessed and how would the results be used and shared?
- In what specific ways would changing the predominant conversation *at our institution* regarding well-being as a core aim result in substantive change? How would implementing those changes be afforded, even if well-being were to be understood as a core objective?

Beyond grounding manifestations of well-being in the specificity of a particular campus climate, the discussion of what facilitates well-being will likely move to such questions as the following:

- Is this the right time to push this initiative given the concerns regarding the cost of higher education?

- Can we maintain conditions of choice of opportunities for students, if well-being is emphasized?
- Can we adequately and efficiently prepare students with the skills needed in a work force, if we broaden purposes and outcomes?

However important, if consideration is given *only* to questions of cost and structure, the institution is likely to overlook the examination and assessment of the evidence for well-being outcomes directly connected to learning and thereby miss how purposefulness does connect to *why:* the institution is invested in providing students with costly research or performance experiences; on what bases it justifies investing in radical alteration of its advising systems; what evidence it has that well-being is linked to learning, and is being achieved by maintaining or lowering the ratio of full-time students to full-time faculty, even when the pressure to cut is prevalent; why it invests (structurally and financially) in students engaging diversity and confronting their own privilege; and why it is important to connect the civic value of a public good with the institution's provision of skills need for meaningful choices such as work.

These are the some of the outcomes that make a difference to the education and to the lives of students. Intentional connection of learning and well-being outcomes results in campus consideration of how the most effective of the opportunities could be scaled and given priority. They would not be add-ons to what is already done or offered; they would result in the institution being more—providing a campus climate of engagement and opportunities to connect deeper learning and the well-being of all students.[15]

Planning change and planning *for* change are defining features of any organization. Changes can be stimulated by directional nudges, or they can be cataclysmic. They can be characterized as the result of bottom-up activities (a groundswell or grassroots effort) or the championing of a committed few. They can be the result of top-down declarations or adopted policies. Change is contextualized. For many within higher education, we have seen changes occur effectively when they draw their source from and connect to prevailing institutional values deeply rooted in its culture.

Historically, external factors have significantly affected institutional change. The passing of the Morrill Act, the GI Bill, the 1965 Higher Education Act, the Carnegie Commission Report, and many other very public declarations shaped purpose and supported change within and outside of higher education. And clearly, increases or decreases in Federal funding, aid policy, State support, and philanthropic support, have been relevant if not decisive to institutions making change. Not to be overlooked, however, are changes that are stimulated and supported internally—the pebble in the pond that results in waves of influence. They have an effect. Those effects often contribute to conversations that when reinforced lead to altered expectations—expectations of families for their children, expectations of what constitutes a career or a profession, expectations and aspirations of how the institution should be promoted and evaluated.[16]

The essays that follow contribute to altering prevailing conversations. They include examination of a model for understanding change in the enterprise of higher education by comparison to the dynamic of change in the enterprise of health care (see E. Lister essay). Others present the use of the curriculum and technological innovation to alter conversations and expectations among faculty (see P. Leyden's look into the future and the C. Schneider essay). Some voices of those leading the discussion of the role of technology in creating change (one of the disruptive forces common now in why higher education must change) present a view that sees disaggregation as a paradigm for learning that is in a struggle for prioritization with an integrative paradigm for learning. Who is lined up on either side of such a tension of paradigms, and is there a prospect of resolution (see the R. Bass essay)?

Change in higher education may be seen and understood not simply as adjusting to disruptive forces, but also as a result of using a strategy of collective conversations to champion a renaissance of its greater purposes, the power and appeal of those greater purposes, and the necessity to attend to their actualization.

## Being "More": Final Words Regarding Community and Institutional Well-being

Institutional or campus well-being can mean seeing the community also as a construct—not some *thing* of physical description, not something static, but an organic and developing whole that exhibits dimensions of its relational character, including how the actions of its members connect to its purposes and values. *Institutional well-being* can also be understood as an expression of its engagement—the internal opportunities it provides to its participants and the patterns of its engagement to the external community.

An institution's commitment to well-being is exhibited by having connections with multiple communities be present and involved in the accounting of real and difficult matters—locally, nationally, and well beyond. The well-being institution serves to encourage students and faculty to welcome being challenged, to persist in addressing those challenges, and most importantly, to be open to receiving something as opposed to thinking they are offering something—replacing privilege with the humility of valuing and respecting diversity and difference.

There are multiple manifestations of the well-being of the institution, and they could be documented well beyond the dashboard of conventional comparative characteristics with peer and aspiration institutions. They should include indicators of where and when the institution offers opportunities for deep learning and engagement, where and when students are expected to risk taking challenges and considering contrarian ideas, and how offices and services function collaboratively. A *prima facie* obligation of the well-being institution is to craft challenging, frequent, and persistent opportunities for learners to be in relation to facts, evidence, risks, doubts, others, difference, the community, alternatives, the conventional and the contrarian, and the expanding boundaries of what counts as real. To cultivate the learner's expectations to be so engaged and to value that engagement are central to the institution's mission—its purposes.

An institution attending to the fullness of its purposes, including well-being, can be a place connected and a place apart. It can understand and value its connections to community, connections that are reciprocal and beneficial to both, and it can have the capacity and courage when needed to be apart from what is accepted as conventional to, indeed, critique it—the courage to support engaged contrarians.

The biochemist who sees the importance of using class or lab time to engage students in understanding what is at stake in why certain research is supported or sponsored and others is not is civically engaged. The mathematics faculty member determining how to mathematically express the pace of drug absorption by liver tissue explicitly connects learning and well-being as much as the community member or college counselor who guides a student to persist through a failure. These examples are often thought to be on the periphery—not to be at the core of the purpose of higher education—nice but not essential. The argument of this volume of essays, however, offers an understanding of the viable and important strategies of engagement in learning, research, teaching, advising, acting, and serving that are at the core, that serve the full purposes of higher education, that place the institution in the lives of its students and in the life of the community. Such deep and guided critical inquiry, immersion in and off campus, sometimes *from* but more often *in* the world, addresses connections as well as separations, knowing and discovering, links judgment to agency in behavior and in the future disposition of its constituents.

The well-being institution can be a context in which students, faculty, and the community flourish—they are *parts of* something greater, but they retain their identities as members of a partnership capable and critical, supportive and contrarian. The external community understands the intent and promise of being a partner in a meaningful collaboration—to create, sustain, and evaluate opportunities and experiences of full engagement—independent, not tokenized, not an object of good will for volunteers, not the recipient of *noblesse oblige* but a partner engaging purposefully with another. The community is a partner and has its own integrity, identity, and value; engagement is the vehicle of connection for institution and community to be well.

*The well-being institution can be a context in which students, faculty, and the community flourish—they are parts of something greater, but they retain their identities as members of a partnership capable and critical, supportive and contrarian*

Granted, the work is hard—how to provide multiple opportunities for relational engagement from first to final years? How to make these opportunities available for distinguishable sets of students—part-time, first generation, or international? How can technology enhance relational engagement and sense of personal agency and identity? How to ensure that students expect to connect campus experiences to off-campus forms of engagement? How to offer opportunities for signature work that reveals greater understanding and possible action? How to insist on honoring the integrity of partners in the community?

But the dominant challenge will be to develop the means to provide the *more* in the promise of higher education—to establish why this effort is valuable in deeper and more lasting ways. And how, as educators and as a community, do we guide students to realize such promise in their own lives and future communities? A university can beat the drum of why and how it can in its policies, and in its practices be *more*—not less. *More* that is not the result of addition but the result of realigning, relying upon the relational features of higher education's full purposes, championing how higher learning is inextricably connected to the civic, to well-being and the forming of greater purposefulness and self-identity, to exploring the larger world and what it will take to live meaningfully in that world.

To be *more* gives priority to justly distributed opportunities and expectations for real engagement across/among the strands in the weave of a network of purposes—engagement that is more than just available—engagement that is guided and supported in the multiple expressions of those connections, opportunities for engagement that are promised and delivered.

NOTES

1. Brandon Busteed, "Is College Worth It?" *Gallup Business Journal*, August 27, 2013, http://www.gallup.com/businessjournal/164108/college-worth.aspx.
2. Allegra Stratton, "David Cameron Aims to Make Happiness the New GDP," November 14, 2010, http://www.theguardian.com/politics/2010/nov/14/david-cameron-wellbeing-inquiry.
3. Sissela Bok, *Exploring Happiness* (New Haven, CT: Yale University Press, 2011).
4. Daniel F. Chambliss and Christopher G. Takacs, *How College Works* (Cambridge, MA: Harvard University Press, 2014).
5. Framing well-being as only a descriptive, even developmental, construct would require assent to the theoretical bases and evidence for developmental hypotheses about maturation as well as learning. These bases appear less widely shared and are less likely to affect the thinking, scholarship, or teaching of most discipline-based faculty. Whereas a conceptual construct and arguments for it that rest on epistemic bases do so. Presenting core meanings of well-being and of learning as sharing an analysis of being relational concepts and not simply descriptive ones opens the conversations across disciplines and divisions.
6. The connections of individual physical health to learning and to higher education objectives can only be mentioned here. See C. Ryff's essay, however, in which she examines why a biological risk factor known as interleukin 6 is implicated in the etiology of various physical health outcomes that are correlated with education levels and inversely correlated with reported levels of well-being. Well-being might, therefore, afford some buffer or protection against physical health risks. Undeniably, physical health, its development, encouragement, and the measurement of its implications, are among the threads in a full examination of the meaning of any complex construct of health, but, regrettably, doing so is beyond the scope of this volume. Ryff's essay includes multiple leads—over 50 citations—as to where that research might go.
7. This insight, the necessary connection of learning to civic engagement, was the early source of the multi-year work of Bringing Theory to Practice and its contribution to the on-going conversation. The success of promulgating the use of the five volume *Civic Series* (2012–2014) aided campus efforts to bring attention to the civic and higher education's consideration of purpose in a democratic society. Emerging has been the cultivation and support of civically minded campuses, each considering what that means and what changes are needed to deepen understanding and local practices and opportunities if higher education is to serve that mission.
8. See Kevin Carey, *The End of College: Creating the Future of Learning and the University of Everywhere* (New York: Riverhead Books, 2015).
9. See Michael Nevradakis, "Henry Giroux on the Rise of Neoliberalism, "*Truthout* Interview, October 19, 2014, http://www.truth-out.org/opinion/item/26885-henry-giroux-on-the-rise-of-neoliberalism and Kwame Anthony Appiah, "What Is The Point of College?" *The New York Times Magazine*, September 8, 2015, http://www.nytimes.com/2015/09/13/magazine/what-is-the-point-of-college.html?_r=0.
10. Ashley Finley, Well-Being: An Essential Outcome for Higher Education, *Change: The Magazine of Higher Learning*, May 11, 2016, 14–19.; Joshua J. Mitchell et al., "Perceptions of Campus Climates for Civic Learning as Predictors of College Students' Mental Health," *Journal of College and Character* 17 (2016): 40–52; Corey L. M. Keyes and Jonathan Haidt, eds., *Flourishing: Positive Psychology and the Life Well-Lived* (Washington, DC: American Psychological Association, 2003); Constance Flanagan and Matthew Bundick, "Civic Engagement and Psychosocial Well-Being in College Students," *Liberal Education* 97, no. 2 (2011): https://www.aacu.org/publications-research/periodicals/civic-engagement-and-psychosocial-well-being-college-students. In addition, there are multiple, campus-based research projects available on the Bringing Theory to Practice website. An example of the studies that arise from such work is Kathy Graff Low, "Flourishing and Student Engagement," *Bringing Theory to Practice Newsletter*, Spring 2010, http://www.bttop.org/newsletters/flourishing-and-student-engagement.
11. Bobby Fong, "Cultivating 'Sparks of the Divinity': Soul-Making as a Purpose of Higher Education," *Liberal Education* 100, no. 3 (2014); "As learning is privatized, treated as a form of entertainment, depoliticized, and reduced to teaching students how to be good consumers, any viable notions of the social, public values, citizenship and democracy wither and die. I am not suggesting that we must defend a rather and sometimes abstract and empty notion of the public sphere, but those public spheres capable of producing thoughtful citizens, critically engaged agents ,and an ethically and socially responsible society" (Henry Giroux, "The Curse of Totalitarianism and the Challenge of Insurrectional Pedagogy," *Counter Punch*, November 29, 2015, http://www.counterpunch.org/2015/09/29/the-curse-of-totalitarianism-and-the-challenge-of-an-insurrectional-pedagogy/.
12. See Derek Bok, *Our Underachieving Colleges: A Candid Look at How Much Students Learn and Why They Should Be Learning More* (Princeton, NJ: Princeton University Press, 2006): 56–82 and Busteed, "Is College Worth It?"
13. Shawn Ginright, *Hope and Healing in Urban Education: How Urban Activists and Teachers are Reclaiming Matters of the Heart* (Abingdon, UK: Routledge, 2015).

14. Finley, Well-Being: An Essential Outcome for Higher Education, *Change.*
15. See Busteed, "Is College Worth It?" Several university counseling centers, e.g., Ohio State University (https://swc.osu.edu/about-us/9-dimensions-of-wellness) and Wake Forest University (https://www.insidehighered.com/news/2014/04/29/wakeforest-u-tries-measure-well-being) provide students with similar taxonomies of well-being as guides for choices and where to locate services.

    Surveys of types of well-being, such as those reported by Gallup, polling of attitudes, and responses to key questions across time periods and cultures include the following: career well-being, social well-being, financial well-being, physical well-being, and Community well-being. Of those five elements, Gallup surveys indicate that those interviewed select career well-being as most important to them followed by financial well-being.

    While it remains to be determined what gains in understanding will be made based on the well-being results from those studies, they do provide important insights and suggest hedonic attitudinal evidence. The tested survey questions regarding well-being could be administered on a campus and repeated at time periods during which various interventions are administered (for example, learning community engagement, deep learning experiences etc.). Then changes in attitudes (feelings) could be measured or even compared to broad-based data banks.

    Attitudes, feelings, and behaviors are individual experiences that can be calibrated. For example, they bring immediate pleasure, have intensity, and can be induced, measured, and compared, even cross-culturally.

    But quite separate from these measurements of attitude are the strands of individual and community flourishing, purposefulness, identity formation, persistence, mindfulness, willingness to risk, and the recognition of the value of the other. These are manifestations of eudaemonic well-being that are less likely to be quantified, may have little to do with immediate pleasure, cannot be induced or easily measured, but are expressed in a life well-lived.

    "We are not suggesting mollycoddling students, but rather providing them with the skills and experiences for both academic and personal success. Emotional health [well-being] at age 26 is the most important indicator of life satisfaction at age 36. And if higher well-being is linked to academic achievement, it will have consequences in the labor market and for broader health and life outcomes . . . All universities market themselves on preparing young people for life—but that means more than leaving higher education with a good degree or being in work six months after graduation. It means making sure that students have the skills and attitudes to be successful, responsible members of society . . . important for their own future and for that of the country," David Bell, Marina Della Giusta, and Antonia Fernandez, "Why We Need New Measures of Student Well-Being," Times Higher Education, August 6, 2015, https://www.timeshighereducation.com/opinion/why-we-need-new-measures-of-student-well-being.
16. Donald W. Harward, "From the Director: Advancing the Greater Purposes of Higher Education," *Bringing Theory to Practice Newsletter*, Spring 2016, http://www.bttop.org/news-events/director-advancing-greater-purposes-higher-education.

PART 1 | Analysis and Meaning

# 1
## ESSAY

# Measuring and Improving the Effect of Higher Education on Subjective Well-Being

*John Bronsteen*

WHY GO TO COLLEGE? The most common reason may well be to improve one's life. To be sure, that is not the only possible reason. For example, people might think college will help them contribute to improving others' lives, or they might think learning has some sort of inherent value independent of its capacity to improve anyone's life. Still, at least one major aspect of the value of higher education is surely its potential to enhance the quality of life of those who receive that education. That aspect is my focus here.

I would like to discuss how to measure and improve the effect of higher education on students' lifetime well-being.[1] To do that, I will start by considering what well-being is and how it can be measured. Then I will describe the obstacles to drawing causal inferences about the effect of higher education on well-being, before giving a brief overview of the existing data on that connection. Finally, I will make suggestions about how higher education might be changed to improve its effect on students' lifetime well-being.

## MEASURING THE EFFECT OF HIGHER EDUCATION ON SUBJECTIVE WELL-BEING

The project of learning how college affects people's quality of life is, unfortunately, quite difficult. For one thing, we need to know what we are trying to measure, i.e., what quality of life is in the first place. Once we know that, we need to find a way to measure it. Finally, we need to figure out how it is affected by college attendance. Let us consider those three challenges in order.

### What Is Well-Being?

If we want to know how college affects well-being, then it would be helpful to know what well-being is. The common philosophical definition of the term well-being, a term often used interchangeably with terms such as quality of life or especially in economics welfare, is how well a person's life is going for her.[2] But what does it mean for someone's life to be going well? About thirty years ago, Derek Parfit famously provided a taxonomy of the three different answers that are most often given to that question.[3] The first is that someone has well-being to the extent that she is happy. In this case, happiness is typically understood to mean something such as feeling good, such that a person's lifetime well-being would be the sum of her aggregate positive and negative feelings throughout her life. The second answer is that someone has well-being to the extent that she satisfies her preferences, that is, gets what she wants. And the third answer is that someone has well-being to the extent that she possesses certain objective indicators such as good health. More recently, a fourth answer has emerged in the form of neo-Aristotelian theories that say someone has well-being to the extent that she has virtue and/or to the extent that she perfects distinctively human capabilities such as the ability to think rationally.[4]

Thus, measuring the effect of higher education on well-being means measuring the effect of higher education on people's felt happiness, or on the extent to which people get what they want, or on the extent to which they have certain objective goods such as health, or on the extent to which they have virtue or cultivate human capabilities.

### Which is it?

This isn't the place to resolve that deep question, but because my topic involves measuring well-being, I will say something about the different relative strengths and weaknesses of these theories in terms of their capacity to supply measurable proxies for well-being. I now turn to that topic.

### The Relative Capacity of Each Theory to Measure Well-Being

Whatever well-being is, we can't find out how it is affected by college unless we can measure it. And some theories of well-being are much easier to measure than others. To understand how one might go about measuring preference satisfaction, objective indicators of well-being such as health, or levels of experiential happiness, we need to look a bit more closely at exactly what each theory claims well-being is.

Let's start with preference theories. These are the favored theories of economists, who typically assume that preference satisfaction means getting what you want and that what you want is revealed by the choices you make. These economists believe that well-being must be revealed by one's choices (and/or one's stated preferences—what people say they want) because to label well-being anything else would be to substitute someone else's judgment for the judgment of the person herself. If Ashley chooses to buy a chair, then according to the standard economic view, we have to assume the chair increases her well-being because otherwise we are telling her what's good for her instead of letting her decide for herself, and that would be paternalistic or even oppressive. In addition, equating well-being with preference satisfaction makes it easy to measure well-being because money can be used as a proxy for the ability to get what one wants.

> *Let's start with preference theories. These are the favored theories of economists, who typically assume that preference satisfaction means getting what you want and that what you want is revealed by the choices you make*

All of this may sound good, but unfortunately there is a problem with it that is so big as to be decisive: People make mistakes. If I choose to eat an apple, but I don't know the apple is poisoned, then it would be crazy to say that eating the apple improves my well-being.[5] Yet the view that well-being is choices (revealed preferences) says just that. Not only is such a theory obviously untenable, but also its untenability is widely understood by philosophers, psychologists, and the general public. Everyone knows that people often lack information, and thus we all expect our democratically elected governments to protect us from potential mistakes we would make. This is why there are health and safety regulations, social insurance programs, and countless other policies aimed at improving people's well-being. In many cases, such policies are obviously not oppressive and enhance well-being greatly.

Thus, philosophers who believe that well-being is preference-satisfaction—and there have been many such philosophers, including prominent ones such as John Rawls[6]—believe that well-being is not people's actual choices but rather the choices they would make if they had perfect information (or at least some amount of information that no one could actually have in real life). And when preference theorists are interested in measuring well-being in real-life circumstances, they often assume that revealed preferences (what people do) or stated preferences (what people say they want) are decent proxies for idealized preferences (what people would want if they knew everything).

There is, however, no support for that last assumption. And indeed there cannot be any support for it because it is impossible to know what people would want if they knew everything. As Connie Rosati has noted, "no actual person could be fully informed, it appears, without violating laws of psychology and physiology."[7] It is impossible to know everything or even to know all the information relevant to a decision. The world is far too complicated, and our brains are far too small, for such knowledge.

Does that matter? Actually, it matters a tremendous amount. When someone makes a choice, she's really making a guess about whether that choice will turn out to be good for her. To know whether it was good for her, we need to know something much different from the mere fact that she chose it. We need to know how things turned out. This is what *she* would have known if she'd had perfect information, but no one can ever have perfect information.

Let me be clear: as a policy matter, it's very often best to let people choose what they want. Among other things, freedom may have value not just as a contributor to well-being, but also independent of well-being. But my task here is to analyze the effect of college on well-being, and to do that I have started by considering what well-being is. So it is relevant for me to note the obvious point that well-being is not people's actual choices, and thus that it is not the amount of money people have to effectuate those choices.

There is also no reason to believe that people's actual choices are good approximations for what they would have chosen if they'd known everything. Even small amounts of additional information often change people's preferences radically, so perfect information (which is an amount of knowledge no one can even imagine having) could reverse people's preferences entirely or change them in any of countless unpredictable ways. We simply have no idea what people's fully informed preferences would be, and it is impossible to find that out or even to make any sort of approximation or educated guess.

So if well-being is fully informed preferences—what people would want if they knew everything—then well-being is impossible to measure or even to approximate.

Therefore, if measuring the effect of college on well-being is our goal, then let us hope that well-being is *not* the satisfaction of fully informed preferences but instead that well-being is happiness, or objective goods, or something else. For the same reasons, this should be one's hope if one aims to measure the effect of anything on well-being or to craft policies that can be expected with any degree of confidence to improve well-being.

Let us therefore move away from preference theories to the second main theory of well-being, which says that well-being is objective indicators such as health. Such indicators may seem much easier to measure than fully informed preferences, but their measurement also has a problem: The theory that well-being is such indicators leaves out a crucial piece of information, namely how to commensurate two or more different indicators.

Consider first a simple, one-item, objective-list theory in which well-being is said to be how long a person lives. That theory is very easy to measure, but of course it is also false: Sally's life goes better for her if she lives 80 happy years than if she lives 80 sad years, despite the fact that her longevity is the same either way. The two versions of her life do not have equal well-being simply because they are equally long.

Objective theories can account for that problem by adding other list items. An objective theory might say, for example, that well-being is a combination of things such as life, bodily health, bodily integrity, senses, imagination, thought, emotions, practical reason, affiliation, [relationship with] other species, play, and control over one's environment.[8] But then the question becomes how to *commensurate* those different list items, that is, how to weigh them against one another on a single scale. Is someone better off if she has a bit more health but one less close friend or vice versa? Without a way to analyze those tradeoffs, an objective list theory cannot tell us how to measure well-being in almost any real-world situation. Such a theory tells us that someone is better off if she has more of a list item than less of it, all else being equal, but all else is virtually never equal. If the answer is that we must simply use our intuition in each case, then the objective list theory has done us little or no good. (After all, the point of having a theory is to reduce reliance on intuition so that when two peoples' intuitions differ, their difference of opinion is not irreconcilable.) If we are going to say, "Well-being is objective goods, and when there is a tradeoff among those goods, then well-being is what people intuit it to be in any given case," then we might as well acknowledge that there is always a tradeoff and therefore say more simply, "Well-being is whatever people intuit well-being to be in any given case," thereby abandoning the pretension that the objective list theory is doing any work.

Given the seeming impossibility of measuring well-being according to preference theories or objective list theories, let us briefly consider the so-called eudaimonic theories, that is, the neo-Aristotelian theories. At the risk of offending many brilliant scholars who find such theories attractive, let me say this: If there is actually any such thing as a eudaimonic theory of well-being, I do not know what it is or could be.[9] Consider, for example, a theory saying that well-being is taking pleasure in virtuous or worthwhile pursuits.[10] Such a theory would dictate that if Jim watches mindless television and takes pleasure in it, then Jim has no more well-being than if he watches mindless television and is made miserable thereby. This cannot be right. No matter how worthless or unvirtuous an activity is, it is still better for the person doing it if (all else being equal) that person enjoys the activity than if that person is made miserable by the activity.

So well-being is clearly connected to enjoyment, but any connection to virtue or to perfecting human capacities seems far less plausible. And if the claim is that well-being *does* involve nonvirtuous pleasures but that it also has a component of virtue that is unconnected with pleasure, then that claim suffers from the same problem noted above about objective list theories. To wit: Such a theory would need some metric for commensurating the different components it says comprise well-being (e.g., virtue and pleasure). Is someone better off with a bit more virtue and a bit less pleasure or vice versa? If the only way to answer such questions is intuition, then the theory might as well say simply that well-being is whatever one intuits well-being to be in any situation. In other words, the theory might as well be the absence of a theory. With apologies for the harshness of the following statement, I believe that once anyone spells out what a eudaimonic theory of well-being is, then it tends to become obvious that such a theory does not make sense.

Finally, let us consider the hedonic theories—the ones saying, as Jeremy Bentham does, that well-being is happiness (which in turn means feeling good).[11] At a glance, happiness might seem much more difficult to measure than either preference-satisfaction or objective goods because happiness is an internal feeling. It may seem that we can observe whether someone has objective goods like health or that we can infer people's preferences from their choices. But as I have explained, preferences and objective goods are far more opaque than they seem. Fortunately, happiness may be *less* opaque than it seems. Psychologists have demonstrated that people's in-the-moment self-reports of their own happiness levels are valid and reliable indicators of how good those people actually feel. In other words, if we simply ask people how happy they are, their answers reflect their true levels of happiness.

How could such a thing be tested? Consider an analogy: the way a researcher might determine whether a scale gives accurate measurements of weight. To do this, the researcher would start by performing tests and retests, putting the same object on the scale multiple times and observing whether the scale gives the same reading each time.[12] The researcher might also re-weigh the object after adding and subtracting some weight from it to see whether the scale accounts for those changes. And the researcher might compare the scale's readouts to those of other scales, especially in cases where many other different kinds of seemingly well-made scales give readouts that agree with one another.

*Psychologists have demonstrated that people's in-the-moment self-reports of their own happiness levels are valid and reliable indicators of how good those people actually feel. In other words, if we simply ask people how happy they are, their answers reflect their true levels of happiness*

The happiness data have been tested in similar ways with encouraging results. Studies of people's self-reported happiness have been replicated with high test-retest reliability (i.e., similar outcomes[13] and levels of self-reported happiness correlate with levels of happiness as measured by criteria such as others' reports[14] and neurological[15] and [16] indicators. Moreover, people's self-reported happiness behaves in ways that make sense. For example, people's happiness initially decreases when they suffer serious injuries, whereas their happiness initially decreases by a smaller amount when they suffer less serious injuries[17] To be sure, there have also been some surprising results, such as people's capacity to adapt over time to both positive and negative life events and people's failures to predict their own adaptation.[18] But so much evidence supports the validity of the data that those few surprises have been taken by psychologists to reflect unexpected truths rather than reasons to reject the studies.

Better yet, studies of self-reported happiness continue to improve. The ideal way to test people's happiness is to ask them to rate how they feel at random moments during the day because people are far better at reporting how they feel right now than they are at remembering how they felt or predicting how they will feel at some other time. Two separate scholars, Matthew Killingsworth and George MacKerron, have each created smartphone apps that beep people at such random moments and prompt them to record their happiness levels.[19] (In return, the apps provide analyses of users' happiness.) Those apps have generated millions of data points about people's happiness, and as psychologists analyze those data in the coming years, their understanding of happiness will increase yet further.

The measurability of happiness is enormously important for several reasons. First, if well-being is happiness, then the data on happiness provide valid and reliable indicators of well-being. Those data can be used to understand the effects on happiness of not only education, but also of health, wealth, work, and so on. They can even be used to help craft governmental policies aimed at improving people's quality of life.[20] Second, even if well-being is not happiness, the different theories of well-being may well converge in many real-world cases. For example, people's preferences are often to be happy.[21] And objective list items such as health often contribute mightily to happiness. In fact, happiness may well be the best way to adjudicate between competing objective factors. For example, if we want to know whether a person benefits more from improved health or from improved relationships with loved ones, the answer may well be whichever one makes the person happier.

> *If well-being is happiness, then the data on happiness provide valid and reliable indicators of well-being. Those data can be used to understand the effects on happiness of not only education, but also of health, wealth, work, and so on. They can even be used to help craft governmental policies aimed at improving people's quality of life*

Thus, the happiness data are not only a good proxy for happiness itself, but also they may well be the best available proxy for the *other* theories of well-being—preferences and objective lists. This is especially so because it is not clear what, if any, other proxies can credibly be used to measure well-being according to those other theories.

### Drawing Causal Inferences

For the reasons given in the previous section, I believe that happiness data provide the best way to measure the correlation between well-being and higher education. Still, it is worth voicing an obvious but still crucial note of caution about any method of such measurement: Correlation is not causation. And drawing causal inferences from correlation is often extremely difficult and error-prone. Yes, doing so is sometimes necessary and the best available option, but the limitations of this approach are nonetheless important to keep in mind.

When measuring the effect of college on well-being, what we really want to know is this: If Jim is a typical person, what is the difference between (*a*) Jim's lifetime well-being if he were to go to college and (*b*) Jim's lifetime well-being if he were not to go to college? In pursuing the answer, one must confront a major obstacle: the impossibility of running Jim's life twice. Without being able to do that, we can never know for sure whether he would have had more well-being with or without college. Either he goes to college or he doesn't, so even if we can measure his lifetime well-being perfectly, we will learn only half of what we need to know.

On the bright side, Jim isn't the only person we can observe. Many people go to college, whereas many others don't, so we can compare those two groups in order to draw inferences about the effect of college on well-being. But those inferences are imperfect. What we really want to know is what each individual's well-being would have been with or without college, and comparing those who went to college with those who didn't is merely a proxy for that information.

How good a proxy it is depends on the way we compare members of each group—those who go to college and those who don't. For example, consider the simplest approach: measuring the well-being of college attendees,[22] measuring the well-being of non-college attendees, and comparing the average levels of well-being for both groups. This would tell us whether those who attend college have higher, lower, or the same levels of well-being as those who don't. But it wouldn't tell us the *effect* of college on people's well-being because the two groups may be different in ways other than college attendance, and the levels of well-being within groups may be attributable to those other differences. For example, suppose it turns out that people are more likely to go to college if they are genetically predisposed to be happy than if they are genetically predisposed to be sad. This would mean that college-goers are happier than others, but that would not be *because* college has any effect on their happiness. (As discussed above, I am focusing on happiness because the hedonic theory of well-being is most measurable and because happiness is clearly at least *one* crucial component of well-being on any plausible theory.)

This concern is not merely hypothetical because there are many known differences on average between the people who go to college and the people who don't. Those differences make it very difficult to isolate the effects of college. To take just one of many examples, people who go to college are raised, on average, by parents with higher incomes than those of the parents of people who don't go to college. Parental income might affect lifetime well-being, so if college attendees have different well-being than non-attendees, that difference could be due to parental income rather than to college. Or it could be due to any of the other differences between those who go to college and those who don't.

Indeed, the difficulties in isolating the effect of college on well-being are equally severe regardless whether well-being is happiness, preference satisfaction, objective indicators, or anything else. Consider the traditional cost-benefit analysis of college, which says that college is worthwhile if it pays for itself by enabling someone to earn more money in his lifetime than he would have earned without it (even considering the cost of tuition and the lost earnings during college years). How do we know whether college pays for itself? To know that, we really want to know whether Jim would have earned more money in his lifetime if he went to college than if he didn't. But Jim lives only once, so we can't know how much money he would have earned in both scenarios and compare them. We can compare the lifetime earnings of those to go to college with the lifetime earnings of those who don't, but the difference can be attributed to college only if the groups are otherwise the same. Perhaps the college attendees earn more in their lifetimes not because they go to college but because, for example, they come from higher-income families in the first place.

If parental income were the only difference between those who go to college and those who don't, there would be a solution to our problem. We could simply compare the lifetime well-being of non-college attendees whose parents have a certain level of income with the lifetime well-being of college attendees whose parents have that same level of income. But parental income is not the only difference between attendees and non-attendees. There are all sorts of other differences, and some of them cannot easily be disentangled from college attendance. For example, suppose we compare Jill, who went to college, with Jack, who did not. Each of them comes from a household with earnings of $50,000 per year. And let us suppose that they also share many other demographic similarities, and that they have the same level of genetic predisposition toward happiness. If one of them has greater lifetime well-being (whatever well-being is) than the other, could we not then attribute the difference to the fact that only one of them went to college?

Unfortunately, the answer is no. We need to ask why, if Jack and Jill are so similar, one attended college whereas the other didn't. If the answer were random chance, then we could isolate the effects of college on well-being. But random chance probably isn't the answer. Maybe Jill's parents placed more value than did Jack's parents on academic accomplishments or on certain measures of success. Or maybe Jill was more driven or ambitious than Jack. Or maybe she simply enjoyed school more than he did. There are countless possible reasons that one person might go to college whereas another might not, and those reasons could themselves affect each person's lifetime well-being. If, say, the Jills of the world have better lives than the Jacks, then we can't know whether that's because they went to college or instead because they had certain other characteristics that made them more likely to go to college but that would have contributed to their well-being whether or not they actually went.

The ideal way to surmount this problem would be to find a situation in which college attendance was randomly distributed across a group of people. For example, imagine a large group of high-school students who all have the credentials to go to college. Now suppose they would all go if they could afford it, but not if they couldn't. If someone distributed grants to a random subset of that group, and if that random subset attended college whereas the other group members did not, then we could track and compare the lifetime well-being of those who went to college and those who didn't to get the answer we seek.

A similar type of strategy was used ingeniously by two scholars who studied the effects of a change in the minimum age for mandatory schooling.[23] Such a change created a natural experiment in which the amount of education was determined by something other than attributes of the students in question. Unfortunately, though, that specific tactic cannot be used for higher education because higher education is never mandatory. Still, the study provides an example of the sort of approach that would be ideal. Another example was used by David Card in the context of assessing the effect of college on earnings.[24] Card compared students who grew up near colleges with otherwise similar students who did not grow up near colleges and found that the former were more likely to go to college for geographical reasons that may have been random in the relevant sense. Although the true randomness of those reasons is still open to question, Card's strategy is another example of the sort of thing that could be fruitful in trying to draw causal inferences about the effect of college on well-being.

One other form of data can also be helpful: longitudinal studies (also called panel data) that are used to track specific individuals throughout their lives. Panel data can be extremely valuable for drawing causal inferences because such data hold constant the most important thing: the individual herself. To see this, suppose we wanted to know the effect of marriage on happiness. We could compare the happiness levels of married people to those of single people, but we could not properly infer causation from those numbers. For all we know, people get married because they are happy rather than becoming happy because they get married. However, if most individuals become happier upon getting married than *they themselves* were before they got married, then the causal inference that marriage increases happiness is more legitimate to draw.

Fortunately, there is much longitudinal data about happiness. Those data are harder to use for education than for, say, income because many of the studies do not start tracking people as children.[25] Some do, however, and they have been used in studies about education. These may provide the best available evidence about the effect of higher education on happiness. Even they, though, require a couple of notes of caution. First, and less importantly to my mind, is the possibility that a person's happiness relative to others at one stage of life is not revealing about that person's happiness relative to others at later stages of life. In other words, suppose Jack and Jill have equal happiness at age 18. Jill goes to college and becomes happier, whereas Jack does not go to college and does not become happier. It seems as though we can draw the inference that college improved Jill's happiness, and perhaps even that college would have been likely to improve Jack's happiness. Indeed, this may well be so. But it is also possible that other differences between Jack and Jill accounted for their similar happiness at age 18 and also for their divergent happiness later on. For example, it is at least possible that certain demographic or socioeconomic factors play a larger role in people's relative happiness at certain points of their lives than at others. This means that relying on panel data does not exempt us from the need to try to hold constant such other factors when possible.

Second and more importantly, there is the danger that college affects people differently depending on the circumstances that drive them either to go to college or not to go to college. Consider this possibility: Suppose the average college attendee is surrounded in high school by friends who also go on to attend college, and suppose the average non-college attendee is surrounded in high school by friends who also do not go on to attend college. It is at least possible that this means college has a different effect on those who go than it would have had on those who don't go. For example, let's say that Allison goes to college whereas Bruce doesn't. Allison and Bruce each report their happiness level as 5 out of 7 at age 18, and they each also report their happiness level at 5 out of 7 throughout their lives after college. It seems from those data that college had no effect on Allison's lifetime happiness and therefore would not have been likely to have any effect on Bruce's lifetime happiness if he had gone to college. Allison apparently gained nothing by going to college, and Bruce apparently lost nothing by not going to college. But for all we know, Allison would have been much less happy (say, 4 out of 7) if she hadn't gone to college because going to college was necessary to keep up with her friends, all of whom went to college like she did. And for all we know, Bruce would have been much happier (say, 6 out of 7) if he had gone to college because in that case he would have jumped ahead of his friends, none of whom went to college. (Or perhaps such jumping ahead would have reduced Bruce's happiness rather than increasing it. Either way, college would have affected him differently from the way it affected Allison, even though he and she started and ended with equal happiness.) If those suppositions were true, then the panel data would mask large effects of education due to the difference between the way in which college affects the particular people who go and the way it would have affected the particular people who don't go.

Still, even this problem is potentially surmountable by, for example, comparing the lifetime happiness of college attendees and non-attendees who went to high schools with similar rates of college attendance. Albeit imperfect, such an approach would be an example of the sort of thing that could be done to address such a problem.

Not enough attention has yet been paid to the effect of higher education on happiness. But ample data exist that could be used to analyze that question, and some of the strategies just discussed could be used to deal with the problems of causal inference. Until then, the best we can do is make use of studies that engage in more traditional forms of statistical analysis such as comparing the outcomes of college attendees with those of non-attendees who are otherwise similar in as many measurable ways (such as parental income) as possible. If people who have similar backgrounds end up with different levels of well-being, and if those different levels correlate strongly with whether the people went to college, then we can tentatively draw the inference that college is responsible for at least some of the difference. That inference is not certain to be correct, but virtually nothing in social science involves certainty. In this case, we can have a modest level of confidence in the results. In the next section I discuss those results by briefly surveying the studies that have been done on the connection between well-being and higher education.[26]

*The Existing Data on the Effect of Higher Education on Subjective Well-Being*
Standard economic theory and conventional wisdom assert that higher education must improve people's quality of life. If it did not, then why would anyone go to college, much less pay vast sums to do so? Moreover, college opens opportunities and often paves the way for levels of achievement, prestige, and income that would have been far less likely to be attained without it. Surely these effects result in improved well-being for college attendees, it is assumed.

*Not enough attention has yet been paid to the effect of higher education on happiness. But ample data exist that could be used to analyze that question, and some of the strategies just discussed could be used to deal with the problems of causal inference*

But empirical studies paint a far murkier picture. In 1984, Robert Witter and his co-authors published an important meta-analysis of studies of the effect of education on subjective well-being (SWB), that is, people's self-reported happiness and life satisfaction. They concluded that the research that had been done "does not reveal any clear trend." Instead, "some researchers have reported a strong relation between education and SWB, whereas others have found almost no relation at all."[27]

One could easily say the same thing about the state of the literature today, three decades after the publication of the Witter et al. paper. Indeed, only twelve years later, Ruut Veenhoven reported that in more recent studies, investigators found a marked downward turn from the results reported by Witter, including a strong correlation between education and life satisfaction only in poor nations. In rich nations, by contrast, newer results showed "even slightly negative correlations with level of education."[28] In other words, college graduates were actually less happy than people with lower levels of education.

Since then, the results continue to be mixed. Although some researchers found a significant positive correlation between education and well-being, such as Stevenson and Wolfers[29] and Yakovlev and Daniels-Leguizamon,[30] others found either no correlation or a negative correlation. Alfred Dockery and others have repeatedly analyzed Australian survey data that show more educated people to be less happy than less educated people.[31] And in two different analyses of data from the World Values Survey, one conducted by Amado Peiró[32] and the other by Ronald Inglehart and Hans-Dieter Klingemann,[33] both found no significant correlation between education and well-being in almost any of the countries they considered, including the United States. Along similar lines, Joop Hartog and Hessel Oosterbeek analyzed Dutch panel data and reached the conclusion that the happiest people were those who had gone to high school but not to college.[34]

Perhaps the fairest assessment of this literature can be found in the following words of Alex Michalos. He asks the question, "Does education influence happiness and if so, how and how much?" Here is his answer:

> *If one defines and operationalizes (1) "education" as highest level of formal education attained including primary, secondary and tertiary education leading to diplomas and degrees, (2) "happiness" as whatever is measured by standardized single-item or multi-item indexes of happiness or life satisfaction, and (3) "influences" as a direct and positive correlation between such measures of education and happiness, then the answers to the basic scientific and philosophic questions are well-known.* Given these definitions, education has very little influence on happiness[35] *(emphasis mine).*

Although Michalos argues for more expansive definitions of education, happiness, and influence, the ones he uses in this paragraph are most relevant for our purposes. And his conclusion accurately sums up the evidence: "Education has very little influence on happiness." Some researchers say that more educated people are happier, whereas others say that less educated people are happier, and still others (perhaps the majority) say that education doesn't correlate significantly with happiness one way or the other.

*Summary*
The most measurable theory of well-being—indeed, perhaps the only measurable one— is the theory that equates well-being with happiness. Happiness, in turn, has been credibly measured via self-reports that are validated by test-retest data and by their correlations with other indicia of happiness such as others' reports and neurological and physiological measures. A large body of work on these self-reports has produced much data on subjective well-being, and those data tell us a lot about what makes people happy.

Without controlled studies or natural experiments in which college attendance is randomly distributed, it is impossible to draw confident conclusions about the effect of college on students' lifetime well-being. All we can do is look at correlation and try to control for other variables—a deeply imperfect but probably still useful enterprise. That enterprise does not yield clear answers about the likely effect of college on people's well-being. And unfortunately, to the extent that it does yield answers, those answers do not appear to be that college makes people happier.

The question, then, is how college might be changed so that it *would* increase most students' lifetime well-being. I offer some thoughts about this question in the next section.

IMPROVING THE EFFECT OF HIGHER EDUCATION ON SUBJECTIVE WELL-BEING
So far, much of what I've said may seem disappointing. It is hard to know what well-being is, and even if we know what it is and can measure it, we may still be unable to reach confident conclusions about college's effect on it. And even if we could draw such

conclusions, the available data do not lend much support to the view that college actually makes people happier.

So let me make a sharp turn and say a few things in this last section that I hope will be far more constructive and optimistic, if perhaps a bit utopian. The data on happiness reveal a lot about what makes people better off, and it would be possible for college to capitalize on those data so as to improve its effects on students' lives.

What do the data tell us? The answers may seem pedestrian but are in fact vitally important precisely for that reason: The key to happiness is often acting on, rather than ignoring, boring facts that people often can't be bothered to care about. For example, the data indicate that other than genetic predispositions, what affects people's happiness the most is whether they get enough sleep.[36] The data also indicate that spending time with other people—especially eating or socializing with friends or family—makes people much happier than they tend to be otherwise.[37] Exercise also increases happiness,[38] as does keeping a weekly gratitude journal.[39] On the other hand, driving in traffic is among people's least enjoyable activities,[40] and they never adapt to it, but it's far less bad if there's someone else in the car for company. Many of the yardsticks by which people often judge their success in life, such as how much money they make[41] and whether they have children,[42] do not seem to increase happiness.

So what does this have to do with college? Let me start with something very specific and then move to something much more general. The specific point is that colleges could simply teach students the findings of hedonic psychology and help the students incorporate those findings into their lives. To take the most banal yet perhaps also the most useful example, consider sleep. Getting enough sleep makes people happier, healthier, and more productive; drowsy driving causes more deaths from car accidents each year than drunk driving; spectacular disasters like the *Challenger* space shuttle explosion and the Exxon Valdez oil spill were caused in part by mistakes made due to sleep deprivation.[43] Considering all of these things, would it be so crazy for colleges to teach their students the importance of getting enough sleep?

Such teaching, in order to be effective, should not just involve telling the students the information and having them read the underlying studies. People's behavior doesn't change just by learning what to do; they have to actually do it. So I think colleges should help students train themselves to develop habits that enable them to be happier. Habit formation is its own crucial subject,[44] and students should be taught how to identify their habits, discard ones they realize harm their happiness, and build new ones they know would benefit them.

If students learned how to create beneficial habits and actually practiced them as part of their educations, then they would be likely to become much healthier and happier throughout their lives. They could also practice spending more time on activities they enjoy, such as active leisure or talking with friends and family, and less time on activities they probably enjoy less (if they are like most people), such as watching TV[45] or web-surfing on social networking sites.[46]

Moreover, students could be taught what makes certain jobs more or less likely to be enjoyable, which could help them choose their future careers. In a perfect world, students trained in the sources of happiness might even some day become leaders in the private or public sectors who work for structural changes that might make society in general more conducive to happiness.

Psychologists have already done most of the hard work of learning what makes people happy. But many millions of people never learn of those findings, and even if they do never make the relatively easy choices necessary to incorporate those findings into their lives. College could solve this problem by teaching students how to be happy and helping them to actually take the needed steps. If it did that, then higher education would surely improve students' lifetime well-being more than it does now.

But there is also a more general point, and it ties in more closely with the traditional mission of higher education. Both the happiness research and common sense indicate that people's well-being is influenced very heavily by interactions with other people. College offers a crucial opportunity for helping students improve those interactions. Not only do students learn to live with others their age and to get along with them in class, in dormitories, and in extracurricular activities, but also the very process of learning often involves understanding others and the relationship between their ideas and one's own.

In college, students come into contact with people and ideas that are different from the ones they are accustomed to and comfortable with. Their previous ways of thinking about things are challenged, and they learn how to deal gracefully with that uncomfortable reality. They also learn how to become people who themselves challenge received wisdom and, ideally, to do so in a respectful and dignified (while still committed) manner. Indeed, the critical thinking skills they hone may even enable them someday to challenge and improve upon the current state of knowledge about happiness itself, some of it contained in the citations in this essay.

Moreover, spending time with one's closest friends is one of the most happiness-promoting activities in human life.[47] Not only do people probably do more of that in college than at any other time in their lives, but also people often meet their closest, lifelong friends in college. Continuing to foster such friendships is undoubtedly one of college's chief advantages, and it should not be taken lightly or for granted.

Of course, college already fosters critical thinking and facilitates deep friendships, so what could it be doing better? Those who believe as I do in the value of the data on subjective well-being take it as a given that a large measure of people's happiness is determined by the way they think about their circumstances rather than by those circumstances themselves.[48] So perhaps college could focus somewhat more on teaching students how to think about their own standing in relation to their peers in ways that are more likely to lead to emotional health and well-being. In particular, people have emotional defense systems that cause them to feel anger toward others if they think those others dislike them. But a reservoir of untapped happiness can be unlocked by letting go of such anger and instead feeling compassion for others—even those who dislike us or have wronged us.[49] Helping students come closer to achieving that lofty goal, or even making them aware of it, would have many benefits. Not only would it directly increase students' lifetime well-being, but also it would facilitate the more traditional learning goals of college because those who confront hostile views with compassion rather than defensiveness are more likely to learn from those hostile views or to critique them thoughtfully. Learning to see other people and their ideas not as threats but as companions, even and especially when doing so is most challenging, is a strength that higher education should be poised to foster.

*Learning to see other people and their ideas not as threats but as companions, even and especially when doing so is most challenging, is a strength that higher education should be poised to foster*

Because the academic mission and core attributes of college are already well-suited to nourishing positive human interaction, anything that improves the way higher education pursues that mission should in turn improve students' lifetime well-being. In that vein, the suggestions that will be made throughout the rest of this volume are likely to be of great value to students and to the institutions that would like to help them lead happier lives.

---

NOTES

1. I am using the phrase "students' lifetime well-being" to indicate that the issue is how much better or worse a person's entire life is if she goes to college than if she doesn't go to college. Thus, I am *not* focusing only on the student's well-being while she is in college.

2. See, for example, Daniel M. Haybron, *The Pursuit of Unhappiness: The Elusive Psychology of Well-Being* (Oxford: Oxford University Press, 2008), 29; L.W. Sumner, *Welfare, Happiness, and Ethics* (New York: Oxford University Press, 1996), 20.

3. Derek Parfit, *Reasons and Persons* (Oxford: Oxford University Press, 1984), 493.

4. See Richard Kraut, *What is Good and Why: The Ethics of Well-Being* (Cambridge, MA: Harvard University Press, 2007); Philippa Foot, *Natural Goodness* (Oxford: Clarendon Press, 2001); Rosalind Hursthouse, *On Virtue Ethics* (Oxford: Oxford University Press, 1999).

5. For two of the many discussions of this point, see Sumner, *Welfare, Happiness, and Ethics*, 128–32 and Daniel M. Hausman, "Hedonism and Welfare Economics," *Economics and Philosophy* 26 (2010): 323.

6. John Rawls, *A Theory of Justice* (Cambridge, MA: Belknap Press, 1971), 408. See also Peter Railton, "Facts and Values," *Philosophical Topics* 14 (1986): 5–31 and Richard Brandt, *A Theory of the Good and the Right* (Amherst, NY: Prometheus Books, 1979), ch. 6.

7. Connie Rosati, "Persons, Perspectives, and Full-Information Accounts of the Good," *Ethics* 105 (1995): 296–325.

8. Martha C. Nussbaum, "Capabilities as Fundamental Entitlements: Sen and Social Justice," *Feminist Economics* 9 no. 2–3 (2003): 33–59.

9. As Daniel Haybron charitably puts it, "The Aristotelian literature has yet to integrate fully with the contemporary literature on well-being, so it is often difficult to tell where an author stands on well-being." Haybron, *The Pursuit of Unhappiness*, 287, n.19.

10. This may be the view of Richard Kraut, one of the leading proponents of eudaimonic theories. See Kraut, *What Is Good and Why*.

11. Jeremy Bentham, *An Introduction to the Principles of Morals and Legislation* (Oxford: Clarendon Press, 1907). Library of Economics and Liberty [Online] available from http://www.econlib.org/library/Bentham/bnthPML16.html; accessed 30 November 2015;

12. Ed Diener et al., *Well-Being for Public Policy* (New York: Oxford University Press, 2009), 68–9.

13. Diener et al., *Well-Being for Public Policy*, 71–2.

14. See Ed Sandvik, Ed Diener, and Larry Seidlitz, "Subjective Well-Being: The Convergence and Stability of Self-Report and Non-Self-Report Measures," *Journal of Personality* 61, no. 3 (1993): 317–42; Heidi S. Lepper, "Use of Other-Reports to Validate Subjective Well-Being Measures," *Social Indicators Research* 44 no. 3 (1998): 367–79.

15. Tiffany A. Ito and John T. Cacioppo, "The Psychophysiology of Utility Appraisals," in *Well-Being: The Foundations of Hedonic Psychology*, ed. Daniel Kahneman et al. (New York: Russell Sage Foundation, 1999), 479; Timothy G. Dinan, "Glucocorticoids and the Genesis of Depressive Illness: A Psychobiological Model," *British Journal of Psychiatry* 164 no. 3 (1994): 365–71.

16. Ito and Cacioppo, "Utility Appraisals," 479.

17. Andrew J. Oswald and Nattavudh Powdthavee, "Death, Happiness, and the Calculation of Compensatory Damages," *Journal of Legal Studies* 37 (2008): S217.

18. See, for example, Timothy D. Wilson and Daniel T. Gilbert, "Affective Forecasting: Knowing What to Want," *Current Directions in Psychological Science* 14 no. 3 (2005): 131–4.

19. See, for example, Matthew A. Killingsworth and Daniel T. Gilbert, "A Wandering Mind Is an Unhappy Mind," *Science* 330 no. 6006 (2010): 932; George MacKerron and Susana Mourato, "Happiness Is Greater in Natural Environments," *Global Environmental Change* 23 no. 5 (2013): 992–1000.

20. John Bronsteen, Christopher Buccafusco, and Jonathan S. Masur, "Well-Being Analysis vs. Cost-Benefit Analysis," *Duke Law Journal* 62 (2013): 1603–89; Cass R. Sunstein, "Cost-Benefit Analysis, Who's Your Daddy?" *Journal of Benefit-Cost Analysis* (forthcoming 2015)

21. Ed Diener, "Subjective Well-Being: The Science of Happiness and a Proposal for a National Index," *American Psychologist* 55 no. 1 (2000): 34.

22. I will use the term "attendees," but of course these measurements could be made just as easily with graduates.

23. Philip Oreopoulos and Kjell G. Salvanes, "Priceless: the Nonpecuniary Benefits of Schooling," *Journal of Economic Perspectives* 25 (2011): 176–78.

24. David Card, "Using Geographic Variation in College Proximity to Estimate the Return to Schooling," in *Aspects of Labour Market Behaviour: Essays in Honour of John Vanderkamp*, eds. Louis N. Christofides, E. Kenneth Grant, and Robert Swidinsky (University of Toronto Press, 1995), 201–22.

25. Even though higher education starts after childhood, the whole point of using the panel data is to know people's happiness levels *before* the higher education begins so as to compare it with those levels thereafter, which requires surveying children.

26. Many thanks to Sonja Starr for a series of enormously helpful conversations about the points made in this section.

27. Robert A. Witter et al., "Education and Subjective Well-Being: A meta-analysis," *Educational Evaluation and Policy Analysis* 6 no. 2 (1984): 165–73.

28. Ruut Veenhoven, "Developments in Satisfaction Research," *Social Indicators Research* 37 (1996): 101–60.

29. Betsey Stevenson and Justin Wolfers, "Happiness Inequality in the United States," *Journal of Legal Studies* 37 (2008): S33–S79.

30. Pavel Yakovlev and Susane Daniels-Leguizamon, "Ignorance Is Not Bliss: On the Role of Education in Subjective Well-Being," *The Journal of Socio-Economics* 41 no. 6 (2012): 806–15.

31. See Haylee Bree Hickson and Alfred Michael Dockery, "Is Ignorance Bliss: Exploring the Links Between Education, Expectations and Happiness." Paper presented at the 37th Australian Conference of Economists, Gold Coast, Australia, September 30 to October 3, 2008; Alfred Michael Dockery, "Happiness, Life Satisfaction and the Role of Work: Evidence from Two Australian Surveys," School of Economics and Finance working paper no. 03.10, Curtin Business School, Perth, 2003; Alfred Michael Dockery, "The Happiness of Young Australians: Empirical Evidence on the Role of Labour Market Experience," *Economic Record* 81 (2005): 322–35; Bruce Headey and Mark Wooden, "The Effects of Wealth and Income on Subjective Well-Being and Ill-Being," *Economic Record* 80 (2004): S24–S33.

32. Amado Peiró, "Happiness, Satisfaction and Socio-Economic Conditions: Some International Evidence," *Journal of Socio-Economics* 35 (2006): 348–65.

33. Ronald Inglehart and Hans-Dieter Klingemann, "Genes, Culture, Democracy and Happiness," in *Culture and Subjective Wellbeing*, eds. E. Diener and E.M. Suh (Boston: MIT Press, 2000): 165–83.

34. Joop Hartog and Hessel Oosterbeek, "Health, Wealth and Happiness: Why Pursue a Higher Education?," *Economics of Education Review* 17 (1998): 245–56.

35. Alex C. Michalos, "Education, Happiness and Wellbeing." Paper presented at the Is Happiness Measurable and What Do Those Measures Mean for Public Policy? Conference, University of Rome, April, 2007.

36. Daniel Kahneman et al., "A Survey Method for Characterizing Daily Life Experience: The Day Reconstruction Method," *Science* 306 (2004): 1776.

37. Daniel Kahneman and Alan B. Krueger, "Developments in the Measurement of Subjective Well-Being," *Journal of Economic Perspectives* 20 (2006): 13.

38. See, for example, Alan B. Krueger et al., "National Time Accounting: The Currency of Life," in *Measuring the Subjective Well-Being of Nations*, ed. Alan B. Krueger (Chicago: Chicago University Press, 2009).

39. See, for example, Robert A. Emmons and Michael E. McCullough, "Counting Blessings Versus Burdens: An Experimental Investigation of Gratitude and Subjective Well-Being in Daily Life," *Journal of Personality and Social Psychology* 84 (2003): 377–89.

40. Kahneman and Krueger, "Developments," 13.

41. Daniel Kahneman and Angus Deaton, "High Income Improves Evaluation of Life but Not Emotional Well-Being," *Proceedings of the National Academy of Sciences* 107 no. 38 (2010): 16489.

42. See, for example, Luca Stanca, "Suffer the Little Children: Measuring the Effects of Parenthood on Well-Being Worldwide," *Journal of Economic Behavior & Organization* 81 (2012): 742–50; Sarah McLanahan and Julia Adams, "Parenthood and Psychological Well-Being," *Annual Review of Sociology* 13 (1987): 237–57.

43. William C. Dement and Christopher Vaughan, *The Promise of Sleep* (New York: Delacorte Press, 1999).

44. See, for example, Charles Duhigg, *The Power of Habit* (New York: Random House, 2012).

45. Kahneman and Krueger, "Developments," 13.

46. Ethan Kross et al., "Facebook Use Predicts Declines in Subjective Well-Being in Young Adults," *PLOS ONE* 8 (2013): accessed November 8, 2015, doi:10.1371/journal.pone.0069841.

47. Kahneman and Krueger, "Developments," 13.

48. There are, of course, limits and exceptions to this. Very few people would be happy if they were impoverished, enslaved, or otherwise denied basic human necessities or rights.

49. Cf. Kevin M. Carlsmith, Timothy D. Wilson, and Daniel T. Gilbert, "The Paradoxical Consequences of Revenge," *Journal of Personality and Social Psychology,* 95, No. 6 (2008): 1316–24.

2

ESSAY

# Eudaimonic Well-Being and Education: Probing the Connections

*Carol D. Ryff*

## INTRODUCTION

For the past 30 years, I have been studying psychological well-being and linking it to a host of other factors, including people's socioeconomic status, their life experiences, and their health. The first section below describes the conceptual origins of the model of well-being I developed, including its links to Aristotle's view of eudaimonia, which he saw as the highest of all human goods. This formulation is contrasted with the hedonic approach to well-being that also has roots in writings from the ancient Greeks. Extensive empirical findings have grown up around both conceptions in recent decades. The second section provides a brief look at what has been learned about the links between eudaimonia and educational attainment. The story therein is straightforward in one sense—better educated people tend to have higher eudaimonic well-being—but complicated in another—there is considerable variability *within* educational strata, and further, issues of causal directionality are not clear. Going forward, two key questions are critical for scientific inquiry. First, does the *kind of education one obtains* matter for eudaimonic well-being? This query is equivalent to asking whether some forms of knowledge and learning are better for nurturing self-realization than others. Secondly, and more incisively, what exactly does higher education do for us as we seek to achieve the best that is within us? The final section will argue that a liberal education, rich in exposure to art, philosophy, and cultural knowledge is key for achieving life-long eudaimonic well-being, with its accompanying virtues of responsible citizenship and civic engagement. Although many have previously advocated for a liberal education, few have emphasized the importance of linking such advocacy to scientific (empirical) research on well-being. Future directions for investigating links between educational experience and eudaimonia will be noted.

## DEFINING EUDAIMONIC WELL-BEING: DISTILLING CORE DIMENSIONS

Over 25 years ago, I called for a new approach to the study of psychological well-being.[1] Although subjective well-being had been studied for decades as a window on the inner lives of U.S. adults, reigning measures assessed primarily happiness and life satisfaction. Such indicators were largely without theoretical foundation, despite extensive literatures in developmental,[2] clinical[3], existential and humanistic psychology,[4] all of which grappled with what it means to be a fully functioning, fully individuated, mature, self-actualized person. My 1989 contribution was to integrate these perspectives by distilling prominent points of convergence among them.[5] Six key components of well-being, shown in the top of Figure 1, identified these recurrent themes. Below them, the figure shows the conceptual formulations from which they were derived.

Definitions of the six theory-guided dimensions of well-being are presented in Table 1.[6] These descriptions of high and low-scoring respondents on each dimension were the basis for developing self-descriptive items to operationalize each component of well-being. The intent in creating such self-assessment scales was to render well-being an empirically tractable subject. The resulting scales have been translated to more than 30 languages and use of them in scientific studies has proliferated over time.[7] More than 500 publications have been generated to date. Numerous investigations examined the psychometric properties of the six-factor model, most of which, particularly when adequate depth of measurement (i.e., sufficient number of items) was employed, supported the original factorial structure.[8] Other studies detailed in the review article examined how various aspects of well-being changed as individuals aged, or as they dealt with particular life transitions (e.g., parenthood, relocation) and other challenges in work and family life (e.g., job stress, parenting a child with developmental disabilities, losing a loved one). Many publications probed links between well-being and health, assessed in multiple ways—how long people live (mortality), their risk for developing disease or disability (morbidity), and their biological risk factors (e.g., stress hormones, inflammatory markers, cardiovascular risk factors). Finally, an important line of inquiry focused on whether these growth-oriented, self-realization, meaning-making aspects of well-being could be modified and improved. Such intervention work has been conducted in clinical, educational, and community contexts.[9] Before examining what is known about empirical links between eudaimonia and education, the above model of well-being will be briefly contrasted with the alternative hedonic conception.

*Figure 1.*

**CORE DIMENSIONS OF PSYCHOLOGICAL WELL-BEING AND THEIR THEORETICAL FOUNDATIONS**

Theoretical Underpinnings

- Maturity (Allport)
- individuation (Jung)
- mental health (Jahoda)
- will to meaning (Frankl)
- self-actualization (Maslow)
- executive processes of personality (Neugarten)
- basic life tendencies (Bühler)
- personal development (Erikson)
- fully functioning person (Rogers)

***Aristotle's Eudaimonia***

## RETURNING TO THE ANCIENT GREEKS: EUDAIMONIA VS. HEDONIA

Aristotle's writings about eudaimonia were conveyed in the *Nichomachean Ethics*, which was not a treatise on human well-being, but rather an effort to formulate ethical doctrines offering guidance for how to live.[10] He opened with the following question: What is the highest of all good achievable by human action? Aristotle believed happiness was the answer, but underscored notable differences among people in what is meant by happiness. In his view, happiness was not about pleasure, or wealth, or honor, or satisfying appetites. Rather it was about "activity of the soul in accord with virtue." This assertion led to the next critical question: What is the nature of virtue? In answering this question Aristotle went to the heart of eudaimonia, arguing that the highest virtue in life is to achieve the

*Table 1.*

## DEFINITIONS OF THEORY-GUIDED DIMENSIONS OF WELL-BEING

| Self-acceptance |
| --- |
| *High scorer:* Possesses a positive attitude toward the self; acknowledges and accepts multiple aspects of self, including good and bad qualities; feels positive about past life. |
| *Low scorer:* Feels dissatisfied with self; is disappointed with what has occurred in past life; is troubled about certain personal qualities; wishes to be different than what he or she is. |

| Positive relations with others |
| --- |
| *High scorer:* Has warm, satisfying, trusting relationships with others; is concerned about the welfare of other others; capable of strong empathy, affection, and intimacy; understands give and take of human relationships. |
| *Low scorer:* Has few close, trusting relationships with others; finds it difficult to be warm, open, and concerned about others; is isolated and frustrated in interpersonal relationships; not willing to make compromises to sustain important ties with others. |

| Personal growth |
| --- |
| *High scorer:* Has a feeling of continued development; sees self as growing and expending; is open to new experiences; has sense of realizing his or her potential; sees improvement in self and behavior over time; is changing in ways that reflect more self-knowledge and effectiveness. |
| *Low scorer:* Has a sense of personal stagnation; lacks sense of improvement or expansion over time; feels bored and uninterested with life; feels unable to develop new attitudes or behaviors. |

| Purpose in life |
| --- |
| *High scorer:* Has goals in life and a sense of directedness; feels there is meaning to present and past life; holds beliefs that give life purpose; has aims and objectives for living. |
| *Low scorer:* Lacks a sense of meaning in life; has few goals or aims; lacks sense of direction; does not see purpose of past life; has no outlook or beliefs that give life meaning. |

| Environmental mastery |
| --- |
| *High scorer:* Has a sense of mastery and competence in managing the environment; controls complex array of external activities; makes effective use of surrounding opportunities; able to choose or create contexts suitable to personal needs and values. |
| *Low scorer:* Has difficulty managing everyday affairs; feels unable to change or improve surrounding context; is unaware of surrounding opportunities; lacks sense of control over external world. |

| Autonomy |
| --- |
| *High scorer:* Is self-determining and independent; able to resist social pressures to think and act in certain ways; regulates social pressures to think and act in certain ways; regulates behavior from within; evaluates self by personal standards. |
| *Low scorer:* Is concerned about the expectations and evaluations of others; relies on judgments of others to make important decisions; conforms to social pressures to think and act in certain ways. |

best that is within us. He invoked the daimon, which is a kind of unique spirit that resides within us all. The central task of life is coming to know one's unique capacities, and then to strive to realize them. Eudaimonia is thus a kind of personal excellence. These endeavors were distilled by the two great Greek imperatives, inscribed on the Temple of Apollo at Delphi—namely, to "know thyself" and "become who you are."[11]

Hellenic culture included other philosophers who puzzled over fundamental questions about what defines ultimate goals in life. Epicurus, for example, argued that the aim is to achieve a happy and tranquil life that is free of pain and includes pleasure.[12] Relatedly,

Aristippus posed that the goal of life was to seek pleasure by maintaining control over adversity and prosperity.[13] Two millennia later, these hedonic ideas appeared in social scientific research on the topic of subjective well-being—that is, how U.S. adults felt about their lives.[14] National surveys were conducted to assess the degree to which Americans felt happy and satisfied with their lives. Such surveys were followed by further psychological studies of subjective well-being[15] and ultimately, by the emergence of "hedonic psychology."[16] Reflecting on the larger field of research, Ryan and Deci[17] posed that hedonia and eudaimonia constituted the two most prominent approaches to the study of psychological well-being. A related empirical study[18] employed a national sample of U.S. adults to document that these two formulations constituted related, but empirically distinct, approaches to the assessment of well-being.

It is worth noting that utilitarian philosophy is implicated in the conceptual history of contemporary research on well-being. Utilitarians sought to promote the "greatest amount of happiness for the greatest number of people." That said, John Stuart Mill (1893/1989), a leading utilitarian, observed that happiness would not be achieved if made an end in itself. Instead, he saw happiness is a byproduct of other more noble deeds, such as caring about the improvement of mankind.[19] Bertrand Russell (1930/1958) further emphasized that happiness is not something that happens without effort; rather it is an experience for which we must strive.[20] Hence, he saw it as a "conquest" that demands zest, active interest, and engagement. These thoughtful points from two famous scholars are interesting that they seem to blend hedonic happiness with striving to lead a worthwhile life (eudaimonia).

The above summary clarifies that well-being is multifaceted—i.e., there is no single right way of conceptualizing it, or studying it empirically. Indeed, in recent decades a great deal of scholarly research has grown up around both hedonic and eudaimonic well-being. Entire scientific journals are now devoted to such inquiry, while mainstream journals in other disciplines (economics, epidemiology, sociology, diverse biomedical fields) now routinely publish findings about well-being. Educational status is regularly part of the reported findings; sometimes as an independent variable (e.g., does educational attainment predict different levels of well-being?), or more frequently, as a covariate (e.g., do the reported findings linking well-being to health, for example, hold up when differences in educational status are taken into account?). Deeper questions involving links between education and the pursuit of individual excellence that define eudaimonia are considered below.

*What is the directional nature of the relationship between education and well-being?*

## EUDAIMONIA AND EDUCATION
Findings from a national sample of U.S. adults, known as MIDUS (Midlife in the U.S., www.midus.wisc.edu) are examined to offer an empirical look at how educational attainment and eudaimonic well-being are connected.[21] The results offer useful information, but also underscore what is not known; thus suggesting possible directions for future inquiry.

*What Do We Know?*
Scientists across diverse disciplines routinely collect information on the educational levels of those included in their research samples. Educational status is thus part of standard demographic information in behavioral and biomedical science, along with gender, age, racial/ethnic, marital status, and so on. Using data from the MIDUS study, initiated in

1995 with over 7,000 U.S. adults aged 25 to 74, we examined how respondents' reports of eudaimonic well-being, across the six dimensions described above, varied depending on their educational attainment.[22] Figure 2 displays what we found—it shows average levels for each dimension of well-being, arrayed separately for men and women, as a function of four levels of educational attainment. The overall story is clear: those with higher levels of education report higher levels of well-being across all six dimensions. The positive associations between education and well-being are somewhat stronger for women than men, as reflected by steeper increments in levels of well-being among the better educated. These patterns may reflect changing educational opportunities among younger compared to older cohorts of women. Such descriptive findings do not adjust for other factors known to account for variation in well-being, such as respondents' age. Before considering that issue, however, it is useful to reflect on the question of causality in these data—that is, what is the directional nature of the relationship between education and well-being?

The positive association between education and well-being may mean that in becoming educated, people experience gains and enhancements in their well-being. Alternatively, it may be the case that those with higher levels of purposeful engagement, personal growth, self-acceptance, and so on, are more likely to persist in getting higher education. Both scenarios are plausible—thus suggesting that educational standing and well-being may be reciprocally related. Nonetheless, there are good reasons to expect that the preponderant direction of influence is the former: namely that becoming educated contributes in multiple important ways to the pursuit of individual excellence. The knowledge acquired on one's

*Figure 2.*

**EDUCATIONAL DIFFERENCES IN PSYCHOLOGICAL WELL-BEING.**

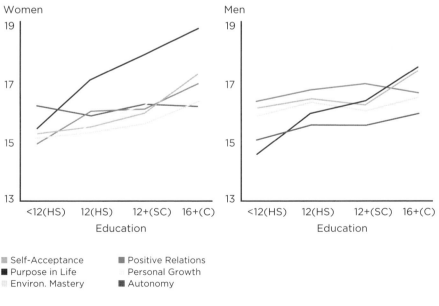

■ Self-Acceptance    ■ Positive Relations
■ Purpose in Life       Personal Growth
■ Environ. Mastery   ■ Autonomy

*Source: MIDUS National Survey*

educational journey not only provides access to resources (income) and opportunities (career positions), it also likely cultivates the skills, strategies, and insights needed to negotiate life challenges and deal with adversity. These questions could be investigated empirically although they rarely are.

Returning to the issue of age influences on eudaimonic well-being, a key point is that the educational gradients in well-being depicted in Figure 2 are not confounded with age. That is, even when age variation is taken into account (e.g., older adults tend to score lower on purpose in life and personal growth than younger adults), the educational differences are still evident *within* age groups. Thus, among older adults, who, on average, score lower on purposeful engagement than younger adults, there is still an educational gradient, wherein better educated older adults score higher on purpose in life than less educated older adults. Similar educational gradients are evident among younger age groups as well. The upshot is that education has a pervasive influence on well-being, even though other factors, such as age (which in part reflects cohort differences in opportunities for higher education as well as life course changes in work, family, and health), are known to matter as well.

A further point worth emphasizing is that averages can be misleading. Considerable variability surrounds the mean scores in all these analyses. Thus, educational status is not, in and of itself, definitive for predicting reported levels of eudaimonia. Among those with only a high school education or less, there clearly are individuals with high levels of purpose, mastery, growth, and so on. In fact, empirical scrutiny of the distribution of scores within educational groups shows that the variability spreads out as one moves down the educational hierarchy. This variability matters for health, where a large body of research on the topic "social inequalities"[23] has documented that those who are socio-economically disadvantaged—typically measured in terms of low levels of education, income, or occupational status—tend to have poorer health. Our research[24] adds an important new angle to that literature. Consistent with prior findings, we document that there is an educational gradient in a biological risk factor known as interleukin-6 (IL-6), which is implicated in the pathogenesis of diverse outcomes (cardiovascular disease, cancer, Alzheimer's). Thus, those with a high school education or less have higher levels of IL-6, on average, compared to those with some college or a college degree. More importantly, we show that among educationally disadvantaged adults, those who report higher levels of well-being have significantly reduced biological risk relative compared to their same education counterparts who reported lower levels of well-being.[25] These findings underscore the potential of well-being to afford protection (a buffer) against biologically-based health risks.

These results offer a glimpse into scientific inquiries that have linked educational standing to well-being and health. Such research is not, however the focus of this essay. Rather, building on such evidence, the aim is to probe more deeply the question— "How and why does education matter for eudaimonic well-being?" Such issues are central to the theme of *Well-Being and Higher Education*—"How might education's greater purposes, including well-being, be realized?"

*What Do We Need to Know?*
Educational status is routinely part of ongoing research on human health and well-being, which makes it puzzling how little is known about what lies behind this omnipresent variable. Put another way, almost never does scientific interest go beyond assessing levels

of educational attainment to consideration of the more penetrating question: *what is the nature of person's education and how does that matter for the individual as well as for society?* Relatedly, among those who have been fortunate to complete a college or university degree, how does the knowledge and training obtained relate to experienced well-being? Some students focus on science, technology, engineering, and mathematics; others pursue degrees in philosophy, history, languages, and the arts. Still others have educational experiences involving a mix of humanities and the sciences. In scientific studies that routinely employ educational status as a key demographic variable, little such information is known—educational status effectively is a black box. Knowing how many years of higher education one has without knowing the content of such education is a major impediment for the questions of interest herein—namely, the challenge of explicating how the pursuit of learning and knowledge translates to lives that are rich in eudaimonia and that may nurture beneficent, well-being functioning communities and societies.

*Among educationally disadvantaged adults, those who report higher levels of well-being have significantly reduced biological risk relative compared to their same education counterparts who reported lower levels of well-being*

Clearly, scientific research could contribute in important ways to understanding how education facilitates, or hinders, the pursuit of personal excellence articulated by Aristotle. The path he envisioned gave explicit emphasis to the task of discerning one's unique talents and capacities. Exposure to diverse realms of knowledge seems to serve this task, particularly when combined with the opportunities to progressively attune one's learning to personal interests and capabilities. However, in laying the foundation of one's higher education, an argument can be made for a broad liberal arts exposure before professional specialization occurs. This stance represents well-worn territory previously advocated by many. I revisit some of these claims below, but with a novel angle—namely, consideration of whether and how a broad liberal arts education contributes to eudaimonic well-being.

## THE EUDAIMONIC CASE FOR A LIBERAL EDUCATION

Many erudite scholars have reflected on what kind of education is needed to nurture full and productive lives. Focusing on childhood, John Dewey, in *The School and Society* (1899), envisioned a progressive education that was guided by active engagement rather than passive learning and that employed Socratic questioning about real-world issues.[26] Similarly, Rabindranath Tagore, winner of the 1913 Nobel Prize in Literature, espoused active engagement of children and gave notable emphasis on the teaching of sympathy and empathy through poetry and the arts.[27] Shifting to higher education in the present context, Martha Nussbaum's *Not for Profit: Why Democracy Needs the Humanities* (2010) calls for a liberal arts education when universities are witnessing an ever diminishing status of the humanities, juxtaposed with the rising ascendancy of science and technology.[28] Fewer students choose to major in literature, art, music, philosophy, or history. Instead, the priority is to obtain educational credentials that will translate to profitable (high salaried) career paths. Relatedly, Hanson and Health, in their book *Who Killed Homer?* (1998), lament the demise of classical education and call for a recovery of Greek wisdom.[29]

Recently, Helen Small's *The Value of the Humanities* (2013) offers a pluralistic argument built around five key arguments. The humanities are to be valued because: (1) they illuminate the meaning-making practices of culture (giving an indispensable role to human subjectivity); (2) they are useful to society in the preservation and curation of culture; (3) they make a vital contribution to human happiness (here Small's draws extensively on the writings of John Stuart Mill); (4) they contribute to the maintenance and health of democracy via teaching skills of critical reasoning, debate, and evaluation of ideas; and (5) they have intrinsic value—i.e., they matter for their own sake.[30] It is notable that Small's third value is directly tied to the experience of well-being, framed as human happiness.

## HUMANITIES CONTRIBUTIONS TO EUDAIMONIA

In articulating a defense of the humanities, Mark Edmundson inadvertently (because it was not his intent) offers guidance for building bridges between education and eudaimonic well-being. His most recent, *Self and Soul: A Defense of Ideals* (2015) asserts that our increasingly materialistic, skeptical culture has lost touch with values (ideals) vitally needed by the human soul.[31] He offers three great ideals—courage, contemplation, and compassion— which he examines via great works of literature and the accompanying argument that these ideals have relevance for contemporary lives. This call for a return to ideals is in the spirit of Aristotle's efforts to distill the highest of all human goods. In an earlier book, entitled *Why Read?* (2004), Edmundson probes deeply into what a liberal, humanistic education can mean for individual "becoming"—what we might call "self-realization."[32]

Edmundson opens with lines from William Carlos Williams: "Yet men die miserably every day for lack of what is found in . . . despised poems."[33] He links the poem to the contemporary context in which we are inundated with input from the internet, television, journalism, advertising, and other forms of what passes for the new. Faced with such overload, he asserts that there may be no medium to help young people learn how to live their lives than poetry and literature. To develop the case, a contemporary philosopher is invoked. Richard Rorty says individuals need to create a vocabulary about their lives; these are words people use to justify their personal actions and beliefs as well as to articulate their deepest self-doubts and highest hopes. Edmundson calls them "final narratives" and underscores that they are alive and dynamic—that is, needing to be challenged, tested, refined over time, and occasionally overthrown.[34] Ralph Waldo Emerson is also brought into the formulation via his view of education as a "process of enlargement in which we move from the center of our being, off into progressively more expansive ways of life."[35] Edmundson's central point is that a liberal education offering rich exposure to great literature is invaluable in building personal narratives and expanding of personal circles.

To sharpen understanding of how the process works, Edmundson asks again and again of poems and novels he considers: Can you live it? Via this query, he pushes the reader to consider whether the literature under consideration offers a new or better way of understanding one's self and others, or points to alternative paths for living a better life. In so probing, the values or ideals, perhaps implicit behind the creative work, are put into action. To illustrate, he considers Wordsworth's famous poem, "Lines Composed a Few Miles Above Tintern Abbey," written in 1798. The context is that Wordsworth's life had become flat—"he lived in a din-filled city, among unfeeling people, and sensed that he is becoming one of them . . . there is a dull ache settling in his spirit."[36] Returning to a scene from his childhood, he remembered himself as a young boy, free and reveling in nature. The return to nature, which is the heart of the poem, reminds him of its role in nurturing his own vitality. "Wordsworth's poem enjoins us to feel that it (the answer to one's despondency) lies somewhere within our research—we are creatures who have the capacity to make ourselves sick, but also the power to heal ourselves."[37]

Not emphasized by Edmundson, but worth noting is that Wordsworth's poetry served the same vital function in the life of John Stuart Mill. In early adulthood, Mill realized something deeply troubling—namely that he did not have happiness, central to the utilitarian philosophy in which he was immersed. Reflecting on his life, Mill described his early educational experiences, which were unquestionably exceptional, but also profoundly deficient. His father began teaching him Greek and Latin at a very young age and then expanded the pedagogy to fields of philosophy, science, and mathematics. Nothing in such learning helped Mill to cultivate the emotional side of his being. In fact, his father was deeply opposed to anything connected to sentiment or emotion. To escape the logic machine he had become, Mill began a quest to feel, and it was the poetry of Wordsworth that ministered deeply to longings in his soul. He credited it for helping him recover from the crisis in his mental history.[38]

Despite this inspiring tale, Edmundson makes clear that most educators in the humanities shy away from teaching literature to nurture inner vitality. Instead, students are instructed in skills of critical thinking, much revered in humanities departments. His view is that critical thinking is often no more than "the power to debunk various human visions. It is, purportedly, the power to see their limits and faults. But what good is this power of critical thought if you do not yourself believe something and are not open to having these beliefs modified?"[39] Students are thus given a cold and abstract language of smug dismissal. Derrida, he notes, clears away what has gone before, but offers nothing in return; he has no positive vision of human development. Thus, despite the rhetoric of subversion that surrounds critical thinking, Edmundson sees much education in the humanities as teaching "the dissociation of intellect from feeling."[40] Here, he invokes Friedrich Schiller who believed a true education ought to "fuse mind and heart" as well as Weber's commentary about "specialists without spirit, sensualists without heart," and finally, Goethe's insight that "it is easy to be brilliant when you do not believe in anything."[41]

For Edmundson, humanism is the belief that it is possible to use secular writing as the "preeminent means for shaping lives."[42] Here he makes explicit his concern with the process of human growth, which can be deeply nurtured by exposure to poetry, art, and literature. We can discover what Blake knew: "that all deities ultimately reside in the individual human heart."[43] Such awareness does not guarantee happiness. Shakespeare's tragedies make clear that certain griefs are not fully negotiable. The point is not to cheer one's self up, but to pursue truths. "We can seek vital options in any number of places. They may be found for this or that individual in painting, in music, in sculpture, in the arts of furniture making and gardening. Thoreau felt he could drive a substantial wisdom by tending to his bean field."[44] In addition, there is no single path, no one human truth about the good life, but many truths and many viable paths. A great humanities education offers "what Arnold called the best that has be known and thought."[45] During pursuit of one's higher education, studying the humanities affords a second chance vis-a-vis how one was socialized earlier. "It's not about being born again, but about growing up a second time, this time around as your own educator and guide, Virgil to yourself."[46]

Edmundson describes his own personal experience, when as a working class adolescent, he read *The Autobiography of Malcolm X*. Through example, the book led him to major discoveries. Malcolm X learned to read and write well in prison, relatively late in life. "In page after rhapsodic page, he describes the joys of reading, the pleasures of expression, the lure of knowledge. Malcom was persuaded, and persuaded me, that you could use the powers you acquired from books to live better yourself and to do something for the people around you."[47] This is what contemporary students who in the "bubbling chaos of popular culture" most need—that is, navigational skills that help them discern the difference between what is worth taking seriously and what is little more than noisy diversion.[48] Effectively, a high-quality humanities education should be there to help one see the differences between distraction and nurturing, vital sources.

*Eudaimonic well-being is not something that people are endowed with at birth —it is not about genetic inheritance or family wealth and background. Rather, it is about a proactive journey of seeking external inputs to find out who one is and how personal capacities can best be brought to life*

Edmundson closes with this vision: "If America leads and inspires the world in the years to come, it will be . . . because here more than anywhere, people are free to pursue their own hopes of becoming better than they are in a human sense—wiser, more vital, kinder, sadder, more thoughtful, more worth the admiration of their children. And it will be because they are free to become who they aspire to be after their own peculiar fashions."[49] These ideas are the essence of Aristotle's eudaimonia. Thus, the great gift of *Why Read?* is the argument that a humanistic education is vital for realizing the best that is within each individual life—it is about taking young minds to a place "where people have fuller self-knowledge, fuller self-determination, where self-making is a primary objective not just in the material sphere but in circles of the mind and heart."[50] It is a journey about achieving humanism's highest promise.

## A Future Scientific Agenda

A central aim of this essay is to underscore that eudaimonic well-being is not something that people are endowed with at birth—it is not about genetic inheritance or family wealth and background. Rather, it is about a proactive journey of seeking external inputs to find out who one is and how personal capacities can best be brought to life. Much of what needs to be taken in requires educational pursuits, not only in early adulthood, but across the life course. Indeed, many have argued that one of the primary benefits of high-quality higher education is that it nurtures a commitment to continued learning, as something vitally needed throughout life. Prior scientific research documents that higher levels of educational attainment are, in fact, linked with higher levels of eudaimonic well-being, but much future scientific work needs to be done. Of great interest and importance is the task of better understanding how the pursuit of knowledge and learning plays a role, perhaps central, in people's becoming—that is, in their self-realization. To begin such inquiry, a worthy hypothesis in need of testing is that a liberal arts education, rich in exposure to the humanities deeply nurtures eudaimonic well-being, both in early adulthood and thereafter. So doing requires tracking varieties of higher education that individuals obtain, or alternatively, have been denied, and linking them to subsequent reported levels of well-being. In the same fashion that scientists all over the world now investigate linkages between personal incomes, or gross domestic products and reported levels of happiness (typically assessed with hedonic instruments), far more scientific scrutiny is needed of how differing varieties of educational training matter for people's sense of mastery, personal growth, purpose in life, positive relationships to others, and so on. These questions are wisely studied while university training is occurring as well as thereafter, when adult lives are being played out in work, family, and community contexts. The central question, which can be put to the test scientifically and that constitutes a reconfiguring of the core utilitarian creed: that is, does a broad, liberal arts education nurture the greatest amount of eudaimonia for the greatest number of people?

---

NOTES

1.  Carol D. Ryff, "Happiness is Everything, Or Is It? Explorations on the Meaning of Psychological Well-Being," *Journal of Personality and Social Psychology* 57, no. 6. (1989): 1069–81.
2.  See Charlotte Bühler, "The Curve of Life as Studied in Biographies," *Journal of Applied Psychology* 19, no. 4 (1935): 405–9; Charlotte Bühler and Fred Massarik, eds., *The Course of Human Life: A Study of Goals in the Humanistic Perspective (*New York: Springer Publication Company, 1968); Bernice L. Neugarten, "The Awareness of Middle Age," in *Middle Age and Aging*, ed. Bernice L. Neugarten (Chicago, IL: University of Chicago Press, 1968), 93–8; Bernice L. Neugarten, "Personality Change in Late Life: A Developmental Perspective" in *The Psychology of Adult Development and Aging,* eds. Carl Eisodorfer and M. Powell Lawton (Washington, DC: American Psychological Association, 1973), 311–35; Erik H. Erikson, "Identity and the Life Cycle," *Psychological Issues* 1 (1959): 1–171.
3.  Marie Jahoda, *Current Concepts of Positive Mental Health* (New York: Basic Books, 1958); Carl Gustav Jung, *Modern Man in Search of a Soul*, trans. W. S. Dell and Cary F. Baynes (London, UK: Routledge, 2001).
4.  Gordon W. Allport, *Pattern and Growth in Personality* (New York: Holt, Rinehart, & Winston, 1961); Viktor E. Frankl, *Man's Search for Meaning: An Introduction to Logotherapy* (Boston, MA: Beacon Press, 2006); Abraham Maslow, *Toward a Psychology of Being* 2nd ed. (New York, NY: Van Nostrand Reinhold, 1968); Carl Rogers, *On Becoming a Person: A Therapist's View of Psychotherapy (*Boston, MA: Mariner Books, 1995).
5.  Carol D. Ryff, "Happiness is Everything, Or Is It? Explorations on the Meaning of Psychological Well-Being," *Journal of Personality and Social Psychology* 57, no. 6. (1989): 1069–81.
6.  This table was previously published in Carol D. Ryff and Corey L. M. Keyes, "The Structure of Psychological Well-Being Revisited," *Journal of Personality and Social Psychology* 69 (1995): 727, and is provided here with the author's permission.
7.  Carol D. Ryff, "Psychological Well-being Revisited: Advances in the Science and Practice of Eudaimonia," *Psychotherapy and Psychosomatics* 83 (2014): 10–28.
8.  Carol D. Ryff and Corey L. M. Keyes, "The Structure of Psychological Well-Being Revisited," *Journal of Personality and Social Psychology* 69 (1995): 719–27.
9.  See Elliot M. Friedman et al., "Lighten UP! A Community-Based Group Intervention to Promote Psychological Well-Being in Older Adults," *Aging & Mental Health*, October 13, 2015, doi:10.1080/13607863.2015.1093605; Chiara Ruini and Carol D. Ryff, "Using Eudaimonic Well-Being to Improve Lives," in *Handbook of Positive Clinical Psychology*, eds., Alex M. Wood and Judith Johnson (Hoboken, NY: Wiley, in press).
10. Aristotle, *The Nicomachean Ethics*, trans. D. Ross, (New York: Oxford University Press, 1925); Carol D. Ryff and Burton H. Singer, "Know Thyself and Become What You Are: A Eudaimonic Approach to Psychological Well-Being," *Journal of Happiness Studies* 9, no. 1 (2008): 13–39.
11. Ryff and Singer, "Know Thyself," 18.
12. Brad Inwood and Lloyd P. Gerson, eds., *The Epicurus Reader: Selected Writings and Testimonia* (Indianapolis, IN: Hackett, 1994).
13. Diogenes Laertius, *Lives of Eminent Philosophers*, trans. Robert D. Hicks (Cambridge, MA: Harvard University Press, 1972).
14. Frank M. Andrews and Stephen B. Withey, *Social Indicators of Well-Being: America's Perception of Life Quality* (New York, Springer, 1976).
15. See Ed Diener, "Subjective Well-Being," *Psychological Bulletin* 95, no. 3 (1984): 542–75 and Ed Diener et al., "Subjective Well-Being: Three Decades of Progress," *Psychological Bulletin* 125, no. 2 (1999): 276–302.

16. Daniel Kahneman, Ed Diener, and Norbert Schwarz, eds., *Well-Being: The Foundations of Hedonic Psychology* (New York: Russell Sage Foundation, 2003).

17. Richard M. Ryan and Edward L. Deci, "On Happiness and Human Potentials: A Review of Research on Hedonic and Eudaimonic Well-Being," *Annual Review of Psychology* 52 (2001): 141–66.

18. Corey L. M. Keyes, Dov Shmotkin, and Carol D. Ryff, "Optimizing Well-Being: The Empirical Encounter of Two Traditions," *Journal of Personality and Social Psychology* 82, no. 6 (2002): 1007–22.

19. John Stuart Mill, *Autobiography* (London, UK: Penguin, 1989).

20. Bertrand Russell, *The Conquest of Happiness* (New York: Liveright, 2013).

21. University of Wisconsin—Madison, Institute on Aging, "Midlife in the United States A National Longitudinal Study of Health & Well-Being," Accessed January 22, 2016, http://www.midus.wisc.edu/

22. Carol D. Ryff, unpublished data.

23. Nancy E. Adler et al., eds., *Socioeconomic Status and Health in Industrialized Nations: Social, Psychological, and Biological Pathways* (New York: New York Academy of Sciences, 1999); Michael Marmot, "Social Determinants of Health Inequalities," *Lancet* 365, no. 9464 (2005): 1099–104.

24. Jennifer A. Morozink et al., "Socioeconomic and Psychosocial Predictors of Interleukin-6 in the MIDUS National Sample," *Health Psychology* 29 (2010): 626–35.

25. Ibid.

26. John Dewey, *The School and Society* (Carbondale, IL: Southern Illinois University Press, 1899).

27. Kathleen M. O'Connell, *Rabindranath Tagore: The Poet as Educator* (Calcutta, India: Visva-Bharati, 2002).

28. Martha C. Nussbaum, *Not for Profit: Why Democracy Needs the Humanities* (Princeton, NJ: Princeton University Press, 2010).

29. Victor Davis Hanson and John Heath, *Who Killed Homer? The Demise of Classical Education and the Recovery of Greek Wisdom* (New York: Encounter Books, 2001).

30. Helen Small, *The Value of the Humanities* (Oxford, UK: Oxford University Press, 2013).

31. Mark Edmundson, *Self and Soul: A Defense of Ideals* (Cambridge, MA: Harvard University Press).

32. Mark Edmundson, *Why Read?* (New York: Bloomsbury, 2004).

33. Edmundson, *Why Read?,* 1.

34. Ibid., 25.

35. Ibid., 30.

36. Ibid., 57.

37. Ibid., 49.

38. Mill, *Autobiography.*

39. Edmundson, *Why Read?,* 43.

40. Ibid., 45.

41. Ibid., 45–6.

42. Ibid., 86.

43. Ibid., 89.

44. Ibid., 111.

45. Ibid., 113.

46. Ibid., 122.

47. Ibid., 125.

48. Ibid., 134.

49. Ibid., 142.

50. Ibid.

# 3
## ESSAY

# Higher Education and Education in Virtue[1]

*Barry Schwartz*

As sociologist Robert Bellah and his collaborators pointed out in their landmark book, *Habits of the Heart*, for a long time in the history of higher education, a significant part of the aim of the university was to shape good people who were good citizens.[2] In some institutions, that aim was reflected in a capstone course taught to seniors by the university president with coursework and dialogue that focused on how to be an ethical, responsible, adult member of society. From a modern perspective, this practice likely seems either quaint or naïve. There is doubt among academics about what being an ethical person means. There is doubt that their own training gives them the expertise to teach it. And there is doubt about whether it is their place to cultivate values in their students. It is not that professors are indifferent to what kinds of people their students become. It is just that they think that *their* roles lie elsewhere. Perhaps they believe, as Plato might, that bad action and misplaced values stem more from error than from evil, so that by cultivating the intellect, they will cultivate ethical commitments as by-products.

Bellah and his co-authors observed all these trends and mourned their loss as a sign of the loss of America's "second language"—the language of civic virtue.[3] But in truth, as the United States has become more and more ethnically, socially, and morally diverse, it has become less and less clear that there actually is a particular or common second language. And if this diversity is true of society at large, it is even more true in the university, where deliberate efforts are made to broaden the range of values and life experiences embodied by students—essentially privileging no particular common second language of civic virtue.

For many, this absence of privilege was the same as *demoralizing* the university. As such demoralization occurred, universities suffered little as a result in the eyes of the public. It continued to be taken as self-evident that higher education was good for students and society at large, and that American colleges and universities did an excellent job of providing it. But in the last few years, the university has lost its halo. Commentators, politicians, and parents are expressing serious doubts about whether colleges are teaching what they should be teaching and about whether they are teaching it well. Demands for accountability are everywhere, spurred in part by the absurdly high cost of a college education and the trillion dollars in student debt. What are students getting for all that money? What *should* they be getting? Yet the concern being expressed is not with the failure of universities to create good people. It is with the failure of universities to create people who can get good jobs.

In a move that typifies this current concern, the Obama White House launched an admirable initiative in 2014 to make college more affordable and accessible. A part of that initiative was an insistence that colleges be held accountable and that federal aid be tied to measures of performance. Accountability was to be measured based on graduation rates and the earnings profiles of graduates in an attempt to measure educational value—not metaphorically but literally—by asking if a college education pays for itself. Very recently, the Brookings Institution moved us a further step in that direction when it introduced a rating system used to rank colleges by the midcareer earnings of graduates, student-loan repayment, and the projected earnings power in the occupations that graduates pursue.[4]

Many academics regard this reliance on financial outcomes as an indicator of educational quality. In comparison to the university described by Bellah et al., this is a blatant instrumentalization of education to the point of Philistinism, yet one cannot reasonably expect students or their parents to shell out a quarter of a million dollars (the price of many highly selective institutions) and be indifferent to what they will earn when they graduate. And besides, if earnings are not a good measure of educational value, then what is? Colleges can't get away with smug silence on that question any longer. Society demands an answer.

*All educators want their students to know how to think, but nobody really knows what this means. We have to do better. We have to specify in greater detail what knowing how to think requires and then ask ourselves if colleges and universities are meeting this goal*

Universities that offer specialized training in specific professions have an answer: We're training the next generation of nurses, accountants, physical therapists, teachers, software engineers, etc. Whether they do it well or not is a legitimate issue, but that they *should* be doing it is not much in dispute. But for programs in the liberal arts, the answers are not as straightforward. You often hear defenders of liberal arts education suggest that their goal is less to teach the specifics of a particular discipline or profession than to teach students how to *think*. It is hard to quarrel with this goal, and it is echoed by those who frequently intone about how fast the technological world is changing and how important it is to have a flexible and innovative workforce. Just as the academy wants to teach students how to think, employers want to hire employees who know how to think.

But what does it mean to know how to think? Is there one right way to think? If so, what is it? All educators want their students to know how to think, but nobody really knows what this means. We have to do better. We have to specify in greater detail what knowing how to think requires and then ask ourselves if colleges and universities are meeting this goal. My aim in this essay is to begin to spell out what knowing how to think requires. In so doing, I will suggest that educating the intellect requires cultivating virtue—virtue of a certain kind but virtue nonetheless.

## INTELLECTUAL VIRTUES

Knowing how to think demands a set of cognitive skills that include quantitative ability, conceptual flexibility, analytical acumen, and expressive clarity. But beyond these skills, I want to argue that learning how to think requires the development of a set of intellectual virtues that make good students, good professionals, and good citizens and the development of non-cognitive skills, such as persistence, identity formation, and purposefulness. I use the word *virtues* as opposed to *skills* deliberately. All of the traits I will discuss have

*Well-Being and Higher Education*

a fundamental moral dimension. I won't provide an exhaustive list of intellectual virtues, but I will provide a short list just to get the conversation started.

## Love of Truth

Students need to love the truth to be good students. Without this intellectual virtue they will only get things right because we punish them for getting things wrong. When a significant minority of Americans reject evolution and global warming out of hand, the desire to find the truth cannot be taken for granted. It has become intellectually fashionable to attack the very notion of truth. You have your truth and I have mine. You have one truth today but you may have a different one tomorrow. Everything is relative, a matter of perspective. People who claim to know the truth, are in reality just use their positions of power and privilege to shove their truth down other people's throats.

This turn to relativism is in part a reflection of something good and important that has happened to intellectual inquiry. People have caught on to the fact that much of what the intellectual elite thought was the truth *was* distorted by limitations of perspective. Slowly the voices of the excluded have been welcomed into the conversation, and their perspectives have enriched our understanding enormously. But the reason they have enriched our understanding is that they have given the rest of us an important piece of the truth that was previously invisible to us. Not *their* (relative) truth, but *the* truth—objective and singular. It is troubling to see how quickly an appreciation that each of us can only attain a partial grasp of the truth degrades into a view that there really isn't any truth out there to be grasped.

> *Love of truth is an intellectual virtue because its absence has serious moral consequences. Relativism chips away at our fundamental respect for one another as human beings. When people have respect for the truth, they seek it and speak it in dialogue with one another*

Finding the truth is hard, and relativism makes intellectual life easier. There is no need to struggle through disagreements to get to the bottom of things if there is no bottom of things. Everyone is entitled to an opinion—the great democratization of knowledge—an alluring concept that leads nowhere. Love of truth is an intellectual virtue because its absence has serious moral consequences. Relativism chips away at our fundamental respect for one another as human beings. When people have respect for the truth, they seek it and speak it in dialogue with one another. Once truth becomes suspect, debates become little more than efforts at manipulation. Instead of trying to enlighten or persuade people by giving them reasons to see things as we do, we can use any form of influence we think will work. This is what political spin is all about. Some few years ago I read an interview with a senior advisor to several presidents. The advisor objected to the very idea that politicians "spin" anything because, he said, there really wasn't anything to be "spun." "Spin," he said, "is all there is."

In what is surely his most profound contribution to American culture, comedian Stephen Colbert coined the term *truthiness* several years ago to capture the distinction between aspiring to say things that have the ring of plausibility and *might* be true and aspiring to say things that actually are true.[5] In coining the term, Colbert called out public figures— politicians and opinion leaders—for their lack of the intellectual virtue of love of truth. In a more serious vein, in the brilliant book *On Bullshit*, the philosopher Harry Frankfurt distinguishes lying from bullshit by pointing out that people who lie know and care about what the truth is, whereas people who bullshit are simply indifferent to whether what they say is true or not.[6] Lying is a social, cultural, and moral problem, according to Frankfurt. But its significance pales in comparison to the significance of bullshit. The aim in cultivating the intellectual virtue of love of truth is not to combat lying; it is to combat truthiness and bullshit.

### Honesty

Honesty enables students to face the limits, the boundaries, and the risks of what they themselves know; it encourages them to own up to their mistakes; and it allows them to acknowledge uncongenial truths about the world. Most colleges encourage a kind of honesty: don't plagiarize and don't cheat. But it is uncommon to see them encourage *face up to your ignorance and error* or *accept this unpleasant truth and see how you can mitigate its effects instead of denying it*. Recognizing the risk of holding an unpopular opinion and the obligation to consider what supports or warrants such an opinion opens students to criticism.

### Fair-Mindedness

Students need to be fair-minded in evaluating the arguments of others. A very substantial body of literature exists in psychology on what is called *motivated reasoning*, our almost uncanny ability to italicize evidence that is consistent with what we already believe, or want to believe, and ignore evidence that is inconsistent. This may be especially true in the moral domain. As the psychologist Jonathan Haidt pointed out in his book *The Righteous Mind*, people use reason more like a lawyer who is making a case than a judge who is deciding one.[7] Lawyers making a case turn a blind eye toward inconvenient truths. Judges do not.

### Humility

Humility allows students to face up to their own limitations and mistakes and to seek help from others. As Carol Tavris and Elliot Aronson indicate in their book, *Mistakes Were Made, (But Not by Me)*, we often hear people use the passive voice when describing failures.[8] Students say things like "I got an A," but "she gave me a C." The desire to own one's successes is perfectly understandable, but students need to learn that they don't get to do that unless they are also willing to own their failures. Admitting mistakes would not be so painful in an environment in which it was routine for people to do so.

### Perseverance

Students need perseverance since little that is worth knowing or doing comes easily, but at the moment, we're cultivating the opposite. Worried that our students suffer from collective attention deficit disorder and will give us bad evaluations if we make them struggle, we dumb down our courses to cater to short attention spans. We assign a TED talk instead of a journal article, a popular (and short) book instead of a scholarly one. We don't appreciate that perseverance—or the related virtue, grit, which has been studied extensively by psychologist Angela Duckworth[9]— is more like a muscle that needs to be developed than a natural resource that needs to be excavated.

*Courage*

Students need intellectual courage to stand up for what they believe is true, sometimes in the face of disagreement from others, including people in authority, such as their professors. And they need it to take risks, to pursue intellectual paths that might not pan out.

*Good Listening*

Students can't learn from others, or from their professors, without knowing how to listen. I often find in discussion-based classes that when I'm speaking, students pay attention, but when one of their peers is speaking, they tune instead to an internal effort to come up with something clever to say themselves (a process, incidentally, that is only exacerbated when teachers make classroom participation an explicit contributor to the final grade). And it also takes the virtue of courage to be a good listener because good listeners know that their own views of the world along with their plans for how to live in it may be at stake whenever they have serious conversations.

*Perspective Taking and Empathy*

It may seem odd to list perspective taking and empathy as intellectual virtues, but it takes a great deal of intellectual sophistication to get perspective taking right. Young children feel for a peer who is upset but are clueless about how to comfort her; they try to make a crying child feel better by doing what would make *themselves* feel better. And teachers at all levels must overcome the curse of knowledge. If they can't remind themselves of what they were like before they understood something well, they will be at a loss at how to explain it to their students. Everything is obvious once you know it.

Perspective taking and empathy pay enormous dividends in professional life. In his wonderful book, *Critical Decisions*, Peter Ubel, a professor and physician at Duke University, makes a compelling case that while the physician paternalism of the old days is happily gone, it has been replaced by an equally inadequate model of patient autonomy in which doctors present the data, and patients make the decisions.[10] Though it is true that doctors can't ultimately tell prostate cancer patients whether or not to have surgery, it is also true that patients don't necessarily have the resources to make a fully knowledgeable decision solely on their own.

Good medical decisions require medical expertise and an understanding of the patient's unique life circumstances. They require shared decision making. But for that sort of doctor-patient conversation, doctors have to be good listeners who are able to take the perspectives of their patients. Moreover, medicine in the developed world has increasingly become a matter of managing chronic disease rather than curing acute disease. But the management of chronic disease (diabetes, hypertension, cardiac insufficiency, musculoskeletal pain) often makes difficult demands on patients to change how they live. A printed list of lifestyle changes is not worth the paper on which it is printed. Most people know what to do. The question is how to motivate them to do it. It takes empathetic, perspective-taking, medical providers to get patients to work as partners in managing their diseases.

Similarly in law, knowledge of the law may be the key to effective advocacy, but by itself, it will not tell lawyers what they have to know about clients who need to be counseled. A good lawyer needs to know the client as well as the law.

And in education, good teachers eschew one-size-fits-all lesson plans and opt instead, to reach each student where she is. However, if the teacher cannot get inside the head of the student, the one-size-fits-all lesson plan is the best she or he can do.

### Wisdom

Finally, students need what Aristotle called "phronesis,"[11] or *practical wisdom*. Any of the intellectual virtues I've mentioned can be carried to an extreme. Wisdom enables us to find the balance (Aristotle called it the "mean")[12] between timidity and recklessness, carelessness and obsessiveness, flightiness and stubbornness, speaking up and listening up, trust and skepticism, empathy and detachment. Wisdom is also what enables us to make difficult decisions when intellectual virtues conflict. Being empathetic, fair, and open-minded often rubs up against fidelity to the truth. As my colleague Kenneth Sharpe and I argue in our book, *Practical Wisdom*, practical wisdom is the master virtue.[13]

My argument for wisdom as the manager of the other intellectual virtues has a parallel in the writings of Thomas Kuhn, whose *The Structure of Scientific Revolutions* changed the way people think about science.[14] Indeed, it changed the way some people think about almost everything. Kuhn argued that scientific progress cannot be understood as a logical, rule-governed advance in understanding that accumulates brick-by-brick, fact-by-fact. There were periods when science seemed to progress in this way, but there were also periods of upheaval when everything changed. Such revolutionary periods were rarely produced by a key new fact. The lesson that many non-scientists drew from Kuhn was that truth was arbitrary and that scientific change was as much about intellectual fashion, or power, as it was about progress. Kuhn was appalled by this conclusion and tried to clarify in subsequent editions of his book that just because scientific advance was not governed by rules did not mean that it was arbitrary.

> Wisdom enables us to find the balance (Aristotle called it the "mean") between timidity and recklessness, carelessness and obsessiveness, flightiness and stubbornness, speaking up and listening up, trust and skepticism, empathy and detachment

Instead, scientists should adhere to what Kuhn called "epistemic values"—simplicity, accuracy, comprehensiveness, fruitfulness—that made some theories better than others. Values are not rules, so scientists can disagree about how important each value is and how well a given explanation exemplifies each value. But scientists do tend to converge on allegiances to certain theories for good and non-arbitrary reasons. This convergence reflects the collective wisdom of scientists. My list of intellectual virtues is meant to play the same role that epistemic values play in understanding good science.

## DEFENSE OF LIBERAL EDUCATION AS DEFENSE OF INTELLECTUAL VIRTUES

In my view, the way to defend the value of college education is to defend the importance of intellectual virtues and then show that the education colleges provide successfully cultivates those virtues. Cultivation of intellectual virtues is not in conflict with training for specific occupations. On the contrary, intellectual virtues will help to create a workforce that is flexible, able to admit to and learn from mistakes, and open to change. People with intellectual virtues will be persistent, ask for help when they need it, provide help when others need it, and not settle for expedient but inaccurate solutions to tough

*Well-Being and Higher Education*

problems. In *The Human Equation*, Stanford business professor Jeffrey Pfeffer argues that the right way to hire is to focus on individuals with the skills you don't know how to train and trust that you can teach the skills you do know how to train.[15] Work places need people who have intellectual virtues, but these places are not situated to instill them. Colleges and universities should be doing this training. But are they?

Few colleges and universities have systematic approaches with which to encourage the development of intellectual virtues. Mostly, their cultivation is left to chance, not to institutional design. Virtues are developed through practice and by watching those who have mastered them. Professors have to model intellectual virtues in their everyday behaviors. The questions we ask in class teach students how to ask questions. How we pursue dialogue should model reflectiveness. Students watch who we call on, or don't, and learn about fairness. We teach them when and how to interrupt by when and how we interrupt. We teach them how to listen by how carefully we listen. If they see us admitting that we don't know something, we encourage intellectual honesty as well as humility. We are always modeling. And the students are always watching. We need to do it better. A good start would be to do it deliberately and not by accident.

Most professors do not have the luxury of teaching small classes and seminars as I do, and it is hard to model intellectual virtues when one is lecturing to three hundred students. Nor do I envision a time when small classes will be commonplace at large institutions. Nonetheless, I think there are practices that can enhance the cultivation of virtue, even if they are imperfect substitutes for teacher-student or student-student dialogue.

In *Poetic Justice* when discussing virtue more generally, the philosopher Martha Nussbaum makes the point that narrative fiction is a good tool for displaying people living virtuous or not so virtuous lives in a way that provides the vividness and specificity lacking in didactic classroom instruction.[16] Providing students with narratives (they needn't be fictitious) of people displaying intellectual virtues may be a good way to make the best of student-faculty ratios that do not freely allow professors to model these virtues themselves.

*Cultivation of intellectual virtues is not in conflict with training for specific occupations. On the contrary, intellectual virtues will help to create a workforce that is flexible, able to admit to and learn from mistakes, and open to change*

## INTELLECTUAL VIRTUES AND LIBERAL ARTS EDUCATION

For the most part, students come to Swarthmore, where I have taught for forty-five years, wanting and expecting that their educations will be broad and their interactions with faculty will be significant. But now even here, this model of liberal arts education is being challenged as students come hell-bent on learning *something* that will make them employable. It seems as though every student at Swarthmore has at least a minor in computer science. Liberal arts education is a precious jewel, and we must do a more serious job of defending it.

An axiom of the social and political upheavals of the 1960s and 1970s was *you can't take down the master's house with the master's tools*. What this means in the context of higher education is that you can't discover the deep limitations of economics by only studying economics. You can't uncover the deep limitations of genetics or evolutionary biology by only studying genetics and evolutionary biology. To see the limitations of a discipline—any discipline—requires a perspective developed at least partly outside of that discipline. General education is not a substitute for disciplinary expertise. However, it is an essential ingredient to keep disciplines from running around in circles and swallowing their own tails. General education enriches the specialized training in the disciplines. Not *every* student of molecular biology needs a general education. However, if no student of molecular biology has a general education, I'm confident that there will be times when those in the field will lose their way. At least some practitioners of molecular biology will have to step away from their laboratory benches periodically to assess whether others in their majestic discipline are pursuing and discovering truths worth knowing.

The challenges to colleges and universities are coming from all sides. The White House wants to make sure that future earnings justify current costs. Parents faced with six-figure tuition bills join the chorus as do students faced with back-breaking debt. As if more pressure was needed, employers want to hire people who can do the job right out of the box; they want plug-and-play employees.

I am not sure that even institutions inclined to resist this pressure will be able to do so. Colleges must articulate their unique value in real detail in a way that makes clear that students who have training in the liberal arts will not only be better people and better citizens, but they will also be better professionals and employees. The right way for colleges and universities to defend themselves is to describe themselves as nurturers of intellectual virtues and then commit to that task.

## Conclusion

In his recent book *The Road to Character, New York Times* columnist David Brooks distinguishes between what he calls "resume virtues" and "eulogy virtues."[17] The former are the skills that get you good grades, good jobs, nice houses, and hefty bank accounts whereas the latter are what make you a good person. Though I think the distinction between skills and virtues is an important one, I also think that Brooks is wrong to imply that resume virtues are all that we need to produce excellence at work, or that eulogy virtues are for what comes after that work has ceased. Eulogy virtues are just as important to becoming good doctors, good lawyers, good teachers, good nurses, good physical therapists, and even good bankers as resume virtues. And they are also important to becoming good children, parents, spouses, friends, and citizens. As Aristotle maintained, virtue is needed for material success just as it is needed for moral success.[18]

And even if academic institutions remain reluctant to reenter the domain of character cultivation, even if they stick to their knitting and focus on the cultivation of intellect, I am confident that if cultivating intellect is understood as cultivating intellectual *virtue*, they will be cultivating good people as a by-product of cultivating good thinkers. None of the intellectual virtues I discussed is *only* an intellectual virtue. Love of truth, honesty, humility, perspective taking, courage, and wisdom will infect the social, cultural, political, and moral lives of students and simultaneously enhance their intellectual lives. Good character and well-being will come along for the ride. Aristotle taught us that happiness is best achieved indirectly as a by-product of excellence.[19] If he was right, then perhaps the best thing that colleges and universities can do to promote the happiness of their students is to cultivate their intellectual virtues.

Notes

1. See Barry Schwartz, "What 'Learning How to Think' Really Means," *The Chronicle of Higher Education*, June 18, 2015, accessed December 29, 2015, http://chronicle.com/article/What-Learning-How-to-Think/230965/.

2. Robert Bellah et al., *Habits of the Heart* (Oakland: University of California Press, 2007).

3. Bellah et al., *Habits.*

4. Jonathan Rothwell and Siddharth Kulkarni, "Beyond College Rankings: A Value-Added Approach to Assessing Two- and Four-Year School," Brookings Institution, April 2015, accessed December 29, 2015, http://www.brookings.edu/~/media/research/files/reports/2015/04/29-college-value-add/bmpp_collegevalueadded.pdf.

5. Stephen Colbert, "The Word—Truthiness," *The Colbert Report* video, 2:40, October 17, 2005, http://www.cc.com/video-clips/63ite2/the-colbert-report-the-word–truthiness.

6. Harry G. Frankfurt, *On Bullshit* (Princeton: Princeton University Press, 2005).

7. Jonathan Haidt, *The Righteous Mind: Why Good People Are Divided by Politics and Religion* (New York: Pantheon, 2012).

8. Carol Tavris and Elliot Aronson, *Mistakes Were Made (But Not by Me)* (Houghton Mifflin Harcourt, 2007).

9. Angela L. Duckworth et al, "Grit: Perseverance and Passion for Long-Term Goals," *Journal of Personality and Social Psychology* 92, no. 6 (2007): 1087–1101.

10. Peter Ubel, *Critical Decisions: How You and Your Doctor Can Make the Right Medical Choices Together* (Harper Collins, 2012).

11. Aristotle, *Nichomachean Ethics*, translated by Robert C. Bartlett and Susan D. Collins (Chicago: University of Chicago Press, 2011): Book VI.

12. Aristotle, *Nichomachean Ethics*, Book II, Chapter 2.

13. Barry Schwartz and Kenneth Sharpe, *Practical Wisdom: The Right Way to Do the Right Thing* (New York: Riverhead Books, 2011).

14. Thomas Kuhn, *The Structure of Scientific Revolutions* (Chicago: University of Chicago Press, 1962).

15. Jeffrey Pfeffer, *The Human Equation: Building Profits by Putting People First* (Boston: Harvard Business School Press, 1998).

16. Martha Nussbaum, *Poetic Justice: The Literary Imagination and Public Life* (Boston: Beacon Press, 1995).

17. David Brooks, *The Road to Character* (New York: Random House, 2015).

18. Aristotle, *Nichomachean Ethics.*

19. *Nichomachean Ethics*, Book X, Chapters 7–8.

4
ESSAY

# Higher Education, the Struggle for Democracy, and the Possibility of Classroom Grace[1]

*Henry Giroux*

TODAY, HIGHER EDUCATION functions largely as a workstation for training a global workforce and for generating capital for the financial elite. Hence, it is not surprising that many of these elite also view the more progressive ideals of higher education as significant threats to the power of the surveillance state, the ultra-rich and religious fundamentalists. Under such circumstances, it becomes more difficult to reclaim a history in which the culture of business is not the culture of higher education. However, this is certainly not meant to suggest that higher education once existed in an idyllic past in which it only functioned as a public good and provided a public service in the interest of developing a democratic polity.

At a time when the public good is under attack and there seems to be a growing apathy toward the social contract or any other civic-minded investment in public values and the larger common good, education must be seen as more than a pathway to a credential or a job. It must be viewed as crucial to understanding and overcoming the current crisis of agency, politics, and democracy faced by many young people. One of the challenges faced by the current generation of educators and students is the need to reclaim the role that education has historically played in developing critical literacies and civic capacities. At the heart of such a challenge is the question of what education should accomplish in a democracy. What work do educators have to do to create the economic, political, and ethical conditions necessary to endow young people with the capacities to think, question, doubt, imagine the unimaginable, and defend education as essential for inspiring and energizing the citizens necessary for the existence of a robust democracy? In a world in which egalitarian and democratic impulses are increasingly abandoned, what will it take to educate young people to challenge authority and in the words of James Baldwin, rob history of its tyrannical power and "illuminate that darkness, blaze roads through that vast forest, so that we will not, in all our doing, lose sight of its purpose, which is after all, to make the world a more human dwelling place?"[2]

Higher education has always been fraught with notable inequities and anti-democratic tendencies, but it also once functioned as a crucial reminder of the pivotal role it might play in enabling students to take heed of, understand, and address social problems in the interests of pursuing a vibrant democracy to come. Understandably, this sounds anachronistic in an age when education is being privatized and instrumentalized. But John

Dewey's insistence that "democracy must be reborn in each generation, and education is its midwife"[3] was once taken seriously by many political and academic leaders. Today, Dewey's once vaunted claim has been willfully ignored, forgotten, or has become an object of scorn.[4]

I have been writing about the relationship between education and democracy in the United States for more than forty years. I have done so because I believe that democracy has become ever more fraught, ever more at risk in the past several decades. If educational institutions choose not to nurture and develop generations of young people who are multi-literate, take on the roles of border-crossers, embrace civic courage, are socially responsible, and display compassion for others, it is possible that the democratic mission of higher education will disappear. I believe that any talk about democracy, justice, and freedom has to begin with the issue of education, which plays a central role in producing the identities, values, desires, dreams, and commitments that shape a society's obligations to the future. Education in this instance provides the intellectual, moral, and political referents for how we imagine and construct a future better than the one inherited by previous generations. Within such a critical project, education is defined not by test scores or the crude empiricism of a market-driven society, but rather by how it expands the capacities of students to be creative, question authority, and think carefully about a world in which justice and freedom prevail and the common good is reaffirmed. Once students leave the university, their actions and choices will be informed by a broader sense of ethical and social responsibilities, and this developing sense of who they are and their relationship to the larger world will be inextricably linked to what kind of world they make for themselves and future generations.

*Under the current regime of market fundamentalism, education is often narrowed to the teaching of pre-specified subject matter and stripped-down skills that can be assessed through standardized testing. This enshrines a pedagogy that kills the imagination and produces what might be called embodied incapacity*

Under the current regime of market fundamentalism, education is often narrowed to the teaching of pre-specified subject matter and stripped-down skills that can be assessed through standardized testing. This enshrines a pedagogy that kills the imagination and produces what might be called embodied incapacity. The administration of education suffers a similar fate. Increasingly, it is too often defined by a business culture and corporate strategies rooted in a view of schooling that reduces it to a private act of consumption. Lost here is the creation of the thinking, speaking, acting human beings who develop "competence in matters of truth and goodness and beauty, to equip themselves adequately for choices and the crucibles of private and public life."[5] In opposition to the instrumental reduction of education to an adjunct of corporate and neoliberal interests that offer no language for relating the self to public life, social responsibility, or the demands of citizenship, young people must take on the challenge of developing critical approaches to education that illuminate how knowledge, values, desire, and social relations are always implicated in power and related to the obligations of engaged citizenship.

Critical education matters because it allows the learner to question everything and complicates one's relationship to oneself, others, and the larger world. It also functions to "keep historical memory alive, to give witness to the truth of the past so that the politics of today is vibrantly democratic."[6] Education has always been part of a broader political, social, and cultural struggle over knowledge, subjectivities, values, and the future. Today, however, public and higher education are under a massive assault in a growing number of countries, including the United States and the United Kingdom, because they represent one of the few institutions left in which young people can be taught to be critical, thoughtful, and engaged citizens who are willing to take risks, stretch their imaginations, and most importantly hold power accountable.

The attack on education is now matched by a war on youth. Consequently, the current generation confronts a number of serious challenges at a time in which civil liberties, long term social investments, political integrity, and public values are under assault from a number of fundamentalist groups that exercise power from a wide range of spaces and cultural apparatuses in an age marked by a politics of disposability.[7] This age is defined by rising numbers of homeless individuals; a growing army of debt-ridden students; entire populations deprived of basic necessities amid widening income disparities, swelling refugee camps, and detention centers that house millions of economic migrants and political refugees; and those displaced by ecological catastrophes. And in addition to these millions, more are contained in prisons and jails, and they are mostly nonviolent, mostly poor, and mostly uneducated. The current generation lives at a time in which local police forces are militarized, drone strikes miss terrorists and wipe out wedding parties, the surveillance state threatens to erase any sense of privacy along with personal and political freedoms, and consuming appears to be the only obligation of citizenship. Legal lawlessness and a politics of disposability are the anti-democratic methods for dealing with those who are unable to pay their debts, violate a trivial rule in school, are unhoused from mental hospitals, or caught jaywalking in poor neighbourhoods, which make them prime targets for the criminal justice system. The politics of disposability have gone mainstream as more and more individuals and groups are now considered without social value and are therefore vulnerable and consigned to zones of abandonment, surveillance, and incarceration.

A culture of fear now drives major, national narratives and in doing so has replaced a concern with social and economic injustice with an obsession regarding the violation of law and order. Fear now propels the major narratives that define social relations and legitimize dominant forms of power freed from any sense of moral and political responsibility, if not accountability. These conditions raise a number of challenges for existing and future generations that they will have to address. What conditions need to be put in place that will enable young people to develop their critical capacities to be change agents? What will it take to dismantle the school to prison pipeline? How will the mechanisms that attempt to turn all black men into criminals in the schools and on the streets be dismantled? How will the widespread anti-intellectualism that enables a culture of thoughtlessness and violence be stopped? What role might education play in putting limits on the growing atomization and isolation of everyday life and the ludicrous assumption that shopping is the highest expression of citizenship?

Education should prepare people to enter a society that badly needs to be reimagined through the ideals of a substantive democracy. Such a task is political and pedagogical. Politically, this suggests defining higher education as a democratic public sphere and rejecting the notion that the culture of education is synonymous with the culture of business.

Pedagogically, this suggests modes of teaching and learning that are designed to produce an informed public, enact and sustain a culture of questioning, and enable a critical, formative culture that advances not only the power of the imagination, but also what Kristen Case calls "moments of classroom grace."[8] Pedagogies that promote classroom grace allow students to reflect critically on commonsense understandings of the world and begin to question, however troubling, their senses of agency, relationships to others, and relationships to the larger world. This is a pedagogy that requires us to ask why we have wars, massive inequality, a surveillance state, the commodification of everything, and the collapse of the public into the private. This is not merely a methodical consideration, but is also a moral and political practice because it presupposes the creation of critically engaged students who can imagine a future in which justice, equality, freedom, and democracy matter.

Taking seriously the role of higher education as a democratic public sphere also poses the challenge of teaching students to become agents of social change. Another is to teach them the skills, knowledge, and values that they can use to organize political movements capable of stopping the destruction of the environment, ending the vast inequalities in our society, and building a world based on love and generosity rather than on selfishness and materialism. In this instance, the classroom should be a space of grace—a place to think critically, ask troubling questions, and take risks, even though that may mean transgressing established norms and bureaucratic procedures. At the same time, it is important to remember that schools are not going to change one classroom at a time. Faculty need to organize not just for better pay, but also to once again gain control over their classrooms by altering the modes of governance that concentrate power in the hands of administrators and reduce most faculty to part-time status. This means building a movement to create a different kind of educational system and a more democratic society. It also suggests that academics need to do more than teach behind the safety of their classroom doors. They should also make efforts to be involved in politics, run for local school boards, become publicly engaged citizens, use the power of ideas to move their peers and others, and work to develop the institutions that allow everybody to participate in the creation of a world in which justice matters, the environment matters, and living lives of decency and dignity matter. In short, they can become public intellectuals willing to create the pedagogical, political, and economic conditions that connect learning to social change and pedagogy to the pressing problems that face the United States and the rest of the globe.

*Pedagogies that promote classroom grace allow students to reflect critically on commonsense understandings of the world and begin to question, however troubling, their senses of agency, relationships to others, and relationships to the larger world*

There are a number of issues that academics in their capacity as public intellectuals can take up and address, of which I will suggest three. First, they can define higher education as a public good for multiple audiences, address a range of important social issues, and lend their voices and analyses to the plethora of alternative public spheres that are opening up online. They could make the important argument that in any democratic society, education should be viewed as a right not an entitlement and suggest a reordering of state and federal priorities to make that happen.

Second, academics need to help ensure that students help to determine the development of their own educations. Students are not customers, and they should have the right to formidable and critical educations not dominated by corporate values; moreover, they should have a say in the shaping of their educations and what it means to expand and deepen the practice of freedom and democracy. Young people have been left out of the discourse of democracy. They are the new disposables who lack jobs, decent educations, hope, and any semblance of a future better than the one their parents inherited. They are a reminder of how finance capital has abandoned any viable vision of the future, including one that would support future generations. This is a mode of politics and capital that eats its own children and throws their fate to the vagaries of the market. If any society is in part judged by how it views and treats its children, American society by all accounts has truly failed in a colossal way and in doing so provides a glimpse of the heartlessness at the core of the new authoritarianism.

Finally, though far from least, there is a need to oppose the ongoing shift in power relations between faculty and the managerial class. Central to this view of higher education in the United States is a market-driven paradigm, the purpose of which it to eliminate tenure, turn the humanities into a job preparation service, and transform most faculties into an army of temporary, subaltern labor. For instance, in the United States, out of 1.5 million faculty members, one million are "adjuncts who are earning, on average, $20K a year gross, with no benefits or healthcare, and no unemployment insurance when they are out of work."[9] The indentured service status of such faculty is put on full display as some colleges have resorted to using "temporary service agencies to do their formal hiring."[10] Record numbers of adjuncts are now on food stamps and receive some form of public assistance. Given how little they are paid, this should not come as a surprise, though that does not make it any less shameful.[11] As Noam Chomsky argues, this reduction of faculty to the status of subaltern labor is "part of a corporate business model designed to reduce labor costs and to increase labor servility."[12] Too many faculty are now removed from the governing structure of higher education and as a result have been abandoned to the misery of impoverished wages, excessive classes, no health care, and few, if any, social benefits. This is shameful and is not merely an education issue but a deeply political matter based on how neoliberal ideology and policy have imposed on higher education an anti-democratic governing structure that mimics the broader authoritarian forces now threatening the United States.

We may live in the shadow of the corporate state, but the future is still open. The time has come to develop a form of higher education in which civic values and social responsibility become central to invigorating and fortifying a new era of civic engagement; a renewed sense of social agency; and an impassioned vision, organization, and set of strategies that can be used to once again make higher education central to the meaning of the ongoing struggle to embrace and live out the promise of a substantive democracy.

---

NOTES

1. I have borrowed the term classroom grace from Kristen Case, "The Other Public Humanities," *The Chronicle Review*, January 13, 2014, accessed December 29, 2015, http://m.chronicle.com/article/Ahas-Ahead/143867/.

2. James Baldwin, "The Creative Process," accessed December 29, 2015, http://thenewschoolhistory.org/wp-content/uploads/2014/08/Baldwin-Creative-Process.pdf.

3. John Dewey cited in Elizabeth L. Hollander and John Saltmarsh, "The Engaged University," *Academe* 86, no 4 (2000): 29–32.

4. This position has been developed fully in the works of a number of educators. See especially Kenneth Saltman, *The Failure of Corporate School Reform* (Boulder: Paradigm, 2012); Alexander J. Means, *Schooling in the Age of Austerity: Urban Education and the Struggle for Democratic Life* (New York: Palgrave, 2013); Diane Ravitch, *Reign of Error: The Hoax of the Privatization Movement and the Danger to America's Public Schools* (New York: Vintage, 2014); and Henry A. Giroux, *Schooling and the Struggle for Public Life* (Boulder: Paradigm, 2005).

5. Leon Wieseltier, "Among the Disrupted," *The New York Times*, January 7, 2015, accessed December 29, 2015, http://www.nytimes.com/2015/01/18/books/review/among-the-disrupted.html?_r=0.

6. Michael Yates, "Honor the Vietnamese, Not the Men Who Killed them," *Monthly Review* 67, no 1 (2015), accessed December 29, 2015, http://monthlyreview.org/2015/05/01/honor-the-vietnamese-not-those-who-killed-them/.

7. See, for instance, Sheldon S. Wolin, *Democracy Incorporated: Managed Democracy and the Specter of Inverted Totalitarianism* (Princeton: Princeton University Press, 2008) and Henry A. Giroux, *The Violence of Organized Forgetting: Thinking Beyond America's Disimagination Machine* (San Francisco: City Lights, 2014).

8. Case, "Other Public Humanities."

9. Junct Rebellion, "How The American University was Killed, in Five Easy Steps," The Homeless Adjunct (blog), August 12, 2012, http://junctrebellion.wordpress.com/2012/08/12/how-the-american-university-was-killed-in-five-easy-steps/.

10. Scott Jaschik, "Making Adjuncts Temps—Literally," *Inside Higher Ed*, August 9, 2010, accessed December 29, 2015, http://www.insidehighered.com/news/2010/08/09/adjuncts.

11. Stacey Patton, "The Ph.D. Now Comes With Food Stamps," *The Chronicle of Higher Education*, May 6, 2012, accessed December 29, 2015, http://chronicle.com/article/From-Graduate-School-to/131795/.

12. Noam Chomsky, "How America's Great University System is Being Destroyed," *Alternet*, February 28, 2015, accessed December 29, 2015, http://www.alternet.org/corporate-accountability-and-workplace/chomsky-how-americas-great-university-system-getting.

# Against the Culture of Acquiescence: Why Students Need Liberal Learning for their own Well-Being as well as the Well-Being of Society

*William M. Sullivan*

THIS IS A PERPLEXING AND DIFFICULT MOMENT for higher education in America. Dissatisfaction is the tenor of much public discussion. Concerns about the cost, value, and efficacy of college have brought back the question of the purpose of higher learning, though not usually in a thoughtful or coherent way. Some would streamline the academy to make it as cost-effective a training system for a national workforce as possible. Others, rightly alarmed at the myopia and stridency of such demands, emphasize the value of critical, detached thinking, particularly as taught in the academic disciplines. A determined but smaller number of voices have emphasized the need to reinvigorate and expand the values of liberal learning to encompass critical intellect and vocational preparation within the broader aim of forming citizens able to understand, reflect, and act with confidence.

The most pervasive attitude, however, is one of disengagement from the larger situation, which mirrors the psychic climate of American society as whole. Like psychological dissociation, disengagement may be tempting to individuals or groups overwhelmed by the forces of disruption. Yet in the aggregate, a stance of disengagement is profoundly maladaptive. The most salient threats to our well-being—the global instability caused by inter-cultural and inter-religious conflict, unguided technological growth and environmental degradation, and the gross economic and social inequalities that are wreaking havoc within an ever more interconnected global society—all require the ability to think incisively and act responsibly as citizens. Coping with the challenges of the twenty-first century demands a widening of perspectives and an enlarged sense of responsibility—exactly the opposite of disengagement.

This mismatch between the challenges we face and the contracting of awareness evident in disengagement make achieving the mission of higher education extremely challenging. The real question is the following: *What strategies can higher education deploy in the face of this engagement deficit for the sake of today's students and for the collective future of our global society?* Two in particular recommend themselves. The first is reinvigoration of the spirit of liberal learning so as to enable all students, not just a select few, to make sense of themselves and the world, to discover meaningful purposes that connect their own well-being with contribution to the larger society. The second is participation in an educational community. To meet the challenges of the present, such communities must intentionally link academic, personal, and career exploration with awareness of sharing a larger life. Such communities of learning are needed if students are to develop the confidence to engage with their times. Imaginatively developed and energetically led, communities of learning that foster student growth in its many dimensions offer higher education its best possibility to address the challenges of the present and renew its own distinctive mission.

## THE ENGAGEMENT DEFICIT: A CULTURE OF ACQUIESCENCE

The urgent need to revitalize the tradition of liberal learning and strengthen academic community emerges with special clarity in the current context of disengagement. The inability to imagine a genuine alternative to a dysfunctional present is a telltale mark of today's culture of acquiescence.[1] In the academy, perhaps the prime symptom of this condition is the fixation on employability as the sole measure of educational value. Of course, in an economic climate of slow growth and radical insecurity, this is understandable. But nevertheless this agenda represents a drastic constriction of perspective that limits the intellectual range of the nation's future workforce and threatens the very adaptability its promoters seek. The complexity of our current challenges demands breadth of mind—real thinking outside the box—and a synthetic sensibility. Reducing higher education's mandate to technical training will constrict the very capacities needed to escape current constraints.

*The most salient threats to our well-being—the global instability caused by inter-cultural and inter-religious conflict, unguided technological growth and environmental degradation, and the gross economic and social inequalities that are wreaking havoc within an ever more interconnected global society—all require the ability to think incisively and act responsibly as citizens*

The larger context is far from inviting. Many Americans are angry. They are also anxious, fearful, and moved by contending concerns and agendas. Redress for racial injustice moves some; others advocate a drastic closing of ranks and raising of barriers to obtain security. Beneath both, like a continuing base note, an ominous but stealthy, long-term, economic inequality has produced a society radically separated into winners and losers, which magnifies the power and influence of the winners to control national policy. It has also inflicted more economic pain on the majority, made life more precarious, and skewed rates of morbidity and mortality well beyond those of any other wealthy nation.[2]

Placed as they are in the midst of these dispiriting realities, today's students have responded in apparently contradictory ways. The recent research of Richard Arum and Josipa Roksa provides a detailed picture of disengagement. They found that a large number of students at a wide range of institutions are simply "adrift." These emerging adults adopt a strategy of simply getting by academically. Their varying burdens of debt notwithstanding, they focus their energies on social life and defer as long as possible entrance into the adult world of career and responsibility. These students are neither strongly driven to achieve nor adequately prepared to make their ways after graduation in careers or life.[3]

By contrast, students at the nation's most selective universities and colleges have been compared by William Deresiewicz to "excellent sheep": highly ambitious, strongly competitive, and self-confident. Their success has become a key purpose in the upper middle class families from which they mostly come. The problem, argues Deresiewicz, is that their success breeds a sense of entitlement and a conspicuous unwillingness to risk questioning the goal of achieving the next rung of success toward which they, like sheep, are being driven by competitive pressure. The nation's ambitious and academically oriented youth are simply "trained to operate within the system, never to imagine how [they] might create a better one."[4]

Like rising levels of depression and anxiety among the young, this bifurcation of student attitudes into drift or unreflective drive for achievement is another symptom of a deep caution about larger commitments and purposes and a constriction of imagination. What these apparently opposed attitudes share is an acceptance of current conditions as inevitable and the consequent adaptation of a wary strategy of limited trust and conditional loyalties. Why is this happening to so many emerging adults? Some blame the spread of attention-stealing communications devices that keep individuals enmeshed in circles of status anxiety and gossip. Others blame the growing fluidity of social relationships and possible styles of living. Still others blame an ever-expanding commercialization of everything from dog walking to child rearing. All of these trends may well contribute to the current confusion and avoidance of hard realities. However, the most plausible explanation is the relentless pressure of constant competition for prestige, economic success, even simple survival that for many people of all classes has overwhelmed other aims.

We live in a society of contracting awareness and diminishing attention in a moment that demands we become more widely aware of and attentive to the complexity of the situation that confronts us. The struggle to stay ahead of the competition, or at least remain afloat, has so engulfed most people's consciousness that there seems to be little if any psychic space or energy left with which to attend the larger reality. As the economic competition becomes more severe, and the consequences of losing more dire, the time horizon contracts. Even among the most successful, the willingness to take risks, to go all out for that fleeting chance, and to subject others to risk has become almost overwhelming. From reality TV to *Wolf Hall*, these imperatives dominate much of popular culture. "If you don't," says the watchword of the hour, "be sure the other guy will!"

Faculty and educational professionals of all kinds have been subject to the same pressures. Faculty, too, are heavily focused on the immediate competitive situation. One's standing within a discipline, academic status, and achievement of tenure—for junior faculty fortunate enough to be able to aspire to it—have taken on such importance that the concerns regarding liberal arts teaching and the preparation of students for purposeful lives are often greeted with suspicion or indifference. Institutions of higher learning seem caught between a sense of mission and what is perceived as tightening constraints on the ability to do anything other than meet the competition. As in the business world, such scenarios are likely to lead to a race to the bottom by cutting costs and cheapening the product.

It is also evident that these tendencies have intensified divisions and conflicts along racial, ethnic, religious, and national lines. These deep divisions—augmented and exacerbated by socio-economic stress—breed resentment, outrage, anxiety, and aggressiveness. They put huge obstacles in the way of common responses to shared problems. Acquiescence becomes a destructive and maladaptive response that leads not only to a closing down, a narrowing of perspective, but also to a decreased willingness to trust others. Acquiescence weakens confidence in the possibility to change the direction of our institutions to realize justice and enhance cooperation and thereby undercuts civic life at its roots. It eviscerates the taproots of interdependence whose support provides individuals with the assurance that by working with others, they can enhance and expand their lives.

## ADDRESSING DRIFT: HUMANISTIC LEARNING
## AND THE RECOVERY OF EDUCATIONAL PURPOSE

The difficulty presented by this pervasive disengagement has resulted in increased attention to student motivation to learn. In summing up a large body of scientific literature on learning, Richard P. Kealing and Richard H. Hirsh emphasize that "learning that sticks, the kind that leads to the kind of changes we expect of college, what we call higher learning, requires rich engagement with new material . . . the outcome of this engagement is a concrete and tangible change in how one thinks and makes sense of the world."[5] Noting that colleges and universities can typically demonstrate only limited success in this core aspect of their missions, Kealing and Hirsh emphasize that learning demands not only cognitive attention, but also engagement of emotional energy, imagination, and perseverance.

In their recent study of the undergraduate experience, sociologists Daniel F. Chambliss and Christopher G. Takacs conclude that "human contact, especially face-to-face, seems to have an unusual influence on what students do, on the directions their careers take, and on their experience of college."[6] They found that the key factors that account for student motivation and therefore engagement in learning were the quality of relationships between students and faculty and the ability of students to find meaningful connections with a campus community oriented toward intellectual and personal development.

Taken together, these findings underscore the continuing relevance of the central teaching practices developed by liberal education, especially the humanistic pedagogies, that build personal relations between faculty and students in the pursuit of a broad understanding of themselves and the world. In other words, contemporary research is helping to reclaim insights and approaches to learning that have been at the historic core of humanistic learning but have for various reasons been neglected. These include involvement of students with their subject matter, their evolving self-understanding and personal development, and the formative aim of educating active democratic citizens. This research-supported approach to teaching and learning, then, holds an important implication about the possibilities opened by today's evolving digital technology. New technologies should be promoted as they prove able to enhance and extend these relationships and pedagogies, not as cost-driven replacements for them.[7]

The signature of humanistic learning and inquiry is its cultivation of a double or bi-focal vision of knowledge. On the one hand, humanistic inquiry values intellectual rigor and cognitive tools of analysis through which persons and events are analyzed from the *outside*. But humanistic learning also seeks to understand the meaning of actions and events from *within*, from the point of view of an engaged participant in the human story. More specialized modes of cognition, including the objectified, analytical view of the sciences (which has proven so powerful for understanding and controlling the natural world), are valuable tools for humanistic inquiry, but their significance must still be sought within the matrix of social, historical forms of life that make up human culture.

Humanistic learning, therefore, can never attend only to the cognitive. It uses critical, skeptical analysis to gain distance and insight. But like the arts, the practice of humanistic inquiry also requires imagination, empathy, and aesthetic and moral awareness. Because such inquiry and the humanistic learning it seeks to promote participate in the human contexts they seek to understand, they must employ critical distance and personal engagement that includes ethical sensitivity and impersonal judgment.

The irreplaceable value of this kind of learning for higher education is that it provides students with a vast and deep cultural fund of human experience. From this they can freely draw as they explore self and world in their search for significance and purpose. Because humanistic pedagogy is necessarily rooted in human history and culture and the history of science and technology, it is in principle open to all areas of human endeavor as subject matter. And this is why the often chilly relations between the disciplines of the humanities and the sciences constitute a significant deficit for liberal learning in today's academy. The scope and urgency of current practical challenges should make better integration across the disciplines a particularly salient priority for those who seek to overcome the culture of acquiescence.

AGAINST THE CULTURE OF ACQUIESCENCE:
RECOVERING THE ENGAGED STANCE IN LEARNING AND LIFE

The import of this bi-focal humanistic stance for higher education in our global era—which demands greater empathic understanding of others and greater responsibility than previously—has been trenchantly argued by William Theodore de Bary. De Bary pioneered the introduction of East Asian studies to the American academy and now proposes a new role for the study of culture and tradition in *The Great Civilized Conversation: Education for a World Community*.[8] In this work, de Bary illustrates the bi-focal, engaged stance of humanistic inquiry.

De Bary urges us to recast the role of humanistic studies so that the texts and artifacts of past traditions of learning from the East and the West become more than simply museums to visit. They are in potential much more: sources of rich comparison and contrast to help us understand the present and provoke questions about how to construe the future. De Bary notes that an educational focus on core or classic texts—a notion resonant in East Asia—was emphasized not only to develop critical thinking skills, but also to propose models for exploration and assimilation. These works include art as well as texts and were intended to expand the imaginations of students. They were to be rich and multi-faceted enough to incite students' own probing and to be useful for their own lives and historical situations.[9]

The value of humanistic pedagogy, de Bary insists, lies in its explicit intent to engage students collectively with issues of living. At its best, active discussion by students with each other and with the instructor leads to the recasting of inherited understandings; students can use these discussions to illuminate other texts and the contemporary situation. In a democratic society that depends upon its citizens for direction, he argues that this pedagogy needs to be a consciously civic one that teaches students "to deal in an informed way with the shared problems of contemporary society."[10] Such discussion can promote and model active civic discourse and exemplify the value and difficulty of civility—a learning by doing.

In today's interconnected but perilous global era characterized by what de Bary calls "a runaway market and technology,"[11] accessing the experiences and reflections of the past and understanding the religious, political, and moral concepts of other civilizations take on new urgency. He points out that the current, economic and national competitive rivalry that exists on a global scale, abetted by explosive technological growth, poses an enormous threat to humanity and the planet itself. Learning of real value, then, must illuminate our engagements and prompt a higher degree of personal and collective responsibility. Such learning may even demand that we change how we approach life.[12] Rather than presenting a reassuring and complacent picture, humanistic learning is intended to hold up a mirror and demand self-reflection and response from the learner and educator alike. Devising the forms of thinking and acting that can link everyday life consciously to these larger challenges and so fulfill the promise of humanistic learning is the pedagogical problem of our age.[13]

## THE PRACTICAL GROUNDING OF LEARNING IN COMMUNITY

It was John Dewey who declared the "ethical principle underlying education" to be "interest in the community welfare, an interest which is intellectual and practical as well as emotional—an interest, that is to say, in perceiving whatever makes for social order and progress and for carrying these principles into execution."[14] Dewey called this attitude "the ultimate ethical habit" and argued that this was the end to which all other aspects of education had to be related.

*Rather than presenting a reassuring and complacent picture, humanistic learning is intended to hold up a mirror and demand self-reflection and response from the learner and educator alike*

Expanded to the concerns with global society and planetary ecology, yet also concretized in social relationships on campus and between the campus and the societies in which it is embedded, Dewey's "ultimate ethical habit" well describes the aim that twenty-first century higher education needs to embody. This is the larger meaning of the concept that liberal learning has a civic purpose.

Andrew Delbanco reminds us that in the face of what he calls the "siege of uncertainty" faced by today's student generation, higher education as a whole is doing far too little to help students cope.[15] Delbanco notes one major reason for this failure: the sense of community that has been "at the core of the college idea" is in danger of being overwhelmed by entropic forces. Without an experience of connection and trust, he emphasizes, students find it hard to achieve one of the most important outcomes of college: learning that "to serve others is to serve oneself" since it is only by participation in a worthy form of social life that personal purpose can be found. This, far more than career success alone, remains the enormous gift that higher education can bestow, "thereby countering the loneliness and aimlessness by which all people, young and old, can be afflicted."[16]

Humanistic learning can most easily find common ground with the recent emphasis on experiential education by attending to the need to build and sustain vibrant, intergenerational, intellectual communities of learning. These efforts have sought to help students put learning to work in actual contexts of social living and thereby to develop habits of inquiry and cooperation so they can go on learn from their experiences. Bringing these educational trajectories into mutually beneficial dialogue and cross-fertilization is one of the emerging frontiers in undergraduate education.

The practical basis for these developments, however, is ultimately the same as that of effective learning of any kind: constructive and mutually responsive relationships based upon the shared purpose of learning. It is worth remembering that the experience of such community is the very source of educational vitality. It is a renewable resource must be carefully tended. Its neglect has weakened the ability of our institutions of higher learning to break out of the trap of acquiescence.

Notes

1. Historian Steve Fraser uses the phrase "age of acquiescence" to characterize the present political situation in the United States in *The Age of Acquiescence: The Life and Death of American Resistance to Organized Wealth and Power* (Boston, MA: Little, Brown and Co., 2015).
2. Richard Wilkinson and Kate Pickett, *The Spirit Level: Why Greater Equality Makes Societies Stronger* (New York: Bloomsbury Press, 2010).
3. Richard Arum and Josipa Roksa, *Aspiring Adults Adrift: Tentative Transitions of College Graduates* (Chicago, IL: University of Chicago Press, 2014), 16–21.
4. William Deresiewicz, *Excellent Sheep: The Miseducation of the American Elite and the Way to a Meaningful Life* (Cambridge MA: Harvard University Press, 2014), 229.
5. Richard P. Kealing and Richard H. Hirsh, *We're Losing Our Minds: Rethinking American Higher Education* (New York: Palgrave Macmillan, 2011), 7.
6. Daniel F. Chambliss and Christopher G. Takacs, *How College Works* (Cambridge MA: Harvard University Press, 2014), 3–4.
7. See William M. Sullivan, "The Coming Digital Disruption: Seizing the Moment for Teaching and Learning," in *Teaching is Touching the Future: Academic Teaching within and across Disciplines,* eds. Heidi Schelhowe, Melanie Schaumberg, and Judith Jasper (Bielefeld, Germany: Universitats Verlag Webler, 2015), 27–37.
8. Wm. Theodore de Bary, *The Great Civilized Conversation: Education for a World Community* (New York: Columbia University Press, 2013).
9. Ibid.
10. Ibid, 46.
11. Ibid, 37–39.
12. The philosopher Peter Sloterdijk has given this perspective a provocative formulation in relation to the challenge of environmental degradation taken from the poet Rainer Maria Rilke in the title of his book, *You Must Change Your Life* (Boston: Polity Press, 2014).
13. I elaborated on these themes in *Liberal Learning as a Quest for Purpose* (Oxford, UK: Oxford University Press, forthcoming).
14. John Dewey, "Ethical Principles Underlying Education," in *The Early Works of John Dewey*, vol. 5, ed. JoAnn Boyelston (Carbondale, IL: Southern Illinois University Press, 1969), 63.
15. Andrew Delbanco, *College: What It Was, Is, and Should Be* (Princeton, NJ: Princeton University Press, 2012), 148–149.
16. Ibid, 148.

# 6
## PROVOCATION

# Is Well-Being an Individual Matter?

*Kazi Joshua*

THERE ARE A VARIETY OF WAYS to approach the human community and how we understand our place in it. For purposes of clarity, I want to suggest that Rene Descartes offered one way: "I think, therefore I am." There are clear implications for this view, in particular, how the individual relates to the community. It suggests a level of autonomy and disconnectedness that I want to argue is a fiction and problematizes the project of collective responsibility and well-being. In fact, it seems to me this is the dominant paradigm that we have applied in higher education. Our talk of collective well-being, high impact practices, civic learning, group work, and community service is in many ways undermined by the emphasis on the individual as the unit of analysis in our work with students.

There is another way to think about the human community and experience. Here I draw from Ubuntu philosophy in which the argument is rephrased as: "I am a person through other persons"[1] or to contrast Descartes, "I belong, therefore I am." The implication is that community is the formative social structure of the individual and, therefore, that the well-being of the community is fundamentally connected to the well-being of the individual. In this model, it would not be possible for individuals to flourish if the community was decaying. I want to suggest that we need to rethink how we have been approaching this whole question of well-being and the project of higher education.

So when we talk about well-being, what do we mean? In *The Well-being Manifesto for a Flourishing Society*, Nic Marks and Hetan Shaw suggest the following: "One of the key aims of a democratic government is to promote the good life: a flourishing society, where citizens are happy, healthy, capable and engaged . . . . Well-being is more than just happiness. As well as feeling satisfied and happy, well-being means developing as a person, being fulfilled, and making a contribution to the community."[2]

The invitation is to think about all aspects of our work with students with this frame in mind. Does our method of evaluating students for admission value students as parts of communities (cohorts) or does it value them as SAT scores, essays, and padded resumes? How does the whole education experience—or the course unit, the credit hour, the transcript, even the diploma–reflect community? The Posse Foundation, one of the most prominent college preparation and youth leadership development initiatives in the country, promotes taking an approach to student cohorts as collectives whose fate in the educational enterprise is tied to the well-being of others.[3] Is there something to be learned from this perspective? If we took that stance seriously, would our methods of assessment, graduation ceremonies, and units of support services change? Might we even be challenged to reconsider how faculty are rewarded and recognized?

Why might understanding well-being as a collective rather than as an individual experience be a compelling case to make? Because we understand that our fate as individuals is tied to each other as parts of community. We understand that the work of elected officials is often hampered because they have paid attention to their own narrow self-interests or those of their parochial districts. There is an emerging consensus that the current arrangements of power do not serve the full purposes of a democratic ideal. The ongoing challenge of civic leadership, like that of learning and of fully becoming, is to explore, to recognize, and to respect while taking account of more than narrow interests. Our educational work, while informative, is also formative.

We know that in real life, individuals rarely work by themselves on matters of social change or on issues that affect large populations. I agree with Albert Bandura when he says, "Many of the challenges of life center on common problems that require people to work together with a collective voice to change their lives for the better."[4] So if part of educating the next generation of leaders is about solving common problems, then it seems that we must craft learning environments in which those skills are taught, and we must also create reward structures in which what we believe is important is valued.

In the end, there are many reminders about how we are connected to each other as human beings–that being human is more than what Descartes suggested. We are reminded by the labor movement's slogan that "an injury to one [is] an injury to all"[5] and by Martin Luther King Jr.'s insistence in his "Letter from Birmingham Jail" that "injustice anywhere is a threat to justice everywhere."[6]

*We were challenged by our students to explore deeply why we were looking at history and not engaging with the unfolding events of our time. Those deep conversations of conscience, of safety, and of privilege forced us to re-chart our course and include St. Louis, MO in our itinerary*

These are more than platitudes. I think we are challenged to consider the well-being of students in the communal contexts in which they live and study. From time to time, we are reminded in our national life that what affects others affects us also. The recent epidemic of Ebola caused national leaders of both parties to agree that this was an area in which action had to be taken. It would be a stretch to simply argue that this was because the well-being of Africans was affected. Rather, it was the realization that we are somehow connected in this globalized world. It is this spirit of collective life and responsibility that I am arguing is central to well-being, and also that we ignore it at our own peril. Justice Stephen Breyer makes the following claim that I believe is consistent with the case that I have been trying to advance here:

> *The future of the American constitutional idea, then, is the future of a shared set of ideals. This implies a shared commitment to practices necessary to make any democracy work: conversation, participation, flexibility, and compromise. Such a commitment cannot guarantee success in overcoming serious problems: terrorism, environmental degradation, population growth, energy security, and the like. But it does imply a certain attitude toward finding solutions—a willingness to explore options, to search for consensus, and not to be "too sure" of oneself, a habit of mind that Judge Learned Hand once defined as the very "spirit of liberty."[7]*

Let me conclude by acknowledging the debt I owe a friend and colleague, a professor of political science at Allegheny College, a member of my community with whom I have had the privilege of sharing some of these ideas. I have learned from him as my thinking has expanded. We were fortunate to teach a course in the summer of 2014 on voting rights as part of a two-year theme at Allegheny. The course included a travel component, and we went to all the key civil rights locations in the South. At the same time, events were unfolding in Ferguson, MO, which appeared to us to be the current site of the struggle for justice and human dignity that we were studying. We were challenged by our students to explore deeply why we were looking at history and not engaging with the unfolding events of our time. Those deep conversations of conscience, of safety, and of privilege forced us to re-chart our course and include St. Louis, MO in our itinerary as a way of recognizing that an injury to one is an injury to all and that whatever affects one, affects all. Our well-being in Meadville, PA could not make sense in the face of the death of Michael Brown. We could no longer be implicated by silence and individual safety.

We understood in that moment, at the insistence of our students, that well-being meant making a contribution to the community. So we were there in St. Louis at the National Day of Action in October, 2014 to bear witness to the possibility that we could stand in solidarity with others because we belonged to the same community.

---

NOTES

1. Relando Thompkins-Jones, "Ubuntu: A Humanitarian's Philosophy," *Notes from an Aspiring Humanitarian* (blog), April 1, 2011, https://www.relandothompkinsjones.com/ubuntu-a-humanitarians-philosophy/.
2. Nic Marks and Hetan Shaw, "A Well-Being Manifesto for a Flourishing Society," in *The Science of Well-Being*, ed. Felica A. Huppert, Nick Baylis, and Barry Keverne (Oxford, UK: Oxford University Press, 2005), 503–531.
3. The Posse Foundation, Inc., "26 Years of Scholar Success," accessed November 30, 2015, www.possefoundation.org.
4. Albert Bandura, *Self-Efficacy: The Exercise of Control* (New York: Worth, 1997), 491.
5. Industrial Workers of the World, "Preamble, Constitution, & General Bylaws of the Industrial Workers of the World," amended through January 1, 2015, http://www.iww.org/PDF/Constitutions/CurrentIWWConstitution.pdf.
6. Martin Luther King Jr., "Letter from a Birmingham Jail," *Atlantic Monthly* 212, no. 2 (August 1963): 78–88, http://www.uscrossier.org/pullias/wp-content/uploads/2012/06/king.pdf.
7. Stephen Bryer, "Wise Constraints," *Atlantic Monthly* (November 2007), http://www.theatlantic.com/magazine/archive/2007/11/wise-constraints/306310/.

# 7
## PROVOCATION

---

# Understanding the Complexities of Well-Being

*Elizabeth Minnich*

To understand well-being as both an immediate, ground-level objective and as a purpose, an end that overarches, braids, and justifies all other tenets of good, democratic education seems to me simultaneously (and obviously) correct and yet difficult to comprehend, a paradox that I fear allows the potential for mistranslation.

## Some Obvious Difficulties

I do not trust some of the paths we might take to try to turn well-being into an effective vision for education in our time. There are many reasons for this difficulty, some that are immediately contemporary. I will start with them, in large part because they are the easiest to critique, even though in terms of real influence, they are also currently the most difficult to dissolve. The most evident issue is the degree to which education has been placed in the economic realm through privatization, which means by definition that profit becomes the bottom-line justification. This market orientation is echoed by political figures, and by rightly, job-scared students and parents who have bought the line (also heavily played by for-profit school recruiters, it should be noted) that seeking anything other than a degree that leads straight to a well-paying job or any job at all is a dangerous luxury.

This *economism*, as I have come to call it for its ideological reductionism and fervency (whether for marketing or from belief, anger, or fear) includes the adoption of business-style management in academe, whether or not it is in actual situations appropriate, in order to fix the failed academic model. What makes economism and one of its prime expressions, managerialism, or any other semi-coherent ends-to-means constructs of what does and ought to matter for educational institutions is, of course, a key (but not simple) question and judgment. It is my own fervent hope that re-focusing on well-being may help us break out of economism and other, singularly-focused purposes that have competed with each other in recent years. To do so, however, we will have to avoid the utterly non-trivial pitfall of reductionism. Of all human undertakings, education may be the very last one upon which we should force the craving for the unambiguous, the strictly comparable, the jargonized, the standard. Unless, of course, we are weary of such demanding, complex, and often messy matters as learning and freedom and wish to nip their full potential in the bud among the young and other aspiring newcomers.

## Reflecting On Complexities of Meaning

Clearly, I believe it is crucial to reflect together on what well-being means, at least when we are speaking of ends, purposes, principles, and values that undergird and overarch efforts to act. We need capacious meanings that allow us to continue to converse, to discover, to disagree about specifics without ultimate clashes. And I would submit that we also need more than a few meanings that are quite different from each other. Our schools differ, and this variation remains important for a welcoming, always renewing democracy. Well-being, richly rather than reductively construed, will surely reflect differently at a religiously-affiliated school; a business school; a state university; a small, secular, liberal arts college; a tribally-affiliated school; a women's college; an art school. How and why that is so again seems to me as obvious and as difficult as democratic education itself.

As stinging flies of the Socratic sort—the ones that wake us from our dogmatic or reductionist slumbers—for our inquiry, I suggest that there are some observations we might consider. To paraphrase Hannah Arendt, human beings have the paradoxical commonality of being each and every one unique.[1] I do not see how we can believe in democracy without taking that as a given or can reach for the similarly paradoxical goal of both democracy and education: shared self-governance.

Entangled Meanings

It may be useful to think here of meanings of the sort that are in play with life, liberty, and the pursuit of happiness and in particular, happiness. Behind Jefferson's use of the term, likely inspired by his much-admired John Locke, is the Greek *eudaimonia* (literally, inhabited by a good spirit: eu = good, daimon = spirit). I understand Jefferson to mean that life should be protected so that we may surpass fear and need into the liberty that allows us, each in our way, to pursue what we cannot finally obtain until the ends of our lives—the deeply satisfying knowledge that we have led good lives. *Good*, we should note meant excellent or good of kind, an exemplar, if you will, of what a human ought to be. In Yiddish, *mensch* captures that meaning well. Simply think of the following: trying to be a mensch, an admirable person of good character and integrity, is simultaneously pursuing happiness. This is a sense of a good life we may be close to losing.

> *Well-being, richly rather than reductively construed, will surely reflect differently at a religiously-affiliated school; a business school; a state university; a small, secular, liberal arts college; a tribally-affiliated school; a women's college; an art school. How and why that is so again seems to me as obvious and as difficult as democratic education itself*

This meaning of happiness lasted for some time in English. Not so long ago we could say such things as, "She was happy in her friends," meaning that she was fortunate to have these friends because they suited and fulfilled what was good in and about her rather than that her friends made her cheerful. However, now the pursuit of happiness may seem to promise a right to pursue individual *pleasure* rather than those older senses that held happiness and virtue as excellence and to entail each other. In fact, I suspect that today we more usually assume the opposite—that virtue is the enemy of happiness *qua* pleasure. Between us and the Greeks, among others, stand Puritans and, I will add, consumerist capitalism.

Perhaps the closest contemporary U.S. meanings to the older definition of happiness in relation to well-being are *self-realization, self-actualization,* and *fulfillment*. We think it a fine thing to pursue self-actualization, which does appear to have some resonance among these terms. These are useful meanings, although I think they remain a bit too selfish and continue a troubling turn away from others, from communal and public life as well as from efforts in both directions to become better, to become good. Of course, the older meanings are even more flawed: to be excellent of one's kind, and therefore happy, was a state of well-being that differed markedly according to which *kind* of human one was supposed to be. The excellence of a woman was not the same as that of the superior male, and on down the unjust, old hierarchy.

Let us look, then, for more capacious meanings that might do what we want with a complicated but resonant notion of well-being.

## MEANINGS REVEALED THROUGH STRUGGLE

Here's another expression of wisdom to keep before us that is associated with the struggle for justice of the women millworkers in Lowell, Massachusetts, in 1912: "Small art and love and beauty their drudging spirits knew. Yes, it is bread we fight for—but we fight for roses too."[2] I believe that people have always wanted more and other from education (as from work) than those with the power to provide or deny it have thought it safe to allow. We have yearned for art, for love, for beauty that surpasses the banal substitutes palmed off on us, a quality saliently captured in the statement of a young Arab living in an isolated, deteriorating *banlieue* on the outskirts of Paris: "I've never seen the Mona Lisa. I want to see it before I die."[3]

And with beauty, we humans, we creatures and creators of meaning, have in our numbers and in our vastly differing situations dreamt of wisdom, of achieving vision that is both acute and far-sighted enough to help us not only find our way through life, but also to do so meaningfully—to let us know that, finally, we do matter. The Myth of the Cave in Plato's *Republic* gives us one such dream, and it still resonates. Plato describes people chained so that they cannot turn their heads and so see only shadows of puppets moved by others behind them cast on a the wall. They are released and led up and out of the cave where they see real things, not artificial ones. Finally they see the sun itself; they become enlightened. Whether or not we believe we can come to know the good, the true, and the beautiful in and of themselves, we are quite clear that we are very tired of being taken in by Colbertian "truthiness."[4] We yearn for insight and hope for wisdom.

Education should then, as is still so often said at graduations, lead us forth into the light from the distortions of ignorance and the powerlessness of many sorts it can perpetuate. It should enable us to seek wisdom—to know, but also to think, with others and for ourselves. How else, other than submission to the dictates of others, are we to find the meaningful lives without which we can be driven to desperation?

I am very serious about this: those who find their lives unilluminated and meaningless—whether rich or poor, educated or not, powerful or powerless—can seek the relief of oblivion and/or utter absorption. They can turn to substance abuse, extremist ideologies and faiths, suicide, the intensities of competition for anything at all, a quest for fame however empty, violence; sheer greed is one thing we get when real hunger is not fed. We are born learning and given any chance at all, we will keep doing so one way or another. This is one of the most admirable and potentially one of the most dangerous drives of our beings. And education ought to be responsive to it.

## Beginning Again: Being Well

Most obviously, well-being means being well. *Well* is an adverb, and *being* is either a noun or a verb used to denote a sort of action, an activity. It is a noun to which we add *ing*—*flowering*, say, or as William James suggested, instead of the static truth, we would do better to think of the activity of verifying.[5] For one thing, we might then be less tempted to assume we possess the truth and so must impose it on benighted others. Gandhi thought the same; he called his political acts "experiments with truth."[6] I repeat, we are exploring meanings that matter.

Consider the differences between *I have life* and *I am living* and between *love* and *loving* and as the condition for any of these, human being. As John Dewey says in the first sentence of *Democracy and Education*, "The most notable distinction between living and inanimate beings is that the former maintain themselves by renewal."[7] The living goes out of existence, ceases to be, when its activities, its relational interactions, cease. This, I suggest, means that while we live, it is how we do so that matters. I cannot be excellent in any way, including morally, if I do not enact that being well. Well-being concerns how we are doing in our living as the humans we are. It is not a mood, a state, an achievement, or a possession.

*Our students need to have their say, as do community members and those who are charged with responsibility for our specific schools—in all their differences. Our world is telling us the purpose of education in desperately inadequate ways; it is time people took up the challenge and together refused and moved past such inadequate definitions.*

How do we do well? This is an evaluation but of what? We may be able to ski well, cook well, or learn well. We can find guidance for these somewhat specific activities. Someone can teach me to cook well, I can be coached in how to learn well, and so on. But where and how do I find out how to *be* well? What activity, what art or sport or project am I trying to become better at or enjoy being good at by doing it well? I am afraid we have to say, at human being—at being a human. But where can I find out how to be a better human? The young French Arab referenced previously, already in trouble with the law, thinks of seeing the Mona Lisa. Close as he is, he never has. He also thinks of religion and of "tying one on."[8] He is hungry; is there a teacher? What kind?

There are all too many candidates wanting to tell us how to *be* better. Religions usually take up that task, as do ethics, morals, and even mores, the modest but personal and important ways a society tells us how we ought to go about our lives. Laws reflect judgment about how we ought to act and reveal—sometimes very dangerously—particular judgments about what and how we ought to be, say of a particular race, sex, or gender, in order to be granted some and not other capacities.

We are in risky territory here, obviously. Who wants others to set the terms for what it means to be human with an eye to evaluation, to excellence and so also to failure, to potential lowering on a scale of human worth? We have seen what happens when some declare themselves members of a master race not to be sullied by sharing the earth with lesser specimens or adopt a one and true religion, or the one political-economic system that can improve human lives.

We have also seen efforts to remedy such arrogance. Efforts at justice have given us concepts such as crimes against humanity. Humanity is then what we all share, and harm to any one or group of us based on denying that is declared radically unacceptable. Similarly, and more often, we have struggled with the faith in the equal worth of all who are citizens in a democracy, and/or with the moral principle that each and every human is, as Kant put it, never to be treated merely as a means, but always as an end.

## Becoming Better Through Education

Education, like every other directed human endeavor, has its purposes. Becoming a better person, including becoming a better citizen, is widely assumed to be one of them. So well-being, how to be human better, would seem already to be something we know about. If we look at what we say, do, and claim, these would include not the kinds of political, judicial, philosophical notions I just touched on but rather on notions of cultural literacy; preparation for work and engagement in civic life; development of ethical reasoning and social and political responsibility; and ability think critically and creatively and to master levels of general and discipline-specific knowledge. We can locate markers of some success in these areas, although of course it is far from obvious, simple, unambiguous, and unarguable just what we are looking for, let alone why. The pretense of stable meanings and strict comparability of many measures papers over real challenges here. Nonetheless, we can do well enough to find agreement and proceed to specify outcomes and evaluative measures, hopefully always open to re-thinking and awareness that scaling is difficult to achieve without distortion.

It is harder to convince ourselves that we know how to feed the deepest hungers of the human mind, heart, and spirit, the ones that lead people to struggle for education against great odds, and if unsatisfied (no education; banal and boring education; too narrow education; cruelly competitive education, privileging the already privileged; irrelevant education), drive us to seek substitute satiation from other sources. We see the results of such failure all the time in our students and on our campuses, and yes, I do think we as educators are responsible, hardly alone, but significantly.

How then might well-being taken as our purpose and our project in all that we do as educators take up this very specific if very large challenge of responding to the drive to become human and do it well through a lifetime? To be another Socratic stinging fly, I believe we wake up. We do not seek simple answers. Rather, we take to the agora, to the public places of campuses and communities, and talk about it together. As scholars, we can bring resources to such a discussion, not to simplify and finish it, but rather to open up, complicate, and inform it. Our students need to have their say, as do community members and those who are charged with responsibility for our specific schools—in all their differences. Our world is telling us the purpose of education in desperately inadequate ways; it is time people took up the challenge and together refused and moved past such inadequate definitions.

This is my first response: for the hardest questions of all, we ought to reach out, not turn inward; take this up in public; practice democracy. We may then find that our inquiry itself responds to needs that people—including we ourselves—may not have known they had but recognize in their satisfaction. Civic engagement is not just for *them*; it is also for *us*. And such engagement is not only about public action, it is also about self-knowledge and learning. It is inquiry, if Gandhi and others are right, in action.

Second, I would remind educators in all roles that faculty are in our realm of academia are what moral exemplars and *mensches* are more broadly. Ask almost anyone to talk about someone who changed his or her life and you will hear about a teacher. Insofar as well-being concerns learning how to be well, it ceases to be abstract. It requires principles, yes, and practices, yes, but it is also a real human experience. Parenting is the same, and coaching, and judging; a rule book simply does not suffice when unique individuals have to find their own ways to relate well to what is general, perhaps even universal. We cannot and ought not all do it the same way. This is why violin students listen to many superb violinists and seek one who is not better than the others, but who inspires them, invites them to find their own ways but now with support. All students are like that, and we need many good teachers to help us begin to imagine ourselves as knowers and to connect to the more beyond ourselves that we seek so hungrily. We need to experience virtuosos of the mind just as we do of the arts, of sports, of leadership. Well-being as a project and purpose of good democratic education entails reaching for excellence not as a singular, absolutized abstraction, but meaningfully, which is also to say, in relation. Teaching is how we humanize thinking and knowing.

NOTES

1. Hannah Arendt, *The Human Condition* (Chicago: University of Chicago Press, 1958), 8.
2. "1912 Bread and Roses Strike," Massachusetts AFL-CIO, accessed December 29, 2015, http://www.massaflcio.org/1912-bread-and-roses-strike.
3. George Packer, "The Other France," *New Yorker,* August 31, 2015, http://www.newyorker.com/magazine/2015/08/31/the-other-france.
4. Stephen Colbert, "The Word—Truthiness," *The Colbert Report* video, 2:40, October 17, 2005, http://www.cc.com/video-clips/63ite2/the-colbert-report-the-word--truthiness.
5. William James, "Lecture VI, Pragmatism's Conception of Truth," in *Pragmatism AND The Meaning of Truth*, introduction by A.J. Ayer (Cambridge, Mass: Harvard University Press, 1978).
6. Mahatma Gandi, *The Story of My Experiments with Truth* (Boston: Beacon Press, 1957).
7. John Dewey, *Democracy and Education: An Introduction to the Philosophy of Education* (New York: Cosimo Classics, 2005), 1.
8. Packer, "The Other France."

# 8
## PROVOCATION

# The University as the Common Enemy of Opposing Views of Well-Being

*Jerzy Axer*

IS THE UNIVERSITY TO REMAIN IN OPPOSITION TO THE WORLD—*extra muros*—and to propagate values differing from those advocated by politicians and endorsed by the state? This used to be my natural way of thinking as a person raised in a state that lacked sovereignty and had a totalitarian system. Luckily, at the University of Warsaw I found a niche in the period from 1964 to 1990, during which time it was something much more than just one of many institutions operating in the captive state. Indeed, it was a veritable Noah's Ark, and its primary task was to convey values under threat into the future—be they intellectual, communitarian, or civic. These expectations proved themselves in times when characters were put to the test: in 1956 (following the anti-Stalinist turn-around) when the will to resume the university's autonomy came to the fore and in 1968 in the context of the anti-Semitic and anti-intelligentsia repressions organized by the communist party. But this was most true in 1981 when Polish universities established themselves as communities of students and teachers.

I was studying and working in a niche that was doubly protected. Not only was the University of Warsaw less subservient toward the authorities than other institutions, but also within its walls groups of people treated the traditions of academic freedom *pars pro toto*—as if they embodied the idea of national freedom. In the university milieu in which I came of age, this value system was passed down in a very traditional way—not explicitly but implicitly—by former officers of the underground Home Army from the time of World War II. Those officers were by then professors who treated their work at the university as the next round in their struggle for individual and collective freedom. In their struggle, teaching was inseparably connected with values. The concept of well-being, if we are to try and refer it to that situation, may be applied as follows: *for the well-being of future generations, we forego our own well-being by not accepting advantages we could otherwise enjoy were we to exhibit a more conformist attitude toward the authorities.*

The well-being of students was to rest upon a continuation of that attitude for as long as the system was to last. Seen this way, the mythical vision of the university as being independent of the City, the Sovereign, or the Church—of the university cultivating the truth—lined up well in our minds with the ethos and dreams of the (indeed marginal) milieu of crypto-opposition. But because of this training, when Poland's political system finally did transition toward democracy beginning in 1989, I couldn't imagine any other university than one that would ensure a strict interlocking of values and teaching and would continue to uphold a critical attitude of standing *extra muros*.

Because the changes involved with Poland's entrance into the globalized world very swiftly unleashed hitherto unknown threats to the idealistic mission of the university, I spent the past quarter of a century endeavoring to reconcile that nonconformist attitude with the new challenges. What I arrived at may be defined as a Polish variety of the liberal arts education, although one I strove to make embrace undergraduate, graduate, and even PhD programs.

But that's all work on the laboratory scale. And hostile to that work are two basic factors that influence university life. The first is interaction with the culture of a nation "thirsty for national profit," to use the terminology of Martha Nussbaum, which demands that the success of a university education be measured in terms of the success of graduates in the labor market.[1] The second is the radical change in the work conditions of academic staff. Teaching has become an obstacle to promotion and one's academic career. As a result, there is no mechanism to encourage the university to shoulder responsibility for anything other than the students' economic well-being.

I view the United States from afar. My fate is that for nearly twenty years I have found support and understanding for our undertakings in Poland in American milieux engaged in the defense and development of the liberal arts education. As a friend from afar, what I have is not knowledge but merely imaginings of the world I visit. And yet what I seem to sense is a set of ever closer analogies between the circumstances of the liberal arts education in the United States and circumstances here in the peripheral world, in which we are experiencing a growing rupture between teaching and values.

Powerful forces external to the university wish to reshape it in such a way as to school people for their chosen defined life path—essentially, career preparation. These forces do so in the conviction that the model for happiness they recommend (that is, their career model and value system) is superior to others and that the role of the university should be to form students who will hitch their own success to the success of that model. Thus, the potential roads they may otherwise choose once they leave the university disappear. The gateway now leads out to a clearly delineated path down which the person formatted by the university strides all the faster, the better they have mastered the instruction obtained during their educations.

This model is ever more unambiguously becoming one in which the success of an education is measured in terms of job production. The student is a client receiving a market product of high price. The humanities—despite their advantages as a resource of rhetorical strategies that help provide students with values—are more and more marginalized due to their low market value.

The second model—one that could be an ally in the renaissance of the university's role as a place for propagating another vision of well-being, one based on communal and democratic values, is today on the defensive. Even so, it is not in essence favorable toward the liberal arts education—especially toward its version that hearkens to the vast body of the arts and humanities from the past. For success is measured here in terms of the amount of shared rights that the community assures itself. The student in this educational model is again a client who—nonetheless differently than in the preceding model—is to be guaranteed a much greater influence on the educational offer. Charges are leveled at the humanities for joining the present with the past in a way that constrains the freedom to creatively build the future.

In these conditions, the university, in trying to maintain its original, autonomous role, has become a joint enemy of the forces predominant in the political world. It is criticized by neo-conservatives for being expensive and inefficient as a means for achieving professional success. At the same time, it is anachronistic in the way it conveys information and continues to demonstrate only a minimum of innovation. On the left, in turn, the criticism concentrates on showing that the university contains too many elements of compulsion, that it does not foster empathy, is incapable of properly heeding the plurality of human identities, and meaningfully contributes to achieving neither the students' nor the faculty's anticipated satisfaction.

The arts and humanities are direly exposed to attacks of this kind. Nor can it be ruled out that the struggle for the restitution of the university's autonomy in the modern world will be lost—at least for a time. And of course, such a setback would spell the marginalization of the philosophy of education in the spirit of the liberal arts education. Even if this were to happen, I deeply believe that a country like the United States, following a period of doubt, would find within its democratic and freedom-loving traditions the will to bring about a rebirth of the educational nonconformism so important for democracy and freedom. It would also find the financial means for building a new, attractive formula, and via its pragmatism, it would make sure that that formula was not at variance with the realities of today's information society.

Why do I believe this? Several days ago in the weekend edition of the leading Polish daily, Barry Schwartz gave an interview in which he stated that he does not believe that people work better in conditions of employment enforced by a system of punishments and rewards.[2] Moreover, he stated that he does not believe that the need to earn money is a good motivation to work. The Polish journalist tried to challenge him on this point and stated that only 14 percent of employers around the world offer another motivation than earnings. But Schwartz was unfazed. "You're a dreamer," replied the journalist. Nonetheless, Schwarz clearly deems himself a realist, and he blames the dissonance between the evidence and his thesis on the fact that people choose the wrong professions.

*The university, in trying to maintain its original, autonomous role, has become a joint enemy of the forces predominant in the political world.*

This view is very convincing for me, as it suggests that the external world treats the university as an enemy because of its differing vision of well-being. Indeed, perhaps we ourselves are not in our proper places. Perhaps we, in choosing careers in academia, are increasingly out of our elements as teachers. For if academia does not assure us market well-being, we confine ourselves to acceptance of our work as a necessary evil. Students have no trouble at all in recognizing this. And so perhaps negotiations with the world *extra muros* on the costly (for society) right to conjoin teaching and values at the university should be commenced by honestly asking ourselves the following: *To which version of the eudaimonia do we give testimony in the decisions and choices concerning ourselves?*

Do we really wish to adopt as our motto the words engraved on the wall at Harvard's Dumbarton Oaks Research Library and Collection in Washington, DC? "Those responsible for scholarship should remember that the humanities cannot be fostered by confusing instruction with education."[3]

If we manage this task, which entails an investment in the long-term, not the short-term, and which reaps reward over generations, and not in the annual budget, then shall we preserve the right to repeat the venerable rituals that accompany the inauguration of the academic year and the ceremonies of conferring doctorate diplomas. For so very long, through these rituals the university has found the meaning of community and has testified to its faith in its role in society. This is the finest distillation of the Latin oath made by newly-promoted doctors: *non sordidi lucri causa sed ut veritas propagetur*— not for sordid gain, but in order to propagate the truth.

---

NOTES

1. Martha C. Nussbaum, *Not For Profit: Why Democracy Needs the Humanities* (Princeton, NJ: Princeton University Press, 2010), 2.
2. Agnieszka Jucewicz, "Chcesz moich talentów i wiedzy w tej firmie? To zrób coś, żeby dało się w niej pracować," November 14, 2015, http://wyborcza.pl/magazyn/1,149284,19181991,chcesz-moich-talentow-i-wiedzy-w-tej-firmie-to-zrob-cos.html?disableRedirects=true.
3. Linda Lott and James Carde, "Garden Ornament at Dumbarton Oaks," Dumbarton Oaks Research Library and Collection Washington, DC, accessed January 16, 2016, http://www.doaks.org/resources/publications/doaks-online-publications/garden-ornament-at-dumbarton-oaks/gardenornament.pdf, 30–1.

# 9

# Education for Well-Being

*Todd Gitlin*

A STUDENT AT THE NEW SCHOOL in Manhattan named Rainesford Stauffer recently published this letter to the editor in the *New York Times*:

> *To the Editor:*
> *As a student who has suffered from depression and anxiety as a result of the crip-pling race toward academic "achievement," I find it disheartening that academic success continuously trumps learning—which is about experience, not perfection.*
>
> *Modern education is no longer an opportunity for furthering knowledge and experience, but instead an endless scramble for perfection.*
>
> *Our goal is not learning anymore, but good grades, good extracurriculars and a good social life. We are stripping students of creativity, curiosity and enthusiasm. Yet we wonder why suicide rates in students have increased?*
>
> *There is no joy in learning anymore, and it is ruining us. It is the pursuit of learning—something that enhances the student as an individual—that we should be chasing in our schools, not impossible perfection.*[1]

The reality he points to will serve as a fine introduction to the topic of my brief essay. Leave aside the difficult, possibly unanswerable questions of whether he exaggerates and whether higher learning ever served creativity, curiosity, and enthusiasm. What he wants is surely justified. The important thing about Mr. Stauffer's problem is not that he has been made depressed or anxious by school but that he has not been educated for well-being. By his account, he has been educated for the opposite: for not-being, for a state of mindless scrambling.

In the contemporary uproar about whether colleges and universities are comfortable enough for their students, the discomfort to which Rainesford Stauffer points is eclipsed. Alarms are sounding because some students of color and some women declare that they are being discomfited in particular ways. Some of their charges are accurate: there *is* a rape culture on campuses (and even more so away from them); there *are* white supremacist attacks; and it is not clear how institutions should respond. Still, in the existing state of headline-seeking alarm, important distinctions are being collapsed, and responsibilities are being garbled. Pulling away from the controversies of the moment for a longer view might help.

Suppose we begin by looking as Aristotle would to the final cause of education, its essential purpose, which is not simply what Student X may want on a given day, or what her parents or friends or cultural authorities may want, or how she feels about her experience then or later. She may, after all, come to change her mind. Part of what her education is for, in fact, is to help her change her mind. Many things could be cogently said about the purposes—plural—of education, but certainly making anyone feel good is not one of them.

The question is not simply what *I* want from education but what *we* need from it—not just *we* the professors or *we* the students or *we* the alumni or *we* the philanthropists or *we* the members of one or another group but *we as a people*, and not simply at this moment, but later on—in other words, what our children and grandchildren will need from it. The question is how to put education to use so that society benefits from a mobilization of intelligence just as individuals flourish. We need to make judgments about education as a social and ultimately as a moral good.

When I think about well-being, it is not simply a matter of ordering up the kind of experience that *feels* good the day I step onto campus. It is more of a matter of imagining the person I want to be, ten or twenty or fifty years later, and asking what that person might *need* down the line. There is also the question of what my larger community, including those yet unborn, will need. The question is not simply what's more fun, or comforting, or flattering to me today as student or teacher, but rather what works toward my well-being in the largest sense and toward the well-being of the larger community (larger not only in space but in time).

Granted, these questions admit of no simple answers, if for no other reason than that as individuals evolve, their judgments evolve, or ought to. Likewise, societies do not think in unison, and as they evolve, their requirements change; in fact, if they are democratic, they *ought* to be subject to change, as they ought also to debate what constitutes their well-being, or what the Greeks called eudemonia, perhaps best translated as human flourishing.

> The question is how to put education to use so that society benefits from a mobilization of intelligence just as individuals flourish

Education, like the rest of the universe of social life, is a cooperative enterprise, a social compact, or it is nothing. Who are the parties to the compact and what is required of them? Obviously students sign up, but it is not so simple to say what they should expect or, indeed, have the right to expect. For one thing, they enter universities in order to change, to become persons who will differ from the persons who signed up and entered. Moreover, the ways they move from their alpha to omega points are not simple or necessarily predictable. A university is a not a mall or a gym. If I join a gym, I expect that if I keep to the discipline, show up, and undertake the exercises recommended, I will end up stronger, more resilient, and so forth. But education of the sort we call higher is harder to judge because the ends are complex.

By way of a quick summary, students have the right to end up *more knowledgeable, more thoughtful, more citizenly,* and *wiser.* That is, they have the right to expect that when they depart, they will know more about the human situation in its historical, philosophical, cultural, geographical, and moral dimensions; that they will have improved their understanding of the natural world; and that they will have learned skills that will make them more employable than they would have been if they had gone without.

By *more thoughtful,* I mean able to reason and to evaluate evidence; able to distinguish between an opinion and an argument; able to give reasons why it would be good to believe one thing or another and bad to believe something else; able to understand why, right or wrong, the people they encounter might believe something different from what they believe. What it means to be *more citizenly* is not simply a function of individual taste because the definition of citizenship depends on the nature of the political society to which one belongs. If the society is autocratic, citizenship is synonymous with a capacity for obedience. If the society is democratic, citizenship is synonymous with a capacity for participation and judgment. Democratic citizenship requires a capacity to think, to know one's mind, to be able to give intelligible reasons for what one thinks, and to understand when it might be desirable to rethink. To be more citizenly is not to be better adjusted or more docile. It is not necessarily to be noisy, but it is to be capable of being more *knowledgeably* noisy. It is to speak better and also to listen better.

The *wisdom* of citizens is intertangled with the wisdom of individuals in that the art of making judgments can only grow when one is challenged by ideas and individuals significantly different from those with which one grew up. There is no curriculum for wisdom, but an encounter with what has passed for wisdom in different human situations cannot help but benefit an inquiring heart and mind.

Well-being is the opposite of protection from contrary, even offensive ideas. Well-being requires openness. It may well require pain.

In college, as a 19-year-old junior (this was 1962), I took a sociology-history course that included a segment on Nazi Germany. One day, we sat in a large auditorium to view the greatest Nazi propaganda film ever made, Leni Riefenstahl's 1935 *Triumph of the Will*.[2] The film was brilliantly shot and edited to hold viewers rapt for almost two hours of spectacles of Hitler-worship and absolute synchronization. No less compelling were the interspersed images of radiant young blonds frolicking in the sunshine in a summer camp atmosphere. The film is a celebration of strength through joy, of eternal life, eternal Reich, eternal surrender, eternal mass murder in the making.

*Well-being is the opposite of protection from contrary, even offensive ideas. Well-being requires openness. It may well require pain*

The class viewed *Triumph,* and then without a break the screen lit up again and we segued directly into Alain Resnais' 1955 *Night and Fog,* one of the earliest documentaries about the Holocaust.[3] *Night and Fog* consists of a bit more than a half hour of footage, recollections, and evocations from the Auschwitz and Majdanek death camps. I recall the long tracking shots of the camp ruins and images of corpses in heaps. In 1962, such images were not yet the virtual clichés they have become.

*Night and Fog* has a voiceover narration that pushes the audience to confront the limits of representation. "Useless to describe what went on in these cells," the narrator says. "Words are insufficient . . . . Is it in vain that we try to remember?" *Night and Fog* is an unbearable film that demands to be borne, a duty imposed upon us by history. It says relentlessly: *Stare at this apotheosis of desolation.*

The two films were, of course, programmed in sequence to jam into consciousness a causal vector from the submissive ecstasies of Nuremberg to the horrors of Auschwitz. You didn't need a diagram. You had a synapse gouged in your mind that shattering afternoon. The audience left in dead silence. We were not issued a trigger warning, nor were we subjected to racist insults. The pedagogical tactic was precisely to produce discomfort, to wound us, to crumple our innocence. Discomfort was the crucible for a teachable moment. Had we not been shocked, jarred, upended, we would have missed the point. Had we been left comfortable, we would have been left ignorant.

The search for well-being is not a sport governed by fixed rules; it is an elusive, never conclusive human quest. It requires a commitment to understand what one does not already understand, but such a commitment is not delivered by any curriculum in and of itself. The mission of the university or college is to supply individuals with a field of mental life upon which all have made a commitment to think. A university is not a place where a herd learns to thinks alike, or to pretend to, or masters a skill set, though that it nothing to sneer at. It is an institution that cultivates intellectual dissatisfaction and stirs the hope that one may improve oneself by encountering and deepening one's understanding of what one does not already know.

Can an aristocracy cultivate well-being? The principle that institutions ought to help human beings flourish permits some room for institutions to select those human beings by criteria that make sense to them—criteria that are conducive to what we have come to call professional standards. There is some value in a conservative vision of a university where well-mannered gentlemen (or persons, now that the membership door has swung open) are selected for their ostensible ability to debate the great books while the hoi polloi are chased away, and the cares of the outside world are barred. In a country as vast and various as the United States, there is a place for that kind of school. But the democratic ethos will not tolerate—*ought* not to tolerate—restricting higher education to that sort of place.

This is not because a college degree is an entry pass for the best paid and most stable employment, though it is generally that as well. It is because democracy requires enlightened activity, activity that contributes to the creation of a society that cultivates the personal flourishing of as many people as possible. A society in which a tiny minority pursues delights on a well-guarded mountaintop while the rest are well-entertained serfs is neither desirable nor realistically possible. What is desirable and possible is a society in which as many people as possible are encouraged to overcome the pettiest inside them in favor of what the greatest democratic leader in history called "the better angels of our nature."[4]

---

NOTES
1.  Rainsford Stuffer, "Letter to the Editor," *New York Times*, January 12, 2016, http://www.nytimes.com/2016/01/13/opinion/reducing-the-stress-on-students.html?_r=0.
2.  Leni Riefenstahl, director, *Triumph of the Will* (1935, Universum Film, Germany), film.
3.  Alain Resnais, director, *Night and Fog* (1955, Argos Films, France), film.
4.  Abraham Lincoln, "First Inaugural Address," March 4, 1861, accessed February 22, 2016, http://www.bartleby.com/124/pres31.html.

# 10
## PROVOCATION

---

# Why Well-Being is Fundamental to Liberal Learning

*Alexander W. Astin*

I WANT TO BEGIN WITH A QUOTE from the late Howard Bowen. Howard was a long-time friend and colleague and in many ways served as a mentor for me. Former president of several colleges and universities and a distinguished scholar of higher education, Howard was one of the few optimistic economists I have known. His aspiration for our country was that it would become "a nation of educated people." The following quote is from his classic book, *Investment in Learning: The Individual and Social Value of American Higher Education*: "Education should be directed towards the growth of the whole student through the cultivation not only of intellect and of practical competence but also of the affective dispositions, including the moral, religious, emotional, social, and esthetic aspects of personality."[1]

Should liberal education concern itself with the well-being of students? In many respects this question borders on the absurd. Yet if we were to recommend that colleges employ *measures* of well-being when they attempt to assess student outcomes, many academics would object: *What does that have to do with higher education? How is that relevant to learning?*

A visitor from another planet, on the other hand, would have little trouble understanding that the student's well-being is fundamental to the aims of liberal education. Just visit the campus of any liberal arts college, and you will be sure to find a health center, a counseling center, a career center, academic support services, recreational facilities, and a financial aid office, not to mention housing and food services of various kinds.

It is therefore puzzling to realize that in the thousands of empirical studies of student development that have been carried out over the past six decades, barely a handful of investigators has incorporated measures of well-being.[2] Probably the closest approximation would be measures of student satisfaction with college, which are frequently included in such studies. However, I have heard many of the same critics who would question the relevance of well-being object to satisfaction measures, either because they are "superficial" or because giving any weight to satisfaction amounts to pandering to students. The same reaction would probably be elicited if one were to propose using measures of well-being.

## WHAT DO WE MEAN BY LIBERAL EDUCATION

A fundamental issue not often addressed in discussions of liberal education is the question of just what it is. Some people seem to believe that such an education can be defined simply in terms of course credits: Take such and such an array of courses, pass them, and *ipso facto*, you've been liberally educated. It doesn't much matter *how* one acquires the requisite credits: in four years or twenty, on a campus or on line, as a resident or a commuter, with a lot of contact with faculty and fellow students or with no such contact, with heavy co-curricular involvement or no such involvement. It doesn't matter. Just collect the right credits and you're done.

This course content view is embraced by those who advocate for replacing traditional liberal education with massive online open courses (MOOCs) and other forms of distance learning because they offer cheaper, alternative means to educate an expanding student population. However, in light of a large body of research that demonstrates that the most critical elements in a high quality, undergraduate education include student-faculty contact, student-student contact, and other campus-based experiences,[3] a liberal arts education consisting mainly of MOOCs seems like a poor substitute.

One has only to visit a few college websites or read a few college mission statements to realize that liberal education is intended to be about much more than simply mastering certain course content. Many institutions are explicitly dedicated to the development of diverse student outcomes that can't be directly linked to specific course content, qualities such as leadership, critical thinking, citizenship, honesty, social responsibility, empathy, and self-understanding. In other words, a liberal education is supposed to facilitate the development of such qualities not merely through exposure to course content, but also through personal interactions with fellow students and faculty, the residential experience, participation in student activities, and similar campus experiences.

*A growing number of educators has been calling for a more holistic or integral education and pointing to the need to connect mind and spirit and to return to the true values of liberal education— an education that examines learning and knowledge in relation to an exploration of the self and one's responsibility to self and others*

In contrast to those who view a liberal education narrowly in terms of course content, a growing number of educators has been calling for a more holistic or integral education and pointing to the need to connect mind and spirit and to return to the true values of liberal education—an education that examines learning and knowledge in relation to an exploration of the self and one's responsibility to self and others. I am speaking here of developing something similar to what Howard Gardner has referred to as "existential intelligence."[4]

THE MEASUREMENT CHALLENGE

When liberal learning is viewed holistically, well-being can easily be incorporated as one of its key objectives, but those of us who believe that the student's well-being should be of central concern to higher education must ultimately come to terms with the definitional issue: *What do we mean by well-being and how should it be measured?* Since meaning refers to well-being at the conceptual level, it is usually expressed verbally, as in a formal definition (e.g., the state of being happy, comfortable, or healthy). Measurement, on the other hand, involves some specified set of operations—usually behaviors or verbal statements from the student—that most often take the form of answers to questions (e.g., rate your current degree of happiness on the following scale). Developing good measures of well-being would ordinarily involve an ongoing byplay between meaning and measurement: Do these words express what we mean by well-being? Does this scale capture that meaning?

## What Research Tells Us

Rather than trying to make a purely theoretical case for the importance of students' well-being in higher education, it can be useful to look at some of the empirical evidence. What can we learn from research about the significance of well-being in the life of college students?

In several longitudinal studies of college student outcomes, we employed a scale that we call Psychological Well-Being, which consists of the student's self-rated degree of emotional health together with negatively weighted self-descriptions that students use to report how frequently they have felt *depressed*, that *my life is* filled with *stress and anxiety*, or *overwhelmed by everything I have to do.*[5] In other words, students who score high on the Psychological Well-Being scale (1) say they experience these three states infrequently, if at all, and (2) they rate themselves high on emotional health.

These studies found that that students' psychological well-being *declines during the college years;* the number of high scorers declines by about one third and the number of low scorers increases by more than half. Apparently, the greater academic demands of college, coupled with the pressures of trying to balance school, family, and a personal life take a toll on students' sense of psychological well-being.

As part a recent national study of college students' spiritual development, we devised measures of five spiritual qualities, one of which seems especially pertinent to well-being.[6] We call it *equanimity.* In the graduate seminars and brainstorming sessions that we conducted while we were developing these spirituality measures, it became clear that equanimity is the quality that most often comes to mind when people are asked to describe a spiritual person. Students with high equanimity scores say they are able to find meaning in times of hardship, feel at peace, see each day as a gift, and feel good about the direction of their lives.

> *Students with high equanimity scores say they are able to find meaning in times of hardship, feel at peace, see each day as a gift, and feel good about the direction of their lives*

One could argue that equanimity in many respects represents another manifestation of well-being. And not surprisingly, equanimity and psychological well-being are positively associated. However, in contrast to psychological well-being, Equanimity actually shows *positive growth* during the college years.

When we explored this apparent contradiction in greater depth, our longitudinal data revealed that a number of diverse activities and experiences can facilitate growth in equanimity during the college years. Specifically, equanimity is most likely to show positive growth when students participate in charitable activities (service learning, donating money to charity, helping friends with personal problems) or when they engage in contemplative practices (meditation, prayer, reflective writing, reading sacred texts). Other positive influences on the student's level of equanimity include study abroad, participation in student organizations, leadership training, interracial interaction, and faculty encouragement to explore spiritual/religious questions. Declines in equanimity during college are associated with majoring in engineering and playing video games.[7]

This is quite a heterogeneous list, but it is still possible to discern a consistent pattern: Students' sense of equanimity appears to be enhanced when they go inside (as in contemplative activities and in exploring religious/spiritual questions) and when they engage with the other (as in service work, foreign travel, and interracial interaction).

We also explored the question of how other college outcomes are affected when a student experiences significant growth in equanimity during the undergraduate years. As it turns out, growth in equanimity during college enhances psychological well-being, academic performance, and satisfaction with the overall college experience.

While these preliminary findings obviously need to be replicated using other measures of well-being and longer-term longitudinal samples, they nevertheless suggest that well-being may be an important student outcome in its own right and point to some potentially important experiences during college that can contribute to a student's sense of well-being.

CONCLUSION

When higher education focuses the bulk of its attention on test scores, grades, persistence, degrees, and other external aspects of students' lives, it is inclined to neglect students' inner lives—the sphere of values and beliefs, moral development, self-understanding, and well-being. At the same time, it is becoming increasingly difficult to argue that higher education should concern itself solely with students' cognitive development—thinking, reasoning, memorizing, critical analysis, and the like—and to argue that the affective or emotional side of the student's life is not relevant to the work of higher education. In fact, I'm persuaded that there is no such thing as pure cognition that can be considered in isolation from affect. On the contrary, since thinking and reasoning almost always take place in some kind of affective bed or context, it defies reality to regard students merely as thinking and reasoning machines.

*As educators and as citizens we need to ask ourselves: What kinds of people will our global society of the future need? While it's obvious that technical knowledge and skill are becoming increasingly important for effective functioning in modern society, better technical knowledge alone will not equip students to deal with many of society's most pressing problems*

As educators and as citizens we need to ask ourselves: *What kinds of people will our global society of the future need?* While it's obvious that technical knowledge and skill are becoming increasingly important for effective functioning in modern society, better technical knowledge alone will not equip students to deal with many of society's most pressing problems: violence, poverty, crime, divorce, substance abuse, and the religious, national, and ethnic conflicts that continue to plague our country and our world. These are problems of the heart, problems that call for greater self-awareness, self-understanding, equanimity, empathy, concern for others, and well-being.

The philosophy underlying the notion of a liberal education implicitly rejects the notion that an excellent education is merely a collection of course credits. On the contrary, liberal education promises to educate the whole student. The broad formative roles that colleges and universities continue to play in our society, combined with their long-term commitment to the ideals of liberal learning, position them well to facilitate the development of students' intellectual and personal qualities so that they might realize their full potential and better serve their communities, our society, and the world at large.

NOTES

1. Howard R. Bowen, *Investment in Learning: The Individual and Social Value of American Higher Education* (Baltimore, MD: The Johns Hopkins University Press, 1977), 33.

2. See Ernest T. Pascarella and Patrick T. Terenzini, *How College Affects Students* (San Francisco, CA: Jossey-Bass, 1991), and Ernest T. Pascarella and Patrick T. Terenzini, *How College Affects Students: A Third Decade of Research,* Vol. 2 (San Francisco, CA: Jossey-Bass, 2005).

3. See Alexander E. Astin, "How the Liberal Arts College Affects Students" *Daedalus* 128, no. 1 (1999): 77–100 and Pascarella and Terenzini, *How College,* 2005.

4. Howard Gardner, *Intelligence Reframed: Multiple Intelligences for the 21st Century* (New York: Basic Books, 1999), 4–60.

5. Alexander W. Astin, *What Matters in College? Four Critical Years Revisited* (San Francisco, CA: Jossey-Bass, 1993), and Alexander W. Astin, Helen S. Astin, and Jennifer A. Lindholm, *Cultivating the Spirit: How College Can Enhance Students' Inner Lives.* (San Francisco: Jossey-Bass, 2011), 121.

6. Astin et al, *Cultivating the Spirit*, 49–62.

7. Ibid, 60–61.

PART 2

# Manifestation and Implementation

# 11
ESSAY

---

# Why Flourishing?

*Corey Keyes*

SCIENTISTS AND INVESTIGATORS of mental illness believe and convey to the public that the treatment, cure, and prevention of mental illness are the only and the best ways to promote the overall mental health of the population. Our nation continues to advocate for doing more of the same thing for mental illness again and again but now expects a different outcome, a cure. Our approach to mental illness is insane. Recent talk of finding a cure for mental illness is promising too much at best or providing false promises at worst. The *Diagnostic and Statistical Manual of Mental Disorders*[1] contains hundreds of purportedly distinctive disorders, each characterized by a collection of signs and symptoms. Will there be a single cure for all? Unlikely. Will we have to wait years for many cures for all mental illnesses? Most likely. What is the cost to all who may become mentally ill while we wait? More suffering and lost life.

Such calls for finding a cure may be effective for persuading the U.S. Congress to devote more financial support to the National Institute of Mental Health. But I believe that promising a cure for mental illness diverts attention and resources away from a second, viable, and complementary approach to mental illness—one that increases happiness. Happiness is no laughing matter, and promoting it might be just what we need to promote good mental health and prevent some cases of common mental disorders.

Happiness, which is also called well-being, represents individuals' evaluations of the quality of their lives. There are two approaches to and types of happiness: hedonic happiness and eudaimonic happiness. The first approach frames happiness as positive emotions and represents the opinion that a good life is measured by feeling good or experiencing more moments of good feelings. The second approach frames happiness as a way of doing things in the world and represents the opinion that a good life is measured by how well individuals cultivate their abilities to function well or to do good in the world. Simply put, happiness is feeling good or happiness is functioning well.

My own and others' research revealed as many as fourteen facets of hedonic and eudaimonic happiness. Those facets are shown in Table 1 on the next page, and represent the items or questions that form my measure of good mental health (i.e., the Short Form Questionnaire of the Mental Health Continuum). The first three items (happy, interested in life, and satisfied) represent emotional well-being, the formal term I use to represent the feeling good approach to happiness. The remaining eleven items represent the functioning well approach to happiness. Of those eleven items, five represent social well-being, which is the formal term for the different ways that we can assess how well an individual functions as a citizen and member of a collective or community. The remaining

*Table 1.*

| SHORT FORM QUESTIONNAIRE OF THE MENTAL HEALTH CONTINUUM |
| --- |
| **Emotional Well-Being** |
| Flourishing requires *almost every day* or *every day* on 1 or more of the following:<br>How often during the past month did you feel |
|   1.  Happy |
|   2.  Interested in Life |
|   3.  Satisfied |
| **Positive Functioning** |
| Flourishing requires *almost every day* or *every day* on 6 or more of the following:<br>How often during the past month did you feel |
|   4.  That you had something important to contribute to society (social contribution) |
|   5.  That you belonged to a community (like a social group, your school, or your neighborhood) (social integration) |
|   6.  That our society is becoming a better place for people like you (social growth) |
|   7.  That people are basically good (social acceptance) |
|   8.  That the way our society works made sense to you (social coherence) |
|   9.  That you liked most parts of your personality (self-acceptance) |
|   10.  Good at managing the responsibilities of your daily life (environmental mastery) |
|   11.  That you had warm and trusting relationships with others (positive relationships with others) |
|   12.  That you had experiences that challenged you to grow and become a better person (personal growth) |
|   13.  Confident to think or express your own ideas and opinions (autonomy) |
|   14.  That your life has a sense of direction or meaning to it (purpose in life) |

six items represent psychological well-being, which is the formal term for the ways we measure how well an individual functions in personal life. The difference between social and psychological well-being hinges on the pronoun and frame of mind: Social well-being reflects our functioning as "we and us" (when I am a member of a larger group), while psychological well-being reflects our functioning as "me and I" (when I am in my private, personal, and intimate sphere of life).

You may have noticed earlier that I used the words *mental health* when referring to happiness. In my own research, I argued that both kinds of happiness together help us to measure and therefore study good, or positive, mental health. I call the pinnacle of good mental health *flourishing* and chose that term to be clear that I am talking about true mental health, not merely the absence of mental illness. I measure mental health in the same way that psychiatrists measure common mental illnesses. To be diagnosed with depression, for instance, one has to have at least one symptom of anhedonia (loss of pleasure or loss of interest in life) combined with four of the seven symptoms of malfunctioning. To be diagnosed with *flourishing* mental health, individuals must experience in the past month *every day* or *almost every day* at least one of the three signs of emotional well–being combined with six or more of the signs of positive functioning. At the opposite end of flourishing on what I call the mental health continuum is *languishing*, which is diagnosed by *never* or *once or twice* during the past month having at least one sign of emotional well-being combined with six or more signs of positive functioning. Individuals who are neither flourishing nor languishing are diagnosed with *moderate* mental health.

Flourishing represents the achievement of a balanced life in which individuals feel good about lives in which they are functioning well. My approach to happiness is consistent with those views of happiness as more than seeking and feeling pleasure. Buddhism, for example, posits happiness as a wholesome and balanced state that includes a meaningful and constructive approach to life. Such a view of happiness is consistent with Aristotle's view of eudaimonia (translated as *eu* = good and *daimon* = soul or spirit) as a deliberate way of being and acting in the world that is virtuous not only for oneself, but also for others and the world.

THE TWO CONTINUA MODEL AND THE NOBLE TRUTHS

While the more complete approach to measuring happiness allows us to approach mental health positively, it has also allowed me to investigate what I consider the most fundamental premise of pursuing happiness: the two continua model. In 1946, the World Health Organization (WHO) defined health not merely as the absence of disease, but also as a state of complete physical, social, and mental well-being.[2] In doing so, the WHO declared a hypothesis that remained untested until very recently—that mental health is more than the absence of mental illness; it is the presence of happiness or well-being. If this hypothesis is supported, it has extremely important implications. First, even if we could find a cure for mental illness tomorrow, it does not mean that most people would necessarily be flourishing in life. In other words, we cannot treat our way out of the problem of mental illness; we must also promote a life of balance in which people can achieve happiness and realize lives in which they can flourish.

I have found strong evidence in support of the two continua model in studies of adults in the United States and the Netherlands, in black Setswana-speaking South Africans, and in youth ages 12 and older in the United States and Australia. We have also shown that positive mental health, as I measure it, is just as heritable as common mental illnesses (depression, panic attacks, and generalized anxiety).[3] We then discovered that the two continua model is encoded in our DNA because barely half of the genes for good mental health are shared with the genes for mental illness. This means we inherit a genetic level of risk for depression while we also inherit a genetic potential for flourishing. However, the absence of or very low genetic risk for depression does not mean a high genetic potential for flourishing. And the presence of high genetic risk for depression does not mean a life doomed for depression because one might also plausibly inherit a high genetic potential for flourishing. What wins, depression or flourishing? It may very well depend on the kinds of experiences that unlock the genes for flourishing and what experiences silence the genes for depression. This focus may come in the future, but right now, the National Institute of Health supports research on genetic risk of mental illness, not genetic potential for good mental health. In other words, we may be looking for the answer to the problem of mental illness in the wrong place by only looking at genetic risk rather than at genetic potential for flourishing.

In a recent study, we found that approximately 75 percent of American college students were free of common mental illness as measured in the past two weeks. Yet only 46 percent of college students were free of mental illness *and* were also flourishing. In short, the absence of mental illness does not imply the presence of mental health among college students,[4] and we found the same thing in adolescents[5] and adults.[6]

Another important implication of the two continua model is that the level of good mental health should differentiate how well people with and without mental illness can function in their lives. All of my research has supported this aspect of the two continua model. For instance, almost 6 percent of college students are flourishing and also have mental illness. These students have a lower risk of suicidal tendencies than the 17 percent of college students who have moderate mental health with a mental illness. Roughly 3 percent of college students who are languishing and have mental illness are at the highest risk for suicidal tendencies. To be more specific, among students who would screen for a current mental illness, 7 percent who were flourishing showed suicidal tendencies, compared to 18 percent with moderate mental health and 28 percent with languishing mental health. When compared to students with mental illness, those currently free of mental illness are less likely to have suicidal tendencies. Yet in this large group of students (i.e., the 75 percent free of a current mental illness), those who are languishing have higher rates of suicidal tendencies than those with moderate mental health, who in turn have lower rates of suicidal tendencies than students who are flourishing. More specifically, among students who do not screen for a current mental illness, only 1 percent of flourishing students showed suicidal tendencies, compared to 4 percent with moderate mental health and 15 percent with languishing mental health.[7]

*Adults with less than flourishing mental health report more physical ailments and chronic disease, miss more days of work, use more health care (more prescriptions, more hospitalizations, more visits for physical, mental, emotional reasons), are more likely to die prematurely, and are more likely to develop mental illness*

In short, anything less than flourishing is associated with worse outcomes for individuals with and those free of mental illness. Adults with less than flourishing mental health report more physical ailments and chronic disease, miss more days of work, use more health care (more prescriptions, more hospitalizations, more visits for physical, mental, emotional reasons), are more likely to die prematurely, and are more likely to develop mental illness.[8]

Here again there are alignments with Buddhist views. The two continua model and its implications share affinities with the Buddhist approach to enlightenment, namely the four noble truths. These truths are as follows: (1) One must first understand the nature of life as consisting of suffering because pleasure and satisfaction are fleeting and life involves sickness, sadness, pain, and death; (2) One must understand the origin of suffering; much of it flows from our desires and expectations that encourage cravings and attachment to things we encounter in daily life; (3) If we can understand our role in producing suffering, we can pursue the cessation of suffering (i.e., nirvana) if we can rid our heart and minds of the hindrances of greed, anger, ignorance, and hatred; (4) The final truth, which is the eightfold path, entails cultivating our ability to function well in life by gaining *wisdom* (right understanding and right aspiration), *ethical conduct* (right speech, right action and right livelihood) and *mental development* (right effort, right mindfulness and right concentration).[9]

So after having grasped the nature and cause of suffering, and after attempting to mitigate it, Buddhists shift greater attention to the task of living good and happy lives. This is done by pursuing wisdom through learning the truth about the imperfect nature of life and human nature and living in a way that mitigates suffering caused by those imperfections. We promote a better life by developing the ethical conduct of speaking truthfully, compassionately, consistently with values and earning a living in a way that does not hurt others and possibly helps others. Last, we promote a good life if we develop our mental capacity by consistently trying to work on it rather than making excuses or procrastinating and by strengthening our minds and attuning them to recognize and live in the present moment and situation.

Using this engaging metaphor or analogy of living or being well together, the four noble truths and the eightfold path illustrate the principles and implications of the two continua model. That is, humans are prone to mental illness, a form of suffering. Mental illness represents a form of imbalance of feeling and functioning, a state of mind and existence consisting of a disinterest in life, sadness, and malfunctioning. But mitigating mental illness through treatment or prevention does not result in a flourishing life. Indeed, one way to overcome our vulnerability to mental illness is to achieve a balanced, wholesome life in which feeling good is connected to our ability to function well.

*We must strive to act in ways that develop our capacity for doing and being good— to contribute to society, to view ourselves and others as fundamentally good, to develop warm and trusting relations with others— so that we come to feel pleasure about living our lives well*

To flourish in life, we must understand that happiness as feeling good may be the aim of our lives, to paraphrase Thomas Jefferson, but virtue (and being in just relation with community) is the foundation for the feeling-good type of happiness. So the absence of suffering does not mean one has achieved nirvana and enlightenment, and the absence of mental illness does not mean one is flourishing. We must strive to act in ways that develop our capacity for doing and being good—to contribute to society, to view ourselves and others as fundamentally good, to develop warm and trusting relations with others—so that we come to feel pleasure about living our lives well.

In 1995, we surveyed a nationally representative sample of U.S. adults, ages twenty-five to seventy-five, and surveyed them again in 2005.[10] Both times we measured good mental health as a continuum as described earlier and for the presence of common mental disorders, including major depression episodes, panic attacks, and generalized anxiety disorder. We found that 18.5 percent of adults had one of three mental disorders in 1995, and 17.5 percent had one of the three in 2005. Although the rate of mental illness appears stable over time, just over half of the cases of mental illness in 2005 were new ones (participants did not have any of the three mental disorders in 1995 but had one of the three in 2005). So between 1995 and 2005, the United States made no progress in reducing the cases of mental illness. While half of the 1995 cases were resolved in one way or another, new cases emerged. These results suggest that the new cases emerged from the group of people who were initially free of mental illness but lost their good mental health, which increased the risk of becoming mentally ill.[11]

*Figure 1.*

## CHANGE IN INCIDENCE OF MENTAL ILLNESS FROM 1995 TO 2005.

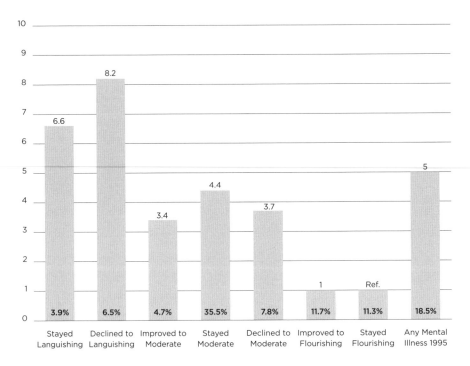

| | Stayed Languishing | Declined to Languishing | Improved to Moderate | Stayed Moderate | Declined to Moderate | Improved to Flourishing | Stayed Flourishing | Any Mental Illness 1995 |
|---|---|---|---|---|---|---|---|---|
| Odds ratio | 6.6 | 8.2 | 3.4 | 4.4 | 3.7 | 1 | Ref. | 5 |
| Percent | 3.9% | 6.5% | 4.7% | 35.5% | 7.8% | 11.7% | 11.3% | 18.5% |

*The odds ratio for a mental illness (major depression episode, generalized anxiety, or panic attack) in 1995 is compared to the odds ratio for positive mental health and any mental illness (major depression episode, generalized anxiety or panic attack) in 2005. The odds ratio is the number at the top of each bar; the percent at the bottom of each bar represents the proportion of adults in each category.*

In Figure 1, the number at the top of each bar represents the number of times more likely that members of that category were to have mental illness in 2005 compared to those who stayed flourishing. Focusing on the numbers at the top of each bar, you will see that adults who declined from flourishing in 1995 to moderate mental health in 2005 were nearly four times more likely to be mentally ill in 2005. The first loss of good mental health—from flourishing to moderate mental health—resulted in a rise in the risk of future mental illness. Adults whose mental health stayed at moderate levels were four and one-half times as likely to have a mental illness in 2005. Those who declined to languishing—almost all of whom had moderate mental health in 1995—were eight times as likely to have a mental illness in 2005. In other words, our nation must protect against the loss of good mental health if it wants to reduce the prevalence of mental illness.

The addition to protection against loss, promotion of positive mental health is important. Individuals who stayed languishing were more than six times more likely to have mental illness in 2005, while those who improved to moderate mental health were approximately three and one-half times more likely to have mental illness in 2005.

Compared to staying languishing, improving to moderate mental health cut the risk of future mental illness by nearly half. Individuals who improved to flourishing—most of whom had moderate mental health in 1995—were no more likely than those who stayed flourishing to have mental illness in 2005. Adults who improved to or stayed flourishing had the lowest risk of developing mental illness. This suggests that we can prevent some mental illness if we help more people to flourish.

The numbers at the bottom of each bar in Figure 1 represent the proportion of the sample that belongs to each category of mental health or mental illness. Because the sample was designed to be representative of the U.S. adult population between the ages of twenty-five and seventy-five in 1995, we can use the percent in each category to esti-mate how much of the U.S. adult population may be in each category of mental health. The percentages of adults who stayed at moderate or improved or declined to moderate mental health, when combined, represent nearly half (48.1% exactly) of the U.S. adult population, and these adults are three to four times more likely to develop mental illness because they have moderate rather than flourishing mental health. The percentages of the sample that stayed at languishing or declined to languishing, when combined, repre-sent one in ten (10.4% exactly) of the U.S. adults who are six to eight times more likely to develop mental illness because they are languishing rather than flourishing.

In short, almost six in ten adults (10.4 languishing + 48.1% moderate = 58.5%) in the study sample were not flourishing as of 2005. This large group of adults was free of mental illness in 1995. Yet those languishing had greater risk (odds ratios between 6.6 and 8.2) of mental illness in 2005 than those adults who *had* mental illness in 1995 (whose odds ratio was 5.0). Adults with moderate mental health had nearly as high of a risk (odds ratios between 3.4 and 4.4.) as adults with a mental illness in 1995. So the amount of any mental illness was 18.5% in 1995 and 17.5% in 2005, which suggests that the United States did not make any significant progress in reducing mental illness. But 52% of adults with mental illness in 2005 did not have any in 1995. Many of 52% of new cases come from the large segment of people that does not have any mental illness but is not flourishing. If we fail to focus on promoting and protecting positive mental health while we emphasize treating current cases of mental illness, we are unlikely to make any progress in reducing the amount of and suffering from mental illness.

## How Can We Pursue Flourishing?

If our or any other nation wants a mentally healthy population, it must take both kinds of happiness seriously. We must promote what we want in our lives, and the concept of flourishing challenges us all to prioritize and balance both kinds of happiness—to feel good about lives in which we can function well. But how do we get there? The two continua model requires us to think of new ways to achieve flourishing because treat-ments that aim to lower the bad do not necessarily increase the good. Just as with the treatment for cholesterol, in which taking statins may lower bad cholesterol but will not increase good cholesterol, mental health therapies aimed at lowering mental illness may not increase mental health.

To that end, colleagues in the Netherlands developed and tested a public health approach to promote mental health based on acceptance and commitment therapy (ACT).[12] The point of ACT is to increase mental flexibility. This flexibility is a competence that includes two interdependent processes: (1) acceptance of negative experiences and (2) choosing to change or persist in behavior based on values or principles. A person who is mentally flexible is willing to remain in contact rather than avoid negative, undesirable, personal experiences. In other words, ACT promotes acceptance of the first noble truth of Buddhism (that suffering exists) because most of us try control or avoid such unwanted private experiences. Rather than reacting emotionally to negative experiences, the ACT program also encourages us to become conscious about making choices toward unwanted experiences based on our values and goals for creating a good life.

Based on ACT, Fledderus et al. developed a course that could be administered to groups of people in a relatively brief period.[13] Their program consists of a two-hour session once per week for eight weeks. Through structured activities, participants are encouraged to discover their values in multiple domains of life, and they are taught how to respond to negativity and adversity based on their own deeply held commitments and values. The course also teaches participants to be open and non-judgmental in personal experiences. The goal is for participants to learn to consistently choose effective responses in any but especially in difficult situations to build behavior repertoires that are flexible and value driven.

Continuing the analogy with the Buddhist strategy for living well, participants in the ACT intervention are learning aspects of the Buddhist eightfold path. They learn that adversity and negativity are natural and they can live in a way that mitigates the problems caused by avoidance or repression of negative experiences. Participants then learn to respond to adversity and negative emotions based on personal values. When compassion meditation is included in the intervention, participants acquire the mindset (and disposition to behave or act) to live in a way that is more beneficial to others and, thereby, themselves. When mindfulness meditation is included, participants learn to strengthen their minds and to appreciate and live (act) in the present moment and situation.[14]

In two randomized controlled trials, one that included mindfulness training,[15] my colleagues found moderate to large effects for promoting flourishing. Because they also measured mental flexibility, they were able to test whether the program enhances mental flexibility and if this enhancement of mental flexibility is the reason for increases in flourishing. In both studies, mental flexibility explained how the program enhanced flourishing. Impressively, the effects of the program were maintained three months later. Unfortunately, the design of the study did not allow for learning how much the inclusion of mindfulness meditation added to the ACT program in promoting flourishing. Yet this is just the beginning of a very important line of research that connects mind and life in a way that promotes what we want more of in our lives: flourishing.

In sum, we must train our minds to focus on what matters, to make conscious choices about how to best respond to the challenges and trials of life, to achieve a better balance of prioritizing feeling with functioning well, and to be compassionate to others and ourselves. No one can or should flourish all the time and everywhere, nor should anyone's flourishing be at the expense of another's. I believe the ACT model can be used to encourage a more sustainable approach to flourishing in life because it is based on promotion of the happiness of others, not just one's own.

NOTES

1. American Psychiatric Association, *The Diagnostic and Statistical Manual of Mental Disorders,* 5th ed., (Arlington, VA: American Psychiatric Association, 2013).

2. World Health Organization, "Health," Geneva, Switzerland: World Health Organization, http://www.who.int/trade/glossary/story046/en/.

3. Corey L. M. Keyes, "Mental Health as a Complete State: How the Salutogenic Perspective Completes the Picture," in *Bridging Occupational, Organizational and Public Health,* ed. Georg F. Bauer and Oliver Hämmig, (Dordrecht, Netherlands: Springer Netherlands, 2014), 179–92.

4. Corey L. M. Keyes et al., "The Relationship of Level of Positive Mental Health with Current Mental Disorders in Predicting Suicidal Behavior and Academic Impairment in College Students," *Journal of American College Health* 60, no. 2 (2012): 126–33.

5. Corey L. M. Keyes, "Mental Health in Adolescence: Is America's Youth Flourishing?" *American Journal of Orthopsychiatry* 76, no. 3 (2006): 395–402.

6. Corey L. M. Keyes, "Mental Illness and/or Mental Health? Investigating Axioms of the Complete State Model of Health," *Journal of Consulting and Clinical Psychology* 73, no 3 (2005): 539–48.

7. Keyes et al., "Relationship of Level."

8. See Keyes, "Mental Health as Complete State" and Corey L. M. Keyes and Eduardo J. Simoes, "To Flourish or Not: Positive Mental Health and All-Cause Mortality," *American Journal of Public Health* 102, no. 11 (2012): 2164–72.

9. Bhikkhu Bodhi, "The Noble Eightfold Path: The Way to End Suffering," Buddhist Publication Society, 1998, http://www.accesstoinsight.org/lib/authors/bodhi/waytoend.html.

10. Corey L. M. Keyes, Satvinder S. Dhingra, and Eduardo J. Simoes, "Change in Level of Positive Mental Health as a Predictor of Future Risk of Mental Illness," *American Journal of Public Health* 100, no. 12 (2010)*:* 2366–71. doi: 10.2105/AJPH.2010.192245.

11. Ibid.

12. See Martine Fledderus et al., "Acceptance and Commitment Therapy as Guided Self-help for Psychological Distress and Positive Mental Health: A Randomized Controlled Trial," *Psychological Medicine* 42, no. 3 (2012): 485–95. doi: 10.1017/S0033291711001206 and Martine Fledderus et al., "Mental Health Promotion as a New Goal in Public Mental Health Care: A Randomized Controlled Trial of an Intervention Enhancing Psychological Flexibility," *American Journal of Public Health,* 100, no. 12 (2010): 2372–78. doi: 10.2105/AJPH.2010.196196.

13. Fledderus et al., "Acceptance and Commitment Therapy."

14. Fledderus et al., "Acceptance and Commitment Therapy" and Fledderus et al. "Mental Health Promotion."

15. Ibid.

# 12
## ESSAY

# College Makes Me Feel Dangerous: On Well-Being and Nontraditional Students
### *David Scobey*

*"To begin is not in the realm of possibilities; only to begin again, over and over again—and therein lies [humanity's] strength."*—Elie Wiesel

## I

Around a seminar table on the wooded campus of The Evergreen State College, a public liberal arts institution near Olympia, Washington, a group of students is telling their stories. They are adult undergraduates in the college's Evening and Weekend Studies Program. I have asked them to talk about their experiences with higher education in the past and (now that they have returned) here at Evergreen.[1] "I couldn't stand the traditional model of college," Jesi says, recalling her first stint as an undergraduate. "Everything was in columns—take these distribution requirements, those disciplines. And learning in columns isn't how I learned. I've always been a worker, and what you find in the work-place is the interdisciplinary model. Everything is connected to everything else." Jesi is a fifty-something mother of five with a long government career in corrections and emergency management; she has returned to college less for her job than for her kids. "I came back because I felt I had let my children down. They were starting to grow up, and I wanted them to go to college. How could I push them without doing it myself?" There is a poignancy to her comment because her son James happens to be sitting next to her; they enrolled in Evening and Weekend Studies together. He too was disenchanted with college the first time around. After dropping out, he found work as an information technology specialist and became a parent, and then as he notes a couple of times, "life took over." Now, a decade later, his academic goals are more job-related than his mother's; he has grown frustrated watching colleagues move ahead of him simply because he lacks a bachelor's degree. Yet something has happened to James' calculus since matriculating: "I thought it would be easy, in and out. I knew IT, and I would just take all the computer classes. But after the first quarter, I changed course. I did Prior Learning from Experience, and it made me realize that I wanted to learn how to write. Now I'm doing non-fiction writing and memoir courses."

One by one around the table, other students describe their previous encounters with college, their reasons for returning, and their experiences so far. Like Jesi, Marcia enrolled for her children. Dorian was prompted by work frustrations and family bonds: "I came back to college because I felt like an angry underling. I had a good job, but I didn't get respect at work. I felt slapped, like I didn't amount to anything without that piece of paper. So I returned to school because of career goals. But my parents are gone, and I also came back for them." There are many such expressions of the emotional—not just economic—stakes of returning to college. Other students describe the sense of anger, embarrassment, even shame that comes with the lack of a degree and conversely the experience of validation that academic progress brings. "I always felt less-than," says Wendy, a naturalist at a wolf conservation center. "I feel like an imposter. Coming here has helped me find my voice. It helps me move through the world. And it's important that I can share this with others like me."

For educators concerned with student well-being, with the importance of well-being to student flourishing and success, this conversation will sound both familiar and strange. The Evergreen undergraduates are articulating some of the most important themes of our work: the disengagement associated with "learning in columns," the energy and joy of collaborative learning environments, and the power of supportive teachers and peers to foster self-discovery and outward exploration. The conversation is a brief for engaged learning, for college experiences that simultaneously welcome students and change them. To use our well-worn phrase, it is a brief for "educating the whole student" and for paying attention to well-being as a condition and consequence of such education.

*This question of well-being for nontraditional students is especially salient when we consider that they have constituted the majority of U.S. undergraduates for the past quarter of a century*

But *which* whole student? For these aren't, of course, the undergraduates that the public (or, I would submit, most academics) have in mind when we talk about the emotional and developmental tasks of college going. They are not recent high school graduates, financially and personally dependent on their parents, organizing their lives and work around central roles as full-time students, forging their academic interests and career plans on the cusp of adulthood. To the contrary: even the younger Evening and Weekend students like James have to pursue their studies in the face of a complex nexus of employment, family, and community factors. No less than traditional collegians, they thrive on educational experiences that connect their aspirations for meaningful work and economic security with opportunities for personal, intellectual, and social development. Yet such integrative learning must fit with the constraints, strengths, hopes, and histories of adult life—with work pressures and ambitions, family responsibilities, the burden of past stumbles with higher education—all of which they bring back to college. What does educating the whole student mean for such undergraduates? What academic practices foster their well-being? Wendy's words suggest the goal beautifully: "Coming here has helped me find my voice. It helps me move through the world." What can we educators do to help students find their voices?

## II

This question of well-being for nontraditional students is especially salient when we consider that they have constituted the majority of U.S. undergraduates for the past quarter of a century. Federal data make it clear: the stereotypical profile of college students—recent high-school graduates financially dependent on their parents, enrolled full-time in two- or four-year institutions—describes only about 26% of undergraduates.

This is almost exactly the same proportion as collegians who are parents. Half of all students are financially independent. Nearly half are enrolled part-time. A majority work at least twenty hours per week while pursuing their studies; about two out of five are employed full-time. An estimated 43% are 25 or older.[2] Of course, not all such undergraduates are enrolled in baccalaureate programs, much less in adult-centered, liberal arts programs such as Evening and Weekend Studies. Yet the Evergreen students belong to a new, nontraditional majority who mainly attend community colleges, for-profit institutions, and non-elite public universities.

This new majority is remarkably heterogeneous. *Nontraditional* is a catch-all rubric for a range of demographic factors (age, employment, family role, enrollment status) and a variety of backgrounds.[3] It includes military veterans and former prisoners; twenty-something food servers and fifty-something parents of grown children; and workers who are unemployed, underemployed, or steadily employed without prospects of advancement. Nontraditional students do not share some core identity or social background. Yet three commonalties are crucial to understanding their well-being. First, as I noted above, nearly all have to fit their educations within a complex ecology of roles and stressors. Their footholds in college are often precarious; from term to term, even week to week, any change in work shifts, family income, children's health, daily schedules, even access to transportation can provoke an academic crisis. "One time my kid was sick with the flu," one community-college student told a research focus group. "And then I got the flu. And that was two weeks out of my math class. Well, all of a sudden, I'd wiped out of math. There was no way I could make it up. There was no leeway."[4]

Second (as the Evergreen conversation underscores) this social complexity is fraught with emotional complexity as well. Nearly every nontraditional undergraduate I've talked with or taught expresses some version of the *less-than* feeling described by Wendy. Returning to school means dealing with the reality of having strayed from the normative script of high-school to college that is so central to the American success story. "I was a thirty-something adult working towards his undergraduate degree (for the third time)," wrote Kevin, a former student of mine, in a course journal, "a task [I] felt [I] should have completed years ago. Academically successful individuals surrounded me daily, and there was an undeniable amount of shame and embarrassment." Prevailing over these feelings and defeating the voice that whispers, "I don't belong here," can itself become a key goal and a signal achievement of college. New-majority undergraduates are clear about the emotional victory and the experience of agency and pride this represents. "I thought that I wasn't college material until I got into this program and started doing well," an interviewee explained in a study of adult working students. "Before I took the initiative to see what I could achieve, I felt really stunted and being in the program has really helped me to just grow so much as a person."[5]

*Returning to school means dealing with the reality of having strayed from the normative script of high-school to college that is so central to the American success story*

But such victories are much too rare. For along with the socio-economic and emotional challenges of returning to college, most new-majority students share a third experience: educational marginality. In myriad ways—from financial aid rules to Federal completion metrics, from the academic calendar to the business hours of student offices—educational policies and practices tend to default to the traditional norm, to penalize students whose lives do not conform to it, and to discourage institutions from investing in such students.[6] The costs of such marginalization are not simply financial and logistical, but also are emotional and cognitive and undermine students' learning and prospects of success. I vividly recall one of my most passionate, creative students bursting into tears unable even to listen in seminar after being stonewalled in the financial aid office. The focus group comment that I quoted above, "There was no way I could make it up. There was no leeway," could serve as the epigram for a host of encounters with inflexible administrators and clueless instructors.

This is not the only story, of course. New-majority students also offer appreciative accounts of educators who have been attentive to their needs, their strengths, and the complexity of their lives. "Night school seems to work real well," another participant told the same focus-group. "There, teachers understand people have other things going on in their lives—parents, work, whatever the situation may be."[7] My point is that no matter the mix of good and bad encounters, nontraditional students must struggle to sustain themselves and their studies, swimming upstream, so to speak, in an academy designed for someone else.

So it should not surprise us that they succeed more slowly and less frequently than their traditional peers. Academic leaders and policy makers are rightly concerned about the low completion rates of all U.S. undergraduates, but attainment rates for new-majority students are even more worrisome. In one national survey, it was estimated that traditional undergraduates seeking bachelor's degrees are three times more likely to graduate than those with at least two nontraditional, demographic markers.[8] Other researchers who focused on discrete nontraditional factors found that "adult students who work 20 hours or more a week are at 'high risk' for failure," and that full-time undergraduates have a six-year completion rate nearly four times higher than part-time students.[9] Facing job, family, housing, health care, transportation, or debt pressures, members of the new majority are at far greater risk of falling behind in classes, missing tuition payments, or dropping out.

*Nontraditional students must struggle to sustain themselves and their studies, swimming upstream, so to speak, in an academy designed for someone else*

## III

Student well-being (or lack of well-being) is clearly at the heart of this story. Many nontraditional undergraduates have languished in their initial experiences with college. Most have to overcome a nexus of barriers (material, social, psychic) to resume their studies. If they progress, it is by tapping sources of resilience and support (material, social, psychic) from their families and communities and from the teachers, mentors, and peers they encounter in school. Success reinforces their well-being and enables them to flourish in their lives and at work in ways that the metrics of promotions and pay raises do not fully capture.

So it is striking that academic leaders and policy advocates have not paid more sustained attention to the issue of well-being for the new majority. Indeed, I would argue, current policy discourse and programmatic innovation in higher education often reinforce the marginalization of these students by ignoring them or by misrecognizing their lives, needs, and goals. I do not mean that we lack research on nontraditional undergraduates.

To the contrary, educational psychologists, economists, and other scholars have produced significant work on their demographics, role pressures, academic experience, and educational outcomes. Yet for the most part, as a leading voice in the field has argued:

> research on undergraduate higher education [has been rooted in] a traditional student profile [that] . . . represented the undergraduate as an on-campus residential student who was solely focused upon the academic pursuits related to future career and life goals and primarily concerned with the key developmental tasks of identity and intimacy formation . . . .Higher education was both a foundation for developing adult identity and competence . . . and a developmental bridge between the family circle and the future adult world of family, work, and societal decision making.[10]

This paradigm, with its stress on the undergraduate's post-adolescent identity formation and entry into the future adult world, has proven enormously generative. It informs much of the best research and practice on student well-being and development, including important work presented in this volume. Yet this framework does not fully speak to the experience of the new majority for whom college is not a launching pad into adult identities and adult roles.

Conversely, a more recent trend among educational thought leaders and policy experts does focus on nontraditional undergraduates, but it does so without paying serious attention to their well-being, emotional needs, or developmental tasks. Indeed it is assumed that they have no distinctive developmental agenda beyond that of acquiring degrees and job skills. To a great extent, this is because the new focus on the new majority is driven by policy advocates—for instance, the National Governors Association or the multi-state consortium Complete College America—whose primary goals are to boost graduation rates and align academic priorities with the dynamics of the labor market.[11] Such completion and workforce goals have emerged as dominant themes in the national conversation on higher education, and they deserve critical examination. Personally I would argue that they are legitimate (as part of a more holistic educational agenda) and dangerously instrumental (if enshrined separately). But this is not the occasion for such a discussion. My point here is that given its stress on targeted, accelerated, training-oriented education, this way of thinking about college for nontraditional students has little to say about their well-being. It treats them as neoliberal ciphers, emptied of emotional or developmental complexity, their inner lives and personal journeys shaped by nothing more than cost and time factors. "Adult learners . . . use a simple calculus," argues Richard Kazis and colleagues in an influential policy brief, "they ask: How can I maximize the economic value of my time in school while minimizing the amount of time I have to spend in classes? They are looking for flexibility, convenience, and accelerated progress to skills and credentials that pay off, as well as better odds for completion."[12]

It's a powerfully simple model of the needs and motives of the new majority, and it leads to a powerfully straightforward policy agenda: streamlined vocationalism. As the student voices I've quoted make clear, it's also inaccurate. Nontraditional students need academic opportunities that take full account of their lives, needs, and goals. To provide such opportunities, educators need models of well-being that also take full account of students' lives, needs, and goals. What should that model look like? We have much work to do in answering this question.

IV

Let's begin by stressing the complexity of the needs that nontraditional students bring to college. Some (such as affordable tuition and engaging teachers) are shared with their traditional peers; others (such as child care support and flexible schedules for courses and administrative offices) reflect their distinct situations. And even among nontraditional undergraduates, these needs are strikingly heterogeneous. The full-time office assistant, the unemployed machinist, and the parent with a part-time job will have divergent time pressures; the middle-aged administrator and the young barista may require quite different levels of help with digital, writing, or financial literacy.

Yet however diverse the needs, they are tightly interwoven within the lives of individual students. When I queried my adult undergraduates at The New School to describe what they wanted the institution to provide, I was apt to hear an eloquent flow of responses. Sufficient financial aid, responsive financial-aid staff, friendly teachers, challenging teachers, advisers who "get it" about their lives, a strong peer community, classes full of snacks, tutoring and academic services with flexible hours, and massage sessions during exam periods ran seamlessly together. Sometimes my students invoked Maslow's famous hierarchy of needs to describe the range of their hopes and frustrations, but I came to think of Maslow's classificatory model (in which the meeting of basic requirements is presumed to be a precondition for higher self-actualization) as too static and, well, hierarchical.[13] What nontraditional students convey is rather the manifold connections among their needs that function like compounds in organic chemistry; each student's life is its own complex molecule in which material, social, intellectual, and emotional factors are bent toward one another and bound together.

Their motivations in returning to college are similarly complex and interconnected. Indeed, I'd argue, the biggest misconception about the new majority—and one of the largest obstacles to their success—is the current conventional belief that their only salient goals are income- and job-related. In saying this, I do not diminish the role of economics in their educational choices; financial security and career advancement (not to mention the affordability of college itself) are as crucial to them as to any other students. Yet perhaps even more than traditional undergraduates, they do not segregate economic goals from academic and personal ones. In one survey of adult prospective students, affordable tuition was ranked as "absolutely essential" by 74 percent of respondents and was second only to "instructors [who] care about students" at 76 percent.[14] Recall Dorian's comment in the Evergreen discussion, with its fluid description of career, family, and emotional motivations:

"I came back to college because I felt like an angry underling. I had a good job, but I didn't get respect at work. I felt slapped, like I didn't amount to anything without that piece of paper. So I returned to school because of career goals. But my parents are gone, and I also came back for them." We can hear a similar fluidity, with financial worries segueing into larger personal dreams, in this community-college student's comment: "I think education is the only way to do better in life . . . like without enough money, if

*Well-Being and Higher Education*

you want to be better and do something . . . be something in life—education is the only way I've found.[15]

As such voices make clear, it is not the desire for a pure and simple pathway to employment that typically drives nontraditional students to college. Rather a compound of goals—financial, occupational, familial, emotional, sometimes communal, and (not least) intellectual—impels them to imagine, each in his or her own way, when, where, and what to study. If educators do not design institutions and programs in recognition and support of this whole spectrum of needs and aspirations—and the interconnections among them—we will simply add to the headwinds against which nontraditional undergraduates have to push, heads down, on their journeys.

V

The first time I mentioned the phrase *self-authoring* to my adult students at The New School, they seemed to sit straighter and take notice. When I followed up by assigning a scholarly article in which the authors used the concept to analyze the goals of nontraditional undergraduates in Australia, they responded to the reading with emphatic assents.[16] By the end of the semester, they had adopted self-authoring as a kind of rhetorical touchstone, a meme for their educational goals and their advocacy for better institutional support.

At first glance, this may seem surprising. As theorized by the psychologist Robert Kegan and elaborated by Marcia Baxter Magolda and other scholars, the concept of self-authorship has served as an influential framework for understanding *traditional* undergraduates and their developmental tasks.[17] It posits a process by which young adults gain mature autonomy and self-direction and move from "relying on external formulas" and "adult guides" to "using [their] internal voice and core personal values to guide [their] life."[18] Magolda parses this developmental journey into three processes that work together to cultivate and activate an individual's internal voice and core values. There must be "cognitive" growth in which s/he creates a belief-system distinct from the guidance of parents and other authorities and tests it iteratively in the face of experience and conflicting world-views; "intrapersonal" growth in which s/he constructs a grounded identity and core personal commitments; and "inter-personal" growth in which s/he develops authentic, mutual relationships that engage others without either conformist deference or defensive stubbornness.[19]

It is easy to see why the self-authorship framework has become a valuable model for undergraduate development in traditional academic institutions. Despite the whiff of individualism in the word itself, Magolda, Patricia King, and other proponents stress the need for a collective fabric of "learning partnerships" that catalyze self-authoring, and it has been widely deployed in the student affairs literature and in the design of undergraduate curricula and student life programming.[20] Indeed the model's key themes—the importance of separating from external authorities and inherited rules, the importance of building autonomous identities and values, and the importance of cognitive development in both—comprise a powerful blueprint for educating the post-adolescent undergraduate to become reflective, self-directed, and socially engaged.

Yet we should not be surprised that members of the new majority also find the idea so resonant. It was conceived as a model of adult (not simply young-adult) development, grounded in longitudinal research that followed interview subjects from college into early middle age. Magolda's tagline for self-authorship—"developing an internal voice to navigate life's challenges"—is echoed uncannily in Wendy's description of her Evergreen experience: "Coming here has helped me find my voice. It helps me move through the world." The force of Wendy's words is clear: for nontraditional students, going to college can itself be an act of self-authoring.

*For most nontraditional students, college is a second act, a project of self-renewal rather than self-creation*

But it is an act that shifts the typical understanding of the concept and inflects it with the distinctive experience of the new majority for whom self-authorship is not a matter of launching an adult identity and forging core values in the face of inherited norms and external authorities. They have usually (if incompletely and imperfectly) undertaken these tasks already. Rather, self-authorship is about self-efficacy, about building the capacity to transform the circumstances and responsibilities that hem in adult life into episodes of a new story, one that new-majority students compose and enact themselves. And it is about claiming that story telling power against a backstory of languishing, a past freighted with unfinished business, and the *less-than* feeling that so often results. For most nontraditional students, college is a second act, a project of self-renewal rather than self-creation. The authoring that it asks them to undertake may seem like a sequel, or the completion of an unfinished chapter, or a correction of the first edition, or a palimpsest in which they overwrite the earlier story without erasing it. But whichever of these metaphors is apt, there is no blank sheet, no page one. Coming to college means overcoming the burdens of the backstory in order to rewrite the future. And that requires collaboration and support.

## VI

What should we do, then, to help nontraditional undergraduates flourish and to foster their self-authoring? Some answers will be clear, I hope, in what I've written. New-majority students deserve educational opportunities that take account of the social, material, and emotional complexity of their lives, of the breadth and interconnectedness of their needs and aspirations. They deserve an educational environment that is similarly broad and integrated in meeting those needs and aspirations. And quite apart from what they deserve, their academic success depends on it.

In this, of course, nontraditional undergraduates are no different from traditional ones. The success of *all* college students depends on integrated support for their material, emotional, social, and intellectual needs—for their self-authoring. Too often the traditional college environment falters in fully offering such support, especially when academic life and co-curricular sociability are misaligned. But at its best, the residential campus works as a kind of total institution for the nurturance of the whole student and embeds academic study in an environment that offers food, shelter, sociability, athletic and creative facilities, spiritual community, and health and counseling services, all aimed at post-adolescent flourishing.

That same environment poorly serves the needs and goals of nontraditional students. Their well-being does not require the compact integration of a residential campus but rather a nexus of infrastructures and services that help them to sustain their studies within the conditions and stressors of their outside lives. The most effective four- and two-year programs are designed to do just that. Evergreen's Tacoma campus and the

Providence based College Unbound, for instance, strengthen engagement and retention by mandating weekly, faculty-led community forums that build mentoring and peer relationships and are scheduled at times and locations that fit the lives of working students.[21] The Accelerated Study in Associate Programs (ASAP) initiative of the City University of New York is similarly student-centered and provides an integrated suite of support and services to low-income, educationally at-risk undergraduates (traditional and nontraditional) in CUNY's community college system. Participants are asked to commit to full-time study, clustered courses, and a gateway seminar that builds study habits and soft skills; they receive intensive advising, tutoring, career services, tuition and fee waivers for all costs not covered by their financial aid, free textbooks, and stipends for public transportation.[22] Were I the Czar of Nontraditional Well-Being, I might add child care support and short-term, supplemental funding for household emergencies.

What makes such best-practice programs so effective is not only their responsive logistics and wrap-around services, as useful as these are, but also their integration of support of an academic experience in which the curriculum and learning climate are similarly student-centered. Weekly forums with faculty mentors and supportive peers, intensive (sometimes intrusive) advising, gateway courses that germinate academic plans while building academic skills—such practices braid together students' personal, career, and intellectual development even as they deepen teachers' and advisers' understanding of students' lives and needs. The result is a specifically new-majority culture of engaged learning. For many faculty, this may entail adjusting expectations and habits that have developed in traditional settings. Especially if teachers come from elite educational backgrounds, it can be difficult to keep in mind just how precarious nontraditional students may feel. "Understanding that you belong on campus—and that an institution believes in that belonging and your potential—are important assets in succeeding as a student," one adult, working, undergraduates notes. "Privileged students most likely take this acceptance for granted…[but] these questions remain open and salient for [nontraditional undergraduates]."[23] This why "instructors who care" score so high in enrollment surveys. It is also why the most effective adult programs, like Evergreen's Tacoma Program and College Unbound, always open their weekly forums by celebrating the academic and personal milestones of students. Such a full-throated culture of welcome enhances persistence and completion, not because it coddles students in need of grit, but precisely because it conveys trust in their resilience and agency.[24]

Of course a culture of welcome means little if the academic experience into which it welcomes students does not foster their success. Adult education research emphasizes that nontraditional undergraduates flourish most when curricular, pedagogical, and credit-earning practices closely engage their lives; draw on their personal, community, and work experiences; and directly advance their goals. As Carol Kasworm summarizes it, nontraditional students value "[learning] engagements that are adult experience-based, challenging, and relevant . . . and that apply to adults' work worlds."[25] Such goals and preferences impel many nontraditional students to pursue career-related degrees. Yet it would be a mistake to equate the desire for "adult experience-based, challenging, and relevant" education with a call for vocational training pure and simple. National data show that new-majority students at four- and two-year institutions distribute themselves broadly across degree programs in health care, business, STEM, and liberal arts or general studies. The most popular areas of study are variously in health care or liberal arts depending on the level of nontraditional factors students display and the type of institutions they attend.[26]

Whatever they study, it is clear that new-majority undergraduates thrive best when they can integrate their learning and credit earning into the fabric of their lives. Research suggests that they persist at higher rates when they can garner credit for prior learning—documented knowledge and skills already gained in non-academic settings—and when they can pursue new opportunities for practice-based learning linked to their current jobs, career aspirations, or unpaid community, creative, and advocacy work.[27] It also points to the value of high-impact practices like community service and project-based learning if these can be made accessible and useful within the time and role constraints of their lives.[28] Indeed, leading adult baccalaureate programs, such as College Unbound and DePaul University's School For New Learning, require that students complete their studies with capstone projects that bring their academic plans to bear on their personal goals in real world settings. Leann, for instance, a recent graduate of College Unbound, developed a business plan for a community performance center. A divorced mother of two with a passion for theater, she long languished in traditional colleges that she found unresponsive to her family situation and for-profit courses that were "low-quality and worthless." By contrast, she loved the blend of peer community, no nonsense mentoring, and student-centered academic planning that she encountered at College Unbound. "All of a sudden, I felt like I wasn't in school," she said, recalling the arc of goal setting, reflection, skill-building, and action that she wove together in her capstone project. Now she is pursuing a master's in theater administration and working part-time as an advisor for incoming College Unbound students.

## VII

This, it seems to me, is what educating the whole student looks like when that student belongs to the new majority.

The vision of well-being that I have tried to capture in this sketch is complex—as complex as the lives of nontraditional undergraduates themselves. It points to the need for institutional infrastructures, student services, learning communities, and curricular practices that work together organically to welcome new-majority students and at the same time challenge them. It calls for academic programs that offer strong guidance from faculty and staff and at the same time offer vibrant and supportive peer communities. Such programs would nurture the inward and outward dimensions of self-authorship and empower nontraditional students (to quote Wendy's words one last time) to find their voices and move through the world.

The academy is filled with committed educators who advance this vision in their everyday work. But higher education as a whole has not done enough to realize it, even as the students who stand to benefit from it have become the majority of our undergraduates. Actualizing this vision will require creativity, institutional will, and resources on the part of academic institutions, faculty, staff, and students themselves. It will also require significant changes in Federal, state, and accreditor policies, but that is an argument for another essay. Yet, as I have tried to show in this essay, we can see glimpses of what it might look like in the research of adult education scholars, the best practices of places like Evergreen, and the voices of students like Wendy.

I hope it is clear that investing creativity, will, and resources in the well-being of non-traditional students is well worth it. When academic programs take account of their lives, needs, and goals, the results are impressive. Participants in CUNY's ASAP program complete their associate's degrees at twice the rate of their peers and at a lower cost per graduate, despite (or rather because of) the extra resources invested in supporting them.[29] Students in College Unbound and Evergreen's Tacoma Program persist and graduate at rates as high as 80%—a level usually limited to select liberal-arts institutions—and Pell Grants cover about two-thirds of tuition in both programs.[30]

Such indicators of cost and completion are important; nontraditional undergraduates (like traditional ones) cannot flourish if they cannot graduate from affordable programs. But the most powerful evidence of student well-being comes from the students themselves. So let me end where I started: listening to the stories of Evergreen undergraduates. The last person around the seminar table that afternoon is named Jesse, "spelled like boys spell it," she tells me. She is a judicial educator in the Washington State court system, and she has come back to school many years after a first, unhappy stint, feeling confident in her subsequent successes and resentful that her lack of a degree has held her back:

> *While I hate to admit this, I often compare myself . . . to others—feeling that a degree doesn't make the person. It is passion, effort, and genuine care that does. I've worked next to a great deal of highly educated individuals who couldn't apply their knowledge to practice, yet they get the interviews and jobs I'm not considered for because I didn't have the paper. It created a great deal of resentment that I have had to figure out how to deal with. It also created a really bad opinion of higher education . . . It was very hard to go back to school and trust that I would not be wounded by it again. And that's what makes Evergreen so different in my mind.*

At Evergreen, in the Evening and Weekend Studies Program, Jesse has flourished, loves the course-work and the writing, and is even considering a career in higher education. "I began to crave college," she tells me, almost fiercely. "College makes me feel dangerous. I hated school before. Now it feels great to be so self-directed."

ACKNOWLEDGEMENT

My greatest appreciation goes to the many students who have shared their stories. It begins with my former students in the Public Engagement Fellows Program of The New School's adult bachelor's program, who first dislodged me from my own cluelessness about the experience of nontraditional undergraduates. In field visits, I learned enormously from students at College Unbound, DePaul University's School for New Learning, and the Evening and Weekend Studies and Tacoma Programs at The Evergreen State College. I am grateful to all of them for letting me publish their words and lift up their achievements. Thanks also to Provost Adam Bush and his colleagues at College Unbound, Dean Marisa Alicia and her colleagues at DePaul, and Dean Sarah Ryan at Evergreen for opening their doors and their work to me.

Dr. Patricia King was a helpful guide through the scholarly literature on self-authorship and a generously critical reader. Don Harward has been, as always, a supportive editor and inclusive leader of the Bringing Theory to Practice project. A decade ago, he invited me into this special community of researchers and educators. I hope that this essay makes clear how much I have learned from them.

NOTES

1. The Evergreen State College has two bachelor's programs for adult working students: the Evening and Studies Program on the main Olympia campus and the stand-alone Tacoma Program an hour away. These have distinct faculties, curricula, and student bodies; both are exemplary in different ways. I discuss each of them at various points in the essay.

2. Thomas D. Snyder and Sally A. Dillow, *Digest of Education Statistics 2013 (NCES 2015-011)* (Washington, DC: National Center for Education Statistics, 2015), Table 303.40, 42, http://nces.ed.gov/pubs2015/2015011.pdf; National Center for Educational Statistics, *Demographic and Enrollment Characteristics of Nontraditional Undergraduates: 2011–12* (Washington, DC: National Center for Education Statistics, 2015), 6, http://nces.ed.gov/pubs2015/2015025.pdf; Sandy Baum, "Student Work and the Financial Aid System" in *Understanding the Working College Student: New Research and Its Implications For Policy and Practice*, ed. Laura W. Perna (Sterling, VA: Stylus, 2010), 5.

3. The National Center for Education Statistics (NCES) defines as *nontraditional* any students with one or more of these seven demographic markers: (1) financial independence, (2) having one or more dependents, (3) being a single caregiver, (4) lacking a traditional high school diploma, (5) delaying college enrollment at least a year after high school, (6) part-time enrollment, and (7) full-time employment (more than thirty-five hours a week) (National Center for Education Statistics, *Who is Nontraditional?* accessed March 5, 2016, https://nces.ed.gov/pubs/web/97578e.asp). Different individuals have varying factors and varying numbers of factors; NCES surveys are used to measure both. The NCES does *not* use age as a marker, but many adult education researchers define students who are twenty-four or older as nontraditional. In this essay I treat NCES factors and student age as criteria of nontraditional status.

4. Lisa Matus-Grossman et al., "Opening Doors: Students' Perspectives on Juggling Work, Family, and College," Manpower Demonstration Research Corporation, 30, published July, 2002, http://www.mdrc.org/sites/default/files/full_466.pdf.

5. Brian Pusser, "Of a Mind To Labor: Reconceptualizing Student Work and Higher Education," in *Understanding the Working College Student: New Research and Its Implications For Policy and Practice*, ed. Laura W. Perna (Sterling, VA: Stylus, 2010), 144.

6. See especially Peggy A. Sissel, Catherine A. Hansman, Carol E. Kasworm, "The Politics of Neglect: Adult Learners in Higher Education," *New Directions For Adult and Continuing Education* 91 (Fall, 2001): 17–27 and David Scobey, "Marginalized Majority: Nontraditional Students and the Equity Imperative," *Diversity and Democracy* 19 (Winter, 2016): 15–17.

7. Matus-Grossman et al., "Opening Doors," 29.

8. Susan Choy, Nontraditional Undergraduates: NCES 2002–012 (Washington, DC: National Center for Education Statistics, 2002), 14 (six-year graduation rates), https://nces.ed.gov/pubs2002/2002012.pdf; Heather T. Rowan-Kenyon et al., "Academic Success For Working Adult Students," in Understanding the Working College Student: New Research and Its Implications For Policy and Practice, ed. Laura W. Perna (Sterling, VA: Stylus, 2010), 93 ("high risk"); Doug Shapiro et al., "Completing College: A National View of Student Attainment Rates—Fall 2009 Cohort (Signature Report No. 10)," Herndon, VA: National Student Clearinghouse Research Center, 17 (part-time graduation rates), published November 16, 2015, https://nscresearchcenter.org/signaturereport10/.

9. Ibid.

10. Carol E. Kasworm, "Adult Undergraduates in Higher Education: A Review of Past Research Perspectives," *Review of Educational Research* 60, no. 3 (Fall, 1990): 345. Peggy A. Sissel, in "When 'Accommodation' Is Resistance: Towards a Critical Discourse on the Politics of Adult Education," in *The Cyril O. Houle Scholars in Adult and Continuing Education Global Research Perspectives*, eds. R.M. Cervero et al. (Athens, Georgia: University of Georgia, 2001), 103–116, similarly argues that adult students are marginalized in higher education research and journalism.

11. See, for instance, Linda Hoffman, Travis Reindl, and Jeremy Bearer-Friend, *Complete to Compete: Improving Postsecondary Attainment Among Adults* (Washington, DC: National Governors Association, 2011); Complete College America, "Time Is the Enemy," published 2011, http://www.completecollege.org/docs/Time_Is_the_Enemy.pdf; and Complete College America, "Four-Year Myth," published 2014, http://completecollege.org/wp-content/uploads/2014/11/4-Year-Myth.pdf.

12. Richard Kazis et al., *Adult Learners in Higher Education: Barriers to Success and Strategies to Improve Results* (Washington, DC: United States Department of Labor, 2007), 15.

13. Abraham H. Maslow introduced his model of human needs in "A Theory of Human Motivation," *Psychology Review* 50, no. 4 (July, 1943): 370–96 and developed it more fully in his 1954 book *Motivation and Personality*.

14. Public Agenda, "Is College Worth It For Me? How Adults Without Degrees Think About Going (Back) To School," 14, published October 23, 2013, http://www.publicagenda.org/pages/is-college-worth-it-for-me.

15. Matus-Grossman et al., "Opening Doors," 33.

16. Lesley Scanlon, "Adults' Motives For Returning To Study: The Role of Self-Authoring," *Studies in Continuing Education* 30, no. 1 (2008): 17–32.

17. See especially Robert Kegan, *The Evolving Self: Problem and Process In Human Development* (Cambridge, MA: Harvard University Press, 1982); Robert Kegan, *In Over Our Heads: The Mental Demands Of Modern Life* (Cambridge, MA: Harvard University Press, 1994); and (among many publications) Marcia Baxter Magolda, *Authoring Your Life: Developing an Internal Voice To Navigate Life's Challenges* (Sterling, VA: Stylus, 2009); Marcia Baxter Magolda, "Self-Authorship: The Foundation For Twenty-First-Century Education," *New Directions For Teaching and Learning* 109 (Spring, 2007): 69–83.

18. Magolda, *Authoring Your Life*, 9–10.

19. Ibid.

20. See the articles in Marcia Baxter Magolda and Patrica M. King, eds., *Learning Partnerships: Theories and Models of Practice to Educate for Self-Authorship* (Sterling, VA: Stylus, 2004) and Peggy S. Meszaros, ed., *Self-Authorship: Advancing Students' Intellectual Growth: New Directions for Teaching and Learning* (San Francisco, CA: Jossey-Bass, 2007).

21. Throughout this section, my accounts of the practices of College Unbound, Evergreen State College's Tacoma Program, and DePaul University's School for New Learning rely on field visits to each program.

22. Susan Scrivener et al., "Doubling Graduation Rates: Three-Year Effects of CUNY's Accelerated Study in Associate Programs (ASAP) for Developmental Education Students," iii, Manpower Demonstration Research Corporation, published February, 2015, http://www.mdrc.org/sites/default/files/doubling_graduation_rates_fr.pdf.

23. Mary Ziskin *et al.*, "Mobile Working Students: A Delicate Balance of College, Family, and Work," in *Understanding the Working College Student: New Research and Its Implications For Policy and Practice*, ed. Laura W. Perna (Sterling, VA: Stylus, 2010), 87.

24. I should emphasize that a culture of welcome with strong, persistent practices of inclusion and support, is equally essential and effective for the success of low-income, first-generation, and nonwhite undergraduates in the traditional student body.

25. Carol Kasworm, "Adult Workers as Undergraduate Students: Significant Challenges for Higher Education Policy and Practice," in *Understanding the Working College Student: New Research and Its Implications For Policy and Practice*, ed. Laura W. Perna (Sterling, VA: Stylus, 2010), 39.

26. See National Center for Educational Statistics, "Demographic and Enrollment Characteristics," for details on the fields of study chosen by associate's and bachelor's students disaggregated by number of nontraditional demographic factors.

27. See Council For Adult & Experiential Learning, "Fueling the Race To Postsecondary Success: A 48-Institution Study of Prior Learning Assessment and Adult Student Outcomes," published March, 2010, http://www.cael.org/pdfs/pla_fueling-the-race and Jovita M. Ross-Gordon, "Research On Adult Learners: Supporting the Needs of a Student Population That Is No Longer Nontraditional," *Peer Review* 13, no.1 (Winter, 2011), https://www.aacu.org/publications-research/periodicals/research-adult-learners-supporting-needs-student-population-no.

28. See for instance, Susan C. Reed et al., "The Effect of Community Service Learning On Undergraduate Persistence in Three Institutional Contexts," *Michigan Journal of Community Service Learning* 21, no. 2 (Spring, 2015): 22–36; Center For Community College Student Engagement, "A Matter of Degrees: Engaging Practices, Engaging Students: High Impact Practices for Community College Student Engagement," published 2013, http://www.ccsse.org/docs/Matter_of_Degrees_2.pdf; and Susan C. Reed and Catherine Marienau, eds., *Linking Adults With Community: Promoting Civic Engagement Through Community Based Learning* (San Francisco, CA: Jossey-Bass, 2008).

29. Scrivener et al., "Doubling," iii.

30. Scrivener et al., "Doubling," iii.

13
<br>ESSAY

# What Constitutes Indices of Well-Being Among College Students?

*Sara E. Dahill-Brown & Eranda Jayawickreme*

## HIGHER EDUCATION AND WELL-BEING
## IN AN ERA OF UNBUNDLING AND ACCOUNTABILITY

American colleges and universities today find themselves confronting a variety of cross-pressures. Traditional brick and mortar institutions of higher learning have been widely criticized in recent years for a variety of perceived failures, for example, that students do not learn well as a result of poor teaching, that they do not graduate in large enough numbers for lack of support, that they graduate in debt because of high costs, and that they stay in debt because they were not adequately prepared for the workforce.[1] These criticisms, among others, have fueled two broad types of responses: one is led by entrepreneurs who would use new technologies to disrupt and unbundle higher education;[2] the other would be used to leverage the power of the state and federal governments to more actively regulate colleges and universities and to hold them accountable for students' academic and labor market outcomes.[3]

Both movements are concerned with measuring student outcomes as a means of increasing transparency in the higher education system in order to help parents and prospective students compare institutions and to facilitate regulation and accreditation. In so doing, they have spurred demand for more data and contributed to changes in the process by which institutions of higher learning are ranked against one another.[4] President Obama and the United Stated Department of Education recently announced the publication of a College Scorecard that draws from all available data on college and universities for a period of nearly twenty years. The most comprehensive effort to increase transparency to date, the College Scorecard includes data on hundreds of variables that range from the number of Bachelor's degrees awarded in the field of history, to the default rate of loans by cohort, to the percent of low-income students who died within two years after matriculation.[5]

Yet for all the apparent breadth of these data, and despite the importance of the outcomes they measure, most agree that the many data points included in the Scorecard and other comparable rankings account for only a narrow slice of the goals that motivate higher education. This is particularly the case for a liberal arts education in which students are expected to study within a broad curriculum that facilitates holistic academic and personal growth; cultivates a sense of civic and social responsibility; and encourages integrative thinking, creativity, and curiosity.[6] It is worrisome that rankings and the easily measured outcomes upon which they rely may reshape institutional priorities and divert resources away from important but less easily operationalized outcomes. Changes in the specific focuses and practices of higher education are inevitable, even desirable, but they should be made consciously and with full information.

Fueled partly in response to the specter of these and other measurements and rankings, and partly by a genuine desire to address health and wellness on campuses, there have recently been calls to refocus attention on the promotion of well-being as a goal of higher education. In addition to fulfilling the intellectual potential of students, this perspective on education argues that higher education can and should facilitate the development of strengths and skills that are intrinsically valuable and promote well-being outcomes across the lifespan. Proponents of this broader and deeper conception of higher education as well as those working day-to-day with college students in many settings may be interested in tailored measures of well-being.

*The measurement of well-being outside of collegiate contexts has garnered increased interest in the last twenty years, especially with the emergence of the field of positive psychology*

Fortunately, the measurement of well-being outside of collegiate contexts has garnered increased interest in the last twenty years, especially with the emergence of the field of positive psychology.[7] Scientists can utilize measures of dimensions of well-being to understand the dynamics and predictors of human flourishing, and institutions and governments pay attention to what is being measured.

## WHY FOCUS ON WELL-BEING?

Well-being is an innately valuable end on its own terms, but individuals who report high levels of well-being flourish in other ways as well, as recent research in positive psychology has shown. For example, those who report high, subjective well-being (defined as feeling satisfied with one's life and having high levels of positive emotions in the absence of negative emotions) are more likely to have better health and possibly even longer lives.[8] High subjective well-being is also causally implicated in further positive outcomes,[9] such as better work performance, better social relationships, and more ethical behavior.[10]

One area that has been the focus of much research has been the relationship between personality and well-being.[11] Steel, Schmidt, and Shultz identified a number of reasons to indicate that the relationship between stable personality traits and subjective well-being should be particularly strong.[12] Among these reasons is the fact that, as Diener and Lucas pointed out, there are theoretical linkages between personality and well-being, and it is apparent that personality factors account for a significant portion of well-being.[13]

Related to this fact, Headey and Wearing found that history tended to literally repeat itself for individuals, that is, the same life events tended to happen repeatedly to the same people.[14] This led them to argue that life events are not completely exogenous but in fact are endogenous to a significant degree and that in the absence of unusual life circumstances, an individual's subjective well-being will remain stable. For example, extraverts generally tend to experience positive events over time, while introverts generally experience negative events. They further claimed that it was possible to predict an individual's life events simply on the basis of that individual's levels of extraversion, introversion and openness

*Well-Being and Higher Education*

to experience. This perspective on well-being, life events, and personality has been termed *Dynamic Equilibrium Theory*.[15] Moreover, adoption and twin research studies by Lykken and Tellegen[16] and Nes and colleagues[17] point to the existence of a happiness *set-point*, that is, over time, an individual's level of well-being appears to remain stable. This set-point is probably related to personality traits rooted in neurobiology.

However, the view that the happiness set-point is immutable has been increasingly challenged, especially in light of evidence that individuals' levels of life satisfaction have been shown to increase over time.[18] For example, life events such as marriage and divorce[19] and unemployment[20] can result in long lasting changes in well-being. In light of such findings, Diener, Lucas and Scollon[21] argued that set-point theory needs to be modified to accommodate evidence that people's personality profiles may predispose them to a particular *non-neutral* set-point, and others have argued that people are generally happy most of the time,[22] that people may have multiple set-points given the multi-faceted nature of well-being,[23] that subjective well-being can change over time,[24] and that there are differences in how individuals adapt to life events such as marriage.[25] Lyubomirsky et al. further argued that long-lasting increases in well-being are possible through a focus on altering one's intentional activity or how one thinks and acts.[26] One important implication of this is that interventions can be designed to increase individuals' happiness *above* their genetic set points.[27]

In addition, Diener found that people from a wide number of countries valued well-being above income.[28] Well-being has also been advanced as an alternative to standard economic and social indicators (such as GNP and levels of education, crime, and health) as a measurement of quality of life. Advocates of this approach have claimed that in combination with objective measures, well-being indicators can provide information that standard indicators cannot.[29] Determining public policy based on economic indicators alone has meant that growing economic prosperity has not been accompanied by an increase in well-being.[30] Many well-being researchers have argued that this paradox needs to be resolved with more emphasis on the expressed well-being of citizens. For example, important predictors of well-being include social capital, democratic government, and human rights. Moreover, not only is well-being seen by many as an important and perhaps the ultimate end, but also well-being can help individuals better achieve other important ends, an argument central to proponents of well-being in higher education.

## WHAT SHOULD BE THE INDICES OF WELL-BEING IN HIGHER EDUCATION?
The promotion of well-being as an outcome of higher education has received increased attention from researchers and practitioners.[31] This interest mirrors the growth focused goals of the progressive movement in education, and it is important to acknowledge that the interest in non-academic outcomes such as well-being among educators is not a new one. Moreover, researchers and educators have identified a number of outcomes that count as positive youth outcomes. These constructs have been variously termed *character* or traits that promote character virtue development, social emotional learning, pro-social behavior, positive youth development, learning mindsets and skills, capacity for accomplishment, thriving, non-cognitive skills, and personal success skills.[32]

Most psychologists are careful to point out that while subjective measures of well-being can provide important information that can inform policy decisions, they are not meant to override other source of information, such as objective measures, those based on the capabilities approach,[33] and standard economic indicators. It should be noted that psychologists emphasize the importance of subjective measures of well-being in part due to concerns about using objective indicators as the sole measures of well-being.[34] One set of concerns stems from the general problem that it is not intuitively obviously which items should be included in a finite set of domains that contribute to or constitute well-being. Also, operationalizing objective domains of flourishing can frequently be challenging. For example, a researcher may be interested in measuring engagement with culture, but does that entail giving equal status to attendance at the opera and fraternity parties? Additionally, while some researchers argue that objective measures of well-being can be clearly observed and empirically verified,[35] the objective data that are frequently cited may not always be accurate, and similar scores on a specific objective indicator could reflect different levels of well-being. Subjective measures of well-being, in other words, can provide unique information that objective measures cannot.

Clearly then, measuring well-being successfully is a challenging task, in part because well-being is multidimensional, a fact recognized by researchers and practitioners.[36] The intrinsic importance of well-being means that assessments relevant to students have been produced and deployed, but the difficulty of the measurement task and the value-judgments inherent have left a number of gaps. No extant measures focused on self-report are attendant to the specific development status of young adults, and at least two include dimensions that focus on the quantifiable value of college for financial security. Ideally, a measure of student well-being complements rather than duplicates extant assessments, focuses on self-report across a number of dimensions, and reflects the best scientific knowledge of well-being and the development of young adults. Below is a list of psychological constructs relevant to or constitutive of student well-being that we have utilized in our past research on well-being in the Wake Forest University student community. We note this list simply to highlight the wide range of skills, abilities, and traits that can arguably be termed relevant to well-being among college students:

Table 1.

**LIST OF WELL-BEING CONSTRUCTS RELEVANT FOR COLLEGE ASSESSMENT**

| Constructs | |
| --- | --- |
| Resilience | Optimism |
| Self-Esteem | Belongingness |
| Self-Acceptance | Personal Growth |
| Purpose in Life | Environmental Mastery |
| Autonomy | Positive Relations with Others |
| Coping | Personal Strength |
| Spirituality | Openness to New Opportunities |
| Open-Minded Thinking | Self-Complexity |
| Locus of Control | Beliefs about Personality Change |
| Group Identity | Identification with Academic Domains |
| Evaluation Anxiety | Satisfaction with Life (Past, Current, Future) and with Specific Life Domains |

The magnitude of constructs relevant to the well-being of college students requires the development of some decision rules to provide clear guidelines with which to identify and select the most appropriate dimensions of well-being for assessment among college students. We present two criteria:

- **The proposed dimension should have a substantive empirical base of research to demonstrate its successful assessment and utility.** Given the significant progress made on research on well-being and personality (non-cognitive traits) in the last twenty years, a proposed dimension should have some identified empirical research base to demonstrate its successful assessment and value in terms of life outcomes.
- **The proposed dimension should be actionable, i.e., colleges should ideally be able to affect changes to students' standing on these dimensions.** While an identified dimension may be important in and of itself or for other valued life outcomes, it should also be actionable in the educational setting. In other words, colleges and other educational institutions should be able to affect changes on students' standing on these dimensions.

Based on these criteria, we propose five broad dimensions that *may* potentially characterize student well-being: subjective well-being, meaning/purpose, belongingness, commitment to others, and grit/perseverance. These dimensions reflect, in our view, the attributes that constitute high student well-being based on the current scientific evidence—attributes that potentially can be changed in the college context, and that are the result of a systematic evaluation of the constructs depicted in Table 1.

## DIMENSION 1: SUBJECTIVE WELL-BEING

The subjective well-being approach is the most ubiquitous method with which to assess well-being in psychology, and much of the research discussed earlier derives from this tradition. Subjective well-being accounts in psychology center on subjective reports of positive emotions and life satisfaction and are used to assess how people feel and think about their quality of life. Subjective well-being accounts incorporate hedonic experiences (momentary positive and negative emotions) and cognitive evaluations of how well life is going more generally. Since both of these elements are subjective (the first is affective and the second is cognitive in nature) this kind of account is termed *subjective* well-being, an umbrella term combining how we think and how we feel about our lives.[37]

Given the benefits of experiencing high subjective well-being (discussed above), promoting it among college students is a worthwhile goal. Moreover, our interest in assessing multiple dimensions of well-being does not obviate the utility of a measure with which to gauge an individual's overall sense of well-being. Indeed, positive psychology researchers have called for the development of national indicators of well-being that can in time achieve the conceptual and methodological sophistication of national economic indicators. Diener recommended that the various facets of subjective well-being (including positive affect, negative affect, life satisfaction, domain satisfaction, and quality of life) be measured separately; that instruments sensitive to changes in well-being resulting from changes in circumstances be utilized, and that short-term and long-term changes in be assessed separately; that instruments used to measure subjective well-being be psychometrically valid (that is, that they consistently measure what they are supposed to be measuring); that current instruments, although comparatively imperfect, can still provide information to policymakers that standard economic indicators cannot offer; and that taking well- and ill-being into account when making policy decisions represents an important part of the democratic process.[38]

## DIMENSION 2: MEANING AND PURPOSE

Hedonic research increasingly argues that while happiness is an aspect of subjective well-being and thus contributes to *hedonia*, the facet of well-being more intimately connected with *eudaimonia* is derived not from pursuing momentary desires but from those experiences that promote growth and "a meaningful life."[39]

Meaning is not entirely isolated from measures of subjective well-being; however, it is positively related to life satisfaction,[40] and pursuing meaningful goals is associated with subjective well-being.[41] Moreover, positive affect may predispose individuals to feel that their lives are meaningful and thus may increase their sensitivity to the potential relevance of a particular situation for building meaning.[42] Another construct, *psychological well-being*,[43] arose as a complementary approach to subjective well-being and includes specific dimensions of well-being that the subjective well-being perspective does not. One of these dimensions is Purpose in Life, defined as "having beliefs that give the individual the feeling that there is purpose in and meaning to life."[44] Having high meaning in life is characteristic of social activists who exhibit high moral excellence in their work.[45] College may be the first context in which individuals begin to answer the question *what does my life mean?*[46] and address hitherto unexamined existential questions that have a bearing on their future well-being. Promoting such existential development has been stated frequently as a purpose of liberal higher education.

*The growth of a sense of commitment to others represents a manifestation of mature civic citizenship, the development of which is arguably one goal of higher education*

## DIMENSION 3: BELONGINGNESS

Ryan and Deci identified relatedness—the importance of feeling a close connection to and being cared for by others—as one of three psychological needs that are principal predictors of well-being along with autonomy and competence.[47] More recent work points to belongingness as a significant predictor of important outcomes, including academic achievement (see below). Moreover, belonging uncertainty has been shown to be harmful in a variety ways, from academic outcomes to health outcomes. Belongingness is a multi-dimensional and malleable construct that is sensitive to factors such as social identity and social environment and is a significant predictor of important outcomes, including academic achievement and health outcomes.

## DIMENSION 4: COMMITMENT TO OTHERS/IDENTIFICATION WITH ALL HUMANITY

In his account of well-being, Aristotle proposed a perfectionist version in which the well-being of an individual is judged by considering how close she or he is to reaching the full potential of humankind. Aristotle's term for this, *eudaimonia*, has been translated variously as flourishing, happiness, or well-being. Defining this good or full life has been a central concern of psychologists, political philosophers, and human development researchers.

Maslow's hierarchy of needs represents one of the earliest attempts in psychology to differentiate between subsistence and flourishing.[48] The hierarchy of different needs emphasizes the importance of fulfilling one set of needs before progressing to other, higher-order needs. Maslow saw these needs as important motivators of human behavior and moreover distinguished between *growth* or higher-level and *deficiency* or lower-level needs.[49] While satisfying deficiency needs helps an individual avoid unpleasant consequences, satisfying growth needs helps an individual achieve a state of flourishing, which Maslow termed *self-actualization*. One component of a self-actualized individual on this account is her commitment to others and even an identification with and concern for all humanity. Recent researchers have shown that people who identify strongly with all humanity are high in dispositional empathy, moral reasoning, moral identity, and universalist values.[50] The growth of a sense of commitment to others represents a manifestation of mature civic citizenship, the development of which is arguably one goal of higher education.

DIMENSION 5: GRIT/PERSEVERANCE

The broad personality trait of conscientiousness had been associated with multiple important life outcomes, including educational achievement and job performance across a wide range of occupations.[51] Moreover, successful completion of high school is predicted by specific facets or sub-traits encompassed by conscientiousness. Researchers have focused on the specific conscientiousness-related trait of grit, defined as perseverance and passion for long-term goals.[52] People high in grit are more likely to persist in achieving long-term goals and to "maintain effort and interest over years despite failure, adversity and plateaus in progress,"[53] meaning that fostering this trait could have positive, long-term effects. More recently, researchers have focused on the importance of grit, optimism, and a growth mindset (the belief that the ability to learn can be improved through effort), and efforts are being made to develop interventions that can successfully increase the prevalence of these factors among student populations.[54] It should be noted, however, that the correlation between grit and the broader trait of conscientiousness is very high,[55] which indicates that grit is a subcomponent of conscientiousness or even a direct measure of the broader trait.[56]

*Students seem to be operating under what social psychologists describe as belonging uncertainty, in which members of socially stigmatized groups feel more uncertain of their social bonds and become more sensitive to issues of social belonging*

ONE EXAMPLE: HOW DOES BELONGINGNESS MATTER AT THE COLLEGE LEVEL?

In February 2013, students, faculty, and staff met to discuss the issues of diversity and inclusion on the Wake Forest University (WFU) campus. In many of these discussions, students expressed anxiety about feeling welcome on campus. Minority, low socio-economic status, non-Greek, and first-generation college students in particular reported feeling out of place and cited multiple instances in which their social identities negatively affected the way they were treated.[57] The feedback from the diversity forum suggested that students seem to be operating under what social psychologists describe as *belonging uncertainty*, in which members of socially stigmatized groups feel more uncertain of their social bonds and become more sensitive to issues of social belonging.[58] Research at WFU has demonstrated that the need for social belonging is a fundamental human motivation,[59] and more recent work points to belongingness as a significant predictor of important outcomes, including academic achievement. Belonging uncertainty is harmful in a variety ways, from academic outcomes to health outcomes. We think that WFU must consider how to improve students' sense of belonging so that they can be healthier, happier, and more successful in their academic pursuits. We further believe that scientifically testing and deploying a social belongingness intervention provides one very promising avenue for addressing the challenges faced by WFU in promoting diversity and inclusiveness among the student body.

### "People Like Me Do Not Belong Here"

When members of underrepresented groups arrive at college, they may see many spheres of college life in which members of their groups are under-represented.[60] Such students may also feel that people from their groups receive lower grades,[61] fit less successfully into the campus culture,[62] and experience various forms of prejudice.[63] They may also feel cut-off from the insider benefits enjoyed by members of the dominant student culture[64] and believe that downplaying their group membership is the only way they can succeed in such an environment.[65] All these factors can lead to belongingness uncertainty that results in a broad-based belief that "people like me do not belong here."[66]

Among other factors (such as questioning the motives of how other people treat them and stress caused by worries about fitting in) such students are more susceptible to social identity threat and stereotype threat that occur when operating in a social context with some measure of anxiety about confirming a negative stereotype about one's social group. Experiencing stereotype threat can disable individuals in a variety of ways and inhibit performance on a wide range of tasks, including academic assessments,[67] ability to pay attention,[68] learning,[69] and even athletics.[70] Often, high achievers who most value high performance in a given domain are most vulnerable to threat and are therefore the most likely to perform at levels well below their ability.[71] Consistent exposure to stereotype threat can cause individuals to devalue or opt out of particular tasks or areas of study, and it is thought to be one component of the way that achievement and attainment gaps between minority and white students and between men and women are perpetuated.[72]

### What Would a Proposed Well-Being Intervention Look Like? Buttressing Social Belonging among First Year Students

Social psychologists have proposed and tested a variety of interventions geared towards improving academic performance in lab and small-scale field settings. The interventions come in two forms: they attempt to establish more inclusive social environments or they seek to inoculate individuals against threat. One intervention from the second group appears particularly promising and has the potential to positively improve social belonging among many groups of students. Building off prior experimental work,[73] Walton and Cohen[74] reported on a study in which they examined the transient nature of belonging anxiety in the face of welcoming teachers and peers. The intervention interrupted the attributions that African-American students made about their levels of belongingness and lead to dramatic improvements in academic achievement, health, and well-being.

One possible response to these impressive findings would be to immediately deploy such an intervention among the student body. However, we believe it is crucial to spend time developing and tailoring an intervention for target students, to first evaluate the intervention experimentally, and pending preliminary results of the evaluation, to implement the strategy more broadly in subsequent years.

## CONCLUSION: A NOTE ON THE RESPONSIBLE USE OF WELL-BEING MEASURES

We wish to close with a note of caution. Measures like the ones we discuss and similar indices used to measure well-being with self-report should be utilized carefully. Generally, they should not be used in any kind of high stakes setting, even when an underlying construct is validated and firmly grounded in a rich body of preexisting research. In other words, there should not be formal consequences or incentives associated with the use of these self-reported constructs at an institution of higher education because these will at best inflate social desirability bias in responses and at worst incentivize gaming.[75] Although we believe measuring well-being can be powerful in a context in which institutional rankings proliferate and measurement of all important outcomes is expected, cross-institutional comparisons using self-reported measures would be similarly unwise. Social context can introduce anchoring or reference biases into the measurement of a particular construct, such as conscientiousness or directly relevant to our project here, grit. Investigators recently found that objective measures of student effort and performance in school were inversely related to self-reported measures of self-control, conscientiousness, and grit among students attending No Excuses charter schools. This finding suggests that school climate heavily influenced students' assessments of their own characters.[76]

Nonetheless, the measurement of well-being is important for facilitating personal and institutional assessments, identifying relative weaknesses, and providing some additional empirical grounding for discussions about the goals and purposes of higher education. However, it is important to take the time to build good measures, validate them in the contexts in which they are to be deployed, use them in tandem with other assessments, and treat the indices that emerge from this careful work as flashlights, not hammers.

NOTES

1. Jon Cowan and Jim Kessler, "How to Hold Colleges Accountable," *The New York Times*, February 19, 2015, http://www.nytimes.com/2015/02/19/opinion/how-to-hold-colleges-accountable.html.
2. Ryan Craig, *College Disrupted: The Great Unbundling of Higher Education* (London: Macmillan, 2015).
3. Michael K. McLendon, James C. Hearn, and Russ Deaton, "Called to Account: Analyzing the Origins and Spread of State Performance-Accountability Policies for Higher Education." *Educational Evaluation and Policy Analysis* 28, no. 1 (2006): 1–24.
4. P.T.M. Marope, P.J. Wells, and E. Hazelkorn, eds., *Rankings and Accountability in Higher Education: Uses and Misuses* (Paris, United Nations Educational, Scientific and Cultural Organization, 2013), http://unesdoc.unesco.org/images/0022/002207/220789e.pdf.
5. U. S. Department of Education, "College Scorecard Data," accessed March 6, 2015, https://collegescorecard.ed.gov/data/documentation/.
6. Association of American Colleges and Universities, *College Learning for the New Global Century: A Report from the National Leadership Council for Liberal Education & America's Promise* (Washington, DC: Association of American Colleges and Universities, 2007).
7. Eranda Jayawickreme, Marie J.C. Forgeard, and Martin E.P. Seligman, "The Engine of Well-Being," *Review of General Psychology* 16, no. 4 (2012): 327.
8. Deborah D. Danner, David A. Snowdon, and Wallace V. Friesen, "Positive Emotions in Early Life and Longevity: Findings from the Nun Study," *Journal of Personality and Social Psychology* 80, no. 5 (2001): 804.

9. Sonja Lyubomirsky, Laura King, and Ed Diener, "The Benefits of Frequent Positive Affect: Does Happiness Lead to Success?" *Psychological Bulletin* 131, no. 6 (2005): 803.

10. Ed Diener and William Tov, "Subjective Well-Being and Peace," *Journal of Social Issues* 63, no. 2 (2007): 421–40.

11. Daniel J. Ozer and Veronica Benet-Martinez, "Personality and the Prediction of Consequential Outcomes," *Annual Review of Psychology,* 57 (2006): 401–421; Kristina M. DeNeve and Harris Cooper, "The Happy Personality: A Meta-analysis of 137 Personality Traits and Subjective Well-Being," *Psychological Bulletin, 124 (1998):* 197–229; Piers Steel, Joseph Schmidt, and Jonas Shultz, "Refining the Relationship between Personality and Subjective Well-Being," *Psychological Bulletin* 134, no. 1 (2008): 138.

12. Steel et al., "Refining the Relationship,"138.

13. Ed Diener and Richard E. Lucas, "Personality and Subjective Well-Being," in *Well-Being: The Foundations of Hedonic Psychology*, eds., Daniel Kahneman, Ed Diener, and Norbert Schwarz (New York: Russell Sage, 1999), 213–229.

14. Bruce Headey and Alexander Wearing, "Personality, Life Events, and Subjective Well-being: Toward a Dynamic Equilibrium Model," *Journal of Personality and Social Psychology* 57, no. 4 (1989): 731.

15. Ibid.

16. David Lykken and Auke Tellegen, "Happiness is a Stochastic Phenomenon," *Psychological Science* 7, no. 3 (1996): 186–9.

17. Ragnhild B. Nes et al., "Subjective Well-Being: Genetic and Environmental Contributions to Stability and Change," *Psychological Medicine* 36, no. 07 (2006): 1033–42.

18. Frank Fujita and Ed Diener, "Life Satisfaction Set Point: Stability and Change," *Journal of Personality and Social Psychology* 88, no. 1 (2005): 158.

19. Richard E. Lucas et al., "Reexamining Adaptation and the Set Point Model of Happiness: Reactions to Changes in Marital Status," *Journal of Personality and Social Psychology* 84, no. 3 (2003): 527.

20. Richard E. Lucas et al., "Unemployment Alters the Set Point for Life Satisfaction," *Psychological Science* 15, no. 1 (2004): 8–13.

21. Ed Diener, Richard E. Lucas, and Christie Napa Scollon, "Beyond the Hedonic Treadmill: Revising the Adaptation Theory of Well-Being," *American Psychologist* 61, no. 4 (2006): 305.

22. Ed Diener and Carol Diener, "Most People Are Happy," *Psychological Science* 7, no. 3 (1996): 181–185.

23. Eranda Jayawickreme, Marie J.C. Forgeard, and Martin E.P. Seligman, "The Engine of Well-Being," *Review of General Psychology* 16, no. 4 (2012): 327.

24. Richard E. Lucas et al., "Reexamining Adaptation and the Set Point Model of Happiness: Reactions to Changes in Marital Status," *Journal of Personality and Social Psychology* 84, no. 3 (2003): 527. Christie Napa Scollon and Ed Diener, "Love, Work, and Changes In Extraversion and Neuroticism Over Time," *Journal of Personality and Social Psychology* 91, no. 6 (2006): 1152.

25. Richard E. Lucas et al., "Reexamining Adaptation and the Set Point Model of Happiness: Reactions to Changes in Marital Status," *Journal of Personality And Social Psychology* 84, no. 3 (2003): 527.

26. Sonja Lyubomirsky, Laura King, and Ed Diener, "The Benefits of Frequent Positive Affect: Does Happiness Lead to Success?" *Psychological Bulletin* 131, no. 6 (2005): 803.

27. Martin E.P. Seligman et al., "Positive Psychology Progress: Empirical Validation of Interventions," *American Psychologist* 60, no. 5 (2005): 410.

28. Ed Diener, "Subjective Well-Being: The Science of Happiness and a Proposal for a National Index," *American Psychologist* 55, no. 1 (2000): 34–43.

29. Ed Diener and Eunkook Suh, "Measuring Quality of Life: Economic, Social, and Subjective Indicators," *Social Indicators Research* 40, no. 1–2 (1997): 189–216; Ed Diener and Martin E.P. Seligman, "Beyond Money Toward an Economy of Well-Being," *Psychological Science In The Public Interest* 5, no. 1 (2004): 1–31; Ed Diener, "Guidelines for National Indicators of Subjective Well-Being and Ill-Being," *Applied Research in Quality of Life* 1, no. 2 (2006): 151–157; Andrew J. Oswald and Stephen Wu, "Objective Confirmation of Subjective Measures of Human Well-Being: Evidence from the USA," *Science* 327, no. 5965 (2010): 576–9.

30. Richard A. Easterlin, "Does Economic Growth Improve the Human Lot? Some Empirical Evidence," *Nations and Households in Economic Growth* 89 (1974): 89–125.

31. Martin E.P. Seligman et al., "Positive Education: Positive Psychology and Classroom Interventions," *Oxford Review of Education* 35, no. 3 (2009): 293–311.

32. Eranda Jayawickreme and Sara E. Dahill-Brown, "Developing Well-Being and Capabilities as a Goal of Higher Education: A Thought-Piece on Educating the Whole Student, in *Handbook of Eudaimonic Wellbeing, ed.,* Joar Vittersø (Dordrecht: Springer, 2016).

33. Martha Nussbaum, "Women's Capabilities and Social Justice," *Journal of Human Development* 1, no. 2 (2000): 219–247.

34. Ed Diener et al., *Well-Being for Public Policy* (Oxford: Oxford University Press, 2009).

35. Diener et al., *Public Policy.*

36. Peggy Swarbrick, "Defining Wellness," *Words of Wellness* 3, no. 7 (2010): http://www.scattergoodfoundation.org/sites/default/files/innovation-submissions/Words%20of%20Wellness-Handout.pdf; Eranda Jayawickreme, Marie J.C. Forgeard, and Martin E.P. Seligman, "The Engine of Well-Being," *Review of General Psychology* 16, no. 4 (2012): 327.

37. Diener and Lucas, "Personality and Subjective Well-Being," 213.

38. Diener, "Guidelines for National Indicators."

39. Richard M. Ryan and Edward L. Deci, "On Happiness and Human Potentials: A Review of Research on Hedonic and Eudaimonic Well-Being," *Annual Review of Psychology* 52, no. 1 (2001): 141–166.

40. Sheryl Zika and Kerry Chamberlain, "On the Relation between Meaning in Life and Psychological Well-Being," *British Journal Of Psychology* 83, no. 1 (1992): 133–145.

41. Edwin A. Locke and Gary P. Latham, "Building a Practically Useful Theory of Goal Setting and Task Motivation: A 35–Year Odyssey," *American Psychologist* 57, no. 9 (2002): 705; Martin E. P. Seligman, *Authentic Happiness: Using the New Positive Psychology to Realize Your Potential for Lasting Fulfillment* (Delran, NJ: Simon and Schuster, 2004).

42. Laura A. King et al., "Positive Affect and the Experience of Meaning in Life," *Journal of Personality and Social Psychology* 90, no. 1 (2006): 179.

43. Carol D. Ryff and Corey L. M. Keyes, "The structure of Psychological Well-Being Revisited," *Journal of Personality and Social Psychology* 69, no. 4 (1995): 719.

44. Carol D. Ryff, "Happiness is Everything, Or Is It? Explorations on the Meaning of Psychological Well-Being," *Journal of Personality and Social Psychology* 57, no. 6 (1989): 1069.

45. Anne Colby and William Damon, *Some Do Care* (Delran, NJ: Simon and Schuster, 2010).

46. Roy F. Baumeister, *Meanings of Life* (New York: Guilford Press, 1991).

47. Richard M. Ryan and Edward L. Deci, "Self-Determination Theory and the Facilitation of Intrinsic Motivation, Social Development, and Well-Being," *American Psychologist* 55, no. 1 (2000): 68.

48. Abraham H. Maslow, *Motivation and Personality* (New York: Harper, 1954); Abraham H. Maslow, *The Farther Reaches of Human Nature* (New York: Viking, 1971).

49. Mahmoud A. Wahbah and Lawrence G. Bridwell, "Maslow Reconsidered: A Review of Research on the Need Hierarchy Theory," *Organizational Behavior and Human Performance* 15 (1976): 212–240.

50. Sam McFarland, Derek Brown, and Matthew Webb, "Identification with All Humanity as A Moral Concept and Psychological Construct," *Current Directions in Psychological Science* 22, no. 3 (2013): 194–198.

51. Mathilde Almlund et al., *Personality Psychology and Economics*, 2011, http://www.sas.upenn.edu/~duckwort/images/publications/AlmlundDuckworthHeckmanKautz_2011_PersonalityPsychologyandEconomics.pdf.

52. Angela L. Duckworth et al., "Grit: Perseverance and Passion for Long-Term Goals," *Journal of Personality and Social Psychology* 92, no. 6 (2007): 1087–1101.

53. Ibid, 1088.

54. Angela L. Duckworth and Stephanie M. Carlson, "Self-Regulation and School Success," in *Self-Regulation and Autonomy: Social and Developmental Dimensions of Human Conduct*, eds., Bryan W. Sokol, Frederick M. E. Grouzet, and Ulrich Müller (Cambridge: Cambridge University Press, 2015).

55. Angela L. Duckworth and Patrick D. Quinn. "Development and Validation of the Short Grit Scale (GRIT–S)," *Journal of Personality Assessment* 91, no. 2 (2009): 166–174.

56. Brent W. Roberts et al., "What is Conscientiousness and How Can it be Assessed?" *Developmental Psychology* 50, no. 5 (2014): 1315.

57. Wake Forest University, *Diversity and Inclusion at Wake Forest* (Salem, NC: Wake Forest University, 2013), http://college.wfu.edu/politics/diversityandinclusion.

58. Gregory M. Walton and Geoffrey L. Cohen, "A Question of Belonging: Race, Social Fit, and Achievement," *Journal of Personality and Social Psychology* 92, no. 1 (2007): 82–96. doi:10.1037/0022-3514.92.1.82.

59. Roy F. Baumeister and Mark R. Leary, "The Need to Belong: Desire for Interpersonal Attachments as a Fundamental Human Motivation," *Psychological Bulletin* 117, no. 3 (1995): 497–529. doi:10.1037/0033-2909.117.3.497.

60. Walton and Cohen, "Question of Belonging," 82.

61. Claude M. Steele, "A Threat In The Air: How Stereotypes Shape Intellectual Identity and Performance," *American Psychologist* 52, no. 6 (1997): 613.

62. Chalsa M. Loo and Garry Rolison, "Alienation of Ethnic Minority Students at a Predominantly White University," *Journal of Higher Education* 57, no. 1 (1985): 58–77.

63. Anthony G. Greenwald and Mahzarin R. Banaji, "Implicit Social Cognition: Attitudes, Self-Esteem, and Stereotypes," *Psychological Review* 102, no. 1 (1995): 4.

64. Leonard Steinhorn and Barbara Diggs-Brown, *By the Color of Our Skin: The Illusion of Integration and the Reality of Race* (New York: Dutton, 1999).

65. Emily Pronin, Claude M. Steele, and Lee Ross, "Identity Bifurcation in Response to Stereotype Threat: Women and Mathematics," *Journal of Experimental Social Psychology* 40, no. 2 (2004): 152–168.

66. Walton and Cohen, "Question of Belonging," 83.

67. Claude M. Steele and Joshua Aronson, "Stereotype Threat and the Intellectual Test Performance of African Americans," *Journal of Personality and Social Psychology* 69, no. 5 (1995): 797–811. doi:10.1037/0022–3514.69.5.797.

68. Michael Johns, Michael Inzlicht, and Toni Schmader, "Stereotype Threat and Executive Resource Depletion: Examining the Influence Of Emotion Regulation," *Journal of Experimental Psychology* 137, no. 4 (2008): 691.

69. Valerie Jones Taylor and Gregory M. Walton, "Stereotype Threat Undermines Academic Learning," *Personality and Social Psychology Bulletin* 37, no. 8 (2011): 1055–67.

70. Jeff Stone, "Battling Doubt by Avoiding Practice: The Effects of Stereotype Threat on Self-Handicapping in White Athletes," *Personality and Social Psychology Bulletin* 28, no. 12 (2002): 1667–8.

71. Jessi L. Smith, Carol Sansone, and Paul H. White, "The Stereotyped Task Engagement Process: The Role of Interest and Achievement Motivation," *Journal of Educational Psychology* 99, no. 1 (2007): 99.

72. Brenda Major et al., "Coping with Negative Stereotypes about Intellectual Performance: The Role of Psychological Disengagement," *Personality and Social Psychology Bulletin* 24, no. 1 (1998): 34–50. A growing body of work exists to demonstrate these various harms and document the evolution of the social psychological literature. Two recent books offer reviews of the research: Michael Inzlicht and Toni Schmader, eds., *Stereotype Threat: Theory, Process, and Application* (Oxford: Oxford University Press, 2011) and Claude Steele, *Whistling Vivaldi: How Stereotypes Affect Us and What We Can Do* (New York: W. W. Norton & Company, 2011).

73. Walton and Cohen, "Question of Belonging," and Geoffrey L. Cohen et al., "Reducing the Racial Achievement Gap: A Social-Psychological Intervention" *Science* 313, no. 5791 (2006): 1307–10. doi:10.1126/science.1128317.

74. Gregory M. Walton and Geoffrey L. Cohen, "A Brief Social-Belonging Intervention Improves Academic and Health Outcomes of Minority Students," *Science* 331, no. 6023 (2011): 1447–51. doi:10.1126/science.1198364.

75. Robert M. Gonyea, "Self-Reported Data in Institutional Research: Review and Recommendations," *New Directions for Institutional Research* 2005, no. 127 (2005): 73–89.

76. Martin R. West, *The Limitations of Self-Report Measures of Non-Cognitive Skills* (Washington, DC: Brookings Institution, 2014), http://www.brookings.edu/research/papers/2014/12/18-chalkboard-non-cognitive-west.

14

# Thriving: Expanding the Goal of Higher Education

*Laurie Schreiner*

IN THE MIDST OF FEDERAL AND STATE ENVIRONMENTS in the United States that are focused almost exclusively on degree completion and gainful employment as the primary indicators of college student success, calls to expand the focus of the goals of higher education to include student well-being may seem a luxury. Yet after more than three decades of considerable attention to institutional retention and graduation rates, with billions of dollars invested in programming and services to support students' timely degree completion, these success rates have changed little.[1]

Among full-time students who enter four-year colleges or universities for the first time, less than 60% graduate within six years,[2] a statistic that has remained relatively stable for more than thirty years. Of greater concern, however, is the lack of progress indicated in the pervasive achievement gap that characterizes the difference in the persistence rates of historically underrepresented students compared to their White and Asian counterparts. While more than 70% of Asian and 62.5% of White students on four-year campuses graduate within six years, fewer than 52% of Hispanic and about 40% of Black and Native American students do so.[3] The income gap is even more stark: 81% of academically qualified, high-income students complete bachelor's degrees within eight years, while only 36% of equally qualified students from low-income families do so.[4]

Given the demographic projections in the United States, most of the growth in new students enrolling in four-year colleges and universities is likely to emerge from populations that have been historically underserved by higher education.[5] Within this landscape, the traditional predictive equations for student success might lead educators to conclude that there is little hope for improving students' odds of success since these equations have tended to emphasize race/ethnicity, household income, generation status, and academic preparation as the most powerful predictors of graduation from college.[6] Even some of the variables added to the persistence equations in the last decade, such as "academic discipline,"[7] "grit,"[8] or "non-cognitive factors"[9] offer scant hope for improving student success odds, as they are grounded in personality characteristics that are not particularly amenable to change. Thus, we would be wise to expand the definition of student success to include more malleable aspects of student functioning, elements that can be changed with intervention and that clearly provide the foundation for not only a good education, but a good life.

In this essay I focus on the construct of *thriving* as a potential way to expand the goals of higher education to include student well-being. Representing the application of positive psychology principles to the historic higher education goals of intellectual and character development, thriving is defined as being "fully engaged intellectually, socially, and emotionally in the college experience."[10] Thriving students are engaged in deep learning and are energized by the learning process, monitor their learning so that effort is applied wisely and strategically to meaningful goals, value multiple perspectives and are appreciative of differences in others, are involved in positive relationships, view their present and future through a lens of realistic optimism, and are committed to enriching their communities.[11] Each of these qualities has been demonstrated empirically to be amenable to intervention and to be connected to other student success outcomes, such as learning gains and degree completion.[12]

## EXPANDING THE GOALS OF HIGHER EDUCATION

Higher education in the United States began with only one goal: "to discipline the mind and build the character."[13] By the 1970s, most institutions had shifted from this one aim to multiple objectives, including research, vocational preparation, a foundation in the liberal arts, service to the community, and regional economic development.[14] At the same time, higher education was becoming increasingly market-driven and consumer-oriented, and by the beginning of the 21st century, a college education was perceived as a commodity that was one's "ticket of admission to a good job and a middle-class lifestyle."[15]

Our current landscape is what I have described elsewhere as a "perfect storm."[16] The most diverse group of students enters higher education from schools that have ill-prepared them for college at the same time that postsecondary institutions have shifted their focus to credentialism and financial sustainability. The promise of higher education, to empower students and broaden their capacity to engage the world as global citizens and whole persons,[17] has narrowed to the point that it is now perceived as simply a steppingstone to a better job. A return to our historic goal of preparing students for productive and meaningful lives of engagement—in the context of a globally interconnected and rapidly changing world—could enable higher education to once again fulfill its promise to a new generation in need.

## THRIVING IN COLLEGE: DEFINING STUDENT SUCCESS HOLISTICALLY

Defining student success primarily in terms of degree completion results in many missed opportunities that could actually enable a greater percentage of students to successfully complete college and to make the most of their postsecondary experiences as preparation for meaningful and fulfilling lives. Although expanded definitions of student success as learning and personal development have surfaced in the last decade,[18] much of the focus has been on behaviors that lead to learning outcomes or on personality characteristics that change little during the college years. What is needed is a definition of student success that is holistic in nature and encompasses academic, interpersonal, and psychological dimensions of a student's experience and also focuses on what is malleable, so that carefully crafted interventions can enable a greater percentage of students to reach their full potential and make the most of their college experiences.

Derived from existing constructs in positive psychology that have been empirically connected to psychological well-being and to traditional student success outcomes such as grades, learning gains, and persistence to graduation, thriving is a holistic view of student success that expands the goals of higher education to include the student's current and future well-being and potential for being a contributing member of the community.[19] In contrast to merely surviving college, thriving implies deriving optimal benefits from the college experience and fulfilling one's potential. Thriving students are vitally engaged in the college experience—not only academically, but also interpersonally and psychologically— in anticipation of full engagement in meaningful and productive lives.

The conceptual framework that grounds the research on thriving consists of Keyes'[20] construct of flourishing, Seligman's[21] well-being theory, and Bean's and Eaton's[22] psychological model of student persistence. Bean and Eaton postulated that students enter college with psychological attributes shaped by their previous experiences, abilities, and self-assessments. As students interact with individuals at the institution, these psychological attributes affect how they interact as well as how they process the interaction itself. Each interaction then shapes their ongoing self-assessment and perceptions of whether the institution is a good fit for them. If the interactions are positive, they result in a greater sense of self-efficacy, an internal locus of control, proactive coping skills, and reduced stress levels. Combined, these positive effects then increase the student's academic motivation and "lead to academic and social integration, institutional fit and loyalty, intent to persist, and . . . persistence itself."[23]

*The most diverse group of students enters higher education from schools that have ill-prepared them for college at the same time that postsecondary institutions have shifted their focus to credentialism and financial sustainability*

An examination of the psychological processes outlined by Bean and Eaton indicates a theoretical connection to the construct of flourishing that has been well-researched in positive psychology.[24] Keyes defined flourishing as emotional vitality and positive functioning that manifest through positive relationships, rising to meet personal challenges, and engagement with the world.[25] The state of flourishing reflects a productive life lived with high levels of emotional well-being.[26] Seligman adds that flourishing incorporates not only engagement and accomplishment in the context of healthy emotions and relationships, but also a sense of meaning and purpose in life.[27] Although little research on flourishing has been conducted within higher education, one notable exception is Ambler's study of the contribution of student engagement to levels of flourishing in the college population. She highlighted the importance of a supportive campus environment as the largest contributor to student well-being.[28]

Combining the psychological well-being implicit in the concept of flourishing with Bean's and Eaton's model of student retention, thriving is conceptualized as optimal functioning in five domains: Engaged Learning, Academic Determination, Social Connectedness, Diverse Citizenship, and Positive Perspective. Each of these domains contains malleable characteristics that can be cultivated within college students. In research with more than 30,000 students at more than 150 four-year colleges and universities[29] and in smaller studies with community college students, adult returning learners, and graduate students,[30] thriving has been established as a reliable and valid construct that mediates the relationship between student characteristics upon entry, campus experiences, and outcomes, such as college grades, learning gains, and intent to graduate.[31] In confirmatory factor analyses, researchers repeatedly demonstrated the strong fit of the thriving construct to national samples of students as well as the internal consistency ($\alpha = .89$) of the instrument designed to measure thriving.[32] The instrument and each domain of thriving will be described below, and research findings on the campus experiences that are connected to higher levels of student thriving will be presented.

## THE THRIVING QUOTIENT

Using a construct validation approach, researchers Nunnally and Bernstein were able to inductively and deductively generate hypothetical scales.[33] The inductive approach to item generation was used in focus groups and interviews with students in five, moderately selective, liberal arts colleges and research universities. The deductive approach to item generation was based on the conceptual model in which malleable, psychosocial factors were connected empirically to student success outcomes.

Using this construct validation developed by Nunnally and Bernstein as a basis, we began our research to develop a reliable and valid instrument to measure thriving in 2007, initially interviewed college students who had been identified by their faculty and peers as thriving, without providing an operational definition of that term.[34] A clear pattern emerged as we asked these students to describe their college experiences in depth and to define what they thought the word *thriving* meant and how it manifested in their lives. These students consistently reported that thriving encompassed academic engagement, self-regulation, awareness of one's strengths, connection to other people and to "giving back," and ability to reframe negative experiences as learning opportunities. Most talked about a sense of meaning and purpose or calling, and many referred to a spiritual foundation that enabled them to view their experiences through a broader lens.

From this inductive beginning, we then incorporated a deductive approach and searched the existing literature for theories of well-being and student success that had established empirical connections between malleable personal qualities and various educational outcomes. This comprehensive search yielded 198 items that then were pilot tested with 2,474 undergraduates at 13 four-year institutions. Each item was expressed as a statement to which the student responded using a 6-point Likert scale with *1 = strongly disagree* and *6 = strongly agree*. The items were hypothesized to cluster on the academic, psychological, and social dimensions of college student thriving and incorporated the concepts of engaged learning,[35] citizenship,[36] openness to diversity,[37] mindset, psychological well-being,[38] academic self-efficacy,[39] perceived academic control,[40] meaning in life,[41] mindfulness,[42] sense of belonging,[43] hope,[44] optimism,[45] resiliency,[46] subjective well-being,[47] spirituality,[48] and self-regulated learning.[49]

Items were eliminated from the pilot version of the instrument based on the following: factor loadings from an exploratory factor analysis, estimates of internal consistency reliability as indicated by Cronbach's alpha, item-total correlations, examination of variability, and examination of the partial correlations of each item with student success outcomes such as intent to persist, GPA, self-reported learning gains, institutional fit, and satisfaction. We eliminated any items that did not contribute uniquely to the variation in at least one student success outcome after we controlled for such student demographic characteristics as gender, ethnicity, generation status, choice of institution at enrollment, and high school grades.

The above process resulted in the elimination of 128 items; the remaining 70 items loaded on five factors in the exploratory factor analysis and had a coefficient alpha of = .86.

The five factors were labeled Engaged Learning, Academic Determination, Positive Perspective, Social Connectedness, and Diverse Citizenship. We then conducted focus groups with students on five liberal arts and research university campuses; these students completed the 70-item instrument and provided significant input on the ease of understanding the wording of the items. After revising the items accordingly, the second version of the instrument was administered to 6,617 undergraduate students at 27 four-year public and private colleges and universities across the United States.

A confirmatory factor analysis (CFA) was conducted to determine the degree to which the five factors identified through exploratory factor analysis fit the new sample. Based on an examination of the fit indices most appropriate for use with large sample sizes, the results of the CFA indicated that the best-fitting model was a five-factor model with a second-order factor that reflected the latent construct of thriving.

THE FIVE DOMAINS OF THRIVING

Through this lengthy process of construct validation, the five latent variables that consistently comprised the higher-order construct of thriving across all samples of college students, regardless of institutional type, emerged as reliable and valid indicators of student holistic well-being.

*Engaged Learning*

Thriving students are energized by the learning process; they connect their current learning with previous knowledge and future goals so that they engage in deep learning that lasts beyond the final exam.[50] Congruent with the component of *engagement* in Seligman's well-being theory,[51] the Engaged Learning domain indicates an absorption and interest in learning, an intellectual vitality that undergirds lifelong learning.

*Academic Determination*

Aligned with the component of *accomplishment* in Seligman's well-being theory,[52] the Academic Determination domain comprises investment and regulation of one's effort, time, resources, and strengths toward achieving meaningful educational goals.[53] Thriving students know that effort is required for success; they also know how to apply their strengths to academic challenges.[54]

*Social Connectedness*

Thriving in college is rarely a solitary pursuit; thus, positive relationships are an integral component of thriving.[55] Based on the construct of *positive relations* established by Ryff and Keyes,[56] the Social Connectedness scale represents the degree to which students are involved in healthy interactions with others they perceive as supportive.

*Diverse Citizenship*

Combining openness to diverse perspectives[57] with a desire to make a difference in one's community,[58] the Diverse Citizenship domain represents the student's engagement with the world. Consistent with the civic engagement goals that have historically characterized higher education in the United States, thriving students "give back" to those around them and recognize that diversity enriches their lives.

*Positive Perspective*

Representing the lens through which students view the world, the Positive Perspective domain represents levels of realistic optimism[59] and is congruent with the *positive emotion* component of Seligman's well-being theory.[60] Students with positive perspectives expect good things to happen eventually and take long-term views of events that enable them to feel confident about their present and future choices. Thriving students perceive negative events as learning opportunities that do not define them; as a result, they tend to be more satisfied with their college experiences.[61]

PATHWAYS TO THRIVING

Investigators who study thriving indicate that it can explain as much as 22% of the unique variance in such student success outcomes, such as college grades, learning gains, satisfaction with college, perception of tuition as a worthwhile investment, and intent to graduate.[62] Therefore, thriving holds potential as a worthy student success outcome in and of itself. Consistent with a more expansive goal of higher education to empower students for meaningful, productive, and fulfilling lives of engagement in the world, thriving can be used as an indicator of the degree to which the programming and services of universities are meeting this ultimate goal.

In the large-scale research conducted to date in the United States, Canada, and Australia, four primary pathways emerged as the most significant contributors to variation in levels of student thriving: (1) campus involvement, including peer interaction; (2) quality and frequency of student-faculty interaction; (3) spirituality, including a sense of meaning and purpose; and (4) psychological sense of community on campus.[63] However, researchers indicate that these pathways contribute quite differently to thriving among students of color in institutions with predominantly white students.[64] For example, campus involvement and peer interaction play different roles in adjustment and success depending on the student's racial identification;[65] students of color experience more incidents of discrimination, less benefits from participating in campus organizations, and greater hurdles to involvement.[66] Likewise, Cole found that student-faculty interactions are qualitatively different and contribute differently to the learning gains of students of color.[67] We confirmed that frequent, student-faculty interaction is a pathway to thriving that varies by race and ethnicity and that enhances the thriving of white students considerably more than students of color. However, we also found that when the quality of these relationships is positive and validates the sense of belonging among students of color, student-faculty interaction is a powerful predictor of thriving regardless of race.[68]

> *Thriving students perceive negative events as learning opportunities that do not define them; as a result, they tend to be more satisfied with their college experiences*

Although spirituality is a pathway to thriving among all students, its connection to thriving among students of color was twice as strong as among White students.[69] Defined as the student's beliefs about the meaning and purpose of life and reliance on those beliefs as a coping mechanism and a lens through which to view the world, spirituality represents transcendence beyond oneself. The largest effects of spirituality on thriving were found among Asian and African American students; spirituality was also a strong pathway for students of color to experience a sense of community on campus.[70]

A psychological sense of community (PSC) is comprised of feelings of belonging, mattering, interdependence, and emotional connections to others in a group.[71] Applied to the campus environment, students with a strong sense of community feel they are part of and contribute to a dependable network of people who care about them, are committed to their well-being, and are able to meet one another's needs.[72] Yet each component of PSC varies by race and ethnicity, and the relative contribution of PSC to thriving varies by race as well.[73] A sense of community on campus consistently contributes the most to the variation in the ability of all students to thrive, but what leads students to experience a sense of community differs significantly across racial groups. For example, involvement in campus activities was the strongest contributor to a sense of community among Latino students, while for African American students it was spirituality, for Asian students it was the fit within their majors, and for white students it was interaction with faculty.[74] For all students of color, however, perceptions of *institutional integrity*, defined as the mission congruence of administrator, faculty, and staff actions, was the strongest predictor of their sense of community on campus that ultimately led to thriving.[75]

## IMPLICATIONS FOR POLICY AND PRACTICE

In an environment in which the academic under preparedness and mental health needs of students are outstripping the ability of many campuses to respond in an appropriate or timely manner,[76] a preventive approach focused on equipping students to thrive has the potential to affect their well-being and success while in college and throughout their lives. The habits of mind implicit in thriving are malleable and are foundational to one's ability to flourish for a lifetime.

Because thriving can be cultivated through intentional interventions as well as through campus experiences that foster a sense of community, there are implications at the individual student level and the institutional level. The implications for individual student thriving are (1) to identify students' strengths of competence and character and teach them how to further develop those strengths and apply them to potential challenges they face and (2) to equip students with coping skills that lead to resilience and well-being. At the institutional level, the implications of the research on thriving are (1) to strengthen the sense of community on campus and (2) to create a thriving campus environment.

## EQUIPPING STUDENTS TO THRIVE

Expanding the goal of higher education to include thriving as a more holistic view of student success that encompasses academic, interpersonal, and psychological well-being will necessitate attention to the needs of individual students and customization of plans for success. Such attention from advisors, student development educators, and faculty should focus on the malleable areas of student need that have the greatest likelihood to affect thriving.

### *Identify Students' Talents at Entrance and Develop Them Into Strengths of Competence and Character that can be Applied to Future Challenges*

A focus on strengths development is integral to thriving, as "people who have the opportunity every day to do what they do best—to act on their strengths—are far more likely to flourish."[77] Strengths development begins with the identification of talents or positive personal qualities that students bring with them into the college environment that can help them achieve,[78] experience psychological well-being, or develop character.[79] An affirmation of those qualities and a validation of the subsequent contribution the student can make to the learning environment sends a message to students at entrance that they already possess the seeds of success and that educators have faith in their ability to succeed, which gives students the confidence needed to transition into unfamiliar environments and to take the risks that are often necessary to fully engage in the learning process.[80]

Once these talents have been identified and affirmed, educators can encourage students to develop them into strengths that can be productively applied toward academic, personal, or relational challenges. Students' strengths can also be perceived as pathways toward reaching their goals and as clues to areas of vocation that might be fulfilling. Regardless of whether the approach emphasizes strengths of competence that produce excellent performance[81] or strengths of character that are the building blocks of virtue,[82] strengths development programs can be deployed within the academic advising relationship,[83] first-year seminars, residence life programming, and peer mentoring programs.[84] Such programs can be effective when students are encouraged to use their strengths more readily, as greater use of strengths has been associated with increased levels of well-being over time,[85] or when students are encouraged to apply strengths to specific situations with greater insight regarding the effect on self and others.[86]

*Equip Students with Coping Skills that Lead to Resilience and Well-Being*
In the midst of an "epidemic of anguish"[87] on college campuses, some experts have suggested that this generation of college students has not developed sufficient resilience to succeed in college or in life. Whether overprotected by middle and upper-class helicopter parents or under-challenged by low-income primary and secondary schools, too many students have not been allowed to experience failure and in the process have not learned how to rebound from adversity in order to succeed.[88]

The key to resilience lies in students' explanatory style, the way they explain negative events that occur in their lives. Thriving students have what Seligman calls an optimistic explanatory style; they perceive negative events as externally caused, changeable, and specific to the situation.[89] This perspective enables them to adapt and bounce back from adversity. In contrast, those who attribute adversity to their own internal inadequacies and perceive such events as stable and global have a pessimistic style that leads to passivity. Such passivity results in a decreased likelihood of exercising proactive coping skills to address the challenge; it also can result in feelings of depression or discouragement that lead to disengagement from active problem solving. As is often the case when problems are not addressed early and effectively, the situation then only gets worse. Reivich and Schatte maintain that this pessimistic thinking is the "number-one roadblock to resilience."[90]

Fortunately, an optimistic explanatory style can be taught to students; Seligman and colleagues experienced considerable success with grade-school students, first-year college students, and members of the American military.[91] Teaching students to perceive failures as temporary setbacks attributable to controllable causes such as insufficient effort or incorrect strategies builds resilience and hope and enables them to approach future events with greater confidence that success is possible. Learning to reframe negative events as learning opportunities is a key skill that advisors can build. For example, an advisor can turn a discussion of low grades into an opportunity to teach the student to reframe the situation and strategize for success the next time. Students equipped with this optimistic explanatory style are more likely to engage in the learning process, which leads to higher levels of academic performance.[92]

## CREATING A THRIVING INSTITUTION

Efforts at the individual student level are necessary but not sufficient. A thriving individual in the midst of a languishing environment will not thrive for long or will not remain in that environment. Thus, the implications of thriving research for a campus-wide agenda are to create the kind of environment that will nourish students so they thrive.

### Strengthen the Sense of Community on Campus

Creating a sense of community on campus is the single best way to help all students thrive. A psychological sense of community is a basic human need that encompasses four key elements: membership, ownership, relationship, and partnership.[93] The failure to attend to this need on university campuses may be one of the reasons for the continuing disparity in success rates across racial and income groups since it may be difficult for students to address academic tasks and personal challenges when this basic need remains unmet. As complex as the solutions may be, creating a sense of community on campus holds the greatest promise for creating an environment in which students can thrive.[94]

Students who report a strong sense of community on campus feel a sense of belonging to a network that challenges and supports them and in which they feel valued and can make meaningful contributions; this network is composed of people who can meet one another's needs.[95] Students with a strong psychological sense of community perceive the institution as committed to their welfare, delivering on its promises, with administrators, faculty, and staff who embody the mission of the institution.[96] Strengthening this sense of community on campus thus involves staff, faculty, and administrators who are committed to collaborative partnerships and who invite students to participate not only in campus activities, but also in campus decisions. These educators will find every opportunity to connect personally to students, connect students to each other, and connect students to the learning process.

*The implications of thriving research for a campus-wide agenda are to create the kind of environment that will nourish students so they thrive*

### Create a Thriving Campus Environment

The sense of community on campus is a key indicator of whether an institution is thriving, but it is difficult for students to thrive if faculty, staff, and administrators are not thriving. A thriving campus is fertile ground for all members to thrive because it intentionally cultivates the conditions that are necessary for human flourishing: positive emotions, meaningful engagement, positive relationships, opportunities for accomplishment, and a sense of meaning and purpose.[97]

Commitment characterizes a campus that is thriving: commitment to the mission of the institution; to student learning, growth, and holistic development; and to one another as partners in the learning process. An unwavering commitment to students' academic, interpersonal, and psychological well-being is embedded in the mission of a thriving campus. This commitment provides a collective sense of meaning and purpose in our work, encourages engagement, and validates each student, staff, faculty, and administrator as members of the community. Thriving institutions communicate this commitment before any member joins the community, beginning with the hiring process when administrators hire only those who love students, want to see them grow, and are equipped to facilitate that process. The commitment continues to be communicated to students as they join the community; attention is paid to helping them feel part of the new environment through symbols and rituals, campus stories, and peer leaders who help them navigate. Faculty and student life educators communicate what it takes to succeed and give students examples of other students like themselves who have done just that.

A thriving campus is one in which members of the community see the contributions they can make, know that they have voices, and know that their input matters. On a thriving campus, leaders communicate expectations and the desire for input and also communicate their responses to such input. Administrators pay attention to student voice on campus committees and are transparent in their decision making, staff carefully examine the level of service they provide students and each other, and faculty have faith that all students admitted to the institution can learn, grow, and succeed under the right conditions—conditions they are committed to providing in and out of the classroom.[98]

A thriving campus also connects people to each other and helps students get to know other students as well as faculty, staff, and administrators. These connections build positive relationships that can provide social support during times of need, but they also introduce students to those whose experiences and perspectives are different from their own. Learning communities are perhaps one of the best examples of specific strategies thriving institutions use to foster these intentional connections. This emphasis on connection also fosters positive emotions that are essential for human flourishing. In their research on positive emotion, Fredrickson and Losada found that organizations are healthy and productive when the positive emotions expressed on a daily basis outnumber the negative emotions 5 to 1.[99] Affirmation, gratitude, and joy outweigh frustration, anxiety, and discouragement on a thriving campus and enable all members to flourish.

Finally, collaborative engagement is the hallmark of a thriving campus; synergy inter-dependence, and commitment to something greater than oneself characterize thriving environments. For higher education, the implication is to break down the silos that fill our campuses. Rather than turf protection, thriving institutions focus on partnerships, meeting one another's needs, and working together toward meaningful goals that cannot be accomplished alone. Team teaching, interdisciplinary scholarship, student-faculty research partnerships, work teams that capitalize on the strengths within the team, ser-vice learning, and partnerships with the local community are just some examples of the practices in which thriving institutions engage. A shared vision fuels these partnerships and sustains the collaborative engagement over time.

CONCLUSION

The model of thriving described in this chapter holds considerable promise for expanding the goals of higher education to include not only academic success, but also psychological well-being. Student development professionals with this goal in mind will organize campus programs and services to help students identify and cultivate their strengths and equip students with the coping skills necessary for resilience and well-being. Faculty with this goal in mind will focus on building a sense of community in the classroom and engaging students in a process of lifelong learning. Institutional leaders with this expanded goal for student success in mind will invest time and effort in creating a campus environment in which staff, faculty, administrators, and students alike are able to experience a sense of belonging and to thrive. Such an approach will provide many more pathways to success for students and enable those who have been historically underserved by higher education to reach their goals.

There is no better time for higher education to expand its goals to include student well-being. Just when the needs and challenges seem most overwhelming, a vision for students to come alive to their potential, build on the strengths they possess despite or sometimes because of their experiences, and make the most of their college years holds promise for enabling a greater percentage of students to succeed. Our students deserve not only to survive, but to thrive.

Notes

1. Erin Hennessy, "New Data Indicate Educational Attainment Continues to Flat-Line," *The AAAED Blog*, October 20, 2010, http://affirmact.blogspot.com/2010/10/new-data-indicate-educational.html.

2. National Center for Education Statistics, "The Condition of Education 2015," May 2015, http://nces.ed.gov/pubs2015/2015144.pdf.

3. Ibid.

4. Bridget Terry Long, "Grading Higher Education: Giving Consumers the Information They Need," December 2012, http://www.brookings.edu/research/papers/2010/12/higher-ed-long.

5. Jeffrey S. Passel and D'Vera Cohn, "*U.S. Population Projections: 2005–2050*," Pew Research Center, February 11, 2008, http://www.pewhispanic.org/2008/02/11/us-population-projections-2005-2050/.

6. Clifford Adelman, "The Toolbox Revisited: Paths to Degree Completion from High School Through College," U.S. Department of Education, February 2006, https://www2.ed.gov/rschstat/research/pubs/toolboxrevisit/toolbox.pdf.

7. See Huy Le et al., "Motivational and Skills, Social, and Self-Management Predictors of College Outcomes: Constructing the Student Readiness Inventory," *Educational and Psychological Measurement* 65 (2005): 482–508 and Stephen B. Robbins et al, "Do Psychosocial and Study Skill Factors Predict College Outcomes? A Meta-Analysis," *Psychological Bulletin* 130 (2004): 261–88.

8. Angela L. Duckworth et al., "Grit: Perseverance and Passion for Long-Term Goals," *Journal of Personality and Social Psychology* 92, no. 6 (2007): 1087–1101.

9. William E. Sedlacek, *Beyond the Big Test: Noncognitive Assessment in Higher Education* (San Francisco, CA: Jossey-Bass, 2004).

10. Laurie A. Schreiner, "The 'Thriving Quotient': A New Vision for Student Success," *About Campus 15*, no. 2 (2010): 2–10,4.

11. Ibid.

12. Laurie A. Schreiner, "Positive Psychology and Higher Education: The Contribution of Positive Psychology to Student Success and Institutional Effectiveness" in *Positive Psychology on the College Campus,* eds. John C. Wade, Lawrence I. Marks, and Roderick D. Hetzel (Oxford, UK: Oxford University Press, 2015): 1–25.

13. Derek Bok, *Higher Education in America, Revised Edition* (Princeton, NJ: Princeton University Press, 2013), 29.

14. Ibid.

15. Deborah Wadsworth, "Ready or Not? Where the Public Stands on Higher Education Reform" in *Declining by Degrees: Higher Education at Risk*, eds. Richard Hersh and John Merrow (New York: Palgrave Macmillan, 2005), 23–38, 25.

16. Schreiner, "Positive Psychology," 3.

17. Carol G. Schneider, "Liberal Education: Slip-Sliding Away?" in *Declining by Degrees: Higher Education at Risk*, eds. Richard Hersh and John Merrow (New York: Palgrave Macmillan, 2005), 61–76.

18. George D. Kuh et al., *Student Success in College: Creating Conditions that Matter* (San Francisco, CA: Jossey-Bass, 2005).

19. Schreiner, "Positive Psychology."

20. Corey L. M. Keyes, "Complete Mental Health: An Agenda for the 21st Century" in *Flourishing: Positive Psychology and the Life Well-Lived,* eds. Corey L. M. Keyes and Jonathan Haidt (Washington, DC: American Psychological Association, 2002), 293–309.

21. Martin E. P. Seligman, *Flourish: A Visionary New Understanding of Happiness and Well-Being* (New York: Free Press, 2011).

22. John P. Bean and Shevawn Bogdan Eaton, "A Psychological Model of College Student Retention" in *Reworking the Student Departure Puzzle,* ed. John M. Braxton (Nashville, TN: Vanderbilt University Press, 2000), 48–61.

23. Ibid, 58.

24. Keyes, "Complete Mental Health," and Seligman, *Flourish.*

25. Keyes, "Complete Mental Health."

26. Keyes, "Complete Mental Health."

27. Seligman, *Flourish.*

28. Virginia Miller Ambler, "Who Flourishes in College? Using Positive Psychology and Student Involvement Theory to Explore Mental Health Among Traditionally Aged Undergraduates" (PhD diss, The College of William and Mary, 2006).

29. See Laurie A. Schreiner et al., "Measuring the Malleable: Expanding the Assessment of Student Success" (paper presented at the annual conference of the Association for the Study of Higher Education, St. Louis, MO, November 14, 2013) and Laurie A. Schreiner et al., "The Thriving Quotient: Advancing the Assessment of Student Success" (paper presented at the annual meeting of the Association for the Study of Higher Education, Vancouver, British Columbia, November 13, 2009).

30. Heather L. Petridis and Laurie A. Schreiner, "Graduate Student Success: Moving from Surviving to Thriving" (paper presented at the annual conference of the Association for the Study of Higher Education, St. Louis, MO, November 16, 2013).

31. Laurie A. Schreiner et al., "The Thriving Quotient: A New Vision for Student Success" (paper presented at the annual conference of the National Association of Student Personnel Administrators, Philadelphia, PA, March 14, 2011).

32. Laurie A. Schreiner, "From Surviving to Thriving During Transitions" in *Thriving in Transitions: A Research-Based Approach to College Student Success,* eds. Laurie A. Schreiner, Michelle C. Louis, and Denise D. Nelson (Columbia, SC: University of South Carolina, National Resource Center for The First-Year Experience and Students in Transition, 2012), 1–18.

33. Jum C. Nunnally and Ira H. Bernstein, *Psychometric Theory,* 3rd ed. (New York: McGraw-Hill, 1994).

34. Schreiner, "The 'Thriving Quotient'," *About Campus.*

35. Laurie A. Schreiner and Michelle C. Louis, "The Engaged Learning Index: Implications for Faculty Development," *Journal of Excellence in College Teaching* 22, no. 1 (2011): 5–28.

36. Tracy M. Tyree, "Designing an Instrument to Measure the Socially Responsible Leadership Using the Social Change Model of Leadership Development," *Dissertation Abstracts International* 59, no. 6 (1998): 1945.

37. Jairo N. Fuertes et al., "Factor Structure and Short Form of the Miville-Guzman Universality-Diversity Scale," *Measurement & Evaluation in Counseling & Development* 33, no. 3 (2000): 157.

38. Carol D. Ryff and Corey L. M. Keyes, "The Structure of Psychological Well-Being Revisited," *Journal of Personality and Social Psychology* 69 (1995), 719–27.

39. Marin M. Chemers, Li-tze Hu, and Ben F. Garcia, "Academic Self-Efficacy and First-Year College Student Performance and Adjustment," *Journal of Educational Psychology* 93, no. 1 (2001): 55–64.

40. Raymond P. Perry, Nathan C. Hall, and Joelle C. Ruthig, "Perceived (Academic) Control and Scholastic Attainment in Higher Education" in *Higher Education: Handbook of Theory and Research,* vol. 20, ed. John C. Smart (Norwell, MA: Springer, 2005), 363–436.

41. Michael F. Steger et al., "The Meaning in Life Questionnaire: Assessing the Presence of and Search for Meaning in Life," *Journal of Counseling Psychology* 53, no. 1 (2006): 80–93.

42. Kirk W. Brown and Richard M. Ryan, "The Benefits of Being Present: Mindfulness and Its Role in Psychological Well-Being," *Journal of Personality and Social Psychology* 84, no. 4 (2003): 822–48.

43. Sylvia Hurtado and Deborah Faye Carter, "Effects of College Transition and Perceptions of the Campus Racial Climate on Latino College Students' Sense of Belonging," *Sociology of Education* 70 (1997): 324–45.

44. C. R. Snyder, "Conceptualizing, Measuring, and Nurturing Hope," *Journal of Counseling & Development* 73, no. 3 (1995): 355–60.

45. Michael F. Scheier, Charles S. Carver, and Michael W. Bridges, "Distinguishing Optimism from Neuroticism (and Trait Anxiety, Self-Mastery, and Self-Esteem): A Re-evaluation of the Life Orientation Test," *Journal of Personality and Social Psychology* 67 (1994): 1063–78.

46. Gail M. Wagnild and Heather M. Young, "Development and Psychometric Evaluation of the Resilience Scale," *Journal of Nursing Management* 1 (1993): 165–78.

47. Ed Diener, "Subjective Well-Being," *Psychological Bulletin* 93 (1984): 542–75.

48. Alyssa N. Bryant, Jeung Yun Choi and Maiko Yasuno, "Understanding the Religious and Spiritual Dimensions of Students' Lives in the First Year of College," *Journal of College Student Development* 44 (2003): 723–45.

49. Paul R. Pintrich, "A Conceptual Framework for Assessing Motivation and Self-Regulated Learning in College Students, *Educational Psychology Review* 16, no. 4 (2004): 385–407.

50. Schreiner and Louis, "Engaged Learning Index."

51. Seligman, *Flourish* .

52. Ibid.

53. Schreiner, "Positive Psychology."

54. Shane J. Lopez and Michelle C. Louis, "The Principles of Strengths-Based Education," *Journal of College and Character* 10, no. 4 (2009): 1–8.

55. Seligman, *Flourish.*

56. Ryff and Keyes, "Structure of Psychological Well-Being."

57. Fuertes et al., "Factor Structure."

58. Tyree, "Designing an Instrument."

59. Charles S. Carver et al., "Optimism," in *Oxford Handbook of Positive Psychology,* 2nd ed., eds., Shane J. Lopez and C. R. Snyder (Oxford, UK: Oxford University Press, 2009): 303–12.

60. Seligman, *Flourish.*

61. Laurie A. Schreiner et al., "College Student Thriving: Predictors of Success and Retention" (paper presented at the annual meeting of the Association for the Study of Higher Education, Vancouver, British Columbia, November 11, 2009).

62. See Schreiner et al., "Measuring the Malleable," and Schreiner et al., "Thriving Quotient."

63. Schreiner, "From Surviving to Thriving."

64. See Eric James McIntosh, "Thriving and Spirituality: Making Meaning of Meaning Making for Students of Color," *About Campus* 19, no. 6 (2015): 16–23 and Laurie A. Schreiner, "Different Pathways to Thriving among Students of Color: An Untapped Opportunity for Success," *About Campus* 19, no. 5 (2014): 10–19.

65. Mary Jane Fischer, "Settling into Campus Life: Differences by Race/Ethnicity in College Involvement and Outcomes," *Journal of Higher Education* 78, no. 2 (2007): 125–61.

66. Schreiner, "Different Pathways."

67. Darnell Cole, "Do Interracial Interactions Matter? An Examination of Student-Faculty Contact and Intellectual Self-Concept," *Journal of Higher Education* 78, no. 3 (2007): 249–81.

68. Schreiner, "Different Pathways."

69. McIntosh, "Thriving and Spirituality."

70. McIntosh, "Thriving and Spirituality."

71. David W. McMillan and David M. Chavis, "Sense of Community: A Definition and Theory," *Journal of Community Psychology* 14 (1986): 6–23.

72. John W. Lounsbury and Daniel DeNeui, "Psychological Sense of Community on Campus," *College Student Journal* 29 (1995): 270–77.

73. Schreiner, "Different Pathways."

74. Ibid.

75. John M. Braxton et al., *Rethinking College Student Retention* (San Francisco, CA: Jossey-Bass, 2013).

76. American College Health Association, *National College Health Assessment: Fall 2015 reference group executive summary.* Retrieved from http://www.acha-ncha.org/docs/NCHA-II%20FALL%202015%20REFERENCE%20 GROUP%20EXECUTIVE%20SUMMARY.pdf.

77. Barbara L. Fredrickson, *Positivity* (New York: Crown Publishers, 2009): 189.

78. Edward C. Anderson, "Strengths-Based Educating: A Concrete Way to Bring Out the Best in Students— and Yourself," *Educational Horizons* 83 no. 3 (2005): 180–89.

79. Christopher Peterson and Martin Seligman, *Character Strengths and Virtues: A Handbook and Classification* (Washington, DC: American Psychological Association, 2004).

80. Michelle C. Louis and Laurie A. Schreiner, "Helping Students Thrive: A Strengths Development Model," in *Thriving in Transitions: A Research-Based Approach to College Student Success,* eds. Laurie A. Schreiner, Michelle C. Louis, and Denise D. Nelson (Columbia, SC: University of South Carolina, National Resource Center for The First-Year Experience and Students in Transition, 2012), 19–40.

81. Marcus Buckingham and Donald O. Clifton, *Now, Discover Your Strengths* (New York: The Free Press, 2001).

82. Peterson and Seligman, *Character Strengths and Virtues.*

83. Laurie A. Schreiner, "Strengths-Based Advising," in *Academic Advising Approaches: Strategies that Teach Students to Make the Most of College*, eds. Jayne K. Drake, Peggy Jordan, and Marsha A. Miller (San Francisco, CA: Jossey-Bass, 2013), 105–20.

84. See Louis and Schreiner, "Helping Students Thrive," and Laurie A. Schreiner, "Thriving in College," in *Positive Psychology and Appreciative Inquiry in Higher Education: New Directions in Student Services*, no. 143, eds. Peter C. Mather and Eileen Hulme (San Francisco, CA: Jossey-Bass, 2013), 41–52.

85. Alex M. Wood et al., "Using Personal and Psychological Strengths Leads to Increases in Well-Being Over Time: A Longitudinal Study and the Development of the Strengths Use Questionnaire," *Personality and Individual Differences* 50, no. 1 (2011): 15–19.

86. Robert E. Kaplan and Robert B. Kaiser, "Toward a Positive Psychology for Leaders," in *Oxford Handbook of Positive Psychology and Work*, eds. P. Alex Linley, Susan Harrington, and Nicola Garcea (New York: Oxford University Press, 2010), 107–17.

87. Robin Wilson, "An Epidemic of Anguish," *Chronicle of Higher Education,* August 31, 2015, http://chronicle.com/article/An-Epidemic-of-Anguish/232721/, para. 1.

88. Peter Gray, "Declining Student Resilience: A Serious Problem for Colleges," *Psychology Today,* September 22, 2015, https://www.psychologytoday.com/blog/freedom-learn/201509/declining-student-resilience-serious-problem-colleges.

89. Martin E. P. Seligman, *Learned Optimism* (New York: Pocket Books, 1998).

90. Karen Reivich and Andrew Shatte, *The Resilience Factor: Seven Keys to Finding Inner Strength and Overcoming Life's Hurdles* (New York: Broadway Books, 2002), 11.

91. Martin E. P. Seligman, Peter Schulman, and Alyssa Tryon, "Group Prevention of Depression and Anxiety Symptoms, *Behaviour Research and Therapy* 45 (2007), 1111–26.

92. Paul R. Pintrich and Akane Zusho, "Student Motivation and Self-Regulated Learning in the College Classroom," in *Higher Education: Handbook of Theory and Research*, vol. 16, ed. John C. Smart (New York: Springer, 2002), 55–128.

93. See McMillan and Chavis, "Sense of Community," and Schreiner, "Thriving in College."

94. Schreiner, "Thriving in College."

95. See David X. Cheng, "Students' Sense of Campus Community: What it Means and What to Do About It," *NASPA Journal* 41 (2004): 216–32 and Lounsbury and DeNeui, "Psychological Sense of Community."

96. Braxton et al., "Rethinking College Student Retention."

97. Seligman, *Flourish.*

98. Laurie A. Schreiner, "Strengths-Oriented Teaching: Pathways to Engaged Learning," in *Paths to Learning: Teaching for Engagement in College*, ed. Barbara F. Tobolowsky (Columbia, SC: University of South Carolina, National Resource Center for The First-Year Experience and Students in Transition, 2014): 77–92.

99. Barbara L. Fredrickson and Marcial F. Losada, "Positive Affect and the Complex Dynamics of Human Flourishing," *American Psychologist* 60, no. 7 (2005): 678–86.

# 15
## ESSAY

# Well-Being and Student Persistence: Reframing Student Success
*Tricia Seifert*

SCIENTISTS HAVE LONG HAD A FASCINATION with reducing each unit to a smaller manifestation. The atom yielded to the electron. Reductionism and disaggregation have been at the heart of scientific advancement and have had implications for other fields. Reductionism in other contexts has often manifested as a quest for the single solution, the silver bullet to fix the problem. In a 2015 speech at the Campaign for America's Future Awards Gala, Lily Eskelsen García, the President of the National Education Association described an encounter with a businessman on an airplane. The businessman asked her to "bottom line" it for him: what was the one single thing that needed to be done to fix public schools? Her response was priceless: "What we really need are fewer people who think there is one single thing that will fix all of our problems in public schools."[1]

While it may be tempting to point out the absurdity of this situation, higher education is not immune to similar thinking. People debate the value and purpose of higher education; they lament its cost and question its return. The higher education bottom line of today is college completion. One need only look at the focus of policymakers, from President Barack Obama and his advancement of his goal that "by 2020, America will once again have the highest proportion of college graduates in the world"[2] to policy influencers within the National Coalition for College Completion, to see that college completion has become *the* measure of student success and as such the measure of institutional success. Without a doubt, college completion is a worthy goal. But should it be the primary measure of success for students or for institutions of higher education? The purpose of this essay is to illuminate why such a measure of success shortchanges students individually and society more broadly.

## COLLEGE IN NEOLIBERAL TERMS
There is good reason to direct energy toward student persistence and completion. The cost of attending a public college in the United States has soared beyond the cost of inflation. According to the National Center for Education Statistics, the average cost of full-time undergraduate tuition, room, and board at a four-year public institution rose from $9,200 in 2001–02 to approximately $17,500 in 2012–13 or by approximately 90 percent.[3] During this same time frame, students at four-year public institutions incurred 55 percent more loan debt: $4,300 to $6,700. Students are worried about debt to the point that this concern influences how they engage in postsecondary education: 40 percent of seniors who responded to the 2015 National Survey of Student Engagement noted

that financial stress affected them to the point that they chose not to purchase required academic materials due to cost.[4]

Institutions also have reason to be concerned with retention and completion rates. Through the Voluntary System of Accountability's College Portrait, institutions report six-year graduation rates. No longer buried on an institution's webpage, this information is available for students and their families to consider and compare when choosing a college. According to the National Conference of State Legislatures, two-thirds of U.S. states use a performance-based funding model to allocate some portion of funding based on indicators. Among these indicators, degrees awarded and course completion are primary.[5] College completion plays a key role not only in terms of student recruitment, but also in terms of retaining state funding.

Beyond college completion, the media and the scholarly literature abound with discussion of how much money graduates of different majors earn. Garrison Keillor has parodied the employment prospects of English literature majors on the radio program *A Prairie Home Companion* for years.[6] Although the U.S. Department of Education ultimately appears to have abandoned the notion of ranking colleges on its College Scoreboard website, it did so only after months of discussing what information to include that would help students rationally value their investments in higher education. Information about the salaries of average graduates by institution is available on the College Scorecard website despite the fact that salary is more a function of what one studies than the institution one attends.[7]

In a model based on two Cs, completion and cash (cost), success is linear. Completion is the necessary condition by which students can begin to earn cash in order to pay back student loans. The reason to attend college is to earn a credential to show employers that one is employment worthy. With sheepskin in hand, the career choices of students are influenced greatly by their desire to maximize cash. Perhaps crass, this is the most instrumental definition of college success and one that bears out in the data.

The Freshman Survey, administered by the Higher Education Research Institute at UCLA, has been used to track student objectives for postsecondary study for more than 40 years. In 1967, more than 85 percent of students identified "developing a meaningful philosophy of life" as an essential or very important objective for higher education. This trend declined precipitously through the decades and hit an all-time low of 39 percent in 2003; it reversed slightly in 2006 to more than 45 percent. Conversely, "being very well off financially" was an essential or very important objective for less than 45 percent of students in the late 1960s, but the importance of this objective has risen steadily over time.[8] The instrumental focus of today's college students has not waned: 86 percent of recent students surveyed identified being "able to get a better job" and 73 percent identified being "able to make more money" as very important reasons for going to college.[9] These numbers are offset by a near equal percentage of students who are motivated "to gain a general education and appreciation of ideas" (71 percent) and "to learn more about things that interest me" (82 percent).[10] Unfortunately, these latter reasons, largely motivations for a liberal education, are rarely discussed in policy circles.

Although students appear to support the neoliberal ideology that success is measured by wealth and a good job, they also hold broad-based learning goals. When one talks to students directly, an even more nuanced notion of success emerges. My research team and I spoke to more than one hundred students from community colleges and universities across Ontario, Canada. We invited them to describe what "student success" meant to them and how their college or university supported their success. The students' definitions included achieving in the classroom, completing their credentials, learning how to contribute meaningfully to their communities, understanding how to manage their lives, and preparing for careers.[11] When we presented our findings, Joe Henry, former Associate Dean of Student Success at Sheridan College, a community college in Canada, commented on how similar our model was to the one that he and his colleagues had developed. Although some may suggest students at community colleges are more vocationally-minded and thus less interested in a more liberal conception of success, the similarity of findings across our two projects with different student population calls into question the purely instrumental and neoliberal motivation for attending college or university often ascribed to today's students.

I've thought a great deal about the data we collected when we asked students, staff, faculty, and senior administrative leaders to define and depict success. In reviewing the drawings and transcripts, the neoliberal and instrumental definition of success as credential to career, or completion to cash, is too reductionist and does not adequately characterize the hopes and dreams of today's college students. Through the advent of quantum mechanics, scientists have come to focus on systems and wholes in order to "understand the complex reality that is the ecosystem."[12] In statistics, one adds a cubic term when the linear term does not sufficiently model the data. As educators and policymakers, I suggest we follow the example of scientists and reframe success from a reductionist, instrumental, and linear model to complex, liberal, and cubic one.

## CUBIC NOTION OF SUCCESS

Figures 1a and 1b depict the general cubic form that provides the basis for this conceptual model of success. Each facet of the cube denotes a different objective. The facets may change in size depending on the individual and may move from a cube to a rhombus. As such, how success *looks* varies by student, which is consistent with findings from my research with Joe Henry and Diliana Peregrina-Kretz.[13] Success is personal, individual, and unique.

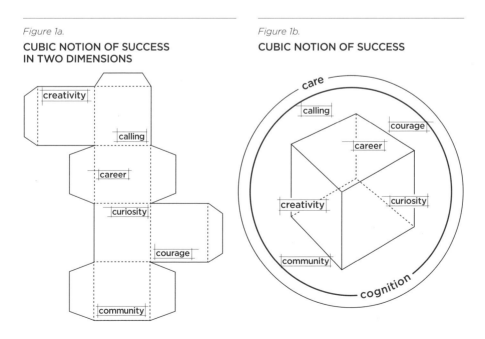

Figure 1a.
**CUBIC NOTION OF SUCCESS
IN TWO DIMENSIONS**

creativity
calling
career
curiosity
courage
community

Figure 1b.
**CUBIC NOTION OF SUCCESS**

care
calling
courage
career
creativity
curiosity
community
cognition

Curiosity is arguably at the heart of the academic enterprise. Fostering students' desire to learn and pursue inquiry is a central component of many institutional mission statements. Students pursue higher education because of an interest in learning more about a topic or a field of study, which often becomes their major. Creativity goes hand in hand with curiosity and is the facet of success that pushes the boundaries of knowledge and expression. Without creativity, society stagnates and reifies the status quo. The questions and problems that face us today will not exist in the same form tomorrow. Science, art, music, and diplomacy wither when past practices and customs are adhered to rigidly. Creative minds are needed to develop possible solutions to the world's intransigent problems, such as hunger, war, and climate change. Creativity and curiosity take root as students respond to an inner calling. When students negotiate and reconcile their internal and external voices to discern what they believe, who they want to be, and who they want to be in relation to others, they author their own lives and are able to hear this calling. Marcia Baxter Magolda calls this process "self-authorship" and asserts that helping students to self-author should be the common goal of 21st century education.[14] It takes courage to listen to one's calling, to look beyond the immediate to see the bigger picture and how one's values are supported or undermined by today's decisions. It takes courage to pursue work that puts food on the table and feeds the soul. A lack of courage often results in college graduates experiencing the "quarterlife crisis" that Alexandra Robbins and Abby Wilner write about so poignantly.[15] It takes courage to ask what Sharon Daloz Parks terms life's "big questions"[16] and perhaps even more courage to "live the questions now" in order to "gradually, without even noticing it, live our way into the answer."[17]

To listen to one's calling takes courage, and to allow that calling to lead one's curiosity and creativity may result in a meaningful career. Theologian Frederick Buechner defined vocation as "the place where your deep gladness and the world's deep hunger meet."[18] A career that unites soul with role helps one attain the epitome of an integrated life.[19] My colleague, David Henderson articulates this beautifully as the place where "one's competence is buttressed by one's compassion."[20] Noted in Figure 1, the success cube exists within the spheres of cognition and care. One is not privileged over the other. Success is not the purview of the head at the expense of the heart. In *The Courage to Teach*, Parker Palmer calls to educators to commit to teaching students' whole beings, their heads and their hearts.[21] If higher education faculty and staff are to be good company on students' journeys as Marcia Baxter Magolda encourages,[22] then institutional success must be recognized in terms of educating the whole student.

Community is a facet of success and a process that contributes to success. Many have talked about the power that a mentoring community has in helping students find the courage to listen to their callings.[23] One need only think of the communes and guilds that existed for centuries to nurture the creative talents and curiosity of members. Community is a key component of student learning. In How College Affects Students, Ernest Pascarella and Patrick Terenzini indicate that interacting with one's peers was one of the most vital and consistently positive predictors of student learning and development.[24]

Community is also a facet of success in that it is a space in which one's gifts and talents— cultivated through courage, calling, creativity, and curiosity and manifested in one's career—may come to fruition. Henri Nouwen, renowned priest, professor, and author, heralded the importance of solitude in order to hear one's voice and community as a place for expressing it.[25] Given the interdependent nature of our world, this is perhaps the greatest benefit for society. Alexander Astin, Helen Astin, and Jennifer Lindholm note that higher education institutions commonly claim a commitment to developing values-based outcomes like character, social responsibility, and citizenship.[26] The problems of the 21st century require more than technical knowledge demarked by credential completion; these problems require graduates with self-awareness, empathy, and a genuine concern for others—the latter two develop in community.

## Success as an Emergent Property

When success is viewed simply as instrumental and linear, it is seen solely as a measurable outcome. Did a student complete her degree? How much money does the graduate make? Diliana Peregrina-Kretz, Joe Henry, and I advance that when success is defined as an outcome in terms of college completion, it "fails to take into account the experiences and connections that influence students' personal, profession, and academic development."[27] We spoke to many students who saw and celebrated success day to day. To them, success was a process. It was how they did on their exams, how they handled uncomfortable conversations with their roommates, how an event they helped to plan on campus was received. Success was the process.

Success as an outcome suggests that upon completion students have *arrived*. The outcome is accomplished; the degree has been earned. This thinking is at odds with a cubic notion of success in which facets, like curiosity and creativity, are intimately connected to lifelong learning. In this regard, success is not an end goal but in the words of Chris Kearns, Vice President of Student Success at Montana State University, "an emergent property."[28] According to Tim O'Connor and Hong Yu Wong, emergent properties "arise out of more fundamental entities and yet are 'novel' or 'irreducible' with respect to them."[29] Success as an emergent property is conceptualized in the model by the arrows that show that the cube is always in a state of revolution.

The cubic notion of success may be considered an emergent property of being well. A host of contributors to this volume have written prolifically on the topic of well-being. I have been deeply influenced by the work of Carol Ryff, Corey Keyes, and Laurie Schreiner. Although the specific construction of well-being varies by author, as Don Harward notes, well-being is the relational activities of being well, as in a life well-lived. Success—in its facets of curiosity, creativity, calling, courage, career, and community—emerges as a property of being well.

*Success as an outcome suggests that upon completion students have* arrived. *The outcome is accomplished; the degree has been earned. This thinking is at odds with a cubic notion of success in which facets, like curiosity and creativity, are intimately connected to lifelong learning*

Herein lies the rub. Current policies do not recognize, let alone reward, students or institutions of higher education for cultivating the emergent property of success. In fact, they actively penalize them. On a student level, students pursue higher education for a host of reasons: most to earn a credential but others to see if they can do it, to gain a skill, or for personal enrichment. Yet according to the website of the Free Application for Federal Student Aid, federal financial aid is available only to the student enrolled "in an eligible program as a regular student seeking a degree or certificate."[30] For students who do not aspire to degrees but need financial assistance, enrolling with the stated reason of seeking a degree is logical even if not accurate. The financial aid policy sends a message to students. Intentionally or unintentionally, it suggests education to spur one's creativity, curiosity, and response to calling in order to contribute to one's community is not valued unless it results in a credential. Students may attend and achieve personal success without attaining degrees, but in the eyes of financial aid policy makers, these students are viewed as policy failures.

From an institutional perspective, measuring success as completion is equally problematic. Institutions that enroll students with low-level degree goal commitment but who need financial assistance are penalized when students who have achieved personal success withdraw without completing their degrees. The individual student's success counts as institutional failure. In the context of performance-based funding metrics in which graduation rates matter, this has implications for state funding in subsequent years. Additionally, the current college completion policy acts as a disincentive for faculty, staff, and leaders in higher education to advise students to pursue programs of study that may be better fits, particularly if these programs are not available at the institution or if making such a change would prolong time to degree. In this case, completion as the measure of reductionist, instrumental, and linear success thwarts the ability of educators to nurture students' complex, liberal, and cubic success. The focus on college completion values the destination—not the journey—which I find antithetical to education.

The six facets that comprise the cubic notion of success are not new to higher education. In fact, one may argue they are at the core of liberal education and Socrates' exhortation to live an examined life. For many, the facets of cubic success are central to the academy and what it means to be an educator. To me, this means igniting students' curiosity and inspiring their creativity to think deeply and critically. It means being good company on the journey as students discern their callings and develop the courage to listen and act. It means helping students identify career paths that make the most of their competence and compassion.

> *The focus on college completion values the destination—not the journey—which I find antithetical to education*

It means modeling engagement in one's community, whether that community is an interpersonal exchange with one other person (a roommate, friend, or family member) or is more broadly one's department, workplace, neighborhood, or city. I see my role as educating students to view learning as a lifelong endeavor, to view success is an emergent property of being well, and to consider that life is about the journey not the destination.

I fear the focus on an instrumental definition of success at the student and institutional level not only shortchanges students and educators, but also shortchanges society. The world is complex, interdependent, and multicultural. Society needs graduates who are able to bring a cubic notion of success to bear on addressing the world's wicked problems. There is a need, nay a demand, for curious, creative thinkers who have the courage to respond to inner callings to contribute to their communities, writ large, as a matter of career. Creating space to educate such graduates, however, requires a fundamental shift in policy and practice.

From a policy perspective, financial aid needs to be available to support students' explorations as well as their degree-seeking intentions. Although completion may still be a goal, it should be complimented by the recognition of each student's progress toward realizing her or his goals. Progress and achievement would then be noted at an individual student level rather than at an institutional level. The Free Application for Federal Student Aid database contains information on all students who receive federal financial aid; goal identification and progress toward goal achievement could be added to the database for students in subsequent years after postsecondary study. Without a doubt, this is an enormous undertaking. Yet the United States need not invent the wheel and can learn from other systems that have implemented similar metrics at other levels of education, such as the Ontario Education Number.[31] This system provides a reliable record of the movement and progress of individual students through elementary and secondary school. With goal attainment measured at the student level, policy aimed at institutional effectiveness could then be used to examine the extent to which institutions have transparent and substantial means of measuring student progress. Institutions are held accountable for processes that facilitate, not foil, student progress. From a practice perspective, measuring progress at an individual student level allows higher education administrators and faculty to better advise students before matriculation and during their courses of study with respect to program fit. Conversations about program fit provide an opportunity to bridge the two solitudes of higher education and high school and bring together high school guidance counselors, college recruitment staff, and academic advisors in meaningful dialogue about college and career.

Reframing success from a perspective that privileges the reductionist, instrumental, and linear conception of completion to career to one that values the complex, liberal, and cubic notion of success will take time. It may require that students demand their educations be about more than the completion of a necessary number of credit hours for a credential. It may require educators demand an opportunity to re-connect to the broader purposes of higher education. It may require employers and society to demand that employees and citizens have the curiosity and creativity to not settle for the simple solution but to push the boundaries to tackle the wicked problems that face our world. If society is to be well, we must recognize and reward higher education faculty and administrators for educating students in ways that help them attain complex and cubic success.

NOTES

1. Lily Eskelson Garcia, "What Teachers Do," speech given at the Campaign for America's Future Awards Gala, October 27, 2015, https://www.youtube.com/watch?v=2zMbspRhqJc.

2. Barack Obama, "Address to Joint Session of Congress," The White House, Office of the Press Secretary, February 24th, 2009, https://www.whitehouse.gov/the-press-office/remarks-president-barack-obama-address-joint-session-congress.

3. National Center for Education Statistics, "Fast Facts," Digest of Education Statistics, 2013 (NCES 2015-011), Chapter 3, https://nces.ed.gov/fastfacts/display.asp?id=76.

4. National Survey of Student Engagement, *Engagement Insights: Survey Findings on the Quality of Undergraduate Education. Annual Results 2015* (Bloomington, IN: Indiana University Center for Postsecondary Research, 2015), http://nsse.indiana.edu/NSSE_2015_Results/pdf/NSSE_2015_Annual_Results.pdf.

5. National Conference of State Legislatures, *Performance-Based Funding for Higher Education* (Denver, CO: National Conference of State Legislatures, July 31, 2015), http://www.ncsl.org/research/education/performance-funding.aspx.

6. Garrison Keillor, "English Majors," transcript from *A Prairie Home Companion* radio broadcast, May 29, 2010, http://prairiehome.publicradio.org/programs/2010/05/29/scripts/english-majors.shtml.

7. Ernest T. Pascarella and Patrick T. Terenzini, *How College Affects Students: A Third Decade of Research,* Vol. 2 (San Francisco, CA: Jossey-Bass, 2005).

8. John H. Pryor et al., *The American Freshman: Forty Year Trends* (Los Angeles, CA: Higher Education Research Institute, UCLA, 2007), http://heri.ucla.edu/PDFs/40TrendsManuscript.pdf.

9. Kevin Eagan et al., *The American Freshman: National Norms Fall 2014* (Los Angeles, CA: Higher Education Research Institute, UCLA, 2014), http://heri.ucla.edu/monographs/TheAmericanFreshman2014.pdf.

10. Ibid.

11. Tricia A. Seifert, Joseph Henry, and Diliana Peregrina-Kretz, "Beyond 'Completion': Student Success is a Process," *Strategic Enrollment Management Quarterly* 2, no. 2 (2014): 151–63.

12. Parker J. Palmer, Arthur Zajonc, and Megan Scribner, *The Heart of Higher Education: A Call to Renewal* (San Francisco, CA: John Wiley and Sons, 2010), 81.

13. Seifert et al., "Beyond Completion."

14. Marcia B. Baxter Magolda, "Self-Authorship as the Common Goal of 21st Century Education," in *Learning Partnerships: Theory and Models Of Practice to Educate for Self-Authorship,* eds. Marcia B. Baxter Magolda and Patricia M. King (Sterling, VA: Stylus, 2004), 1–36.

15. Alexandra Robbins and Abby Wilner, *Quarterlife Crisis: The Unique Challenges of Life in Your Twenties* (New York: TarcherPerigee, 2001).

16. Sharon Daloz Parks, *Big Questions, Worthy Dreams: Mentoring Young Adults in Their Search for Meaning, Purpose and Faith* (San Francisco, CA: Jossey-Bass, 2000).

17. Rainer Maria Rilke, "Letters to a Young Poet," no. 4, para 2, 1903, http://www.carrothers.com/rilke4.htm.

18. Frederick Buechner, *Wishful Thinking: A Theological ABC.* (New York, Harper & Row, 1973), 95.

19. Palmer et al., *The Heart.*

20. David Henderson, personal communication, November 23, 2015.

21. Parker J. Palmer, *The Courage to Teach: Exploring the Inner Landscape of a Teacher's Life* (Hoboken, NJ: John Wiley & Sons, 2007).

22. Marcia B. Baxter Magolda, "Helping Students Make Their Way to Adulthood: Good Company for the Journey," *About Campus* 6, no. 6 (2002): 2–9.

23. Robert J. Nash and Michele C. Murray, *Helping College Students Find Purpose: The Campus Guide to Meaning-Making* (San Francisco, CA: Jossey-Bass, 2010); Parks, *Big Questions*; Palmer, *Courage to Teach*; and Tricia A. Seifert, "What's So Funny about Peace, Love, and Understanding? Or, Why Higher Education is Finally Talking about Faith, Belief, Meaning, and Purpose," In *Making Meaning: Embracing, Spirituality, Faith, Religion, and Life Purpose in Student Affairs,* ed., Jenny Small (Sterling, VA: Stylus, 2015), 58–80.

24. Ernest T. Pascarella and Patrick T. Terenzini, *How College Affects Students* (San Francisco, CA: Jossey-Bass, 1991).

25. Henri J. Nouwen, *Reaching Out: The Three Movements of the Spiritual Life* (New York, Image, 1986).

26. Alexander W. Astin, Helen S. Astin, and Jennifer A. Lindholm, *Cultivating the Spirit: How College Can Enhance Students' Inner Lives* (San Francisco, CA: Jossey-Bass, 2011).

27. Seifert et al., "Beyond Completion," 160.

28. Chris Kearns, personal communication, November 23, 2015.

29. Tim O'Connor and Hong Yu Wong, "Emergent Properties," *Stanford Encyclopedia of Philosophy*, published September 24, 2002, substantive revision June 3, 2015, para. 1, http://plato.stanford.edu/entries/properties-emergent/.

30. Free Application for Federal Student Aid, "Am I Eligible to Receive Financial Aid," accessed March 12, 2016, https://fafsa.ed.gov/help/fftoc03a.htm.

31. Ontario Ministry of Education, "Ontario Education Number (OEN)," accessed March 12, 2016, http://www.edu.gov.on.ca/eng/document/brochure/oen/.

# 16
## ESSAY

# What Does Doing Good Mean?
# Well-Being and the Civic Purpose
# of Higher Education

*Andrew Seligsohn*

IN COLLEGES AND UNIVERSITIES ACROSS THE UNITED STATES—and increasingly around the world—student engagement in activities focused on service and that otherwise affect the social or public good has become a norm. The activities themselves vary widely and range from short-term volunteerism to sustained participation in ongoing efforts aimed at lasting social change. And the variation does not stop there: activities may be undertaken through the curriculum or the co-curriculum, during the academic year or during breaks, through highly structured programs or on the fly.

But across this variety, there are two presumptions that characterize these many efforts. The first is that they benefit a community beyond the campus. The second is that students benefit from participation in activities that are intended to achieve community or public benefit. The first presumption is open to legitimate challenge: while we have many examples of student engagement producing significant results, we lack comprehensive empirical data about the likelihood that such activities will actually create the desired community benefits, and we lack data about the magnitude of the benefits that do accrue. While there are promising efforts to document the effect on significant social indicators of university engagement broadly, these projects are in their early stages, and they do not even attempt to disaggregate forms of engagement. With respect to the public effect of student engagement service and work, there is no compelling evidence.

The focus of this essay, however, is on the second presumption and, in particular, on one version of it: that students *as people* are better off for having participated in activities intended to provide social benefit. My interest in this presumption is not so much empirical as conceptual. What is meant when it is claimed that it is good for students to engage in work to benefit communities? What sort of work is in mind? What sort of good is expected to emanate from that work? What assumptions about colleges and universities are built into the conceptual apparatus through which student community action is understood?

These questions are worth exploring because how we think about the good that students derive from engagement activities is likely to influence how we build programs and opportunities for students. Moreover, our thinking about these issues may inform decisions about whom to include in shaping these opportunities and in shaping colleges and universities more broadly. One reason for pursuing these questions is that we often drill down very deeply on quite narrow questions about what students gain from engagement. We might survey students on their experience of efficacy or analyze data to answer specific questions about student persistence in college. These are important questions, and my own organization, Campus Compact, has often been involved in seeking to answer them. Still, it is sometimes valuable to step back and ask very different kinds of questions about students: *What forces cause students to feel dislocated and unsafe? What factors can help them feel whole and sufficiently secure to embrace challenges?* The recent unrest on college campuses, frequently characterized by calls from students from underserved communities for safe spaces, reminds us that many students do not feel that they are in environments conducive to their thriving. We need to listen to what students are saying about what will change that experience, and we need to analyze the way we engage all students to see how we can create environments that support their well-being.

How then should we address the question of the effect of civic and community engagement as higher education experiences on students? My approach is to examine relevant aspects of the two realities these efforts connect. One reality is the social and political landscape into which our students venture from our campuses. The other reality is that of our institutions of higher education themselves.

*What forces cause students to feel dislocated and unsafe? What factors can help them feel whole and sufficiently secure to embrace challenges?*

When our students head out into the world, much of their lives and careers will take place on and against a landscape of inequality—a landscape that has seen the intensity of inequality increase dramatically during the last half century.[1] The political language popularized during the Occupy Movement (the 99 percent and the one percent) has become a widely recognized shorthand to refer to the fact that the overwhelming majority of new wealth since the 1970s has accrued to a tiny fraction of the population—those already at the top of the income and wealth distribution. As the uprisings in Ferguson and Baltimore and the wave of protests on colleges campuses in 2015 have all made clear, accelerating economic inequality interacts with longstanding racial injustice to produce increasing social volatility. Indeed, it would be difficult to explain the dynamics of the 2016 Republican presidential nomination battle without reference to a backlash against people of color and their demands for equity and justice.

In short, our students set forth from our campuses to undertake their socially beneficial endeavors in a country in which inequality is both increasingly pervasive and increasingly salient. However, it should be noted—and I will return to this point later—that many students do not relate to these inequalities in a homogenous way. While it would appear that students on some campuses reflect conventional expectations about college, primarily residential student populations, many campuses serve predominantly first-generation students from low or moderate income families, and their expectations and experiences should not be assumed to be conventional. Thus, we make a mistake if we begin with the premise that student service work involves privileged students seeking to help those who are less fortunate than themselves. That happens, but it is far from universally the case. Moreover, that framing of student civic engagement is not conducive—and in fact, possibly detrimental—to realizing the good, both the individual and the public good that engagement can produce.

Because of the significance of inequality for the social justice efforts of students, it is worth examining the texture of contemporary American inequality in greater detail. Two recent books provide a useful starting point for the inquiry: Robert Putnam's *Our Kids: The American Dream in Crisis*[2] and Ta-Nehisi Coates' *Between the World and Me*.[3] Putnam's central concern is economic inequality, while Coates' is contemporary race and racism. These vastly different works have in common a focus on the lived experience of inequality and injustice, and they are thus fitting entry points for a consideration of the world in which the lives and community engagement of our students unfold.

First, a brief detour to consider categories and vocabulary: as Putnam notes, there are various ways of identifying the layers in the class stratification system of the United States, for example, according to income, wealth, or education level.[4] Similarly, there is no single racial divide in the United States, since many different ethnic identities are racialized in the United States. For a set of reasons having to do with simplicity, clarity, and the practices of these two authors, I will generally use the terms *wealthy* and *poor* to refer to those on the winning and losing sides of the class divide. And in the context of race, I will primarily focus on the divide between white and African-American experience. Neither of these approaches is adequate to the complexity of the world I am describing, but both, I hope, are reasonable compromises under the circumstances. It should also be noted that race and class are not inter-changeable concepts. There are rich and poor African-Americans and rich and poor whites. Because of the history of race discrimination, African-Americans are more likely to be poor than whites, but due to their greater proportion of the population, in absolute terms there are more poor whites in the United States than poor Africa-Americans. So we need to be careful in the way we use these concepts, but we should not be so careful that we refuse to discuss issues at the core of public life.

Putnam's book takes the broad and complex phenomenon of exploding economic inequality and uncovers its significance in the lives of real people on both sides of the growing divide. As the book's title suggests, Putnam is particularly concerned with the opportunities available to young people whose experiences are increasingly shaped, in nearly every facet, by the class positions of their families. He begins with his own home-town, Port Clinton, Ohio, and compares the early experiences and life courses of members of his high school graduating class, the class of 1959, with those of young people in Port Clinton today. The comparison reveals the first key element of the book's argument: while the life chances of students graduating high school in 1959 were not determined primarily by the class circumstances of their families, for today's young people they are.

For the class of 1959, the public institutions, social structures, and family relationships that provided the scaffolding for the experiences of children and young adults did not vary significantly depending on class position. For example, working class children had access to relationships with adults at all points along the class spectrum and thus had relatively easy access to information about topics such as applying to and paying for college. Today, for a set of inter-related reasons detailed by Putnam, the situation is vastly different. Children born without class privilege find themselves without access to the information and supports necessary for changing their own circumstances.

And that is the second major component of Putnam's argument: what differs about the experiences of children growing up on either side of the class divide now is nothing short of *everything*. Rich and poor children experience different family structures, different parenting practices, different communities, and different schools. There is no space outside the space of class difference, and in every domain, the differences have the effect of reinforcing and magnifying class inequality. If a wealthy child was to spend time in the world of a poor child, nearly every aspect of the experience would be unfamiliar, and the reverse is equally true. Unlike differences in, for example, religion, that might create an experience of unfamiliarity (but that do not, in the contemporary United States, correspond to specific patterns of opportunity), the class-based differences experienced by children connect directly with their opportunities to change their class positions. For example, stress caused by instability negatively affects children's cognitive development. Poor children are systematically more likely to experience such stress because of the difficulty their caregivers will face in trying to maintain stable housing, consistent employment, a physically safe environment, and access to appropriate health care. That means poor children are likely to perform less well in school, which diminishes their prospects of getting out of poverty. It is not only that poor and wealthy children live in different worlds, it is also that those worlds are built to replicate the inequalities they embody.

While Putnam identifies an expansion of the gap in lived experience corresponding with the expansion of the economic gap during the last 50 years, he does not paint an idyllic picture of the past. Instead, he acknowledges that certain inequalities, such as those grounded in race and gender, have always been highly problematic in American life and were in many respects far worse during the early years of the lives of the members of the class of 1959 than they are today. His point is that during the more class egalitarian period of the mid-20th century, the economic opportunity structure ran counter to race and gender inequality and allowed many families to improve their positions from one generation to the next. In contrast, today nearly everyone is locked into their existing economic ranks, and the space between the upper ranks and the lower ranks is growing. One implication is that African-Americans who managed to get into the upper ranks economically are now able to take advantage of the benefits of the new structure. Overall, however, the growth in class inequality hurts African-Americans because they are more likely to find themselves on the losing end of the new rigidity in class structure.

*It is not only that poor and wealthy children live in different worlds, it is also that those worlds are built to replicate the inequalities they embody*

Putnam's work leaves us with a few crucial conclusions. First, our students' lives before and during college are shaped by the inequality landscape. Within some institutions, all—or virtually all—of the students come with a shared experience of having traveled the smooth path of privilege or of having fought their way across the deep divide that prevented most of their peers from getting to college. Many institutions make multiple efforts to attract and provide multiple learning opportunities for students from a diversity of class backgrounds, but the challenges of succeeding in doing so are great. Among the challenges is that of recognizing that it will be nearly impossible to attract students for whom class has not shaped their experience (privileged or suppressed) even if the insularity of their worlds may have prevented them from knowing that. The challenge to the institution is to understand and account for inherent inequalities that are the reality of all of their students and are similar to the decline of the middle class; inequality differences prevail on any campus.

Second, when college students engage with members of low-income communities through their college programs or courses, they are either re-entering a world that has profoundly shaped them or they are entering a world that is distinct in nearly every respect from their own and in which they are implicated. For wealthy students, this form of engagement involves complexity far greater than is captured by concepts such as *communicating across difference* or other similar conceptual frameworks often used to prepare students to enter unfamiliar communities. The difference involved is hierarchical and morally non-neutral because the structures that have diminished opportunity for those at the bottom are the very same ones that have created opportunity for those at the top. Students from contexts of privilege are not simply encountering people with different ways of living, although they are doing that; they are also encountering people whose lives are negatively affected by the very policies that have enriched privileged families and that are maintained by the disproportionate political power of people in their class.

Third, the pervasiveness of the inequalities that serve as barriers to opportunities for poor people create an a implicit criticism of the work of college students who are engaged in service, for example, because the realities of the inequalities and their pervasive and pernicious consequences lead the institution to a position of downplaying the reality of the inequalities in order to preserve the possibility that their students' work will result in feeling relevant or inspiring (withholding pointing out that limited efforts of the kind college students typically undertake are unlikely to make a meaningful difference to the public good).

The increasing inequality context in the contemporary United States means that for many students, the social good that results from their actions is not necessarily aligned with the well-being feelings or individual good brought by such actions. Students can find themselves feeling dislocated, guilty, diminished in the eyes of peers, in conflict with or embarrassed by their families, and otherwise unsettled. If these risks are to be mitigated and any balance of individual well-being and the realization of the public good achieved, much will depend on the institutional context in which student engagement is undertaken, a point to which I will return later.

In *Between the World and Me,* Ta-Nehisi Coates illuminates deep truths about American life through a memoir written in the form of a letter to his son. It is a personal narrative with a public purpose: to characterize the daily reality of life for African-Americans in the context of persistent racism. Coates tell his son that "racism is a visceral experience, that it dislodges brains, blocks airways, rips muscle, extracts organs, cracks bones, breaks teeth."[5]

The contrast with Putnam's method could not be more stark. Putnam tells the story of class inequality by matching detailed interviews with a vast body of statistical evidence. Coates tells his son that "the sociology, the history, the economics, the graphs, the charts, the regressions all land, with great violence, upon the body."[6] He means that the forms of documentation of racial inequality available to social science can never capture the experience of fear and vulnerability of people existing in a society that permits and promotes violence against the bodies of black people. Coates writes in the aftermath of the well-publicized killings of Michael Brown, Eric Garner, and Tamir Rice, but he writes with recognition that there is nothing new about the phenomenon of those in positions of power committing acts of violence against black people without consequence to themselves.

Despite the differences in approach, Putnam's and Coates' work converge on a recognition of the deep damage done to young people who grow up in environments saturated with violence and the fear of violence. Putnam illustrates this point through the story of a young man he calls Elijah, who spent his childhood in extreme poverty, bouncing from one family member to another, witnessing and experiencing violence at every turn.[7] For Coates, who grew up in an entirely African-American world in West Baltimore, the fear of violence began with the realities of living in a world beyond police protection in which strength and the willingness to harm established dominance. It was reinforced by the violence of parents who feared that allowing their son to remain peaceful would put him at risk. Eventually, the daily risk of facing police violence became the central focus of his fear, not least because a college friend was shot and killed by police in an incident of unaccountable official violence.

In Coates' interpretation, the pervasiveness of violence has a hold not only on African-Americans, who constantly experience themselves as under threat, but also on whites who are trapped in a constant need to deny the ongoing significance of racial violence. White Americans, he says, "have forgotten the scale of the theft that enriched them in slavery; the terror that allowed them, for a century, to pilfer the vote; the segregationist policy that gave them their suburbs."[8] Their forgetting is due to a desire to remain in "the beautiful Dream" of American exceptionalism: "I am convinced that the Dreamers, at least the Dreamers of today, would rather live white than live free."[9]

It is this world, with its persistent inequality, its racialized violence, and its profound need to deny these realities with myths of equality of opportunity and colorblindness, to which we send our college students to do good. Indeed, we send them into the very teeth of these inequalities to seek to create equality of opportunity where there is none. In the best case, we prepare students thoroughly for these ventures with an understanding of the context, of their role in it, and of the limitations inherent in their efforts. We encourage them to analyze and reflect on the realities they encounter, their responses to them, and how all of that connects with larger social and political issues. We guide them to resources and opportunities to take further action in ways that fit with their values. If we assume that all of the right things are done by higher education professionals, what good do we expect—or at least hope—will come of these endeavors for students? How will they be changed in ways that are beneficial? And what more might have to be true of our colleges and universities for us to have confidence that students will be able to realize these benefits?

It should be acknowledged that many practical benefits accrue to students from participation in socially beneficial actions. Students develop useful skills in areas such as problem solving, communication, and project management, among many others. These practical skills are not my focus here. They are important, but they are not unique to engagement in action oriented toward social justice and the public good. In principle at least, students can acquire the same skills through participation in, for example, high-quality internships in the for-profit sector. We are seeking experiences that accrue to the individual well-being of students *because* they are actions taken for the public good and with cognizance of the pervasive inequalities that influence them.

One candidate for such a benefit is the opportunity for students to step outside the myths that hold poor people and people of color responsible for the challenges they face.

As Putnam amply demonstrates, it is not the case that everyone in the United States has an equal opportunity—or even a meaningful opportunity—to succeed. The deck is stacked against poor children. For college students from wealthy families, simply seeing the conditions under which poor children must seek to develop themselves can be powerful, and it is all the more powerful when combined with the kinds of learning a well-designed college course can provide. Understanding the daily experience of life in neighborhoods saturated by violence—criminal violence, police violence—can be transformative for students who have experienced an assumption of security. Recognizing basic truths about our world contributes to individual well-being by allowing us to ground relationships with others on honesty and mutual understanding. When that recognition of inequalities informs efforts to serve social justice or the public good, students personally become aware of self and others. Participating in deceptions that justify one's privilege is harmful because it undermines deep connections with others, so coming to terms with the painful realities of the lives of those excluded from privilege contributes to the good of participating students.

At the same time, there is no guarantee that this exposure—even when properly situated in an educational context—will produce the real understanding needed to achieve these benefits. For many students, the reality is more complicated. For those who come from privilege and have campus experiences in which little attention is given to deep inequality, the encounter with inequality may be jarring and difficult to assimilate. Students may be forced to see their colleges, their home communities, even their families as cynically pursuing their own good while ignoring those on whose backs their wealth and security are built, or they may come away reinforcing a stereotypic judgment that preceded their experience, which is analogous to blaming the victim.

*Recognizing basic truths about our world contributes to individual well-being by allowing us to ground relationships with others on honesty and mutual understanding*

The situation is yet more complex for students who themselves come from poor communities, regardless of race. Recent evidence has shown that substantial numbers of students confront poverty daily while in college.[10] These students, of course, do not benefit from the demystification of the American class system; as Coates and many of Putnam's informants make clear, those without privilege are keenly aware that others have it. Still, they might earn self-claimed benefits, not those simply permitted by the privileged, in two ways. Those from low-income backgrounds might benefit from the experience of taking informed action to contribute to their own communities or communities facing similar challenges. Moreover, while students from poor communities might feel some ambivalence about how their own families and communities fit in a broader culture that often blames people for their poverty, the opportunity to learn about structural inequality and take action to challenge it has the potential to move students past feelings of shame and toward an experience of confidence and efficacy. Students from low-income backgrounds may also benefit from seeing their wealthier peers come to a deeper understanding of underserved communities. I have seen this in my own work with students manifest as palpable relief on the part of low-income students that wealthier students have discovered that poor neighborhoods are populated primarily by good people seeking to improve their lives and communities. Rather than feeling as if they must choose between hiding or explaining where they come from, these students could claim common ground for honest discussions with peers from a variety of contexts.

As with the forms of well-being that might be cultivated among wealthier students, these outcomes are speculative. It is possible that the need to move back and forth between worlds, and to do so with people whose life experiences are radically different from one's own, might simply be disorienting to low-income students. They might find that the kinds of defenses they need to build up in order to soldier through a world not built for low-income, first-generation students—one that treats them as other—are eroded by frequent context-switching. They might be frustrated by the confusion of their peers and discomfited by the need to choose between vernaculars. And they along with their wealthier peers might be disillusioned by the fact that the institutions sending them back into their communities to do socially beneficial work are not themselves engaged in efforts to achieve social justice.

To be clear, I am not arguing against engaging students in public work to overcome economic and racial inequality. On the contrary, I am considering the pitfalls of engaging students in that essential work in order to identify what colleges and universities must do to maximize the likelihood that these experiences achieve their goals to serve the well-being of the individual. The promise for high and low income students is that engaged action to pro-mote equality will render them whole, whether by freeing them from ahistorical myths or by liberating them from the need to conceal who they are. The peril is that the reverse will be true, that students will find the disjuncture between the world of the campus and the world beyond so destabi-lizing that their well-being will be diminished rather than enhanced. The question is how to achieve the rewards of engagement while avoiding its risks. The argument for doing so is compelling when we recognize the possibility for students to achieve lives rich with mean-ingful relationships, grounded in deep understanding of social and political realities, and oriented toward positive change. In other words, the goodness of a life saturated with the results of taking action to create communities that live up to their own best ideals is emphatically worth pursuing. At the same time, the risks of generating or reinforcing cynicism or alienation must be mitigated.

*The behavior of the institution as a whole matters in the individual experiences of students*

This risk-reward context brings us back to the role of the university. The best way to reduce the likelihood that students will experience debilitating contrasts between their own work toward justice and the reality of their campuses is for colleges and universities to make deeper and more substantive commitments to democratic values. Colleges and universities can do that by integrating civic engagement into the curriculum; prioritizing community-based research; reforming tenure and promotion standards to reward engagement; and re-orienting practices in purchasing, employment, real estate development, admissions, and financial aid to focus on advancing the interests of historically marginalized communities. In the best case, these efforts would be undertaken in a coordinated fashion to maximize their effect and demonstrate to students and communities beyond the campus that the institution is committed in practice to the principles it espouses to its students.

Evidence grounded in systematic research supports the conclusion that the behavior of the institution as a whole matters in the individual experiences of students. Robert Reason and Kevin Hemer analyzed data from the Personal and Social Responsibility Inventory and concluded that the degree to which high impact practices such as service learning are effective in cultivating civic values in students depends in part on the extent to which students believe their colleges are actually committed to the values cultivated through the experience.[11] Students notice if institutions ask them to do as they say, not as they do. If the institution is not living according to its stated values, students are less likely to embrace those values and are therefore less likely to achieve the well-being that results from civic participation in the long run.

If colleges and universities are to facilitate their students' achievement of the well-being that comes from beneficial social action, they will have to fulfill their own public purposes. Doing so does not require an extraordinary commitment beyond what ought to be expected of institutions that are publicly subsidized directly or through tax exemption. It simply requires colleges and universities to recognize that they exist to serve the public good through their teaching, research, and institutional action. In the end, then, the situation of the college or university parallels that of the student. Student well-being depends on coming to terms with the complex and difficult realities of our world. Sometimes, those realities threaten our identities, but in the end, we benefit from reckoning with that rather than denying it. We benefit from facing the contradiction and seeking to resolve it through action in the world. The same is true for institutions. Consistently acting in the service of public goods is not easy for institutions that face constant financial challenges and many other threats. In the short run, it seems to make more sense to accept contradictions between the values embedded in the student experience and the expediencies of running a large and complex institution. In the end, though, it is a self-undermining approach, as students, alumni, and key external stakeholders increasingly insist that colleges and universities acknowledge the contradictions in their approach and resolve them.

---

NOTES

1. See for example, Timothy Noah, *The Great Divergence: America's Growing Inequality Crisis and What We Can Do About It* (New York: Bloomsbury Press, 2012).
2. Robert D. Putnam, *Our Kids: The American Dream in Crisis* (New York: Simon & Shuster, 2015).
3. Ta-Nehisi Coates, *Between the World and Me* (New York: Spiegel & Grau, 2015).
4. Putnam, *Our Kids*, 50.
5. Coates, *Between the World,* 10.
6. Ibid, 10.
7. Putnam, *Our Kids*, 110–17.
8. Coates, *Between the World*, 87.
9. Ibid.
10. See for example, Clare Cady "Students Shouldn't Have to Choose Between Books and Food," *Chronicle of Higher Education,* February 28, 2016, http://chronicle.com/article/Students-Shouldn-t-Have-to/235519/ and Sara Goldrick-Rab and Katharine M. Broton, "Hungry, Homeless and in College," *New York Times*, December 4, 2015, http://www.nytimes.com/2015/12/04/opinion/hungry-homeless-and-in-college.html?_r=0.
11. The Personal and Social Responsibility Inventory is an instrument designed through the Core Commitments initiative of the Association of American Colleges and Universities and housed at Iowa State University's Research Institute for Studies in Education. Robert Reason and Kevin Hemer's analysis was shared with me by Reason in an e-mail message on February 4, 2015. I discuss these results in more detail in "Colleges and Universities as Exemplars in the Development of Citizens," *Journal of College & Character* 17, no. 1 (2016): 1–7, http://dx.doi.org/10.1080/2194587X.2015.1125369.

# 17
PROVOCATION

# Student Well-Being as a Function of Identity Development

*Elsa Núñez*

When I left for college, many of my friends and family said that I would go away and never come back, or worse yet, that I would change—and not in a positive way. My mom and dad probably feared it too, but they loved me, so if I changed, in whatever way, they were okay with it as long as I became a college graduate.

I, however, swore I would never change, and I would always be a ghetto girl from the projects. Yet in my freshman year of college, the questions of who I was and where I fit in this great American society began to haunt me.

One of the social indicators among Hispanics is language, and among Puerto Ricans, the way you pronounce certain words in particular indicates class. Swallowing the final syllable suggests you are uneducated or part of the lowest social strata. The word *lado*, for example, means side; I pronounced it my entire eighteen years before college as *lao*, dropping the *d*. At some point, after heart wrenching self-debate, I decided that I would always, for the rest of my life, drop the d when I went home, so that when I spoke with pre-college friends or my family, I would show them I had not changed.

Today, like me, many of our students come to college with issues of identity based on class, sexual orientation, race, and ethnicity. As President of Eastern Connecticut State University, I am concerned about retention and graduation rates, though we have the highest rates of all the public state universities in Connecticut. Part of our focus has been on the issues of identity that our students face. This focus, we believe, is crucial to our impressive outcomes and central to our students' well-being.

The focal point of this essay is well-being—the quality of a student's life—and its effect on learning. Through impressive studies led by Bringing Theory to Practice and others, we have come to recognize that how students feel about themselves and the world around them is central to their motivation and capacity to learn. For instance, significant work has been done to show how experiential learning and community engagement positively affect students' well-being—how those practices contribute to a student's social and psychological health.[1] I would like to direct my comments to another important aspect of student well-being: how our campuses can best support the development of gender, racial, and class identity. In a brief essay, I cannot give you a comprehensive analysis of these issues, but I think I have found some interesting ideas that may provoke more thought and discussion.

First, on the matter of gender. Even though researchers suggest that sexual awareness and the development of gender identity take place at an earlier age than fifty years ago, eighteen-year-old freshmen on college campuses are still exploring their sexuality—some for the first time—in an environment that is new and unfamiliar. They are living away from home. They are managing freedoms they have not had previously and dealing with multiple layers of uncharted territory: new academic expectations and opportunities, new living conditions, new social circles.[2]

One could well argue that gender is the most fundamental element of personal identity—more basic than ethnicity or social class. To explore, confirm, and embrace one's gender identity while going through all the other discoveries inherent to being a college freshman is a significant process for all students, regardless of their gender or sexuality. How college campuses provide support during this process is as critical to a student's acclimation to and success on campus as any other element of personal identity.

One of the first researchers to speak about gay and lesbian sexual identity as a normal developmental process rather than a disease or condition to be treated was Vivienne Cass in 1979.[3] Cass articulated six stages of identity development, including identity confusion and identity tolerance. Embedded in her writings were discussions of denial and rejection of one's sexual orientation. We have come a long way in twenty-five years. Reflecting the evolution of our society's acceptance of the lesbian, gay, bisexual, transgender (LGBT) community, the stages of gender identity development have also evolved. A baseline of tolerance and acceptance by LGBT individuals and their straight counterparts has evolved to a baseline of identity integration and public pride. Even so, individual students as well as LGBT groups on campus must still be supported to move through the process of gender identity development.

> To explore, confirm, and embrace one's gender identity while going through all the other discoveries inherent to being a college freshman is a significant process for all students, regardless of their gender or sexuality

In focusing on gender identity development among heterosexual students, Roger Worthington and his colleagues note that while "virtually all literature regarding sexual orientation is situated in volumes designed to address lesbian, gay, and bisexual (LGB) issues," similar research on heterosexual sexual identity is "all but nonexistent."[4] Worthington and his co-authors discuss the importance of providing heterosexual students with the same resources as LGB students to help them explore, affirm, and internalize their gender identities. By engaging in a frank and supportive discussion of sexual identity on college campuses, gender identity becomes a common developmental process shared by all students, regardless of their sexual orientations.

Second, on the matter of race. While discussions of gender and sexual orientation usually have two axes—male and female, straight and gay—in comparison, the issue of race on our campuses has many foci. For the purposes of this brief provocation, I want to focus on three: Latino, African American, and white.

Part of the issue of racial identity development across all races and ethnicities is the need to educate people about the definitions of those terms. The inaccurate terminology we use to describe the groups I just mentioned is a symbol of the need for more education regarding race and ethnicity. For instance, Latino or Hispanic does not constitute a race or an ethnicity. More than 20 nations of origin are represented under the umbrella term Latino. The Pew Research Center found that 52 percent of young Latinos (ages 16–25) identify themselves by their nations of origin: Cuban, Puerto Rican, Mexican.

They are more likely to identify themselves as Americans (24 percent) than as Latinos (20 percent).[5]

In the same way that much of the early research on gender identity focused on minority subgroups (gays and lesbians), most of the literature and discussion about racial identity on college campuses focuses on minority students—African Americans and Latinos in particular. In the 1990s, Janet Helms advanced a White Racial Identity Development Model that focused on developing racial awareness as a key component of white racial identity.[6] Helms and Tina Richardson acknowledge that racism exists and that confronting one's own racism as a white person ("abandonment of white privilege") is central to the development of white racial identity. Only by interacting with students of color in trusting, positive, campus environments and activities can white students confront and respond to their own racism and at the same time build relationships and develop non-racist, white identities.[7]

Helms and Richardson delve into racial identity for minorities and make the point that the development of racial identity is similar for all people of color, regardless of race, and involves cognitive, emotional, and behavioral changes in response to "surmounting internalized racism in its various manifestations." Early stages in racial identity development include conforming to racial stereotypes, even to the point of trying to "act white"; advanced stages include expressing a positive racial self-identity, actively rejecting and combating racial stereotypes, and developing positive individual and group self-expression.[8]

On our campuses, we need to create a deeper, more substantive understanding of race, ethnicity, and culture. For instance, while celebrating Latin American Awareness Month and Hispanic Heritage Month, we also need to celebrate Mexican history, Puerto Rican holidays, and Guatemalan culture—to name just three possibilities—so that students from those countries can share their pride and so white students can begin to understand the nuances and richness of racial, ethnic, and cultural diversity. In addition, in our classrooms, we need to extend the intellectual discussion of race and culture to include deeper meanings.

Third, on the matter of socioeconomic class. Education, income and wealth, prestige conferred on the basis of family history, where you live, the make of car you drive, the clothes you wear—these are all symbols of class. How do students on campuses perceive these distinctions? In a 2014 study of hundreds of college students at a northern California public university, investigators focused on the issue of class identity. They hypothesized that that social class would be less important to students' self-identity than gender or ethnicity. Instead, they discovered that the majority of students saw social class as most central to their identities, a finding that crossed all social classes in the study. They also found that interacting with peers on campus became a central condition for students to examine, understand, and reconcile their class identities. In these peer interactions, students clearly recognized class distinctions in speech, dress, etiquette, and behavior.[9]

During interviews, students expressed a wide range of emotions. Affluent students expressed guilt, denial, and justification—although one student described privilege as a "blessing and a curse"—while lower-income students expressed anger and also pride in working hard and earning everything they had. One interesting outcome was the prevalence of the myth of meritocracy and the American Dream in the visions of lower-income students. Whereas affluent students understood the potential for downward mobility, students from low-income families repeatedly envisioned some point in the future when they would surely be able to "move up."[10]

How can we affect this class consciousness on our campuses? As with gender and race, we need to help students develop their personal identities in terms of class and also provide opportunities for them to understand how class affects their peers and the world at large. From the study cited above, we can see that peer interaction on our campuses is a series of teachable moments. We can add to those interactions with planned activities that help students from all classes learn from each other, including residential hall activities, community service opportunities, intramural teams, and campus organizations.

On an intellectual level, we need to raise the level of discussion of income inequity on our campuses. Recently, the head of the Federal Reserve Board wrote that income inequity threatens our social order and economic future as a nation.[11] Students need to engage in that discussion, not only in terms of using their own experiences and peer comparisons, but also by engaging in a discussion of the effect of income inequity on our nation and the global community.

*Developing healthy attitudes among majority students— those who are heterosexual, white, and middle-class— is every bit as important as programming to support identity development for minority populations*

In conclusion, gender, race, and class are elements of the personal and group identities of each person and every student on our campuses. So what are the key takeaways regarding the issue of identity development in these three areas, and how we can support our students as they learn more about themselves and their fellow students?

When we talk about identity development on our campuses, we inevitably think about how best to support minority groups based on ethnicity, sexual or gender identity, or socioeconomic status. As the literature clearly suggests, developing healthy attitudes among majority students—those who are heterosexual, white, and middle-class—is every bit as important as programming to support identity development for minority populations.

While developing their identities, it is important for white students to acknowledge institutional racism and take steps to understand, respect, and support ethnic minorities. It is important for heterosexual students to move from tolerance to affirmative support of their friends with different sexual identities. It is important to have middle-class students look past the perspective of privilege to understand that the efforts to address income inequity must run parallel to steps taken to support gender, ethnic, and economic minorities on campus. At the same time, all students—by engaging in shared activities and discussions on gender, race, and class—can develop deeper intellectual understanding of those issues. They can develop, internalize, and celebrate their own personal identities while better understanding and supporting students who may fall outside of their own groups. This is all important to each student's well-being.

One of the most important decisions I made in my life was to continue to drop the *d* in the presence of my family and old friends, and to this day we are very close.

NOTES

1. See George D. Kuh, *High-Impact Educational Practices: What They Are, Who Has Access to Them, and Why They Matter* (Washington, DC: Association of American Colleges and Universities, 2008); Jean Jaymes West and Donna Simmons, "Preparing Hispanic Students for the Real World: Benefits of Problem-Based Service Learning Projects," *Journal of Hispanic Higher Education* 11, no. 2 (2012): 123–135; Janet Eyler, Dwight Giles, Charlene Gray, and Christine Stenson, "At a Glance: What We Know About the Effects of Service Learning on College Students, Faculty, Institutions and Communities, 1993–2000: Third Edition" August 31, 2001, http://www.compact.org/wp-content/uploads/resources/downloads/aag.pdf.

2. See Freya Sonenstein, Joseph Pleck and Leighton Ku, "Levels of Sexual Activity Among Adolescent Males in the United States," *Family Planning Perspectives* 23, no. 4 (1991): 162–167; American Psychological Association, Task Force on Gender Identity and Gender Variance, "Report of the APA Task Force on Gender Identity and Gender Variance," Washington, DC: American Physiological Association, 2009, https://www.apa.org/pi/lgbt/resources/policy/gender-identity-report.pdf.

3. Vivienne C. Cass, "Homosexuality Identity Formation: The Cass Model," *Journal of Homosexuality* 4, no. 3 (1979): 219–235.

4. Roger L. Worthington, Holly Bielstein Savoy, Frank R. Dillon, and Elizabeth R. Vernaglia, "Heterosexual Identity Development: A Multidimensional Model of Individual and Social Identity," *The Counseling Psychologist* 30, no. 4 (2002): 496–531.

5. See Pew Research Center, "Latino Youths Optimistic But Beset by Problems," December 11, 2009, http://www.pewhispanic.org/2009/12/11/latino-youths-optimistic-but-beset-by-problems/; Pew Research Center, "Between Two Worlds: How Young Latinos Come of Age in America," Updated July 1, 2013, http://www.pewhispanic.org/2009/12/11/between-two-worlds-how-young-latinos-come-of-age-in-america/.

6. Janet E. Helms, *Black and White Racial Identity: Theory, Research, and Practice* (Westport, CT: Praeger, 1990).

7. Janet E. Helms and Tina Q. Richardson, "How 'Multiculturalism' Obscures Race and Culture as Different Aspects of Counseling Competency," in *Multicultural Counseling Competencies*, eds. Donald B. Pope-Davis and Hardin L. K. Coleman (Thousand Oaks, CA: Sage, 1997).

8. Ibid.

9. Virginia Thomas and Margarita Azmitia, "Does Class Matter? The Centrality and Meaning of Social Class Identity in Emerging Adulthood*," Identity: An International Journal of Theory and Research* 14, no. 3 (2014): 195–213.

10. Ibid.

11. Jeffrey P. Thompson and Timothy M. Smeeding, "Inequality and Poverty in the United States: The Aftermath of the Great Recession," Washington, DC: The Federal Reserve Board, 2013, http://www.federalreserve.gov/pubs/feds/2013/201351/201351abs.html.

# 18
## PROVOCATION

# Student Narratives and Well-Being
### *Thia Wolf & Amalia Rodas*

MANY YEARS AGO, in a literacy course aimed at preparing students to work as writing consultants in our bustling writing center, I found myself in an intriguing tussle with a bright young woman who "really hated" the course reading and content. These readings highlighted inequities in education that frequently lead first generation students from low-income backgrounds to perform at lower levels in college courses than their more privileged counterparts. The angry student—we'll call her Sue—a first-generation student, whose family lived in poverty, took exception to this critique; she had always performed well in school, and she felt that theories of inequity made her individual accomplishments less important. One day, perhaps two thirds of the way through the semester, Sue turned to me as I walked near her during a class break and said, "The question isn't if I can understand this material or if I can apply it. The question is, 'Who will I be if I decide to believe this?' Because I will never be the same if I decide that I do believe this and that this is what I want to think about."

I ask us to aim for this moment of recognizing the self in the curriculum. As teachers, we like these moments, but all too often we do nothing to foster them. Sue came to her critical insight and was able to value the course material on her own. Although I supported her in the usual ways—through assigning pertinent reading, entering into discussions, responding to her writing, and meeting with her during office hours—I did nothing intentional to help her uncover the meaning of the course's relationship to her construction of herself.

While this hands-off teaching approach to students' development of their identities in the midst of college coursework is quite common, I wish to argue here that it hampers them emotionally and practically. In fact, by ignoring the importance the self-narratives in classroom contexts of our students, we signal to them that how their learning affects their developing senses of themselves does not actually matter and is not a part of college work.

Seminal research by Hazel Markus and Paula Nurius on the construction of "possible selves" indicates that our self-concepts are based not only on our accomplishments and direct experiences, but also on the ways we can imagine ourselves in new and future contexts. Possible selves "are different and separable from the current or now selves, yet are intimately connected to them."[1] These selves arise and are explored through ongoing, everyday narrative behaviors, for "[n]arrative practice lies at the heart of self-construction."[2]

If we in higher education are to take seriously our responsibility to support and enhance the psychosocial development and well-being of students in college, we need to care about and help them work critically with the narrative behaviors they use when authoring their lives—their stories of their "now selves" and the future-oriented stories of their "possible selves." But using narrative as a meaningful intellectual and emotional activity for making sense of the self in the college context is not part of most of our teaching repertoires, perhaps because stories are seen in many disciplines as less important than facts or evidence. Yet stories are the evidence that each of us uses to decide which information, people, and experiences are important to us and what the likelihood of success might be for our now and future selves in varied fields of study.

To illustrate the important functions of self-narrative in the life of a developing college student—and to highlight missed opportunities for intentional narrative work with students in the context of higher education—I turn to a story I have witnessed unfolding over the past five years. Amalia Rodas, a first-generation college student from a low-income, Guatemalan-American family, has worked beside me (literally—we share an office) since she completed our peer mentor training course five years ago and began to work in the First-Year Experience Program. In order to capture her story appropriately, I interviewed her this semester and asked her to go over material I had gleaned from a variety of conversations in the workplace over the years. She read and responded to a draft of this essay to ensure that she is represented in ways that are resonant for her and accurate from her point of view. I asked to list her as a co-author of this essay, and she agreed that she would allow me to do so. Listening to her narrative from start to finish has taught me something about her conceptual model of herself in college that I had previously missed and left me wishing I had asked her to tell me her full story sooner.

*Stories are the evidence that each of us uses to decide which information, people, and experiences are important to us and what the likelihood of success might be for our now and future selves*

Amalia, now twenty-three years old, entered college at eighteen. She is the eldest child—and the first to go to college—in a large family with hard-working parents:

> *My mom had me when she was sixteen. She had six children by the time she was thirty-four. My father worked for fifteen years taking care of a house for wealthy people. I didn't know that my parents were poor until I was older. We said a lot of, "Why can't we have what the other kids have?"*

Amalia's decision to come to California State University, Chico had little to do with the college itself. The theme of decision making and acting without necessary information appears in her narrative in more than one place.

> *I picked Chico State by a process of elimination and also some random elements. I didn't want to go to San Marcos because it was too close to home. I got accepted to CSU, East Bay, but one of my teachers said it would be expensive to live in that area. San Bernardino accepted me, but I hadn't heard from them about financial aid right away, and then I heard from Chico that I had been accepted and gotten financial aid, so I picked Chico.*

Amalia's story about going to college was sketchy at this point, and she had no clear model of college at the heart of her determination to go there. She describes herself as quiet, keeping "most of me to myself." When college acceptance letters arrived, she told herself, "'Oh, this is real. I guess I am going.' I didn't have clear ideas about it beyond that." Without others actively seeking to hear her story, the underdeveloped quality of her narrative of herself in college was not apparent to the high school teachers who sought to help her gain college entrance.

She describes her first year in college as a "culture shock." "There were no brown girls where I lived, only white girls. My one Hispanic friend I made in the dorms didn't stay in college." After a series of difficult arguments with her father that resulted in the temporary loss of contact with her family in her sophomore year, she describes long periods of attending some classes only intermittently while she became increasingly sleepless, exhausted, and physically ill.

Her model of schooling for the first several years of college was entirely grade dependent: "If my GPA was low, I would raise it up the next semester so that I could stay in school. So my transcript goes up and down because I'd respond to having a bad semester by following it with a good semester." Permanent change in this habit did not occur until after she had entered her major in the School of Social Work in the second semester of her junior year. The School uses a cohort model that allowed her to build a sense of connection with classmates: "I noticed other people came in and participated, so I finally started taking notes and participating. I started sitting in the front of the class instead of the back. I asked questions. I realized that I want to learn, I want to do things with my education, not just pass class."

The contrast between Amalia's school narrative and her performance at work in the First-Year Experience Program is striking. While she was not in her early years with the program always reliable, her extraordinary capacity for problem solving allowed her to rise to the top. She rapidly became a member of the student Executive Committee, created and supervised a large-scale public event for freshmen in sustainability courses, and acted as personal assistant to the director. In time, with appropriate work reviews, discussions, and reflection on her behaviors, she became a model employee. "I was so successful at work," she says, "that it was really a blow when I had to face the fact that school wasn't seeing me the same way."

*Nothing in the college context helped Amalia to investigate her model of college, her model of herself in college, or her goals for her possible selves in relation to those models*

Amalia's pattern of doing poorly some semesters and then "making up for it" by doing well in other semesters resulted in a consequence she was not positioned to predict: her best performances did not result in acceptance to graduate school. "The Advisor told me there was no way I would get in. I said, 'But see here, in this semester and this one I did really well.' That is when he told me that you have to do well overall."

Nothing in the college context helped Amalia to investigate her model of college, her model of herself in college, or her goals for her possible selves in relation to those models. She believed that her developing love of learning, her newfound commitment to her major, and her demonstration of being able to do well when she put her mind to it would tell her story adequately to anyone who reviewed her graduate application. The result was rejection and devastation: "When I learned they wouldn't even consider me for the graduate program, I thought that nothing I had done had really mattered. I thought that I had learned how to love learning and do well in college too late. The hope the advisor held out to me was that I could reapply sometime later in my life after finding work related to my field and proving myself there. The road seemed very long just to be able to come back to school."

For those who want to know the ending to this story, it is fortunately a happy one. An unexpected conversation with a faculty member in the Public Administration Program at CSU, Chico, resulted in an invitation to apply to their graduate program and an acceptance to begin graduate work in the spring. When Amalia describes the effect of being accepted, she weeps: "I am so excited about this. I feel I can do something for first-generation students in school; that's what I want to focus on—the policies that help them or hold them back."

Amalia has demonstrated the resilience to re-invent herself in the college context, to move learning to the heart of her school-going enterprise, and to change her social worker possible self to a public administrator possible self. As she prepares for this future, she says, "I care about doing work that will genuinely be of use to people who otherwise will struggle in the ways I have."

Amalia's story serves as a cautionary tale to those of us who work in college settings. Too many moments in this narrative reveal the lack of needed information and concept-building activities that could have changed her understanding and behavior sooner. Without access to her ongoing narratives, however, neither Amalia's teachers nor her advisors understood her struggles or the potentially self-defeating flaws in her thinking.

*Student narratives have the potential to teach us about our effects on students and at the same time support students' conceptual understanding of college and their construction of effective current and possible selves in courses and programs they encounter*

During her first several years of college, as she gradually matured into a competent, curious, and empathetic adult, Amalia simultaneously continued school behaviors that mirrored her behaviors in high school where she "did enough to pass a class, but just the minimum." Her conceptual model of college as different from and more meaningful than high school did not begin to develop until she neared her senior year; even then, she did not understand how her student self was viewed in the college context until she pursued entrance to graduate school.

What then can we, those working directly with students in higher educations, do differently? What is it I want to provoke myself and my colleagues to do when I consider how Amalia's evolving narrative could have been a useful part of her work in college courses to ensure her success, not only in meaningful preparation for work or engaged learning, but also in developing into a more well version of herself?

Narrative work with students comes in many possible forms and can be used in each and every discipline. Student narratives have the potential to teach us about our effects on students and at the same time support students' conceptual understanding of college and their construction of effective current and possible selves in courses and programs they encounter. Here are four suggestions:

1. Ask students for short written narratives at the start of the semester about how they came to be in your course and what their past relationships to the material might be. Pay attention to these stories as you work with students throughout the term, refer to them, and invite students to add to them.

2. Ask students to do reflective writing that recounts *the story of my learning* at key moments in the semester. Have students reread these and chart changes in their learning during the term. Ask them to write about how this matters to them as they are and as they might be in future years.
3. Help students see their possible selves should they pursue work in your discipline. Share with them what the lives of anthropologists, biologists, or engineers are like. Ask them if they would they like such a life? Why or why not? How can this course help them to see their possible post-college selves more clearly?
4. Find ways to make student stories part of your course material. These can be learning stories or relevant personal stories. Invite the whole student into the classroom, then teach students that their narratives are helpful to their learning rather than beside the point.

Neither Sue nor Amalia should have had to find themselves in the curriculum entirely on their own, and each of them suffered while trying to do so. Making their narratives a part of the curriculum would have given faculty who wanted to support student development and well-being access to their storylines as they worked to construct themselves in college. While narrative assignments and narrative classroom exchanges are used in a handful of disciplines and often employed as part of civic education, I challenge every educator in every discipline to ask for and listen to students' stories about themselves—as learners, as members of the college community, and as complex human beings developing possible selves.

NOTES
1   Hazel Markus and Paula Nurius, "Possible Selves," *American Psychologist* 41, no. 9 (1986): 954–69.
2   James Holstein and Jaber Gubrium, *The Self We Live By* (New York: Oxford University Press, 2000), 104.

# 19
## PROVOCATION

# Well-Being and Agency:
# Political Education in a Time of Crisis

*Brian Murphy*

IN THE HEDONIC AND EUDAEMONIC meanings of well-being, agency matters. Well-being is the sense of being an agent or actor, or it is the practical action required to sustain oneself or one's community. We understand the interdependency of sense and being only in actual lived experience, in the contexts of work and family and learning in which our students live. Well-being can only matter as an intention in higher education if we who teach have a deep and close understanding of the lived experiences of our students, the challenges and violence that often circumscribe their agency, their prospects for agency, and their future.

It would be a weak and narrow understanding of our students' prospects if we approached their well-being, or the agency required to be well, only through the lens of their individual circumstances or only with a view of their individual agency. Of course it is true that providing the context for individual growth and development, a growing sense of capacity and ability, is what any college or university professes to provide. But surely it is not enough to engage students in capacities that allow them to survive alone, or pretend to, in a market world. Surely agency must mean more.

This is not an abstract issue. Any sober view of the next fifty or sixty or seventy years—the adult lives of many of our students—suggests that the issues that will most matter are those that require political intervention. Climate change and global warming, growing structural and institutional inequality, racism, ideological violence, the rise of fundamentalism in multiple guises, the use and deployment of technology—all of these require the intervention of governments and the development of public policies. All of these will require that young people be capable of acting together politically.

Put another way, all of these issues require the exercise of public power for resolution; none can be solved by the market alone. An education on agency must include an education on power and its uses, the dynamics of political organizing and building coalitions, the negotiation of economic and social interests, and the uses and abuses of public discourse. Any student who graduates from an American university or college without some grounding in these public issues might have a sense of well-being, might actually have a limited sort of agency in a career, but will be the recipient of public or corporate decisions made by others through a process over which he or she exercises little agency.

We are, it must be said, paddling upstream to act on these ideas in American higher education to develop programs and projects and campus cultures that facilitate the development of political sensibility among our students. There is among too many of us a deep suspicion of politics and a confusion of the political and the partisan, which works, of course, to keep students away from power and its uses. While many others of us believe it is entirely possible to abjure partisan declarations and yet engage with politics or insist that students are educated on the public issues that will dominate their lives and their communities, we are not the majority. But I think we confront a deeper issue than the fear of partisanship: the notion that the purpose of an education is uniquely personal achievement in preparation for a vocation.

This trope, a deep vocationalism in virtually all public discourse about higher education, and the reduction of our purposes to job and career preparation, makes it hard to stand up for a deeper humanism that prepares students for careers and for public lives. Donors, legislators, community leaders: we too often fear them and seldom engage them in the political purposes of our institutions. Or we argue that the skills and capacities of the marketplace are also civic skills, and vice versa, as if preparing students for the one prepares them for the other simultaneously.

*A deep vocationalism in virtually all public discourse about higher education, and the reduction of our purposes to job and career preparation, makes it hard to stand up for a deeper humanism that prepares students for careers and for public lives*

This is an argument from weakness, or from a (prudent) assessment that the current politics surrounding our institutions will punish those of us who insist that our students learn about public issues and about how to lobby, argue, organize, and vote. This avoidance of politics, sometimes prudent, reduces a core aspect of agency in the lives of students or in the lives they will live once they leave us. Whatever its sources and reasons, the argument that we are only about careers and vocations for individuals is an implicitly reactionary position, one that limits our students' options and prospects for engagement in the issues that must be decided through politics.

The consequences of leaving political education to someone else or divorcing the substantive civic meanings of careers from the narrow gaining of discipline-based skill sets are quite different for students who already come from privilege than for students from marginalized communities. The former can be said to need a political education precisely because they will inherit the structural privileges that give them power, but the latter need it more. Any college or university that educates the vast majority of American young people— community college, comprehensive state university, even a larger and accessible state-funded research university—has a responsibility to engage its students in public and civic learning if well-being is going to mean anything more than feeling good.

One could argue, of course, that to the degree students of privilege and students lacking privilege learn about the stakes in global warming or the consequences of gross economic inequality, it is more possible to build broader political and social coalitions capable of addressing these issues and saving the planet in the bargain. But whatever our views of the way through the current crises, all of us who work in poor and marginalized communities have learned one unfortunate lesson: education of the middle class has not actually given our students the tools they need to battle for their own interests or defend their communities.

Those of us who argue that well-being must include the civic or that students need to develop the civic and political skills of democratic agency—whatever their careers—do so with a certain sense of urgency. We stand at an historic turning point in post-war America, in which the broad social consensus that growth would generate equality is unraveling and the sense of progress that dominated the narrative of the Boomer years is now broadly doubted. More to the point, the assumption that many of us had during the civil rights era, that America could genuinely afford to give all its citizens an equal chance, is questioned by growing segments of our country. Never has politics itself generated such cynicism and doubt. Voter alienation, the distrust of the democratic system, and a longing for magical leadership all combine with an astonishing ignorance about public issues.

These are frightening tendencies in a country with enormous military power and technologies of vast capacity for surveillance and control. The prospect of a shrinking electorate, gerrymandered on top of voter alienation, makes democracy itself fragile.

There are several ways we could respond to this crisis, including to ignore it. Or if there is a crisis, one argument goes, *It doesn't have much to do with us; its development is long-term and its solutions outside our role. If we do our work well, educated men and women will come into their own political views and act as they like.* Taken one step further, we could argue that a serious liberal education, by virtue of its robust insistence on deep analytic skills that cross disciplines and its equal insistence on the arts and imagination, would prompt among young people an openness to the world and a capacity for critical literacy when confronted by political leadership that lies and deflects or by economic and environmental crises that demand public action. Implicit in this argument is the idea that the republic is safe because broadly educated people will care for it.

But one simple question is, *How's this working out for us?* In too many universities and colleges, we are graduating competent and literate persons who have never studied civic issues deeply or had the practical experience of solving public issues. Even among those of us who care deeply about liberal learning and the role of the arts and imagination in higher education, there is often hesitation about political engagement or about insisting that our students confront civic issues. In practical terms, this results in a failure to have civic requirements for graduation or move community engagement from the margins to the center of a curriculum or a campus.

If higher education takes its democratic role seriously, it has to go beyond civic learning or the formality of teaching about civic institutions. This appears quite obviously necessary in a country where huge percentages of our people cannot name the three branches of government and cannot name the men and women who represent them in Congress. But making sure students know these bare minimums or learn the rudimentary outlines of history and geography must be joined with two other learnings, both of which have everything to do with well-being.

*In too many universities and colleges, we are graduating competent and literate persons who have never studied civic issues deeply or had the practical experience of solving public issues*

First, the growing diversity of America requires a sensibility of inclusion and respect and a capacity to work with groups and individuals different from oneself. This is one civic skill, at least, in which there is an echo in the career conversation: business managers in the new America consistently request that employees work collaboratively across differences. But a sensibility of inclusion and an openness to difference are absolutely required for political change; anyone who actually practices politics in most American cities knows that multi-cultural and multi-ethnic coalitions are the future. We need to emphasize the degree to which this capacity depends on a certain emotional and intuitive openness, a personal connection to the other in which individuals see themselves in others.

This happens unevenly, I would argue, on most campuses and in classrooms and even less so in the increasingly popular e-classroom. Yet it does happen on campuses at which there is intentional leadership to raise issues of diversity and inclusion, and it is one of the reasons diversity is an actual necessity on college and university campuses. But it takes more than the formality of diversity; it also takes a certain willingness to be open about race and class and privilege among faculty and staff and student leaders themselves. When students can talk, even if guardedly at first, about their own experiences of race and class and gender, when they can tie together the formalities of academic discourse and analytics with these experiences, when they are given the room to speak and listen, then something deeply personal can emerge, and a community can develop.

These conversations are often messy and can lead to disruption and conflict. Look at the multiple instances in which discussion of micro-aggressions and race prompts tough arguments and tougher judgments and tests the protocols of campus discussion, and you can see why lots of colleges and universities are wary. Yet it is only when these issues are aired in all their complexity and tension that a deeper listening and learning can happen.

One could argue—indeed many do—that the generation of community among difference is a good in itself or that the deeply personal transformations associated with a genuine regard for the other is a sign of maturity. But the forms of public agency required in the current social transformation of the country require these dispositions as well.

Second, an education in democratic practice is one in which practical experience matters. To learn about the formalities of power without engaging power does not adequately prepare students for confronting the issues that define our current crisis. If we are hopeful that students learn political engagement, we must support their initiatives and their involvement. And indeed on many campuses across the country, there are initiatives around voter registration and voter mobilization or local organizing around rent, transportation, minimum wages, police violence, poverty, race relations, immigration, and the rights of undocumented persons. Whatever the particular focus or issue, when students come off campus and engage or engage on the campus itself, they experience of public life in a way that can link the abstract to the concrete, the personal to the social.

## How Can We Ground These Reflections in a Specific Context?

De Anza College is a large and diverse community college, one of 113 public community colleges in California. We have 23,000 students who reflect the ethnic, class, cultural, and linguistic diversity that is California (and soon the nation). We have a reputation for excellent academic work, high transfer rates to universities, and successful, technical programs. Our student success and persistence rates are always among the highest in the state and country. At the same time, roughly 85 percent of our students lack college-level math and compositional skills when they first enroll. We have large percentages of poor and first generation students, many of them immigrants, many of them undocumented; their ages vary widely, and many are raising families. Despite their test scores coming in, we know these students are incredibly talented and capable: more than 70 percent of them speak at least two languages and have navigated the complexities of race and class and poverty to get themselves to us and stay. They are joined by other students better prepared in formal terms who choose to start with us.

How do we think about agency for these students or about an education that adequately prepares them to live in the increasingly divided and inequitable world of Silicon Valley, California, the United States? We start with an appreciation of their current strengths, of the agency and perseverance that bring them across the valley on two-hour bus rides, of their determination to work two jobs and raise children while studying. We start with the power they already have—name it, identify it, call it out—after all too many of them have not thought of themselves as successful, much less as powerful. In our first-year program we call it "decolonizing your education," and bring education itself into view as an object of reflection and action rather than as an assumed environment one navigates silently and alone.

At one level, our programs are conventional. We offer credits and degrees and transfer programs, and we aim for self-consciousness on the part of students as they each choose their majors, their course patterns, and their future work. All colleges and universities do this, more or less successfully. We know our students want transferable credits and skills and the personal choices that come from gaining them. At the same time we are clear that the college wants more for our students, and the students themselves demonstrate time and time again that they want more as well. They want educations for their contexts; they want to understand inequality, poverty, racism, gender, and religious conflict; they want to intervene in the social process; they want to gain the experience of engaging in public issues, fighting for policies and projects, organizing—not all of them, of course, but a large and growing number of them.

*How do we think about agency for these students or about an education that adequately prepares them to live in the increasingly divided and inequitable world . . . ?*
*We start with an appreciation of their current strengths, of the agency and perseverance that bring them across the valley on two-hour bus rides, of their determination to work two jobs and raise children while studying*

For a growing number of our students, in other words, well-being cannot exist alone in the growing agency of the singular self that prepares to fit into a system that has already proven itself too indifferent or too callous. For any college campus with significant numbers of non-white students, the escalating violence against young men of color is deeply frightening. For those of us in Silicon Valley, the coexistence of deep poverty and enormous wealth is in your face: 30 percent of children in Santa Clara County go hungry while 70 percent of the country's venture capital is invested within twenty miles of the campus. On a campus of great cultural diversity, the easy proclamations of racism and nativism by presidential candidates are taken personally.

So the college must lead. We have programs in social change leadership, community conversations on race and xenophobia, a new graduation requirement in sustainability, an institute for "democracy in action." We have an activist student government with an independent budget that supports public representation of student interests and multiple student organizations that reflect different political and social perspectives.

More important, we have an increasing number of faculty who actively seek ways to connect their courses to contemporary issues and who encourage their students to organize and play roles in their communities. This is not restricted to the social sciences but extends into our most technical programs. Accounting students provide tax assistance in poor communities, auto tech students make the single largest annual donation in Silicon Valley to the local food bank, and environmental science students work in local environmental struggles. De Anza students were among the most active organizers in a recent state tax initiative, provided leadership for a local minimum wage campaign, and are now organizing around rent control, housing, and local public transportation campaigns. They led the campaign to have our foundation become the first community college foundation in the country to divest from fossil fuels.

Finally, we are trying to create a public environment in which there is constant dialogue on the core issues of our region and of the nation. This means public debate on race and gender; annual programs on civil liberties and civil rights; conferences on global poverty and climate change; presentations of public art, poetry, and the spoken word; and a free speech area in which religious debate and music compete for time and audiences. We have a commuter campus, and our students stay on campus twice as long as the national average, have an annual Occupy tent city, and often challenge the college administration on our own issues (parking, student wages and hours, environmental sustainability).

In this real place with real students, I have seen a blossoming of talent, and generosity, and civic skill. Students have taught us the need to take care of each other and to ask for help because institutional change is hard and demanding. In our social change leadership certificate program, our faculty offer sections on self-care, the dynamics of non-violent communication, and cultural humility. The students create a space in which they can provide comfort and care for each other, deconstruct their work and its frustrations, and learn to listen. These too are civic skills, part of gaining a sense of agency that can be sustained over a lifetime.

De Anza College is one of 230 community college campuses across the country that have joined together in a national coalition committed to the principle that our students deserve an education in democracy. There is not a singular template for what the Democracy Commitment means, and each college acts in its own particular environment. There are multiple initiatives, curricular forms, community projects and programs, and a deep pluralism in the theoretical (or ideological) dispositions of our campuses. But at its core is a view of student agency, the belief that our students must learn to act in the public world and join with others to solve public issues.

Citizenship without agency is abstract and meaningless. Well-being without agency is illusion, and well-being without the capacity for action in the face of crisis is a contradiction in terms.

# 20
## PROVOCATION

---

# Spirit, Truth, and the Bright Colors of Books: Institutional Well-Being and Productive Disorder at a Black Women's College

*Mona Phillips*

*"Helga Crane sat alone in her room, which at that hour, eight in the evening, was in soft gloom. Only a single reading lamp, dimmed by a great black and red shade, made a pool of light on the blue Chinese carpet, on the bright covers of the books which she had taken down from their long shelves, on the white pages of the opened one selected, on the shining brass bowl crowded with many-colored nasturtiums beside her on the low table, and on the oriental silk which covered the stool at her slim feet."*—NELLA LARSEN, Quicksand[1]

*"Three great things are necessary for the spiritual equipment of an institution of learning: Freedom of Spirit, Self-Knowledge, and a recognition of the Truth. These are trite phrases, but they are none-the-less eternally true; and first of all comes Freedom of Spirit."*—W.E.B. DU BOIS, "Diuturni Silenti"[2]

THERE IS PANIC IN THE AIR. I can taste it. It follows me into the classroom, my office, my grading, my interactions with students who are in their own state of panic about money, debt, lost and wasted time—panic.

Words buzz around me and come at such a pace as to form one word: *innovationtechnologyassessmentinquirybasedlearningactiveclassroomstedexonlineoutcomes-valueadded*—word panic masquerading as progress. Colleges and universities compete for students they are not sure they really understand but are certain are different in some fundamental way than students of the past. The Department of Education's policies are crafted inside of an ideology of statistics. *The Chronicle of Higher Education, Academe,* and other publications offer some comfort: Yes! A humanities professor in Oregon, for Pete's sake, has just written my truth. I am not alone in my panic and disorder.

I work, however, in an institution—a historically black college for women—that is situated in a particular racial and gender political national context that harkens back to the early 20th century. Historically black colleges and universities (HBCUs), and more recently, women's colleges, carry the extra burden of proving themselves just as good because options are open to college-bound black and female students that were not there in previous centuries, and race remains a stubborn marker of value. As HBCUs and women's colleges enter the competition for the best students, the often unspoken recruitment message must be: We are good—*too*. Our campuses are wired—*too*. We have state-of-the-art wellness facilities—*too*. Our students are actually *more* likely to get into top flight medical and professional schools.[3]

In the early twentieth century, Negro colleges were not historically black, and train station depots clearly identified the traveling statuses of *women* and *colored*. It was in those pre post-racial times that W.E.B. Du Bois named the question: "How does it feel to be a Problem?"[4] It was in the pre-racially complex times that Anna Julia Cooper gave us the beautifully crafted dilemma of a traveling middle-class, well-educated, elite Black woman: "Under which head do I come?"[5] Nella Larsen in *Quicksand* and later Alice Walker in *Meridian*, in similarly cruel times, could ponder the regimentation and obedience that ordered Naxos and Saxon, their fictional Negro colleges. It was in the time before the Negro college became historically black that Du Bois exhorted Fisk University in a 1924 speech that it must tell the truth about Southern racism, and that the college's emphasis on discipline was killing ideas.[6] In those less-wired times, black intellectuals asked: What is the cost of order in Negro colleges? Where is Truth? Where is the institutional embrace of the "lovely, lovely, brightly colored books?" It could certainly be argued that Du Bois's *Truth* and *Spirit* and Larsen's brightly colored books are concepts embedded in contemporary discussions about the efficiency of the liberal arts and humanities, but there is some value in threading today's debates through history since the past is always with us, and evidence of experience was not always reduced to a statistically significant relationship between two variables, thereby freeing the tongue and the pen.

I am suggesting three things in this essay: first, the questions asked by black intellectuals in previous centuries should be asked now by historically black and majority colleges and universities; second, the intellectual well-being and spirit of historically black institutions depend on us saying out loud what we know to be true, especially since our deep frustration and orderly anger with the latest dictates from the Department of Education and regional accreditation bodies have not commanded respect;[7] and third, the larger arena of American higher education would benefit from the forceful assertions of *Truth* and *Spirit* coming from colleges and universities that are now historically black and timid women's colleges.

What, specifically, would Du Bois's and Larsen's *Truth and Spirit* and colors look like, sound like in the twenty-first century?

Historically black and women's colleges can now perhaps question their institutional histories and release them from the traditional narrative of triumph. Brown and Emory Universities, in Du Bois's *Spirit* of intellectual and political confidence, systematically unpacked their histories to reveal slave trade profits and other racial complexities. Students and faculty at Princeton are now asking whether it is fitting to have President Woodrow Wilson occupy such a prominent place in their institutional narrative without scrutiny of his attitudes and policies about race. Lovely, productive disorder and intellectual energy would emerge from the self-examination of HBCUs of our founders and luminaries: What were their attitudes toward race and class? Is it possible now to insert "lifelong, committed partners" in official descriptions of my college's founders Harriet P. Giles and Sophia B. Packard and perhaps give rise to an environment in which we begin to name out loud the ways in which heteronormativity is at the core of *everything we do?* Who knows?

Perhaps following the lead of HBCUs, other colleges may decide that examination of one's own past is not a luxury only wealthy colleges can afford.

Are HBCUs the ones to say aloud that education in the United States is located simultaneously in discourses and ideologies of merit, progress, uplift, hope, and change—as well as systems of profit and commodification that require education to be new, different, and responsive to shifting demands of the market? That education's simultaneous location in the country's founding ideals and capitalism produces the notion of generationally-unique students, new pedagogies, webinars, pamphlets, work-shops, consultancies, administrative posts, and bureaucracies? I suggest that since the panic-inducing creation of the new and improved has particular implications for the *Spirit, Truth* and brightly colored books at colleges and universities that always must prove their value, there are no better places to take the lead in naming and resisting panic than those very colleges and universities—HBCUs and women's colleges.

I have said very little about students in this essay, and that is intentional. Writing and talking about our students at HBCUs and women's colleges can be tricky if we try to avoid describing them as different. Yes, there are questions to be asked about differential preparation, what (most, by the way) students do not know about U.S. history, and their reluctance to engage with what I am optimistically calling "brightly colored books."[8]

But I am most concerned here about the intellectual table we set for students, and I am advocating that the HBCU asks hard questions about itself, the enterprise in which we are engaged, and that we say out loud *what we know to be true*. In fact, our students are embedded in their own locations of productive disorder, political agitation, and information sharing, such as #Blacklivesmatter; #Sayhername; lesbian, gay, bisexual, transgender, queer, intersexual, asexual activist organizations; blogs; and Facebook. I wonder if students come prepared for productive disorder, and we give them strenuous rigidity and a "machine," not Helga's "sumptuous purples and deep reds."[9]

> *I am most concerned here about the intellectual table we set for students, and I am advocating that the HBCU asks hard questions about itself, the enterprise in which we are engaged, and that we say out loud what we know to be true*

Productive disorder always reveals inner tensions and competing interests and ideologies. In a disordered institution, drawing on the scholarship done by Black women at HBCUS and women's colleges, we would theorize and talk out loud about male privilege and whiteness *inside* HBCUs, subjects too often marginalized or taboo.[10] Just think how the often cramped and predictable conversations about racism and patriarchy in higher education would be blown open when HBCUs confidently enter the ideas arena with knowledge claims about our own lovely disorder? Taking our own students lead, we should do it before someone does it *for* us.

Often colleges that correctly perceive themselves to be policed, scrutinized, and judged more than others strive to present the most ordered faces possible to the world. But to what end? As Du Bois said in 1924, "They [know] 'Jim Crow' cars; they know the effects of disfranchisement; they know personal and persistent insult. You cannot teach these children honesty as long as you dishonestly deny these truths which they know all too well."[11]

NOTES

1. Nella Larsen, *Quicksand* (New York: A.A. Knopf, 1928), 1.
2. W.E.B. Du Bois, "Diuturni Silenti," in *The Education of Black People* (New York: Monthly Review Press, 1973), 65.
3. Kimberly M. Jackson and Leyte L. Winfield, "Realigning the Crooked Room: Spelman Claims a Space for African American Women in STEM," *Peer Review* 16 (Spring 2014): 9–12.
4. W.E.B. Du Bois, "Of Our Spiritual Strivings" in *The Souls of Black Folk* (Rockville, MD: Arc Manor, 2008), 162.
5. Anna Julia Cooper, *A Voice from the South* (New York: Oxford University Press, 1988), 96.
6. "Diuturni Silenti," 66.
7. Danielle Douglas, "Historically Black Schools Say Obama's Policies Have Fallen Short," *Washington Post*, March 6, 2015, https://www.washingtonpost.com/business/economy/historically-black-schools-say-obamas-policies-have-fallen-short/2015/03/06/8ad96c70-bc71-11e4-bdfa-b8e8f594e6ee_story.html.
8. See Michael W. Clune, "Degrees of Ignorance," *The Chronicle of Higher Education*, December 6, 2015, http://chronicle.com/article/The-Gutting-of-Gen-Ed/234453 and Nicholas Carr, "Is Google Making Us Stupid? What the Internet is Doing to Our Brains," *The Atlantic*, July/August, 2008, http://www.theatlantic.com/magazine/archive/2008/07/is-google-making-us-stupid/306868/.
9. Larsen, *Quicksand*, 1–7.
10. Kelly M. Mack, Claudia M. Rankins, Cynthia E. Winston, "Black Women Faculty at Historically Black Colleges and Universities: Perspectives for a National Imperative," in *Beyond Stock Stories and Folktales: African Americans' Paths to STEM Fields (Diversity in Higher Education, Volume 11)*, edited by Henry T. Frierson and William F. Tate (Bingley, UK: Emerald Publishing Limited), 149–164; Josephine Bradley, Deborah Cook, Deidre McDonald and Sarah North, "We, They and Us: Stories of Women STEM Faculty at Historically Black Colleges and Universities," *Doing Diversity in Higher Education: Faculty Leaders Share Challenges and Strategies*, edited by Winnefred Brown-Glaude (New Brunswick, NJ: Rutgers University Press, 2008), 103–118; Alma Jean Billingslea-Brown and Gertrude James Gonzalez de Allen, "Discourses of Diversity at Spelman College," *Doing Diversity in Higher Education*, ed. by Brown-Glaude, 39–60; Florence Bonner, "Addressing Gender Issues in the Historically Black College and University Community: A Challenge and Call to Action," *The Journal of Negro Education: Black Women in the Academy: Challenges and Opportunities* 70 (Summer 2001): 176–191.
11. Du Bois, "Diuturni," 71.

PART 3

Facilitation:
Curricular,
Pedagogic and
Across Boundaries

# 21
ESSAY

# The Well-Being University

*Nance Lucas & Paul Rogers*

THE PURPOSE OF A COLLEGE DEGREE is to prepare students to be engaged and responsible citizens and to equip them with knowledge and skills to live their lives authentically with *greater meaning and purpose*. Of course, this includes cultivating a life of meaningful work, yet too often, students begin their college careers selecting academic majors because they want to follow someone else's path, or they want to please everyone but themselves. It is not unusual to hear the story of a graduate who lands a high-paying job on Wall Street only to discover a few years later that her life is void of passion and intent.[1]

A recent example unfolded when a group of five undergraduate recipients of an endowed scholarship for student well-being met with the donor during a recognition luncheon at George Mason University. As students began to introduce themselves, the donor asked them to talk about how they selected their academic majors. One of the students talked passionately about her dreams of wanting to be an elementary school teacher since she was in the eighth grade. She described how she wanted to make a difference in children's lives through education. As she was applying for colleges and looking at schools that offered education degrees, her mother showed her the household monthly bills and explained that she could not survive on a teacher's salary. Her mother persuaded her to major in health sciences so that she could get a "good job" upon graduation. The student proceeded to tell the donor that she was majoring in nursing. All but one of the remaining students in the room shared similar stories. Their conversations continued about their yearning to find greater meaning and purpose in their lives despite the practical reasons for how they selected their academic majors.

A successful college education today extends beyond preparing students to think critically, communicate well, and solve complex problems. These time-honored educational processes and outcomes remain vital to prepare students for the challenges of the 21st century workforce. Our opportunity (and our obligation) in higher education is to go further— to create and sustain educational environments in which students can fully examine what it means to have lives *well-lived*. Beyond the goal of helping students get good jobs upon graduation, we can embrace an expanded set of outcomes that will truly prepare students for today's rapidly changing, multifaceted, and interconnected world.

Focusing on well-being in college can help guide students towards life paths that include experiencing greater meaning, pursuing higher goals, giving to others, and thriving in life's many important domains. Increasing students' well-being during college can lead to a greater likelihood of degree completion and a positive effect on their emotional and psychological health.[2] When institutions of higher education commit to increasing students' well-being, they are, in fact, preparing them to address real world challenges with a deeper sense of compassion and connection to others in an integrated world that includes many diverse communities. As we envision a world in which more people are thriving and fewer are languishing, our graduates will be leaders in contributing knowledge and tools that can facilitate optimal human functioning.

The development of a multidisciplinary science around well-being has made it possible for diverse organizations and institutions to create conditions that cultivate and support the well-being needs of their members. Entire countries such as Bhutan, Ecuador, and the United Kingdom have made policy changes that support human flourishing. These include the development and implementation of rigorous indexes and measures, such as the Gross National Happiness (GNH) index, which is used to measure health and well-being beyond traditional economic indicators. Companies such as Google, General Mills, and Green Mountain Coffee have made large-scale changes and commitments that positively facilitate employee well-being.[3] While some might question whether their motives in making these investments are strictly for bottom-line purposes, programs like these are having a positive effect on the emotional and physical health of employees.[4] And the roster of countries, companies, and municipalities that are making well-being a top priority is growing.[5]

*Entire countries such as Bhutan, Ecuador, and the United Kingdom have made policy changes that support human flourishing*

Higher education is also increasingly paying attention to well-being, even though well-being, from our perspective, has a long history in the academy and the disciplines. Historically, many university and college mission statements aspired to the holistic education of students and encouraged them to formulate philosophies of life embedded in ideals of responsible citizenship and civic engagement. The humanities, of course, have always been grounded in central notions of what it means to live *fully* in a complex and interdependent world; the social sciences and natural sciences have a strong record of contribution to human flourishing (e.g., in medical and health sciences, social justice, psychology, and sociology). And while these ideals remain embedded in the central premise of a successful college education, the unfortunate rise of vocationalism[6] and an overemphasis of institutional ranking systems have distracted our attention away from a commitment to the holistic education of our students.

There are many additional compelling reasons for universities and colleges to make major commitments to students' well-being. Chief among these is the growing number of students who enter our ranks with documented emotional health concerns. The emotional health self-ratings of students dropped to the lowest point in history in 2014 at 2.3 percentage points lower than entering college freshmen in 2013.[7] In 2014, college counseling center directors reported monumental increases in students with significant emotional and psychological health issues in the last five years.[8]

We have an uncommon advantage today in advancing the goal of transforming undergraduate education with well-being as a core purpose of higher education for philosophical and pragmatic reasons. This requires an inclusive, coherent, and comprehensive agenda and, perhaps more importantly, a genuine commitment from all levels of our institutions to make well-being a responsibility of faculty and staff that spans programmatic and structural boundaries.

## The Case for a University-Wide Commitment to Well-Being

In December 2013, George Mason University included well-being as one of twelve strategic goals in its 2015-2025 strategic plan. Our vision at George Mason University is to become a model "well-being university"—a place at which students, faculty, and staff learn what it means to have lives well-lived and how to respond well to a full range of emotions and challenges. A series of grassroots efforts preceded this highly visible institutional commitment to become a model well-being university. These early efforts created favorable conditions that allowed major stakeholders from across the institution, including students, to shape this agenda.

As early as 2005, undergraduate and graduate academic courses on the science and practice of well-being appeared in the course catalog. University leaders (faculty and staff) and alumni were introduced to strengths-based leadership approaches and appreciative inquiry methods.[9] In 2009, a university-wide center dedicated to advancing the science and application of well-being was established with a major gift. This center began immediately to sponsor conferences, workshops, mini research grants for faculty, and other programs offered in partnership with other university units. An undergraduate, living-learning community with the theme of mindful living was created to expose students to formal knowledge and life enhancing skills. An academic minor, open to all students, in consciousness and transformation was created.

> *Our vision at George Mason University is to become a model "well-being university"—a place at which students, faculty, and staff learn what it means to have lives well-lived and how to respond well to a full range of emotions and challenges*

Throughout the institution, it was becoming evident that this movement was unfolding and the tent was getting bigger. By 2013, well-being had become a unifying force that attracted faculty members from a wide range of fields and disciplines and student affairs professionals from varying programs and services. It became apparent that questions and issues of well-being extended beyond the conventional disciplines of psychology, philosophy, and religious studies to include economics, education, sociology, music, dance, and integrative studies, as examples.[10]

Partnerships and collaborations between academic and student affairs to facilitate students' well-being were well underway. The value of these relationships cannot be overstated, as these partnerships played vital roles in expanding programs, finding shared interests, and moving the vision forward in surprising ways. For example, faculty researchers worked with student affairs colleagues to examine existing institutional student data and create new surveys that expanded traditional approaches to measuring student success and retention. Working with the athletic department, researchers and administrative faculty members designed and carried out an experiment using mindfulness practices with Mason's men's and women's basketball teams. While the bottom-up efforts met the top-level declaration serendipitously, other shifts were happening organically within the institutional culture. Well-being became a unifying force for students, faculty, staff, and university leaders.

## The Ripple Effect

In leading change, the process is as equally important as the outcome.[11] At Mason, intentional efforts were made to build a coalition, create a vision from the bottom up, and empower others to act. Kotter outlines these steps in leading transformations and explains how change efforts often fail when these phases are skipped in the process.[12] Other leadership scholars argue that a shared vision developed by individuals at all levels of an organization is a more effective leadership approach that results in lasting change.[13] At Mason, these efforts came together most visibly in the formation of university-wide learning communities on well-being. The learning communities became the vehicle for crafting a shared vision and agenda on institutionalizing well-being and allowed major stakeholders to take ownership of the strategies to reach these shared goals. Intentional efforts were made at the onset to practice shared and collaborative leadership while acknowledging the opportunities and challenges of leading a major institutional change effort.

The first well-being learning community launched as a grassroots effort in 2013 and included university leaders, faculty, staff, and students from across the institution. This group was charged with creating a blueprint for Mason's well-being university initiative.

Early on, the group coalesced around a clear commitment to measuring well-being and using those results to design programs and services that positively affect the well-being of students and employees. Not surprisingly, definitional issues came to the fore-front of the conversation. This was a complex and challenging task given the diverse range of disciplines and backgrounds of the learning community members. After nearly six months of discussion and debate, a university-wide definition of well-being emerged that met the group's criteria in terms of measurement, communication, and programming. At Mason we have defined well-being as *building a life of vitality, purpose, resilience, and engagement.*

Strategic priorities were identified, including integration of well-being courses in the general education program and in academic and career advising. The university entered a formal partnership with The Gallup Organization to assist in measuring attitudes regarding well-being among undergraduate students and alumni. Gallup's StrengthsFinder operating system was installed, and students, faculty, and staff were able to access this self-discovery tool on talent identification for free.

Making StrengthsFinder available widely assists the institution in creating and sustaining a strengths-based culture, one of the primary goals of the initiative. Many instructors have used this assessment to help establish learning communities in the classroom; academic advisers are using StrengthsFinder to increase students' self-efficacy and agency as they make decisions about their academic majors and career choices. An academic college embedded this assessment in two core required courses for its majors and provided faculty development for instructors and the college's academic advisors. A university-wide entity was formed, Mason Strengths Academy, the goal of which is to provide resources and ongoing learning for all community members.

In 2014, a second well-being university learning community was formed to lay the foundation for the well-being agenda and to raise greater awareness among all university stakeholders. This learning community played a critical role in advocating for integrative efforts. It also guarded against a temptation toward fragmentation in which student affairs claims responsibility for the well-being of students, and human resources assumes this role for staff and faculty. Learning community members served as ambassadors and helped to create and lead a wide variety of programming that included a month-long, university-wide celebration and inquiry on well-being called *Spring into Well-Being*, a common book reading for incoming students focused on well-being, and a series of faculty and staff development activities and student-led programs. Upper-class students developed a well-being peer educator program designed to inspire students to engage in their own self-development and to expose students to the wide range of university resources focused on well-being. Major units worked together to create employee certificate programs and faculty curriculum transformation projects on well-being.

## The Well-Being Ecosystem

Striving for institutional coherence of efforts and engagement resulted in a greater commitment to what we came to see as an emerging and vibrant well-being university ecosystem (see Figure 1). Central to this ecosystem is a set of core values that guide the evolution of this initiative—using a grassroots approach, maintaining support from the institution's senior leadership, sustaining academic and student affairs partnerships, sharing common language (definitional and learning outcomes), and working from a shared set of priorities. The ecosystem model demonstrates the breadth and depth of Mason's well-being university and also serves as means to measure our progress. The well-being ecosystem model is meant to be dynamic and fluid, and invites a diverse set of stakeholders to advance the various dimensions. For example, a university well-being measurement advisory committee was formed to provide consultation on institutional surveys on well-being and on other unit-level measurement activities that include well-being domains. Committee representatives include senior research faculty, institutional assessment office staff, student affairs educators, and well-being university learning community liaisons.

*The well-being ecosystem model is meant to be dynamic and fluid, and invites a diverse set of stakeholders to advance the various dimensions*

---

Figure 1.

**THE WELL-BEING UNIVERSITY ECOSYSTEM AT GEORGE MASON UNIVERSITY.**

| Curricular Offerings | Co-curricular Programming | Measurement & Assessment | Student-Led initiatives |
|---|---|---|---|
| Faculty/Staff Employee Offerings | Top-level Leadership and Support<br>Grassroots Participation<br>Academic & Student Affairs Partnerships | | International Multi-cultural Dialogue |
| Alumni & Community Programming | Commitment to the Commons<br>(Shared vision, language, strategic goals, champions, etc.) | | Strengths |
| Interdisciplinary—Cross-unit Leadership (Learning Communities) | Financial Resources & Commitment | Ongoing/Strategic Communication | Infrastructure<br>People<br>Spaces<br>Trails |

GEORGE MASON UNIVERSITY

## CHALLENGES AND OPPORTUNITIES MOVING FORWARD

Making a university-wide commitment to well-being is a bold goal and one that introduces a new value proposition about what a successful college education includes. These efforts are aimed at helping students early on in their college careers to achieve greater purpose and meaning in their lives. Ideally, students will become more resilient, know how to establish quality relationships, experience equanimity in adverse situations, and live life in congruence with their core values.

This type of commitment also comes with challenges. Current realities can seem antithetical to a well-being agenda and can result in tensions that cannot easily be mitigated by this vision. For example, the effects of state budgets on tuition hikes, faculty workload increases, and growing gaps in faculty and staff salaries seemingly detract from our ideals of human flourishing. After decades of civil rights passages, social justice issues continue to be unresolved and in some cases are exacerbated by our very institutional cultures. Sexual violence continues to plague campuses and makes gains in well-being nearly impossible for victims. Institutional senior leaders face growing pressures that distract them from a focus on promoting a well-being agenda. For naysayers, late adopters, and cynics, well-being can become a moniker for why becoming a university committed to well-being is an untenable goal.

However, from our perspective, these same challenges and tensions provide vital insights that can be addressed using well-being as a framework to create conditions that facilitate human flourishing within our locus of control. This requires greater risk taking and vulnerability in bringing stakeholders together to deeply examine structural and political structures that might hinder progress on advancing a well-being agenda. Well-being can be a unifying force at institutional levels and for all of higher education.

---

NOTES

1. Nance Lucas, "Put on a Well-Being Face," *Mason Spirit Magazine* Winter (2016): 24–7.
2. Barbara Buck, Sheila R. Carr, and Jan Roberston, "Positive Psychology and Student Engagement," *Journal of Cross-Disciplinary Perspectives in Education* 1, no. 1 (2008): 28–35 and Lindsay G. Oades et al., "Towards a Positive University," in *Positive Psychology in Higher Education*, ed., Acacia C. Parks (New York: Routledge, 2013).
3. David Gelles, *Mindful Work: How Meditation is Changing Business From the Inside Out* (New York: Profile Books, 2015); Nance Lucas, "When Leading with Integrity Goes Well: Integrating the Mind, Body, and Heart," in *Developing Ethical Leaders: New Directions for Student Leadership*, ed., Arthur J. Schwartz (San Francisco, CA: Jossey-Bass, 2015), 61–9.
4. Kim S. Cameron et al., "Effects of Positive Practices on Organizational Effectiveness," *Journal of Applied Behavioral Science* 47, no. 3 (2011): 266–308; Fred Luthans and Carolyn M. Youssef, "Emerging Positive Organizational Behavior," *Journal of Management* 33, no. 3 (2007): 321–49.
5. Paul Rogers and Nance Lucas, "The Time is Right to Prioritize Well-Being in Higher Education," *Bringing Theory to Practice Newsletter*, Winter (2016). http://www.bttop.org/node/7023.
6. Dan Berrett, "The Day the Purpose of College Changed," *The Chronicle of Higher Education*, January 26, 2015, http://chronicle.com/article/The-Day-the-Purpose-of-College/151359/?cid=at&utm_source=at&utm_medium=en.
7. Robert P. Gallagher, *National Survey of College Counseling Centers 2014* (Alexandria, VA: International Association of Counseling Services, Inc., 2014), http://www.collegecounseling.org/wp-content/uploads/NCCCS2014_v2.pdf.
8. Ibid.
9. Barry Conchie and Tom Rath, *Strengths Based Leadership: Great Leaders, Teams, and Why People Follow* (New York: Gallup Press, 2008); Jeanie Cockell and Joan McArthur-Blair, *Appreciative Inquiry in Higher*

*Education: A Transformative Force* (San Francisco, CA: Jossey-Bass Publishers. 2012); David Cooperrider, Diana Whitney, and Jacqueline Stavros, *The Appreciative Inquiry Handbook: For Leaders of Change*, 2nd edition (Brunswick, OH & San Francisco, CA: Crown Custom Publishing, Inc. & Berrett-Koehler Publishers, Inc., 2008).

10. See "History of Well-Being at Mason," George Mason University Well-Being University Initiative, http://wbu.gmu.edu/history-2/ and "Well-Being Academic Courses at Mason," George Mason University Well-Being University Initiative, http://wbu.gmu.edu/academic-courses/undergraduate-courses/.

11. Susan R. Komives, Nance Lucas, and Timothy R. McMahon, *Exploring Leadership: For College Students who Want to Make a Difference* (San Francisco, CA: Jossey-Bass, 2013).

12. John P. Kotter, "Leading Change: Why Transformation Efforts Fail," *Harvard Business Review* March-April (1995): 59–67.

13. Adrianna J. Kezar, Rozana Carducci, and Melissa Contreras-McGavin, *Rethinking the "L" Word in Higher Education: The Revolution of Research on Leadership: ASHE Higher Education Report,* Volume 31, Number 6 (San Francisco, CA: Jossey Bass, 2006).

# Curricular Infusion of Well-Being and Science

*Joan B. Riley & Heidi G. Elmendorf*

TRADITIONALLY PERCEIVED AS DISCIPLINES that deal principally with evidence-based knowledge and cognitive learning dimensions, the sciences are unlikely disciplines in which to expect faculty to integrate affective and meta-cognitive learning goals or to provide students the opportunity to examine issues of well-being. The common structure of science courses and many other evidence-based disciplines—a structure that often includes a wide content scope, a large number of enrolled students, and a lecture format—reinforces this perception that well-being is unlikely to be an intentional goal. So why and how do faculty in the sciences assume the responsibility of incorporating a dimension of well-being into their courses?

## THE CHALLENGES ACROSS HIGHER EDUCATION

Issues of well-being are important concerns to all students; they understand that challenges to their own goals, identities, and emotional lives can affect their academic success and impede their progression toward graduation. Many respond to the suggestion that they take the opportunity to seek help; self-identification of stress, for example, is ubiquitous. It is hardly surprising that at many colleges and universities, counseling centers and health services report seeing increasing numbers of students.

Colleges must confront problems associated with student well-being as challenges, yet exactly who can and should address these challenges may be unclear. While faculty most often interact with students directly, their roles in higher education are traditionally circumscribed to those of scholars and teachers. Consequently, and often purposefully, faculty establish boundaries to emphasize these roles in the way they conduct their courses—to separate the personal from the intellectual. At the same time and despite these constructed boundaries, faculty cannot ignore the fact that many of our students struggle with complications regarding their well-being and that this fact negatively affects their learning. These effects are clearly evident in our classrooms where we observe behaviors such as sporadic class attendance, missed assignments, and inconsistent quality of work. How especially in the disciplines like the sciences, where faculty are asked to be disinterested scholars and yet engaged professors, can support of student well-being be recognized as valued?

## GOALS OF THE ENGELHARD PROJECT

In a November 2013 speech, Georgetown University President John DeGioia described the university's responsibility to our students as the following: "Our explicit way of supporting young people engaged in the most important work in which they can be engaged:

learning to know themselves and identifying the conditions that will provide for an authentic, flourishing life."[1] We created the Engelhard Project at Georgetown University as a pathway to address this challenge and to positively influence our community by bringing efforts to educate the whole student into the classroom, no matter the discipline.[2] The project intentionally targets courses with large enrollments of first and second year students to create a course culture that builds community and changes the relational dynamic between students and faculty.[3] The project works with faculty to find curricular content in their courses that connects to issues of well-being—a process we call *curricular infusion*.

To be considered part of the project, a course must include a wellness topic framed by readings and class conversation, a visit by a campus health professional or resource person, and reflective writings. While these core elements may seem basic, the freedom to shape their context allows faculty to apply them in a great variety of unique, engaging ways to fit best within disciplinary contexts and existing course structures. These courses are then internally referred to as *Engelhard courses*. However, this designation is not listed in any registration materials so as to avoid self-selection bias or self-consciousness among student participants, most of who enter without specific expectations or even awareness of the curricular infusion component.

*Collectively, the project has reached 15,126 students in 358 courses over the ten-year period of 2005 to 2015. More than one-third of our first year students take Engelhard courses*

While the Engelhard Project began with disciplines and courses that already dealt with well-being as part of the content, it is striking how broadly the project has reached into the curriculum at Georgetown. The project now includes courses across the humanities, arts, social sciences, math, and sciences that range in format from large introductory level courses to upper-level seminars, including those taught by tenure-line research professors, full-time teaching faculty, adjunct faculty, and graduate students. Collectively, the project has reached 15,126 students in 358 courses over the ten-year period of 2005 to 2015. More than one-third of our first year students take Engelhard courses.

Students are not the only individuals affected by the success of the project. Faculty are motivated to participate for many reasons: an awareness of the importance of these issues and a need to engage with them in the classroom; a curiosity about new and innovative pedagogies and the benefit of working with like-minded colleagues; a desire to improve their teaching and earn respect from colleagues and students; a goal to deepen disciplinary learning by connecting course material to well-being issues; and a desire to improve their relationships with students.

## PEDAGOGICAL CHALLENGES IN LARGE INTRODUCTORY SCIENCES COURSES

The greatest numbers of first- and second-year students are enrolled in introductory courses within disciplines, and thus these courses represent our primary targets for curricular infusion. Yet we have found that these courses, especially in evidence-based disciplines like the sciences, also present some of the greatest barriers to curricular infusion because of their size and perceived content. In the following paragraphs, we focus on two courses from within this category of pedagogically-challenging courses and describe how curricular infusion was used not only to overcome the challenges, but also to help us collaterally minimize many other problems that too often plague introductory courses. We believe that the challenges and solutions we faced and found are common across a wide disciplinary spectrum of introductory courses, such that readers may draw useful connections and contrasts to their own teaching.

One of us (Elmendorf) teaches Foundations of Biology I. This course includes lecture, laboratory, and recitation components and serves as the first required biology course at Georgetown for a wide range of science majors and premedical students. The course has a required broad scope of content that leads students through the foundational concepts in biochemistry, cell biology, molecular biology, developmental biology, and physiology. Broadly, the course has two learning goals beyond those described in the syllabus: first, to give students a sense of how to develop an intellectual community and second, to offer them an opportunity to understand the boundaries of a discipline and to gain comfort with the inherent uncertainty of marking an area as the unknown. The course features a significant amount of group work and reflective and analytical writing in addition to traditional exams.

The other of us (Riley) teaches Health Promotion and Disease Prevention. In this course, undergraduates in human science are introduced to the theory and application of health promotion principles. Students explore the evidence, issues, and controversies in health promotion. The laboratory, which serves as the space for the curricular infusion component of the course, allows student groups to apply content material to their lived experiences as students. The course provides meaning and engagement for science students by helping them to translate the bench evidence into practice. The class demonstrates how science discovery and evidence are applied to improve health and well-being while taking into account the complexity of health. Students learn that health is more than simply the biology of each person—it is complex and the result of social and physical environmental determinants.

Building a strong intellectual community in educational settings is a desirable goal but a logistical challenge in larger classes. Simplistically, intellectual communities require basic knowledge of the members of the community, and large courses often preclude even simple name recollection for faculty and students. The absence of community within the large course classroom creates a sense of isolation for students. This is particularly acute among first-year students who are our primary constituency because they have not yet had the time to develop strong peer support networks independent of course settings, and large courses often exacerbate the loneliness many students experience when transitioning to college. For faculty, designing a course that works to build community requires a responsive teaching style, yet teaching large courses often feels like steering the Titanic with little chance for last minute changes in direction. A true learning community depends on the ready exchange of ideas and feedback among students and between faculty and students. But such an exchange can be hampered by the sheer size of the classroom population.

*Large courses often exacerbate the loneliness many students experience when transitioning to college*

Introductory courses also cover a great breadth of topics. This is dictated by the *internal curricular demands* of the various science departments (introductory courses are used to provide students with exposure to the breadth of a discipline) and by *external curricular demands* as set by graduate programs that many students will be entering (e.g., the GRE and MCAT exams required for admission to graduate and medical schools, respectively). In the academy, we talk about the coverage of content, yet it is often noted that the term *coverage* is a double entendre in that the effort to get through (cover) material can obscure (cover) its meaning from students. From a student's perspective, the consequence of the fast-paced movement through a wide array of topics results in an emphasis on content mastery rather than deeper learning goals. Because these courses are often required within the curriculum, students consequently feel the pressure to achieve, and genuine learning can too often take a back seat to the push for memorization and the rote recall needed for high grades. Faculty also feel the pressure of the clock and calendar relentlessly advancing and can hesitate to add anything new to an already packed syllabus or to deviate beyond necessary material. External demands for coverage can overwhelm better pedagogical instincts, and faculty course evaluations can suffer when students struggle to keep up. Further extending the content to include a well-being curricular infusion module runs the risk of potentially exacerbating this content burden.

The concepts featured in introductory courses also can seem quite abstract, disconnected, and unnecessarily complex to students who often enter a discipline without a foundational framework to help them organize their new knowledge. Introductory courses deal in broad rules and too often ignore the context that could allow students to recognize the real world implications and applications of the concepts or explanatory rules. Often, an attempt to make the material more relevant by mentioning seminal discoveries or pivotal thinkers (typically historical references) only serves to distance the lesson from the students, as this strategy does not encourage them to counter the topic from their own perspectives or make any real connections—cognitive or non-cognitive.

## IMPLEMENTING CURRICULAR INFUSION

In the course Foundations of Biology I, we integrate Engelhard curricular infusion through a research paper in which students explore the genetic and environmental bases of a mental health topic of their choosing. Many students select topics that have affected them or their families and friends directly, so in our predominantly 18–19 year-old population, we often see papers on addiction, depression, anxiety disorders, attention deficit hyperactivity disorder, etc. When writing the paper, students are required to use the primary scientific literature and leverage their nascent knowledge of foundational molecular, genetic, and neurobiological principles to explain the latest research. Students develop their projects during face-to-face time in the course and in an online environment with feedback from faculty, teaching assistants, and peers.

In the Health Promotion course, students use the Georgetown community as the target audience for their health promotion projects. They conduct a community needs assessment, identify gaps in services, and design health promotion strategies to meet an identified need. Exploring the evidence of the scope of the problem and best practices to address the need allows students to work in teams to explore strategies while applying course concepts of behavioral change, social marketing, and program evaluation.

The curricular infusion of well-being topics builds intellectual community and reduces students' feelings of isolation in the larger courses by heightening their awareness of themselves and their peers. The connections forged by the discussions and the sharing of written work create and accelerate the development of a community of learners. Importantly, the community includes students, course faculty, and teaching assistants. Students see faculty as more caring and approachable, which changes the relational dynamic between faculty and students. A student said it best when she described her Engelhard faculty as "present" in the classroom and, as one faculty member commented, "I need to bring all of me into the classroom."

For faculty, this inclusion in the course community can prove disruptive to a traditional approach that isolates their sphere of influence and addresses only the cognitive dimensions of learning. We have found that this is not an easy transition for many of our colleagues, but investigators clearly indicate that engaging the affective and meta-cognitive dimensions of learning deepens students' cognitive gains when the goal is higher order learning.[4] And for many faculty, the reward of serving as mentors as well as instructors to their students is well worth the inevitable bumps that result from a pedagogical shift. Most report that they enjoy teaching more and see their students more clearly. They are better able to recognize the complex demands and challenges students experience in their daily lives. Perhaps not surprisingly, many find that their teaching evaluations improve after participation in the Engelhard Project.

We have found that curricular infusion—despite augmenting already hefty course content—also helps to overcome the superficial learning tactics that dominate the approach of many students to introductory courses. Instead, it creates an environment that empowers students to take ownership. This innovative pedagogy allows for the creation of time and space for reflection through which students make meaning of their learning. In doing so, it erodes the barrier presented by the abstract concepts and facilitates learning in an environment that allows students to realize that the content they are learning is more than simply a collection of facts. In our courses, this pedagogical approach helps students recognize that science matters and that scientific concepts are applicable to issues important to them in their own lives. By asking students to make meaning of the scientific principles that underlie well-being, curricular infusion fosters a climate that encourages and promotes inquiry and creates opportunities for students to explore, ask questions, and discover. Students come to recognize that ideas are dynamic, not static. They develop skills in asking questions and become comfortable with a notion of the unknown. The literature becomes easier to read because students see it as more relevant and more engaging. Students experience the Eureka effect because the science makes sense of an aspect of their lived experiences through a new personal connection to the course material.

*By asking students to make meaning of the scientific principles that underlie well-being, curricular infusion fosters a climate that encourages and promotes inquiry and creates opportunities for students to explore, ask questions, and discover. Students come to recognize that ideas are dynamic, not static*

Curricular infusion also helps to destigmatize the many challenges of college faced by new students by inviting them to examine their own lives in their own community with its social and physical obstacles and challenges to wellness. It helps students normalize their experiences and relate them to those of their classmates. In group work, students must practice empathy in response to the personal narratives of classmates, and in reflections, students have the opportunity and permission to grapple with their own turbulent emotions. The discussions and activities provide an intellectual opening into emotionally fraught issues and create an opportunity to learn about well-being from a more scholarly point of view.

Initiating similar conversations that infuse well-being into learning in a more residential life environment could be seen as intrusive, presumptuous, and unwelcome by students and the value quickly dismissed. But when such infusion is done in academic settings, students take the topics seriously. Their initial motivation may be extrinsic (e.g., grades), but the intellectual aspects inevitably serve to provide the essential intrinsic motivation necessary for ownership. Instead of telling them answers, curricular infusion provides opportunities for students to develop questions and explore evidence along a path they have helped to craft—and have lived. Students and faculty also gain knowledge of campus resources to help them overcome personal challenges. The partnership between faculty and counseling professionals on the campus gains a public face in the classroom and further brings validity to the discussions. Students can make use of campus resources to find professional help with a personal challenge, to encourage a friend to seek help, or to better understand a friend's behavior.

Overall, curricular infusion allows students to engage with a classroom topic in connection to reflection on their own lives, their own communities and identities, and their own obstacles and challenges to wellness. Using academic content as the platform to incorporate well-being in our courses in an open and non-judgmental manner establishes the salience of our students' learning.

## Affecting Campus Culture from Within the Classroom

The Engelhard Project changes classroom pedagogies and has created a culture of caring faculty by providing a framework in which whole student education is recognized. Curricular infusion broadens and strengthens awareness of the narratives of student lives and awareness of health and wellness resources, including the possible connections that bridge learning and well-being.

*Faculty find a community of peers with whom to discuss teaching and learning across disciplines and how to create meaningful learning experiences—a rare opportunity that they benefit from sharing*

Some faculty experience teaching in the Engelhard Project as transformative in their development. Others experience incremental benefits as they integrate curricular infusion into their courses. We have not yet encountered a faculty member who has experienced negative outcomes. Collaboration creates intellectual capital. Faculty find a community of peers with whom to discuss teaching and learning across disciplines and how to create meaningful learning experiences—a rare opportunity that they benefit from sharing. These conversations are inclusive and provide common ground among non-tenure-line faculty, adjunct faculty, and tenured faculty. The community of practice that has evolved has enabled faculty and staff across divisions and lines to feel embedded in the culture as valued participants in university life. Faculty are able to share strategies and assignments, which allows for cross-disciplinary engagement and breaking down the silos of departments, schools, and academic/student affairs.

Students cite the Engelhard Project as one of the transformative experiences of their undergraduate years and write to us about it in later semesters and even after graduation. We have also seen an increase in in the number of undergraduate and graduate students who seek to serve as teaching assistants in Engelhard courses due to their own positive experiences. Students report in reflective writing assignments that they are better able to apply their scientific knowledge to real world problems and to find meaning in the abstract and detailed intricacies of the disciplines. They come to value the epistemology of the disciplines, the excitement of scholarship and research at the boundary between the known and unknown, and the vibrant and essential nature of communities as areas for intellectual exploration and learning. They gain awareness of mental health issues on campus and can better utilize resources, help friends, and contextualize their own challenges. In short, the assumed gap between the non-cognitive and the cognitive is bridged, personal becomes intellectual, and the intellectual becomes personal.

We have been struck by how readily faculty have integrated the Engelhard Project into an astonishing diversity of courses. The goals of the project have been adapted to fit into a broad array of pedagogical styles, disciplinary content, and course structures. Students from first-year to post-baccalaureate status and from the humanities to the sciences consistently remark on the impactful nature of curriculum infusion, referencing the Engelhard Project in course evaluations, reflective writings, direct communications with faculty, and peer mentoring of other students. They are searching—as college students always are—for deeper meaning in their lives, and the Engelhard Project brings that meaning into our classrooms. It deepens disciplinary engagement and strengthens our community. It grounds education in our collective and shared humanity.

---

NOTES

1. John DeGioia, "Remarks at the Launch of 'Designing the Future(s) of the University'" (speech presented at Georgetown University, Washington, DC, November 20, 2013), http://president.georgetown.edu/speeches/designing-the-futures-launch.html.

2. "The Engelhard Project for Connecting Life and Learning," Georgetown University, accessed December 29, 2015, http://engelhard.georgetown.edu/.

3. Edilma Yearwood and Joan Riley, "Curriculum Infusion to Promote Nursing Student Well-Being," *Journal of Advanced Nursing* 66, no.6 (2010): 1356–64.

4. Jean Lave and Etienne Wenger, *Situated Learning: Legitimate Peripheral Participation* (Cambridge: Cambridge University Press, 1991).

## 23
### ESSAY

# Bringing Together the Humanities and the Science of Well-Being to Advance Human Flourishing

*James O. Pawelski*

WELL-BEING IS A GLOBAL AND PERENNIAL CONCERN related to human experience. A basic level of physical well-being is necessary for any experience at all, and a large proportion of our individual and collective efforts is aimed at finding the oxygen, water, food, and shelter necessary to sustain life. In addition to merely sustaining life, however, we are also deeply concerned with its quality, and for that reason we seek to thrive physically, mentally, and socially. Observing the pervasive human interest in well-being, Aristotle went so far as to argue that well-being, or *eudaimonia*, is the "end at which all actions aim" and that everything we do is ultimately for the purpose of flourishing.[1]

Given the centrality of the quest for flourishing in human experience, it is to be expected that well-being should be a central concern of higher education. Indeed, all stakeholders of a university have an interest in promoting the theoretical understanding, empirical measurement, and practical cultivation of human flourishing. Well-being is a complex and dynamic psychosocial construct, and understanding and advancing it requires ongoing collaborative and interdisciplinary efforts. The question of well-being is just as important for academics as for student services, for the sports program as for the business office, for the faculty and administrators as for the students, for custodians as for program coordinators, for parents as for the community surrounding the campus. Each individual, group, department, and administrative unit in a college or university should continually inquire as to the role he, she, it, or they play in defining and furthering flourishing.

In this chapter, we will focus on the question of well-being as it relates to the humanities, a cluster of studies that have traditionally provided much of the core curricular material for education across time and culture. From the earliest socialization of newborns to the advanced studies of doctoral students, literature, music, art, history, religion, philosophy, and other similar studies provide foundational learning. In recent days, there has been increasing debate on the value of the humanities in our society. Educators, politicians, and members of the general public are placing a renewed emphasis on the importance of science, technology, engineering, and mathematics (STEM) and on the overall goal of employability as an outcome of education. These individuals often downplay the importance of the humanities and consider them to be more ornamental than practical. An important way to assess the value of the humanities is to consider them from the standpoint of the "eudaimonic turn" that is underway in our culture in general and that is also making its way into the humanities themselves.[2] This eudaimonic turn consists of an explicit acknowledgment that well-being is a central value of human experience. In the present context, we will focus on the eudaimonic turn in the humanities: its importance, the necessity of balance, and the benefits of scientific collaboration.

## THE IMPORTANCE OF THE EUDAIMONIC TURN IN THE HUMANITIES

Although media reports that the humanities are in crisis may be overstating the case, there is cause for concern. With enrollments in humanities courses declining in many colleges, some universities closing down entire programs, and vocal politicians actively discouraging students from majoring in the humanities, administrators and scholars are concerned about what this portends for the future of the humanities.

Louis Menand, professor of English and American literature and language at Harvard University, has argued that there is a "crisis of rationale" in the humanities—that scholars are not in agreement on the purpose of the humanities and thus not able to communicate their importance to the general public.[3] Geoffrey Galt Harpham, formerly President and Director of the National Humanities Center, argues that "humanists today must find ways to reactivate the links between their practice and the larger interests of a society based on individual freedom and self-realization."[4]

The humanities play a complex role in society. An understanding of that complex role must begin with the acknowledgment that they are valued in various ways in different contexts and thus have a range of uses. In some contexts, they are prized for their economic value, with sales of music, art, and literature closely tracked to assess their worth as investments or as ways of making a living. In other contexts, they are prized for their professional value, with acquisition of knowledge, ability to critique, or mastery of medium leading to career advancement. In still other contexts, they are prized for their entertainment value, and their absorbing content is taken up by many as a means of rest and relaxation.

*The subject matter of the humanities often explores the understanding and cultivation of those factors that make life worth living, and this points to the eudaimonic value of the humanities, their value for living life well*

These uses of the humanities are certainly important, but they do not exhaust their role in our society. A look at the content of the humanities themselves indicates a very different way in which they are valued. The subject matter of the humanities often explores the understanding and cultivation of those factors that make life worth living, and this points to the eudaimonic value of the humanities, their value for living life well. For a variety of reasons, it is easy for the economic, professional, and entertainment value of the humanities to eclipse their eudaimonic value. Each of these uses is advanced by strong interests, banks of data, and powerful organizations. The eudaimonic value of the humanities, however, although underdeveloped and frequently forgotten, is no less important, and its advancement is one of the most pressing prerequisites for well-being in higher education.

A growing number of scholars, creators, and teachers in different sectors of the humanities are calling for increased attention to their actual and potential value for human flourishing. They are, in effect, calling for a eudaimonic turn in which well-being is explicitly acknowledged as one of their central values. This is perhaps nowhere more advanced than in the study of literature. Three years ago, a dozen literary scholars wrote a series of critical essays, published under the title *The Eudaimonic Turn: Well-Being in Literary Studies*, on what it might mean for literature to have a eudaimonic value and how this value might be accessed.[5] More recently, a group of scholars published *On Human Flourishing: A Poetry Anthology*, a collection of poems composed throughout time that explores various topics of well-being.[6]

As to the concern expressed by Menand, this focus on the eudaimonic turn may help to provide a unifying rationale for the humanities. If well-being is recognized as a central concern of the humanities, this gives scholars a common language to describe some of the ultimate aims of their work. This does not, of course, mean that it will result in agreement, but it at least gives scholars a common framework within which to debate. A eudaimonic turn, with its promise of a unifying rationale for the humanities, could help revitalize the humanities and each of its disciplines by inviting them to join together in an inspiring project of historic proportions: a renewed examination of the question of well-being relevant for our times. This would require an enormous collaborative effort and would enable the humanities to make important contributions toward defining well-being and its various constitutive parts. Such a eudaimonic turn could help unlock and develop far more of the well-being value of the humanities than we now access. It could yield new knowledge and insights about well-being as scholars explicitly examine questions related to well-being in their various disciplines. A eudaimonic turn could also help scholars develop a rationale for their own work as they ask how it relates to the central concern of well-being.

This focus on the eudaimonic turn may also help the humanities connect with the larger interests of society. Well-being is a notion that resonates deeply with those outside academia, so an explicit focus on well-being in the humanities would connect them with an important, widely-shared human purpose. Using the language and rationale of well-being could help scholars in the humanities guide and frame the work they do in a way that could connect powerfully with administrators, funding organizations, government agencies, and the general public. Interestingly, many grant applications in the sciences require researchers to indicate how their work, if funded, would support the greater good. A eudaimonic turn in the humanities would allow scholars in these disciplines to indicate more readily and in more understandable ways how their work also supports the greater good.

THE NECESSITY OF BALANCE

For the eudaimonic turn to be most effective, it is crucial to maintain an important balance that is difficult to achieve in the humanities. In the last few decades, a great deal of the work in the humanities has been undertaken from the standpoint of critical theory. As Moores points out, such a standpoint frequently employs what Paul Ricoeur called a "hermeneutics of suspicion," with the goal of reading texts against the grain to discover their hidden meanings and in particular to reveal the pernicious effects of various psychopathologies and undesirable ideologies.[7] Moores indicates that this can be a worthwhile enterprise for identifying obstacles to well-being, but that it is less helpful for understanding the nature of well-being itself and how it can be cultivated. He cites more than two dozen literary scholars who, in various ways, are pushing against the constraints of the hermeneutics of suspicion and employing what, borrowing another of Ricoeur's terms, he calls a "hermeneutics of affirmation." Prominent among these scholars is Rita Felski, whose manifesto *Uses of Literature*[8] and more recent *The Limits of Critique*[9] point out that suspicion has become hegemonic in literary studies and has led to an overbearing emphasis on the negative. Instead, she develops a "positive aesthetics" with a rich phenomenological and pragmatic exploration of four fundamental uses of literature: recognition, enchantment, knowledge, and shock.[10]

In theology, scholars are beginning to ask whether a balance has perhaps been lost, with an overemphasis on sin and suffering and an underemphasis on joy and flourishing. Ellen Charry, a theologian at the Princeton Theological Seminary, has begun to develop what she calls a "positive theology."[11] In *God and the Art of Happiness*, she examines views on happiness in the history of Christian theology and considers why there has been no well-developed doctrine of happiness in Christianity. She then attempts to develop just such a doctrine under the name "asherism," roughly the Hebrew equivalent of eudaimonia.[12] More recently, Miroslav Volf, Director of the Center for Faith and Culture at the Yale Divinity School, has begun the Theology of Joy Project. Noting that joy is hardly considered by modern theologians, he is leading an interdisciplinary initiative "to build a transformative movement driven by a Christian articulation of the joy that attends the flourishing human life."[13]

*In theology, scholars are beginning to ask whether a balance has perhaps been lost, with an overemphasis on sin and suffering and an underemphasis on joy and flourishing*

The situation these scholars diagnose in literary studies and in theology is similar in many ways to the situation Martin Seligman diagnosed in psychology nearly twenty years ago. In his Presidential Address to the American Psychological Association in 1998, Seligman argued that psychology had come to focus almost exclusively on pathology at the cost of neglecting mental health and the things that make life most worth living.[14] He suggested the founding of "positive psychology" as a subfield of psychology to focus on the best things in life. In the years since, positive psychology has flourished, with profound effects not only for psychology but also for other fields, including medicine, neuroscience, economics, organizational studies, education, and sociology.

In each of these domains, as well as in humanities disciplines such as literary studies and theology in which a turn toward the eudaimonic is in various stages of development, a question arises as to the relation between methods that focus on what is undesirable and those that focus on what is desirable. Are the former negative, and must they somehow be replaced by the positive? Are they wrongly focused on ill-being instead of well-being? Do they somehow constitute a dysdaimonic obsession, from which we must rescue inquiry via a eudaimonic turn? Such a perspective is much too narrow. It confuses inquiry with the subject of that inquiry. If the subject of inquiry is negative, it does not necessarily follow that the inquiry itself is negative; conversely, if the subject of inquiry is positive, it does not necessarily follow that the inquiry itself is positive. Some other criterion is needed to make that determination, and a comprehensive approach to well-being can help provide such a criterion.

One way to approach well-being comprehensively is to begin with the insight emphasized by Martin Seligman, Mihaly Csikszentmihalyi, and other psychologists in the founding of positive psychology that the positive is not simply the absence of the negative but rather that they are two different kinds of things.[15] Seligman identifies the positive with things that are preferred and the negative with things that are dispreferred.[16] Building on this insight, I would like to suggest a way to carry out a comprehensive analysis of any situation by means of a eudaimonic profile, a broad picture of those things that support or hinder eudaimonia in a particular situation (see Table 1).

This eudaimonic profile is based on a mapping of the conceptual space of the positive and the negative.[17] According to this conceptual mapping, well-being can be supported directly through promotion or maintenance of what is preferred or indirectly through mitigation or prevention of what is dispreferred, and it can be thwarted directly through aggravation or entrenchment of the dispreferred or indirectly through destruction or obstruction of the preferred. Further, each of these relations to well-being has a dynamic mode that is concerned with increasing or decreasing and a conserving mode that is concerned with maintaining or avoiding.

There is a temptation to label a mode of inquiry in terms of its subject (positive because it studies positive emotions, negative because it studies negative emotions), in terms of its approach (positive because it is affirmative, negative because it is suspicious), or in terms of its beneficiaries (positive because it applies to psychologically healthy persons, negative because it applies to psychologically non- healthy persons). The eudaimonic profile allows us to move beyond labeling a mode of inquiry based merely on its subject, approach, or beneficiaries to considering it in terms of its overall effects on well-being. Understood broadly, those things that support well-being are positive and those things that undermine it are negative.

The eudaimonic profile, however, also allows us to move beyond a simple dualistic appraisal of modes of inquiry as positive or negative. It allows the consideration of the effects these modes have on promoting and maintaining well-being and on mitigating and preventing its loss. In addition, it raises questions of possible unintended negative consequences in the form of aggravation and entrenchment of the dispreferred or the destruction and obstruction of the preferred. Each of these quadrants has an important effect on the overall eudaimonic results of inquiry and must be considered if we are to arrive at a comprehensive picture.

This move to a eudaimonic profile emphasizes the importance of balance. If the ultimate goal is well-being, then we must make sure that no helpful approach is left out and that

*Table 1.*

**EUDAIMONIC PROFILE**

| Positive | Negative |
|---|---|
| *Directly positive*—presence of the preferred <br> • Promotion—increasing the preferred <br> • Preservation—maintaining the preferred | *Directly negative*—presence of the dispreferred <br> • Aggravation—increasing the dispreferred <br> • Entrenchment—maintaining the dispreferred |
| *Indirectly positive*—absence of the dispreferred <br> • Mitigation—decreasing the dispreferred <br> • Prevention—avoiding the dispreferred | *Indirectly negative*—absence of the preferred <br> • Destruction—decreasing the preferred <br> • Obstruction—avoiding the preferred |

none is overemphasized. The context of the situation indicates the best approach for the best outcome. This approach allows us to move from a corrective stance to a comprehensive one, from merely arguing for what has been left out or undervalued to arguing for all that would support well-being. More than simply making the case for certain neglected modes of inquiry, we seek to examine the relation of all modes of inquiry to well-being. A balanced eudaimonic approach means that we can avail ourselves of direct and indirect methods for increasing comprehensive well-being. It also means that we must think carefully about the best approach for any given context and that we must consider the entire eudaimonic profile to judge the overall effects of any particular action.

## THE BENEFITS OF SCIENTIFIC COLLABORATION

One reason it is easy for the eudaimonic uses of the humanities to be eclipsed by their economic, professional, and entertainment uses is that the latter are supported by data. The economic value of a painting can be appraised based on the sale price of similar works, the professional value of a scholarly publication can be judged by a journal's impact factor, and the entertainment value of the song can be estimated by the number of times it is played on the radio. Admittedly, these types of metrics are not absolutely precise, but they are crucial for guiding decisions by auction houses, tenure committees, and record labels. Unfortunately, empirical evidence for the well-being value of the humanities is much harder to come by. To generate such data, the humanities could benefit from a strategic collaboration with the science of well-being.

This suggestion is sure to raise objections. Some scholars have taken the principled stance that the humanities deal with things that simply cannot be measured and so should not be judged based on empirical evidence. Although it is doubtless true that the humanities cannot be measured (indeed, it is difficult to understand what that would mean), at least many of their effects certainly can be. Policy and public opinion are more and more guided by empirical evidence, and those things that cannot be measured—or can be measured but are not—are increasingly at a disadvantage. To refuse to look for ways to measure the empirical effects of the humanities is to be careless with the enormous cultural treasure they represent, to deny them even the possibility of acquiring the empirical evidence necessary for their support in data-driven decisions, and to put them in danger of being cut off from the resources they need to survive. If methods of measurement are not perfect, a more constructive approach than simply boycotting them would be to work with the scientists who create and use them to improve their effectiveness.

*Policy and public opinion are more and more guided by empirical evidence, and those things that cannot be measured—or can be measured but are not—are increasingly at a disadvantage*

Unfortunately, empirical evidence for eudaimonic outcomes is scarce at all levels of higher education. In a recent article in the *New Republic*, humanist scholars Gordon Hutner and Feisal Mohamed at the University of Illinois point out that university administrators are making decisions without adequate means to measure the contributions made by the humanities.[18] This is corroborated by conversations Brandon Busteed, Executive Director of Gallup Education, reports having had with dozens of college presidents and trustees who claim that the purpose of a college education is to improve students' lives and yet admit that they do not have a way to measure this outcome.[19]

Defenders of the humanities frequently claim that they enrich and improve our lives, that they increase empathy and critical thinking, that they give our lives greater meaning. Yet there is a paucity of empirical evidence to support these claims. Of critical importance is knowing not only to what extent they are generally true, but also how they are specifically borne out in various contexts: in particular activities, courses, and majors and for learners with varied psychological profiles, different individual experiences, and diverse demographic backgrounds.

Data are necessary to advance the well-being value of the humanities. To the extent we can measure the effects of particular approaches and endeavors on various aspects of well-being, to that extent we can use empirical methods to help identify best practices and choose the most fitting means to achieve specific eudaimonic goals. Furthermore, scientists who are experts in creating interventions and in studying their effects may be able to provide helpful advice to humanities scholars, teachers, and practitioners on how to maximize the well-being effects of engagement with the humanities in various contexts.

The work of gathering data to assess and advance the well-being value of the humanities will need to proceed carefully. It must not be over-reliant on one particular method of measurement. It must involve populations that are sufficiently large and diverse. It must include studies employing qualitative and quantitative research methods, cross-sectional and longitudinal designs, and correlational and causal approaches. It will also need to be well-grounded conceptually, to which end Louis Tay, Melissa Keith, and I have proposed a conceptual model to guide future empirical research.[20]

The expected benefits to the humanities from a strategic collaboration with the science of well-being extend beyond the generation of data in a variety of ways. First, such a collaboration could help humanities scholars learn more about scientific endeavors in this domain, thus making humanities scholarship more informed and more relevant to contemporary debates. Second, important new areas of endeavor could open up for humanities scholars, in which they could make important contributions toward defining well-being and its various constitutive constructs in ways that could deepen the scientific work being done in these areas. Third, scientific research may provide empirical ways of settling long-standing disputes in various humanities disciplines.

*Collaboration could help humanities scholars learn more about scientific endeavors in this domain, thus making humanities scholarship more informed and more relevant to contemporary debates*

The benefits to be had from a strategic collaboration between the humanities and the science of well-being would not flow simply in one direction; such a collaboration is also likely to provide significant benefits for science. First, humanities scholars could help situate the project of understanding well-being historically and show how people in various times and cultures have understood well-being. What is the range of perspectives that have been held regarding well-being? Are there commonalities that hold across different contexts? How might historical insights help us develop our own notions of well-being more comprehensively and effectively? Darrin McMahon's books *Happiness: A History*[21] and *Divine Fury: A History of Genius*[22] are outstanding examples of the way intellectual histories of well-being and related concepts can help shed light on current notions of human flourishing, help us avoid the dangers of presentism, and allow us to benefit from the perspectives of others in different times and places.

Second, informed by these historical and cultural perspectives, humanities scholars could conduct conceptual analyses of well-being and its constitutive elements. The more clearly we understand what we mean by these concepts, the more we can avoid merely verbal disputes about them.[23]

Third, humanities scholars could help scientists develop more robust empirical constructs to be tested. In the past several decades, scientists have sought to operationalize powerful notions such as hope, love, curiosity, gratitude, and optimism so as to render them amenable to empirical study. These scientific attempts have led to well-funded research programs whose results have been shared with the public. Yet few would argue that the constructs scientists are measuring have fully captured the meanings of the cultural terms they use.

Finally, this collaboration may advance scientific research on the cultivation of well-being in a variety of contexts. Scientists frequently use a number of techniques connected with the humanities in their research on well-being, and humanities scholars may be able to help them use these techniques even more effectively to enhance established or new interventions. Psychologists who develop interventions to help victims of trauma create narratives to facilitate post-traumatic growth, for example, may benefit from collaborating with humanities scholars skilled in the creation and interpretation of narrative. Psychologists studying creativity may benefit from collaboration with creative writing instructors to understand better how to create writing prompts to elicit creativity in measurable ways. Humanities scholars may also be able to help scientists create more effective and more easily distributable interventions for cultivating well-being. Culture is one of the richest resources available for the enhancement of well-being, and we are steeped in music, literature, art, and movies from infancy. Interventions that can tap into the depth of meaning in these experiences may help create shifts more readily than interventions that require more effortful and less familiar activities.

Thus, collaborating on well-being can bring important benefits to the science of well-being as well as to the humanities. Far *more* important, though, are the benefits it may bring to humanity. Students in colleges and universities are required to take humanities courses of various sorts. Many of these students see these courses as drudgeries, hoops that must be jumped through to reach their educational and vocational goals or simply to avoid getting into trouble. Being more explicit about the role the humanities can play in individual and social well-being could help these students connect more powerfully with the humanities and transform scholastic captives into captivated students of the humanities. A shift from extrinsic to intrinsic motivation among students would no doubt help them do better in their classes and quite possibly in their lives.

What would a eudaimonic transformation of the curriculum look like? Doubtless, much would remain the same. This should not be too surprising, given the claim that the humanities already are implicitly about well-being. Some things, however, would change as teachers and professors begin to ask explicitly how the courses they are teaching support the individual well-being of their students and the collective well-being of society. Instructors in critical thinking classes who currently look to blogs and letters to the editor for arguments to critique may decide to spend some time examining arguments that typically appear in students' self-talk. Teaching students how to apply their knowledge of fallacious reasoning to their own automatic thoughts is the foundation of cognitive therapy, and goes back to Stoic methods for cultivating the mind. For the students who take critical thinking classes each year, this could amount to a prophylactic against rising levels of depression, anxiety, and other mental illnesses.

Creative writing instructors might also add modules to their curricula based on research that shows the well-being value of expressive writing. James Pennebaker,[24] Laura King,[25] and others have found that writing about an important event in one's life over the course of several consecutive days can lead to various significant psychological and health benefits. Without changing their curricula dramatically, teachers could include an expressive writing module that would have the dual benefit of giving students an engrossing writing prompt and the possibility to benefit from several other well-being outcomes at the same time.

Theater instructors and directors might expand the scope of their work. Thespians are experts in character development; they are masters of creating characters on the stage. The skills they hone on the stage, however, are also directly relevant to the development of one's character off the stage. Such skills include a remarkable ability to regulate one's emotion and to be mindfully aware of one's own body and the effects different postures and movements can have on oneself and others. These skills can have an enormous effect on well-being. To take one example, Amy Cuddy, Associate Professor of Business Administration at the Harvard Business School, has found that holding certain postures (which she calls "power posing") for as little as two minutes can have significant physiological and psychological effects, increasing the ability to cope in stressful situations, leading to greater tolerance for risk, and resulting in increased performance on job interviews.[26] Clearly, the skills thespians learn are important for well-being in a variety of ways, yet we rarely think of connecting the skills necessary for developing characters on stage with the character development skills so important in life.

*If it is true that well-being is a central concern of human experience, then it behooves us to find ways of understanding, expressing, evaluating, sharing, and organizing that experience to support higher levels of flourishing for more people*

These are just a few of a plethora of possible ways courses in the humanities could be modified to realize more of their well-being potential. In addition to adding modules to specific classes, entire courses could be created with the goal of supporting the psychosocial well-being of students.[27]

CONCLUSION

If it is true that well-being is a central concern of human experience, then it behooves us to find ways of understanding, expressing, evaluating, sharing, and organizing that experience to support higher levels of flourishing for more people. One promising way of doing so is by means of a eudaimonic turn in the humanities. An explicit focus on well-being could help the humanities identify a unifying rationale, connect with the larger interests of society, and restore their balance. Furthermore, bringing the humanities together with the science of well-being could help advance empirical inquiry in this important area through greater conceptual nuance and clarity, more robust constructs, and a powerful new approach to positive interventions. Most importantly, however, a collaboration between the humanities and the science of well-being stands to benefit humanity by opening up new ways of transforming the quality of human experience in the interests of greater flourishing.

*Acknowledgement*

The research in this chapter was made possible through the support of a grant from Templeton Religion Trust. The opinions expressed in this publication are those of the authors and do not necessarily reflect the views of Templeton Religion Trust.

---

Notes

1. Aristotle, *Nicomachean Ethics*, trans. H. Rackham (Cambridge, MA: Harvard University Press, 1926), I.vii.8.
2. James O. Pawelski, "What is the Eudaimonic Turn?" in *The Eudaimonic Turn: Well-Being in Literary Studies,* eds. James O. Pawelski and D. J. Moores (Madison, NJ: Fairleigh Dickinson University Press), 1–26.
3. Louis Menand, "The Marketplace of Ideas," American Council of Learned Societies Occasional Paper No. 49, published 2001, http://archives.acls.org/op/49_Marketplace_of_Ideas.htm.
4. Geoffrey Galt Harpham, *The Humanities and the American Dream* (Chicago, IL: Chicago University Press, 2011).
5. James O. Pawelski and D. J. Moores, *The Eudaimonic Turn: Well-being in Literary Studies* (Madison, NJ: Fairleigh Dickinson University Press, 2013).
6. D. J. Moores et al., eds, *On Human Flourishing: An Anthology of Poetry* (Jefferson, NC: McFarland, 2015).
7. D. J. Moores, "The Eudaimonic Turn in Literary Studies," in *The Eudaimonic Turn: Well-being in Literary Studies,* eds. James O. Pawelski and D. J. Moores (Madison, NJ: Fairleigh Dickinson University Press, 2013), 26–63.
8. Rita Felski, *Uses of Literature* (Malden, MA: Blackwell, 2008).
9. Rita Felski, *The Limits of Critique* (Chicago: University of Chicago Press, 2015).
10. Felski, *Uses of Literature*, 22.
11. Ellen Charry, *God and the Art of Happiness* (Grand Rapids, MI: William B. Eerdmans, 2010).
12. Ibid.
13. Yale Center for Faith & Culture, "Theology of Joy & the Good Life," para. 1, http://faith.yale.edu/joy/about.
14. Martin E. P. Seligman, "The President's Address," *American Psychologist 53* (1999): 559–62.
15. Martin E. P. Seligman and Mihaly Csikszentmihalyi, "Positive Psychology: An Introduction," *American Psychologist* 55 (2000): 5–14.
16. Martin E. P. Seligman, *Authentic Happiness* (New York: Simon & Schuster, 2002).
17. James O. Pawelski, "Defining the 'Positive' in Positive Psychology: Part II. A Normative Analysis," *Journal of Positive Psychology* 11, no. 4 (2016): 357–365.
18. Gordon Hutner and Feisal G. Mohamed, "The Real Humanities Crisis is Happening at Public Universities," *New Republic,* September 6, 2013, https://newrepublic.com/article/114616/public-universities-hurt-humanities-crisis.
19. Brandon Busteed, "Is College Worth It?" *Gallup Business Journal,* August 27, 2013, http://businessjournal.gallup.com/content/164108/college-worth.aspx#1.
20. Louis Tay, James O. Pawelski, and Melissa Keith, "The Role of The Arts and Humanities in Human Flourishing: A Conceptual Model," (unpublished manuscript, 2015).
21. Darrin M. McMahon, *Happiness: A History* (New York: Atlantic Monthly Press, 2006).
22. Darrin M. McMahon, *Divine Fury: A history of Genius* (New York: Basic Books, 2013).
23. James O. Pawelski, "Defining the 'Positive' in Positive Psychology: Part I. A Descriptive Analysis," *Journal of Positive Psychology* 11, no. 4 (2016): 339–356; Pawelski, "Defining the 'Positive:' Part II."
24. James Pennebaker, "Writing About Emotional Experiences as a Therapeutic Process," *Psychological Science* 8 (1997): 162–6.
25. Laura King, "The Health Benefits of Writing About Life Goals," *Personality and Social Psychology Bulletin* 27 (2001), 798–807.
26. Dana Carney, Amy Cuddy, and Andy Yap, "Power Posing: Brief Nonverbal Displays Affect Neuroendocrine Levels and Risk Tolerance," *Psychological Science* 21 (2010): 1363–1368.
27. James O. Pawelski, "Character as Ethical Democracy: Definitions and Measures," *Journal of College and Character* 5, no. 9 (2004):1–43. doi:10.2202/1940–1639.1398.

# Honoring the Humanity of Our Students

*David Schoem*

EVERY STUDENT WE ENCOUNTER is a person of extraordinary intellectual, personal, social, and spiritual potential. Students on our campuses and in our classrooms are first and foremost our society's collective children: the living, breathing future of our nation and global society. They come to us as eager, active learners, seeking to find meaning in their own lives while hoping to enhance the life of our society and planet as highly advanced members of a humane civilization.[1]

Yet in our increasingly corporate institutions of higher education, we too often prioritize the value of the dollar above the value of the individual person, the power of technology above the power of teacher-student relationships, the importance of testing above the importance of learning, and the centrality of the brain above the human capacity of the whole person.[2] While some in higher education rightly look for new initiatives, new practices, new programs, and new technologies to improve learning and student success, others point to the longstanding roles of good teaching, good teachers, good learning environments and learning communities, and good teacher-student relationships.[3]

## TEACHING THE WHOLE STUDENT

I have learned first-hand from many wonderful university colleagues who bring a long-standing and dedicated commitment to good teaching. These teachers emphasize building strong relationships that often extend throughout a student's undergraduate years and beyond, and they prioritize mentoring students to help them realize their potential and lead informed lives of purpose and fulfillment. I have seen numerous examples of students whose lives have been transformed by good teachers. The worlds of these students have been opened up in classes filled with new perspectives and new ways of thinking. They have discovered their rich, evocative, personal voices from teachers who listened closely and carefully to them. These students have discovered their true passion in life through an opportunity to explore ideas and thoughts with their teachers. They have been encouraged and supported by teachers who believed in them and supported them. In some cases such support has provided students the resilience to overcome societal and institutional bias and prejudice based on their racial, religious, or sexual identities and to flourish in their personal and professional lives.

I witnessed the teacher who was able to successfully reach out to a student who stopped attending classes, wasn't leaving her room, and wasn't responding to exhortations from student life to seek counseling assistance. This professor, however, was able to get a response from the student, and together they walked to the counseling center to address her depression. Another faculty member I know stood by a student who was overwhelmed by the wealth, racial privilege, and entitlement of her classmates and became terribly insecure about her intellectual abilities and capacity in the classroom. The faculty member stood by this student throughout her college years, and she went on to become a leader on campus and later completed her PhD.

When one instructor learned that a racist flyer had been placed on the residence hall door of an African American student in his class, he met with the student and with his permission brought the issue to the attention of the entire seminar. The class lent their emotional and community support to the student, and again with the student's permission, they organized a campaign to support an inclusive community throughout the residence hall. Along the lines of the *Not in Our Town* campaigns,[4] every door in the residence hall soon had a flyer that affirmed student commitment to a racially inclusive and welcoming community.

> When faculty develop relationships with students, support them as whole beings, and touch their souls, students are motivated and inspired to learn, think critically, discover, question, succeed academically, graduate from college, and flourish personally, socially, spiritually, and civically

Many of us have seen the wide-eyed excitement of students in class or office hours who have discovered new perspectives or insights. They may have realized there is an intellectual door opening for them to a new field of study; or have re-imagined their lives and relationships in new, constructive dimensions; or have found new confidence in their own thinking and ability; or have discovered, even for the moment, a deeper level of meaning in their lives.

For other students, teachers took a special interest in them as future poets, doctors, musicians, business persons, conflict mediators, writers, parents, elected officials, lawyers, social workers, engineers, clergy members, or teachers, which resulted in their success. These teachers typically mentored their students not only during their classes, but also throughout their undergraduate studies and sometimes into their professional lives.

## THE IMPORTANCE OF TEACHER-STUDENT RELATIONSHIPS

Despite the current negative rhetoric directed toward teachers in our society,[5] scholars and educators are very familiar with the strong evidence that good teaching matters to students, student learning, and their persistence and graduation. Good teachers understand the importance of honoring their humanity and of giving genuine attention to each, individual student. They focus on student learning, and they also recognize that students learn best when they are valued as whole beings in the classroom and in the college. Treating students as just corporally detached intellects and consumers is not a winning strategy for learning or success. Our students come to the classroom and campus for learning, discovery, and critical inquiry with their whole lives and histories intact. When faculty develop relationships with students, support them as whole beings, and touch their souls, students are motivated and inspired to learn, think critically, discover, question, succeed academically, graduate from college, and flourish personally, socially, spiritually, and civically.[6]

Good teachers tend to be democratic, experiential, empathetic, and they encourage purposefulness in students' lives. They create a safe space (more recently dubbed a "brave" space"[7]) in their classrooms for reflection, active hope, dialogue, and perspective taking.

These instructors encourage integrative learning, active listening, meaningful engagement with people from different backgrounds, exploration of beliefs, and investigation of inequalities. They utilize integrative pedagogy and pedagogies of hope.[8]

## TEACHING AND LEARNING IN COMMUNITY

One of the ideal institutional models for focusing on the humanity of our students is the learning community, which is rooted in the traditional notion of the scholarly community. Structured as residential learning communities or curricular communities, these models at their best integrate the curricular and co-curricular aspects of the college experience. They seek to provide, in community, the essential support for learning deeply, wrestling with ideas, finding meaning and purpose in life, and building close faculty-student relationships.[9]

Community is a foundational principle in the literature on schooling and learning,[10] yet it is often set aside as an organizing principle as colleges and universities become larger and more corporate. In today's academy, the value of the individual star and the prize winner, be it the faculty member or student, too often takes precedence over the learning community. Fierce competition tears apart trust and collaboration among students and faculty, and courses that are graded on the curve to insure failure wreak havoc on any sense of common purpose in study and learning. On large campuses without learning communities, the plague of social isolation and anonymity works to build a sense of impersonality and devaluing of life and humanity itself. The current popularity of the *I'm Shmacked* YouTube videos[11] illustrates the anomie of drunken optics and the wasteland of what should be the rich, vibrant, life-affirming community on the college campus.

I have worked with many learning communities throughout my career: studying in one, directing others, overseeing a campus network, and consulting with many others. These learning communities consistently invigorate faculty teaching and scholarship, engage students in learning and meaningful relationships, and build community within the larger campus. In recent years I have worked with the Michigan Community Scholars Program,[12] a residential learning community that focuses on deep learning, community building, meaningful service learning and community engagement, intercultural under-standing, intergroup relations, and dialogue. The program mission statement reads in part, "Faculty, staff, and students seek to model a just, diverse, and democratic community, and wish to make a difference throughout their lives as participants and leaders involved in local, national and global communities."[13]

In its emphasis on diversity, the program has in recent years achieved a balance of about 50 percent students of color and international students, including close to 30 percent underrepresented students of color and 50 percent white students. Each week, the program's Intergroup Relations Council holds formal dialogues or more informal hot topic lounge discussions that are led by trained student facilitators.

Although students come from a variety of neighborhoods and schools across the country, their common interest in making a difference in the world helps them to bridge their different backgrounds and experiences and to engage thoughtfully and energetically with one another. They feed off one another's shared commitments and fuel a palpable energy of ideas and activities in their living space in the residence hall. Students take a common course together that focuses on the central themes of the program and provides advice to help smooth the transition to college. They also select a small enrollment, first-year seminar and a community service learning course from a menu of courses taught by faculty who are committed to the program's mission and typically teach in classrooms in the residence halls. Students take their learning from the classrooms back to the corridors of their living spaces and continue their learning in informal discussions and interpersonal relationships on a 24/7 basis.

These learning communities have their foundation in the Oxford-Cambridge model of close faculty-student relationships, tutorials, dining together, and common social and athletic clubs that later shaped the Harvard-Yale House and Residential Colleges communities.[14] They later expanded their purview to emphasize the development of engaged democratic communities as conceptualized by Alexander Meiklejohn at the University of Wisconsin.[15] These learning communities emphasize the same notion of deep learning in community, a new, inclusive vision of a diverse democracy, close faculty-student relationships, and a strong sense of value in the humanity and worth of each individual student, teacher, and staff member of the community.

## Meaning Making and Healthy Learning Environments

The learning environment is of considerable importance in terms of a student's personal, social, and academic success. Student mental health issues on college campuses have reached concerning rates,[16] which has led some in higher education to worry about epidemic levels of stress, anxiety, and depression.[17] In addition, campus climate issues of racial incivility, micro-aggression, outright racism, and levels of sexual assault and rape obviously create unsafe environments that are hostile to learning and academic success and to personal, social, and intergroup growth and development.

Many campuses, in response, have increased the budgets of their counseling offices, safety departments, health services, and in some cases student life diversity staff to support students who face mental health concerns, hostile climates, or who have been sexually assaulted. Campuses also have begun to think about the hard work of addressing the broader educational, social, and structural issues that serve as the foundation of these problems. They have instituted new orientation programs, provided ongoing support and educational service centers, and given public voice to the need for and the importance of a healthy and safe campus climate.[18] These issues are deep-seated, however, and will require far more sustained effort to achieve the kind of campuses at which students from all different social identities feel and experience the same sense of ownership, empowerment, comfort, and safety as do students from dominant social identity groups.

With regard to mental health issues, however, the addition of more counselors only serves to showcase the heavy volume and intensity of problems that students face rather than to address the root causes. While mental health issues are certainly not the exclusive domain of college campuses, the stress level caused by high-pressure, high-stakes exams, weed-out courses, and intensive competition on every front creates conditions that intensify mental health issues such as stress, anxiety and depression. Giving students an opportunity to pet a therapy dog one day prior to final exams may give some momentary comfort, but it does little to ameliorate the underlying, daily, stress-inducing conditions that negatively affect the lives of many students on too many college campuses.

If we truly believe in the worth and humanity of each of our students rather than thinking of them as customers or consumers in a large corporate enterprise, we must rethink how we educate our students, the attention we give to the learning environment in our classes and academic departments, and the overall climate we foster for students from all social identity backgrounds. How do we possibly justify requiring our students to endure four years of high-stress learning, hostile social climates, and potentially violent campus life in order to receive college degrees? I know we would not tolerate such an approach for people we love and respect as extraordinary individuals seeking to learn and find meaning and purpose in their lives.

## How Current Practice De-values the Humanity of Our Students

For too long in higher education, we have tolerated, rewarded, and made as the standard the opposite of honoring the humanity of our students. Rather than taking responsibility for student learning, we enroll students in large classes with little faculty-student contact. We honor the grandiose lecture performed before hundreds of students. We put on a pedestal and promote faculty who are aloof from students or are too busy doing more important research to spend time with their students. In doing so, we deny many otherwise outstanding faculty the opportunity to be good teachers and teach the whole student because the professional rewards lie elsewhere.[19] At many colleges, the standing joke is that the campus teaching award is the kiss of death because those who receive it are certain not to be granted tenure or a future on that campus.[20] As a result, we have created a generation of passive and stressed-out student learners who look to be entertained and strive to get the grade and credential rather than a rich education. *Will this be on the test?* and *Why didn't I get an A?* are the basis for too many faculty-student interactions.[21]

> *How do we possibly justify requiring our students to endure four years of high-stress learning, hostile social climates, and potentially violent campus life in order to receive college degrees?*

Even more harmful, particularly in introductory STEM and economics classes, are the high-stakes tests given as early as the first semester in college. Typically given in large lecture classes, these tests have a curved grading system that guarantees failure for a certain percentage of students. In guaranteeing the failure of students in weed-out classes, even in some of the most selective institutions, we unnecessarily destroy student dreams and opportunities for learning and future professional lives, and those weeded-out are disproportionately women and underrepresented students of color. Higher education does the sorting job for industry rather than focus on its own enterprise: educating students.[22]

I have seen far too many cases of students who have been harmed by the weed-out, test-oriented, big lecture course.

- A student sits in my office, distraught. Her dream is to be a doctor, but she tells me that she is failing introductory chemistry. She is very bright, studies hard, and goes to office hours, but the 600-student lecture class with high-stakes exams doesn't work for her. She came to college with an excellent high school profile and the highest hopes and ambitions, but things are not working out as planned. She meets weekly with a therapist at the campus counseling office.
- Another student comes to my office. She tells me that she just got her grade back from her first exam in introductory economics. She is crushed. Her dream is to gain admission to the university's business school. But as bright and hardworking as she

is, she received a D on her exam. The class is graded on a curve, so there is a pre-determined institutional decision that a certain percentage of students will get grades of D and E. She tells me how hard she studied and how bad she feels. She's embarrassed to tell her friends or her parents. I recommend that she get a personal tutor, which has become a commonplace practice for students in this class who can afford this expensive but essential help.

These cases represent the tip of the iceberg. Every fall semester I have more of these interactions with distraught students. Introductory chemistry, economics, and math are often the triggers. Although I occasionally have this discussion with a male student, in most cases female students are most willing to express their pain, and underrepresented students of color are well-represented with white female students. A smaller number of male students share similar stories but usually not until a semester or a year after the fact. They relate the same disappointment and distress after their hidden tears have dried.

What's the lesson here? Is it one of students not working hard enough or overestimating their abilities in highly competitive college classes? Is it one of students who are ill-prepared by high school for demanding college standards? Is it one of students who do not know how to study or manage their time for college learning?

While there is some truth in all of these explanations, I am convinced that the dominant story is one of inadequate and ineffective approaches to teaching that are rewarded through tenure and promotion structures that minimize the importance of teaching and through financial savings from oversized classes that come at the cost of teacher-student relationships, student learning, and in too many cases, broken lives. It is a story of universities that have taken on the cutthroat business of industry by using introductory courses, originally designed to engage students in learning about and experiencing new fields of study, to lop off or lay off those who get low grades. Rather than being about teaching and learning, higher education becomes a blunt instrument for gatekeeping and maintaining the social inequalities and stratification in society. Unfortunately, despite all the rhetoric, higher education continues to privilege the most wealthy and educationally advantaged white students while reinforcing the inequality of society and victimizing women and especially underrepresented students of color.[23]

Yes it is true that some students overestimate their ability, some come underprepared for college-level classes, and some don't yet know how to properly study and manage their time. And I have had ample personal experience with the view of many faculty that student failure in these introductory courses is the student's fault and that their courses serve to separate out the worthy students. I couldn't disagree more. Both the analysis of why students fail in these classes and the approach to teaching are terribly flawed.

Unfortunately, today with the multitude of technological advances and opportunities available to enhance good teaching, unless we are very careful and intentional, we stand on the precipice of multiplying the wrongs of our denigration of teaching. Massive open online courses, commonly known as MOOCs, are currently presented to higher education as a way to offer a college education to the masses at a very affordable price. Absent in the conversation is any mention of good teaching. We are entering a new era of the super-star lecturer who performs for and entertains an online audience comprised of thousands, even tens of thousands, of students and uses the latest technologies without any in-person contact, any meaningful teacher-student relationships, or any nod to the value of good teaching and good teachers. For low income students, including many underrepresented students of color, this new approach to teaching in higher education is a recipe for disaster. Many of these students have in too many cases struggled through underserving public high school educations and have gotten by only with intelligence, grit, persistence, and the inspiration and commitment of a caring teacher or mentor.[24] Student failure will be attributed to the student, and blame will be plentiful. As is the case with community colleges, America's political and educational elite will tell its low income families that they were given every opportunity to learn and advance themselves, that they had the most renowned scholars in the nation as their lecturers, and still they failed.[25]

Learning analytics is another popular tool whose leading advocates seem to be following a similar pattern. Data culled from years of college classes provides clear evidence of the longstanding inequitable performance outcomes across race and gender in introductory STEM courses taught in the traditional lecture-testing format.[26] Yet it is very disappointing that rather than insist that faculty change their teaching approach in these classes to address the inequity, the first innovation to come from the learning analytics movement has been a new, high-priced, robotic counseling reform known as *e-coaching*—no human contact necessary.[27]

I want to be clear that my criticism is not of the internet, data, or technology as opportunities to enhance student learning. It is, rather, the way technology is being imagined and used as an excuse not to demand more from faculty to make substantial, non-trivial, changes in their approaches to large, introductory STEM and economics classes and as a cheap replacement to remove good teachers from the classroom and from our students.[28] What students really want and need are some human teachers with whom they can learn and to whom they can relate.

*What students really want and need are some human teachers with whom they can learn and to whom they can relate*

SEIZING THE PLATFORM FOR HONORING THE HUMANITY OF OUR STUDENTS

Students who have arrived at our institutions of higher education deserve access to outstanding teaching and teachers who will support their learning and development so they can grow and flourish as individuals and as active, contributing citizens of our diverse democracy. Such teaching and teachers are indeed present right now on our campuses, but they work against the tide of institutional structures and rewards that place greater value on other activities.

Ultimately, it will take a reconceptualization of higher education's approach to students, the learning/scholarly community, teaching and learning, and teacher-student relationships. My hope is that we will recognize that our students are whole people and that they represent our collective humanity. The primary goal of higher education should not be limited to job training for industry and the corporate world with a narrow and restrictive vision of students as consumers and customers on the path to becoming future employees. We should elevate our vision to see that all of our students hold the capacity to realize our society's full humanity and our role is to help them discover meaning and purpose for their own lives as they study and learn with bright, caring, creative teachers and mentors.

## NOTES

1. See Alexander W. Astin, Helen S. Astin, and Jennifer A. Linholm, *Cultivating the Spirit: How College Can Enhance Students' Inner Lives* (San Francisco, CA: Jossey-Bass, 2011); Arthur W. Chickering, Jon C. Dalton, and Liesa Stamm, *Encouraging Authenticity and Spirituality in Higher Education* (San Francisco, CA: Jossey-Bass, 2006); Raine Eisler, *Tomorrow's Children: A Blueprint For Partnership Education in the 21st Century* (Boulder, CO: Westview Press, 2001); Robert J. Nash and Michelle C. Murray, *Helping College Students Find Purpose: The Campus Guide to Meaning-Making* (San Francisco, CA: Jossey-Bass, 2010); Parker J. Palmer, *The Courage to Teach: Exploring the Landscape of a Teacher's Life* (San Francisco, CA: Jossey-Bass, 2007); Robert D. Putnam, *Our Kids: The American Dream in Crisis* (New York: Simon and Schuster, 2015).

2. See Anthony Cody, *The Educator and The Oligarch: A Teacher Challenges The Gates Foundation* (New York: Garn Press, 2014); William Deresiewicz, *Excellent Sheep: The Miseducation of the American Elite and The Way To A Meaningful Life* (New York: Free Press, 2014); Henry A. Giroux, *Education and the Crisis of Pubic Values: Challenging the Assault on Teachers, Students, and Public Education* (New York: Peter Lang Publishing, 2012); Michael Fabricant and Michelle Fine, *Charter Schools and the Corporate Makeover of Public Education: What's at Stake?* (New York: Teachers College Press, 2012); Diane Ravich, *Reign of Error: The Hoax of the Privatization Movement and the Danger to America's Public Schools* (New York: Alfred Knopf, 2013).

3. See Paul Goodman, *The Community of Scholars* (New York: Vintage Books, 1962); Parker J. Palmer and Arthur Zajonc, *The Heart of Higher Education: A Call To Renewal* (San Francisco, CA: Jossey-Bass, 2010); Fred M. Newman and Donald W. Oliver, "Education and Community," *Harvard Educational Review* 37, no.1 (1967): 61–6.

4. Not in Our Town, accessed January 16, 2016, https://www.niot.org/about.

5. See Ravitch, *Reign of Error*; Karl Weber, *Waiting for Superman: How We Can Save America's Failing Public Schools* (New York: Public Affairs, 2010).

6. See Linda Darling-Hammond, *The Flat World of Education: How America's Commitment to Equity Will Determine Our Future* (New York: Teachers College Press, 2010); Andrew Delbanco, *College: What It Was, Is, And Should Be* (Princeton, NJ: Princeton University Press, 2014); Sonia Nieto, *Why We Teach Now* (New York: Teachers College Press, 2014); Sonia Nieto, *What Keeps Teachers Going?* (New York: Teachers College Press, 2003); Sharon Daloz Parks and Laurent A. Parks Daloz, *Common Fire: Leading Lives of Commitment in a Complex World* (Boston, MA: Beacon, 1997).

7. See, Brian Arao and Kristi Clemens, "From Safe Spaces to Brave Places: A New Way to Frame Dialogue Around Diversity and Social Justice," in *The Art of Effective Facilitation: Reflections from Social Justice Educators*, ed. Lisa M. Landreman (Sterling, VA: Stylus Publishing LLC, 2013): 135–150.

8. David Schoem, "Transforming Undergraduate Education: Moving Beyond Distinct Undergraduate Initiatives," *Change Magazine* 34, No. 6 (2002): 50–55.

9. See Ernest L. Boyer, *College: The Undergraduate Experience in America* (New York: Harper and Row, 1997); Kenneth A. Feldman and Theodore M. Newcomb, *The Impact of College on Students* (San Francisco, CA: Jossey-Bass, 1969); Faith Gabelnick et al., eds., *Learning Communities: Creating Connections Among Students, Faculty, and Disciplines* (San Francisco, CA: Jossey-Bass, 1990); Richard Guarasci and Grant H. Cornwell, *Democratic Education in an Age of Difference* (San Francisco, CA: Jossey-Bass, 1997); Jody Levine Laufgraben and Nancy S. Shapiro, *Sustaining and Improving Learning Communities* (San Francisco, CA: Jossey-Bass, 2004).

10. See Jacqueline Ancess, *Beating the Odds: High Schools as Communities of Commitment* (New York: Teachers College Press, 2003); Peter Block, *Community: The Structure of Belonging* (San Francisco, CA: Berrett-Koehler Publishers, 2009); Goodman, *Community of Scholars*; Newman and Oliver, "Education and Community;" Palmer and Zajonc, *Heart of Higher Education*.

11. ImShmacked TV, YouTube, accessed January 16, 2016, https://www.youtube.com/user/ImShmackedTV.

12. See David Schoem, "Modeling a Diverse and Democratic America: The Michigan Community Scholars Program," *About Campus* 10, no. 5 (2005): 18-23; Joseph A. Galura et al., *Engaging the Whole of Service-Learning, Diversity, and Learning Communities* (Ann Arbor, MI: University of Michigan, 2004).

13. University of Michigan, Michigan Community Scholars Program, "Mission, History, Goals & Highlights," accessed January 16, 2016, https://www.lsa.umich.edu/mcsp/aboutus/missionhistorygoalshighlights.

14. Mark Ryan, *A Collegiate Way of Living: Residential Colleges and a Yale Education* (New Haven, CT: John Edwards College. Yale University, 2001).

15. Adam R. Nelson, *Education and Democracy: The Meaning of Alexander Meiklejohn, 1872–1964* (Madison, WI: University of Wisconsin Press, 2001).

16. Jake New, "Fragile Mental Health," *Inside Higher Ed,* February 5, 2015, https://www.insidehighered.com/news/2015/02/05/incoming-students-emotional-health-all-time-low-survey-says.

17. See Lynn E. Swaner, "Linking Engaged Learning, Student Mental Health and Well-being, and Civic Development: A Review of the Literature," *Liberal Education* 93, no. 1 (2007); https://www.aacu.org/publications-research/periodicals/linking-engaged-learning-student-mental-health-and-well-being-and; Richard Kadison and Theresa Foy DiGeronimo, *College of the Overwhelmed: The Campus Mental Health Crisis and What to do About It* (San Francisco, CA: Jossey-Bass, 2004).

18. Katherine Rosman, "On the Front Line of Campus Sexual Misconduct," *The New York Times*, September 26, 2015, http://www.nytimes.com/2015/09/27/fashion/on-the-front-line-of-campus-sexual-misconduct.html?_r=0.

19. Dorothy E. Finnegan and Zelda F. Gamson, "Disciplinary Adaptations to Research Culture in Comprehensive Institutions." *Review of Higher Education* 19, no. 2 (1995):144–77.

20. Nancy Van Note Chism, "Teaching Awards: What Do They Award?" *Journal of Higher Education* 77, no. 4 (2006): 589–617.

21. Alfie Kohn, *What Does It Mean to be Well-Educated?* (Boston, MA: Beacon Press, 2004).

22. Joel Spring, *The Sorting Machine: National Educational Policy Since 1945* (New York: David McKay, 1976).

23. Samuel Bowles and Herbert Gintis, *Schooling in Capitalist America: Economic Reform and the Contradictions of Economic Life* (Chicago, IL: Haymarket Books, 1977).

24. See Steve Kolowich, "Doubts about MOOCs Continue to Rise, Survey Finds," *Chronicle of Higher Education*, January 15, 2014, http://chronicle.com/article/Doubts-About-MOOCs-Continue-to/144007/; Thomas Leddy, "Are MOOCs Good for Students?" *Boston Review*, June, 14, 2013, http://bostonreview.net/us/are-moocs-good-students.

25. Burton R. Clark, "The 'Cooling Out' Function in Higher Education," *American Journal of Sociology* 65, no. 6 (1960): 569–76.

26. Tim McKay, "Learning Analytics at U-M: An Update and Agenda for 2013–15," University of Michigan, Center for Research on learning and Teaching, September 13, 2013, http://www.crlt.umich.edu/sites/default/files/resource_files/LATF%20SLAM%20Kickoff%202013_0.pdf.

27. Mary C. Wright et al., "Better than Expectations: Using Learning Analytics to Promote Student Success in Gateway Science," *Change* 46, no. 1 (2014): http://www.changemag.org/Archives/Back%20Issues/2014/January-February%202014/better_abstract.html.

28. Sherry Turkle, "Talk to Me: How to Teach in an Age of Distraction" *Chronicle of Higher Education,* October 2, 2015, http://chronicle.com/article/How-to-Teach-in-an-Age-of/233515; Susan Pinker, "Can Students Have Too Much Tech?" *The New York Times,* January 30, 2015, http://www.nytimes.com/2015/01/30/opinion/can-students-have-too-much-tech.html.

# Well-Being and Being Safe:
# Do Guns Change Social Interactions?
# A Missouri Case Study[1]

*Jonathan M. Metzl*

MISSOURI IS POISED TO BECOME the latest state to allow guns into college classrooms. The Republican state senate is currently (as of March, 2016) finalizing deliberations on a bill that, if passed, will remove restrictions on carrying concealed weapons on college campuses across the state.[2] For supporters, allowing students, professors, and staff to carry weapons to school is a matter of safety and self-defense. "Making good people helpless doesn't make bad people harmless," claimed Republican State Senator Bob Dixon during Senate hearings on campus-carry legislation.[3] Meanwhile, critics point to data suggesting that college campuses are already among the safest places in the United States for college-age persons precisely because these campuses function as gun-free zones.[4]

The specter of loaded firearms in the context of college classrooms raises particular concerns[5] in no small part because the dynamics of learning[6] often depend on professors challenging students to step beyond their comfort zones and because students and professors engage in daily high-stakes negotiations about matters such as grades, attendance, and participation. But beneath these concerns lies a broader set of questions: do guns change the ways that people interact with each other? And does the presence of firearms in sites of learning change the types of thinkers, doers, and citizens that colleges and universities aim to produce?

The effect of guns on people's daily interactions emerged as a central theme in interviews I conducted with everyday Missourians when I was in the state to talk to people about legislation that paved the way for campus carry. During the past several years, the Missouri legislature overturned regulations on the open-carry of firearms,[7] lowered the legal age to carry a concealed gun to 19, and repealed requirements for comprehensive background checks and purchase permits. Armed citizens soon appeared with increasing prominence in previously gun-free public spaces, forcing non-armed citizens to adapt.

For instance, I met a man named John Steen who now thinks twice about shopping at Sam's Club. Steen, a 66-year old Vietnam veteran who works in Kansas City, used to stop by the wholesale megastore on his way home from his job as a home health care provider. But that was before he saw armed white men stroll through the aisles exerting what gun proponents describe as their "unalienable" rights to carry firearms into public spaces including retail stores.[8] For Steen and other African Americans in Kansas City, the result was often intimidation: "I see white guys and their sons walking around Sam's Club, Walmart, and other places where we shop, strolling with guns on their hips like it's the wild west," he told me. "They're trying to be all macho, like they have power because of their guns, walking down the aisles. It just makes me . . . stay away."

Ironically, Missouri used to have among the strictest gun laws in the nation, including a requirement that handgun buyers undergo background checks in person at sheriffs' offices before obtaining gun permits.[9] But starting in 2007, an increasingly conservative legislature and citizenry relaxed limitations governing practically every aspect of buying, owning, and carrying guns. Concealed carry led to calls for open carry, which then led to Amendment 5, which effectively negated the rights of cities or towns to pass or enforce practically any form of gun control.[10]

What followed was a state of affairs that was referred to in *The New York Times* as a "natural experiment" to test whether more guns led to more safety and less crime.[11] Instead, according to researchers, the opposite occurred: gun deaths soared when it became easier for people to buy and carry firearms in the state. A team of researchers led by Daniel Webster, Director of the Johns Hopkins Center for Gun Policy and Research, analyzed extensive crime data from Missouri and found that the state's 2007 repeal of the permit-to-purchase handgun law was associated with a twenty-five percent increase in firearm homicides rates. Between 2008 and 2014 the Missouri gun homicide rate rose to forty-seven percent higher than the national average.[12]

*The specter of loaded firearms in the context of college classrooms raises particular concerns in no small part because the dynamics of learning often depend on professors challenging students to step beyond their comfort zones and because students and professors engage in daily high-stakes negotiations about matters such as grades, attendance, and participation*

Missouri's startling rates of gun death made national news.[13] Yet beyond the headlines, many Missouri residents with whom I spoke worried that the Show Me State's famous neighborliness and hospitality might give way to interactions based in trepidation and mistrust. For example, Missourians like Steen worried about the ways that guns heightened racial tensions. And indeed, the implications of white citizens brandishing guns in mixed race settings played out *writ large* in downtown St. Louis when, after the passage of Amendment 5 and just months before protests began in nearby Ferguson, white Missouri open-carry advocates paraded through the streets waving handguns, long guns, and assault rifles.[14]

For Rev. Dr. Cassandra Gould, events such as these illustrate a double standard through which society codes white gun owners as "protectors" and black gun owners as "threats." As Pastor of Quinn Chapel A.M.E. Church in Jefferson City, Gould led an intense debate among her congregants after the shooting in Charleston that yielded a decision to ban guns in their house of worship. For Gould, "even though I want us to be protected, I can't escape the fact that these are the same guns that are oppressing communities of color in our state."[15] This disparity in the way certain races are perceived in relation to weapons is one that may also be salient to consider within the realm of higher education—particularly as more institutions seek to reimagine their practices to be more equitable and culturally-sensitive.

Some Missouri parents fret about firearms when their children play. In a state in which there are now virtually no remaining laws prohibiting the carrying or owning of guns, Missouri now leads the nation in accidental shootings by toddlers—instances where young children find unlocked guns and accidentally discharge them.[16] In response, the Missouri chapter of Moms Demand Action signed onto a BE SMART campaign to promote safety steps, including training parents to secure guns in their homes and ask about proper firearm storage before dropping children off at a friend's house.[17] As Becky Morgan, Missouri Chapter Lead for Moms puts it, "This is a new step to parents are taking to look out for our children's safety. We already ask about food allergies, pet allergies and pools. Now we ask if firearms are in the home, are they stored properly out of children's reach?"[18]

Thoughts about gun proliferation even affect exchanges in the halls of power that passed gun legislation in the first place. Democratic Missouri State Representative Stacey Newman worries that many legislators and their staff carry concealed weapons during heated debates on the House floor: "With new laws, capital security can no longer ask lawmakers to check their firearms at the door," she explained. "And I often find it quite unnerving that the people I'm working with or arguing against might well be carrying secret guns during our legislative sessions"[19]—a sentiment relevant to, perhaps, a safeness needed in academic environments in which risk taking and active discussion can thrive. To be sure, notions of an armed society are precisely what many pro-gun-rights Missourians and legislators envision and support. Linda Hopkins, owner of Smokin' Guns BBQ in North Kansas City, welcomes customers who carry concealed weapons and feels far more angered by "food prices and intrusive government regulations."[20] And Missouri was recently cited in *Guns & Ammo* as a top state for gun owners due to legislation allowing concealed carry: "Known once as one of the last holdouts against CCW, the Show Me State is now ahead of the curve when it comes to gun rights."[21]

But a number of the Missourians with whom I spoke felt otherwise, and their concerns seemed to provide broader context for questions of self-other relationships, power relations, safety, and conflict resolution that lie at the core of debates about allowing guns into college classrooms. Newman, the state representative, particularly worries about the effect that allowing guns will have on the "psyches of our children," who go to college to learn and grow in a safe environment and instead may soon encounter classrooms where guns and armed confrontations remain "constant possibilities." For Newman the issue hits home: her daughter attends grad school at the University of Kansas, a campus that already allows concealed firearms: "As a parent this is just my worst nightmare."[22]

Meanwhile Steen, the home health provider, has seen enough of guns in his lifetime. "I was in Vietnam with the US Military, I saw what it means to draw a gun and shoot another person, it's devastating. Trust me . . . most of these people have no idea."[23]

---

NOTES

1. Editor's note: Beyond the cultivation of curricular opportunities, pedagogical innovations, and the multiple structural ways in which a campus culture facilitates learning and well-being, there is the question of what else the campus must be and support if it truly is to attend to its full purposes. Is safeness an undeniable, crucial element of the campus culture? Must an institution committed to well-being recognize that its constituencies feel and be secure? By introducing an actual current prevailing challenge at play in the state of Missouri—the permissibility of guns, even concealed, on campus—Dr. Metzel's provocation opens and provokes consideration of what being safe might mean in relationship to a culture of well-being and learning. The directions of subsequent discussion could be as diverse as judicial interpretation of the right to bear arms to the exploration of what institutions can require as part of any contract for student admission, to the employment of faculty and staff. Beyond those discussions, the provocation could open an even broader window to what being a safe environment can mean. Does it clarify the negotiation of campus judicial policies and their harmony with

criminal law? Does it speak to whether there ought to be trigger notices to alert students to materials that would negatively affect their senses of being safe? These topics are high on the list for anyone considering what a supportive environment for well-being must be. Insights and practices to help guide thinking through these issues and related ones can be found in several earlier essays in *Well-Being and Higher Education* (see for example the essay by Barry Schwartz) and on both the National Association of Student Personnel Administrators (NASPA) and the National Association of College and University Attorneys (NACUA) web sites.

A version of this article first appeared in The Conversation: Jonathan M. Metzl, "Are Looser Gun Laws Changing the Social Fabric of Missouri?" The Conversation, March 10, 2016, https://theconversation.com/are-looser-gun-laws-changing-the-social-fabric-of-missouri-55800.

2. Jon Swedien, "Sen. Dixon Files Bill to Allow Concealed Carry On Missouri Campuses," *Springfield New Leader*, December 2, 2015, http://www.news-leader.com/story/news/politics/2015/12/02/sen-dixon-files-bill-allow-concealed-carry-missouri-campuses/76684966/.

3. Mallory Daily, "Bill to Allow Concealed Carry on Missouri Campuses Sparks Strong Reactions For and Against," St. Louis Public Radio, January 27, 2016, http://news.stlpublicradio.org/post/bill-allow-concealed-carry-missouri-campuses-sparks-strong-reactions-and-against.

4. Armed Campuses, "Guns on Campus' Laws for Public Colleges and Universities," accessed April 2, 2016 from http://www.armedcampuses.org/.

5. Rio Fernandes, "A PowerPoint Slide Advises Professors to Alter Teaching to Pacify Armed Students," *The Chronicle of Higher Education*, February 24, 2016, http://chronicle.com/article/A-PowerPoint-Slide-Advises/235418.

6. Matthew Watkins, "UT Architecture Dean Cites Campus Carry as a Reason for Departure," *The Texas Tribune*, February 25, 2016, https://www.texastribune.org/2016/02/25/ut-architecture-dean-cites-campus-carry-reason-dep/.

7. Tara Dodrill, "Open Carry Ban Overturned in Missouri," *Inquisitr*, November 11, 2014, http://www.inquisitr.com/1602089/open-carry-ban-overturned-in-missouri/.

8. Danny Wicentowski, "Gun Rights Supporters Head to Gateway Arch, Citygarden to Test Missouri's New Gun Laws," *Riverfront Times*, October 20, 2014, http://www.riverfronttimes.com/newsblog/2014/10/20/gun-rights-supporters-head-to-gateway-arch-citygarden-to-test-missouris-new-gun-laws-updates.

9. Sabrina Tavernice, "In Missouri, Fewer Gun Restrictions and More Gun Killings," *The New York Times*, December 21, 2015, http://www.nytimes.com/2015/12/22/health/in-missouri-fewer-gun-restrictions-and-more-gun-killings.html?_r=0.

10. Ballotpedia, "Missouri Right to Bear Arms, Amendment 5 (August 2014)," Accessed April 2, 2016, https://ballotpedia.org/Missouri_Right_to_Bear_Arms,_Amendment_5_(August_2014).

11. Tavernice, "In Missouri," para. 3.

12. Daniel Webster, Cassandra Kercher Crifasi, and Jon S. Vernick, "Effects of the Repeal of Missouri's Handgun Purchaser Licensing Law on Homicides," *Journal of Urban Health* 91, no. 2 (2014): 293-302.

13. Tavernice, "In Missouri."

14. Wicentowski, "Gun Rights Supporters."

15. Jonathan M. Metzl, "Are Looser Gun Laws Changing the Social Fabric of Missouri?" *The Conversation*, March 10, 2016, https://theconversation.com/are-looser-gun-laws-changing-the-social-fabric-of-missouri-55800.

16. See Christopher Ingraham, "People are Getting Shot by Toddlers on a Weekly Basis This Year," *The Washington Post Wonkblog*, October 14, 2015, https://www.washingtonpost.com/news/wonk/wp/2015/10/14/people-are-getting-shot-by-toddlers-on-a-weekly-basis-this-year/ and Mary Sanchez, "Why the gun lobby wants to arm children," *The Kansas City Star*, February 26, 2016, http://www.kansascity.com/opinion/opn-columns-blogs/mary-sanchez/article62741097.html.

17. Adrian Pelliccia, "Everytown and Moms Demand Action #NotAnAccident Index Finds at Least Five Unintentional Child Shootings in Missouri in 2015, Moms Demand Action, May 14, 2015, http://momsdemandaction.org/in-the-news/everytown-and-moms-demand-action-notanaccident-index-finds-at-least-five-unintentional-child-shootings-in-missouri-in-2015/ and Everytown for Gun Safety Support Fund, BE SMART, Join the Campaign to Reduce Child Gun Deaths," Accessed April 2, 2016, http://besmartforkids.org/.

18. Metzl, "Are Looser Gun Laws," para. 24.

19. Ibid, para. 29.

20. Ibid, para. 32.

21. Keith Wood, "Best States for Gun Owners 2015," *Guns & Ammo*, July 21, 2015, http://www.gunsandammo.com/network-topics/culture-politics-network/best-states-for-gun-owners-2015/.

22. Metzl, para. 32.

23. Ibid, para. 33.

# 26
PROVOCATION

# Well-Being and the
# Community College Mission

*Dr. Amanda Hyberger*

*"In the coming years, jobs requiring at least an associate degree are projected to grow twice as fast as jobs requiring no college experience. We will not fill those jobs—or keep those jobs on our shores—without the training offered by community colleges."*
—President Barack Obama[1]

IN AN INCREASINGLY COMPETITIVE world economy, America's economic strength depends upon the education and skills of its workers. To meet this need, President Obama set two national goals: by 2020, America will once again have the highest proportion of college graduates in the world and community colleges will produce an additional five million graduates.[2]

The urgent need for an increasingly educated workforce and the important role that community colleges play in maintaining America's preeminence in the world are indisputable, but for many of us who have dedicated our lives to community colleges, there is undeniable fear in this realization. Although eager to assume this role, the inability to find easy solutions for closing the degree attainment gap at our institutions has profound implications to our nation's future. On one hand, community colleges are gaining ground in terms of academic respect, including increased appreciation for the long-standing focus of faculty on teaching, learning, and classroom innovation. On the other hand, there is increasing pressure to produce similar results in the same timeframe but with fewer resources than universities with entrance requirements.

In many ways community colleges themselves have helped bring about this current impasse. Exceedingly successful at creating open-access institutions, community colleges now face a seemingly impossible task in this new era of accountability. We have multi-faceted faculty who teach fully on-line, hybrid, and ground courses as well as those who teach early morning, evening, and weekend courses. We have excessively lenient admissions policies that have fostered last-minute registration and inadequate preparation for the first day of classes. We administer our own placement tests and summer-bridge courses that allow multiple opportunities to avoid remedial courses. We accept late work, partial work, and even poor quality work at times in hopes of inspiring, graduating, and improving the lives of our students. Most importantly, our student population is naturally diverse demographically and socio-economically. This is one of our greatest assets, but it also makes it difficult to successfully meet the Presidential goal. These diverse students have various personal reasons and timelines for attending college. Within a given course, a faculty member can anticipate part-time and full-time students, remedial and honors students, advanced high-school students, adult learners, and even university transfer students.

As a result of this openness and subsequent diversity, and perhaps even more than prestigious universities that rigorously select students most likely to succeed, the community college access environment has been a survival of the fittest model. For decades, community colleges have expected to graduate much smaller numbers of students than were admitted. Instead, we have celebrated the many students who crossed the finish line but at a much slower pace and with more remediation than would be permitted at universities. Access has meant opportunity for all, and that was where a good deal of the attention was focused. So unfortunately students, especially non-remedial students, have often gone unguided and been left to navigate their college experiences and financial resources on their own. Many students without mentors or family with collegiate experience wander through our halls isolated and confused. In recent years as extensive safety nets have been put in place, there has been a logical fear that hand-holding students through to graduation simply extends high school and is not preparation for the real world.

*Especially suffering in this environment are first generation college students, who are crucial to meet the goal of an increasingly educated workforce*

So how do we answer the nation's call and reallocate energy and resources to student-centered learning without sacrificing access? What will be needed to truly affect America's status in the global economy, to graduate more students, and to graduate life-long learners who are self-reliant, creative, adaptable, and eager to positively affect their communities and chosen professions? How do community college professionals, especially those in direct, day-to-day contact with students, influence policy makers and at least have an open channel to offer sound advice for allotment of financial resources?

Before any of these questions can be answered, we in higher education must recognize and acknowledge the challenges that prevent growth in the number of quality graduates. Putting monetary issues aside long enough to discuss ideas, we must focus our community leaders and policy makers on the current realities of our classrooms. The primary challenge that needs to be discussed openly and honestly is that an alarming number of our entering students are academically unwell. A seemingly endless number of factors may contribute to this situation: lack of educational support in the family structure, eroded self-confidence due to poor performance on standardized testing, poor work ethics, or lack of understanding of how personal interests align with college majors or professions. Whatever the root causes, before improvements can be made, America must own the reality that although most people recognize the importance of a college degree, our instant-gratification society does not naturally develop disciplined, open-minded, eager learners. Especially suffering in this environment are first generation college students, who are crucial to meet the goal of an increasingly educated workforce. Instead, this population demonstrates lower literacy rates than counterparts in other nations.[3]

To achieve the President's goal of an additional five million graduates—and more importantly of high-functioning graduates who can be competitive in a global world—we as a society need to attend to the academic wellness of our students. Academic wellness should not be confused with mental wellness; a person coping with a mental illness may or may not be succeeding academically. Academic wellness deals with a student's intrinsic desire to learn, passion for a given field, confidence that deep learning is possible, and developed life skills to make academic pursuits a reality. Instead, low self-esteem, low self-expectations, and lack of motivation represent the base-line reality for many entering freshmen. Unfortunately, these students often do not see themselves as *unwell* but as *unsmart*.

A student cannot learn, retain, and build upon previous learning without the confidence that learning is possible in the first place. A student does not likely think, "The reason I'm having trouble with this concept is that I'm a first generation college student from an underserved and failing high school." He or she likely thinks and has thought for years, "I'm not good at this subject" or "This class requires more papers than I can possibly write." Largely, new students enter community colleges intimidated and unfocused instead of excited about learning and experiencing new opportunities. No computer program, remedial course, or co-requisite course can make deep learning possible until the hearts and minds of students are healed and motivated. We must not view them as they often see themselves; for our nation's sake, we must recognize them as unwell and able to be restored. If we truly understand and have empathy for this crisis, then we can begin to shift attention and resources toward potential solutions. Perhaps one such needed shift is one of perspective—that in fact it is not the student who is unwell but the system itself.

Restoring the academic health of our students and institutions across the nation will require the wisdom on the part of college administrators, communities, grantors, and the Federal Government to allocate resources toward solutions that have potential to affect pre-collegiate education and the patience to allow experienced and passionate educators the time and space to be creative and dynamic. Already throughout the nation, high impact practices, such as learning communities, service-learning, and undergraduate research, have shown great potential but need nationwide support and multiple levels of implementation to realize their full potential. EPortfolio initiatives, which encourage students to attend to possible connections among ideas or methods through reflection, are still on the rise, but best practices are still being developed and much is still to be discovered. High impact practices and ePortfolio are not easy blueprints for success but must to be tailored to local communities and used as springboards for collaboration with businesses and community organizations, especially when implemented in community colleges.

*A student cannot learn, retain, and build upon previous learning without the confidence that learning is possible in the first place*

Local businesses and community partners are often underutilized or ill-used assets. When these local leaders are brought to campus, they usually encounter only the most polished and prepared students. They meet with our student leaders and soon-to-be-graduates at career fairs or perhaps through internships or experiences in clinics. All of these things have their place, but rarely do we introduce leaders to the student likely to fail or one that could potentially embarrass the institution. What would happen if we were courageous and worked to help our community leaders understand the academically unwell student? What if in the same spirit of internships, there were *preternships* open to all entering students? Radical but not impossible. What if service learning activities with community organizations could be opportunities to volunteer and reflect and also to explore a career and meet potential mentors in a selected field of interest? How would such partnerships change local policy conversations? How would what we gain from such conversations serve to help us understand the unwell culture of the institution? It is not hard to imagine that discussions in board rooms would be radically different—perhaps even revolutionary—for educational reform.

The opportunities to discuss and affect the wellness and success of all students open wide as we invite local businesses to the campus to work with students during their first semesters, a time during which they do not generally expect to receive this kind of support or interest. For community college students, discussing career, financial, and work ethic issues with real world mentors quickly separates the new college experience from the previous high school or failed college experience. In addition, these partnerships could help students understand that their financial aid is an investment by the community and that their futures matter to the people and businesses around them.

The needs of our nation will hardly release community colleges from their current responsibilities and challenges. Faculty across the nation could be whispering by the department copiers, "We can increase the number of graduates tomorrow. We just need to inflate grades and lower our standards." Fostering quality, well graduates who are eager and able to compete globally is much more difficult. Students require education in life skills, mentoring, and opportunities to practice and reflect on their behavior in conjunction with and prior to coursework to gain confidence and build positive connections with their campuses and larger communities. We must believe our students are capable of deep and connective learning and build that belief into the mission and actions of community colleges. Such a transition is possible on a national scale if those who interact with students do so with compassion and the courage to begin meaningful conversations.

---

NOTES

1. The White House, "Building American Skills Through Community Colleges," Accessed January 10, 2016, https://www.whitehouse.gov/issues/education/higher-education/building-american-skills-through-community-colleges.
2. Ibid.
3. Organization for Economic Cooperation and Development, "OECD Skills Outlook 2013 First Results from the Survey of Adult Skills," Revised November 2013, http://skills.oecd.org/OECD_Skills_Outlook_2013.pdf.

# 27
## PROVOCATION

---

# The Morehouse Mystique and the Collective Well-Being Imperative

*John Silvanus Wilson Jr.*

*The school is a mill into which students are thrown as grain into the hopper for the grinding of a grist that shall improve the world.*
—From the final letter written by Henry Lyman Morehouse
Fiftieth Anniversary Ceremony of Morehouse College, 1917

Educators, psychologists, and sociologists have tried for years to understand or decode the *Morehouse Mystique*—the Morehouse style of education that can be as elusive as it is illuminating. In simple terms, it refers to the manifestation of particular characteristics that define the institution and its unique approach to nurturing the well-being of its students. At Morehouse, the purpose of producing an enriched student is to produce an enriched people, community, nation, and world. At no time in the College's history has well-being been defined or approached as an exclusively individual desideratum. Students continue to be intellectually and psychologically prepared to improve the world. And to that end, well-being is measured not merely by the ability to compete and work in the world one enters, but also by the ability to imagine and work for the world one wants his or her children to enter. Thus at Morehouse, the primary measure of institutional and individual value has always been tied to the common good or to the collective well-being.

A Morehouse graduate named Martin Luther King, Jr. is by far the most remarkable example of this tie between the campus learning experience and the collective imperative to well-being. When King entered Morehouse in 1944, he was reading at an eighth grade level and aspired to be a doctor or lawyer. By the time he graduated in 1948, based largely on the institution's approach to nurturing him, he was already on a life trajectory that would eventually yield a Nobel Peace Prize, a national holiday, and a granite memorial on the National Mall.

King is singular but not alone.

Consistent with its early emphasis on producing "preachers and teachers," Morehouse continues to graduate many leaders for the nation's major pulpits and for various educational institutions, including nearly 50 college presidents. Three historically black universities have been named in honor of Morehouse men.

Morehouse has also produced numerous public servants, including at least eight mayors, five U.S. congressmen, and at least 16 other legislators of stature from at least 14 states. Morehouse men have been leaders of social and civil rights organizations, including the National Association for the Advancement of Colored People, the National Urban

League, the Southern Christian Leadership Conference, the United Negro College Fund, and Africare. Similarly, Morehouse graduates have served in senior national roles as a U.S. Surgeon General, Deputy Secretaries of Commerce and Education, and U.S. Secretaries for Health and Human Services and Homeland Security.

Morehouse alumni in science and technology have led large laboratories, generated pioneering research, founded multiple high-tech companies, and blazed new trails in on-line education. In the medical fields, Morehouse has produced countless physicians; one Morehouse graduate founded a medical school, another spearheaded leading-edge cancer research, another helped to eradicate the Guinea worm disease and is a MacArthur Fellow, another led the National Institute of Biomedical Imaging and Bioengineering, and yet another led the National Science Foundation.

*The Morehouse College definition of individual well-being has always been tied to the greater good or to the collective well-being of those far beyond the Morehouse campus*

One Morehouse graduate won multiple Olympic gold medals, one won a Super Bowl ring, and another won major league baseball's Most Valuable Player award in the World Series.

Morehouse men have been lauded musicians, composers, and Grammy-award-winning producers, and many have received critical acclaim on Broadway. One Morehouse man is a breakthrough filmmaker and won an honorary Oscar, and another only recently slipped to second place after reigning for years as the top revenue-grossing actor in cinematic history.

Morehouse has produced four Rhodes Scholars, more than any other historically black college or university, including a 2016 recipient in computer science.

In the aggregate, these distinguished alumni have reached high levels of personal achievement and community service, and their accomplishments are the stuff of the Morehouse institutional brand.

How did the Morehouse approach to student well-being, as infused into campus traditions and culture, help to prepare King and so many others to be reformers and transformers of the ways of the world and not merely conformers to them?

This essay highlights the roots of the Morehouse approach to student well-being and reveals a leadership style that has been stable yet adaptable and adoptable for years. It reveals a character-driven pedagogy that has helped to consistently produce a disproportionately high number of leaders who operate in the public interest.

THE CAMPUS POSTURE

Grounded in history, the Morehouse College definition of individual well-being has always been tied to the greater good or to the collective well-being of those far beyond the Morehouse campus. That institutional posture was set early on before the College graduated even 100 students. And Morehouse's aggressive embrace of a unique institutional identity was tightened by an often-misattributed response to a pivotal historic event.

On September 18, 1895 within four miles of the Morehouse College campus, Booker T. Washington delivered a defining speech at the Atlanta Cotton States and International Exhibition. The ten-minute articulation of how to improve race relations in the South would later be dubbed, "the Atlanta Compromise." Southern racial tension had remained high since emancipation, and there was little agreement and less imagination about whether and how the races could live, develop, and work together. Washington's speech was an eloquent proposal designed to relieve those tensions and release the nation from a quandary with which it had struggled too long.

With profound curricular and pedagogic implications, the Compromise offer fueled the subsequent debate about the purposes of black higher education, which was itself a version of the well-being debate. In Washington's view, the eight million Negroes were to remain in the South as a full third of the southern population, and they were to focus much of their training and work in agriculture, mechanics, commerce, and domestic service. Washington proposed that vocational-industrial education for African Americans would ease racial tensions as they learned to eschew civil, social, and political rights in order to "dignify and glorify common labour, and put brains and skill into the common occupations of life."[1] Washington made stark contrasts to the liberal arts alternative by insisting, "there is as much dignity in tilling a field as in writing a poem," and "the opportunity to earn a dollar in a factory just now is worth infinitely more than the opportunity to spend a dollar in an opera-house."[2]

According to multiple reports, the predominantly white audience received him enthusiastically then and later, and his accommodationist outlook drew written praise from President Grover Cleveland. But among those in the crowd to hear him that day was a Roger Williams University professor named John Hope who, instead of joining the thunderous applause, became what one biographer described as "the first black intellectual to publicly oppose Washington."[3]

In a series of speeches beginning in early 1896, Hope spoke forcefully about the need for a "liberal" or "higher" education for "a certain percentage of our people."[4] Similarly, one of Hope's white friends who served as the executive secretary of the American Baptist Education Society, Henry Lyman Morehouse, also pushed for a different approach to ensure the equality and well-being of blacks. In April of 1896, he published a brief essay in the periodical, *The Independent*, entitled "The Talented Tenth."[5] Hope and Morehouse argued that some institutions ought to specialize in developing servant leaders who would be preeminent, world-class thinkers devoted to uplifting the race.

Within two years, Atlanta Baptist College president, Dr. George Sale, recruited Hope to serve as a classics professor and bookkeeper. As only the seventh professor and second black professor at that time, he impressed the institution's leaders, including Henry Lyman Morehouse, who was serving as a trustee. Hope also became close friends with another impressive professor at neighboring Atlanta University, W.E.B. DuBois, who arrived in Atlanta the year before.

By 1903, DuBois popularized the Talented Tenth theory originated by Hope and Morehouse and expanded on the idea in his best-selling work, *The Souls of Black Folk*.[6] By 1906, John Hope had become the first black president of Atlanta Baptist College, and he would serve for 25 years; by 1913, Atlanta Baptist College would be renamed Morehouse College in honor of Henry Lyman Morehouse, the institution's biggest fundraiser, defender, and friend.

Meanwhile, Booker T. Washington's advocacy of vocational-industrial education captured the attention of the nation, secured the endorsement of southern whites, and garnered unprecedented resources from northern philanthropists. As he pushed for a narrow function of education, best-suited, he thought, for the entire race, the leadership at Morehouse College simultaneously assumed a different institutional posture and laid the foundation for a broader and deeper manifestation and measure of well-being. John Hope and Henry Lyman Morehouse courageously set the stage to establish student well-being as more about making a life than a living and as more relational than personal. At Morehouse, making a whole, new person was pointless if that person was not also equipped and motivated to make a whole, new world. This foundational perspective engendered a unique approach to well-being around which subsequent Morehouse leaders would shape a powerful campus culture. One particular leader was chief amplifier and architect of that distinctive and fruitful culture.

THE CAMPUS CULTURE

When Benjamin Elijah Mays began his 27-year presidency of Morehouse College in 1940, he was already aware of the manner in which John Hope had established a unique institutional identity and posture toward well-being. Mays shared Hope's values and ambitions for the institution. Therefore, he resolved to build upon the foundation set by Hope by developing a campus culture reflective of the College's assumed position as shaper of an African American intellectual vanguard.

*John Hope and Henry Lyman Morehouse courageously set the stage to establish student well-being as more about making a life than a living and as more relational than personal. At Morehouse, making a whole, new person was pointless if that person was not also equipped and motivated to make a whole, new world*

At a time when many college presidents had been trained as ministers, Mays brought more than the conventional Christian outlook to his role. Mays's global view and holistic approach to student development took into account stubbornly held social attitudes and beliefs about the presumed limitations of African American students, especially black males. Moreover, he sought to shatter such presuppositions with a strident confidence that Morehouse students could succeed in every field of human endeavor. Through his educational philosophy and approach to well-being, Mays took aim at longstanding social barriers to African American achievement and simultaneously prodded students to eschew and unlearn habits of thought and behavior that had for years inhibited such achievement.

Accordingly, he saw an important need for Morehouse to deliberately, consistently, and positively reshape the self-perception of its students. Concerned with personality development, he recognized that once students were freed from perceived, race-based constraints, they would be more motivated to aspire and strive for academic and professional excellence. Two years into his presidency, Mays proposed a blueprint for a dynamic campus culture and community that featured four important institutional inputs and a new set of character traits to be exhibited by the best of its students and graduates.

First, the campus was to be a model for democratic practices. Instead of centralizing all of the power on campus in the office of the president, Mays favored new levels of empowerment for students and faculty. The purpose of this empowerment was to develop more responsible citizens and progressive leaders. In this way, Morehouse was to operate as a microcosm of the type of society that he envisioned. Succinctly put, a taste of on-campus democracy would sharpen students' taste for off-campus democracy.

Second, the campus was to be community-minded in the sense that it would resist becoming the kind of highbrow institution that tended to produce graduates with what Mays called "better-than-thou" attitudes. Instead, Mays wanted students, faculty, and entire departments to assist surrounding communities and offer a range of services that included teaching in Sunday schools, providing accounting help to small businesses, and helping low-income mothers to manage their money more effectively through budgeting.

Third, the campus was to promote solid citizenship, especially as measured by voter participation. The goal was to develop what Mays called "a real democracy in the United States," and this would be a foundation upon which to promote and advance democracy worldwide.

Fourth, Mays saw an enormous opportunity to develop a new kind of scholarship that would be free of prejudice and bias. In his view, the pressure to generate scholarship in accord with established, prejudiced mores had crippled many white scholars. This left a dire need for what Mays called "scholars of the first magnitude." Mays believed that within a fifty-year period, Morehouse and other black colleges could successfully produce some of the best scholars in the nation.

Mays also masterfully used a messaging strategy, the key elements of which were derived from the scholarship of a 1923 Morehouse graduate and mystic theologian, Howard Thurman. Students continue to be encouraged to discover for themselves what Thurman called "the sound of the genuine,"[7] or their authentic voices, or their agency moments. In accord with the common advisory, "the two most important days of your life are the day you are born and the day you find out why," students are encouraged to have their second days or their why days on the campus of Morehouse College.

Similarly, for decades, graduating seniors at Morehouse have been encouraged to honor their alma mater by living their lives according to another mandate captured best by Thurman: "Over the heads of her students, Morehouse holds a crown that she challenges them to grow tall enough to wear!"[8]

Finally, the collective well-being injunction has lived at Morehouse ever since John Hope and Henry Lyman Morehouse were wise enough to embed it in the Talented Tenth imperative. The messaging about it is voluminous, varied, and richly associated with the brand of the College.

These and other organizational characteristics, goals, and strategies remain woven into the fabric of the structured programming of the campus, from annual student orientation ceremonies, to weekly assemblies and chapel experiences, to annual homecoming, anniversary, commencement, and reunion rituals and traditions. And because Mays worked hard to ensure that faculty would also embrace and promote these goals, they were carefully integrated into the College's formal curricular and extra-curricular offerings. More importantly, they were the substance of what has come to be known in education as "the hidden curriculum."

## THE HIDDEN CURRICULUM

Mays peerlessly utilized what more contemporary educators refer to as the *hidden curriculum*. As the term implies, students are challenged to read the less obvious values and signs in the campus setting as guideposts for success in and beyond the classroom. Not long after enrolling, students detect the nonacademic rules, assumptions, and expectations that inform, frame, and add texture to their experiences. More than the formal curriculum, the hidden curriculum influences the adaptation of students and faculty and profoundly affects the overall process of teaching and learning. And when effectively infused into the culture or fabric of the campus, the hidden curriculum can greatly inform and enrich the student's sense of worth and self-esteem.

In the Morehouse context, the hidden curriculum was woven into the College's hallowed learning environment in order to create and maintain a culture of high expectation that was reinforced and strengthened by the top-down weight of institutional and moral authority. Mays and his faculty successfully created a new culture, community, and ongoing conversations about the high calling of their students. The reach and power of their work underscores the designation of hidden (infused) and curriculum (tutelage). They promoted overarching and socially relevant values and expectations, and their messaging remains of unique and timeless value.

Although Mays and his colleagues never used the term *hidden curriculum*, they generated a label for its product. Those who mastered it were said to exhibit the *Morehouse Mystique*. Meeting the requirements and mandates of the mystique—intelligence, integrity, oratorical excellence, honesty, compassion, agency, servant-leadership—also positions students to become Morehouse men. Every student who enrolls has this potential.

> *The mystique remains the basis for a distinctive institutional voice because it references a brand of liberal arts preparation for life and living that continues to be uniquely available at Morehouse College*

Morehouse men are challenged to reflect these virtues, while feeling called to pursue greatness, to be consequential, and to make a meaningful difference in the world. The mystique remains the basis for a distinctive institutional voice because it references a brand of liberal arts preparation for life and living that continues to be uniquely available at Morehouse College. In this regard, the mutually reinforcing formal curriculum, informal co-curriculum, and hidden curriculum combine to synergistically produce something truly unique. Understandably, Mays believed these three levers accounted for the special, intangible something called the Morehouse Mystique. In Mays' view, if that special something was ever lost, Morehouse would run the risk of becoming, in his words, "just another college."

## THE CAMPUS TRAJECTORY

This overview of the historical and social foundations of the Morehouse approach to well-being—the Morehouse Mystique—has broad implications and contemporary relevance for higher education at large. What Hope and Mays did for Morehouse was timely and timeless. Their values, posture, campus culture, programming, and messaging persist at Morehouse to this day and are at the heart of the institution's identity and appeal. Beyond that, their educational legacy provides us with insight into how institutions can be built to last and ideally positioned to sustainably produce improvers of the world's well-being.

The 120-year-old decision to reject an unnecessarily narrow view of black education and instead to courageously promote the prerequisites of social justice was not without cost. As a practical matter, the noble vision of Hope and Mays was not then or since rewarded with the kind of transformational external support that Booker T. Washington enjoyed at the height of his leadership of the celebrated Tuskegee Institute. Still they held to their particular definitions of institutional and student well-being, secure in the knowledge and faith that support would eventually come from external champions of liberal arts education and friends of higher education in general who understood and appreciated their far-reaching vision. And then as now, history has proven them to be right, even if Morehouse is as yet unrewarded with the kind of investment that yields financial impregnability.

Leaders since Hope and Mays have understood that the institution's distinctive mission is inextricably tied to the nation's interests, including the realization of the highest expression of a national identity. From the start, the purpose of Morehouse College was tied to the reason to invest in it —namely to make a better nation and by extension a better world. The educational experience is designed to ensure the well-being of the individual student and to equip him to make a living and a life. However, the true value of the Morehouse student's well-being is not assessed on campus before graduation; it is assessed off campus when the graduate takes his rightful place as a responsible and productive citizen.

Finally, Hope and Mays created an investment-worthy platform to attract a steady stream of capable and committed students, faculty, and staff. By doing so, they adeptly positioned Morehouse College to become and remain a first-choice institution for high-minded individuals who aspire to teach and learn in a decidedly mission-driven campus environment. The Morehouse experience, outcomes, and trajectory all yield many vital, world-changing lessons for 21st century learning communities and those who lead them.

---

Notes

1. U.S. Survey Course, "Booker T. Washington Delivers the 1895 Atlanta Compromise Speech," http://historymatters.gmu.edu/d/39/, paragraph 4.
2. Ibid, paragraph 11.
3. Leroy Davis, *A Clashing of the Soul: John Hope and the Dilemma of African American Leadership and Black Higher Education in the Early Twentieth Century* (Athens, GA: University of Georgia Press, 1998), 92.
4. Davis, *A Clashing of the Soul*, 90–91.
5. Henry Lyman Morehouse, "The Talented Tenth," *The Independent* 48 (1896): 1.
6. W. E. B. Du Bois, *The Souls of Black Folk*, (Mineola, NY: Dover Publications, 1994).
7. Howard Thurman, "The Sound of the Genuine: Spelman College Baccalaureate Address" (speech, May 4, 1980).
8. "Crown Forum," Morehouse College, http://www.morehouse.edu/academics/degree_requirements/crown-forum.html.

# 28
## PROVOCATION

---

# Mobilizing Campus Communities for Well-Being

*Theodore E. Long*

WHAT EMERSON CALLED "DRAWING OUT THE SOUL"[1] was once thought to be a core purpose of a college education. Indeed, the work of shaping and nourishing human beings flourished in the early years of American higher education, especially in small, residential, relatively homogeneous colleges. An echo of that emphasis is often found in the college mission statements of today. However, for the most part, as higher education grew and prospered, the cultivation of student well-being was disconnected from the central activities of higher education in the following ways:

- Hyper-specialization separated well-being from faculty work;
- Increasing institutional size diminished personal engagement;
- Increasing diversity added complexity to the meaning and circumstances of well-being;
- Decreasing residency uncoupled students from a community context for development; and
- Higher education focused more on its business than its mission and purpose.

As a result, we have abandoned well-being as a central focus and forgotten what it means to educate students in that way.

If the cultivation of well-being is to become a vital element of higher education under these new circumstances, the intentional and systematic mobilization of entire institutions is required. We cannot expect that a few ad hoc initiatives will be sufficient to renew this core purpose or to ensure its ongoing practice. Reconnecting well-being to the heart of higher education will only succeed through a focused and disciplined collective effort led by highly committed leaders who are able to achieve six essential conditions for sustaining this important aspect of learning. Here I outline these six conditions as an agenda for mobilizing campus communities. They are not listed in order of priority or temporal sequence, which will vary according to the specific situation of each institution. Each is necessary to build a successful campus program, but none of them alone can get the job done; only the entire set will be sufficient to do so.

## EDUCATE THE COMMUNITY

We cannot assume that faculty and staff are sufficiently knowledgeable about well-being to develop and carry out effective programs to nourish it. We do have some campus specialists in what I will call "well-being remediation"—counselors, medical staff, and perhaps some judicial officers—who help students regain their balance in the face of personal distress or unhealthy behavior. They are important, but many people think of them just as part of the institutional M.A.S.H. unit that gets students back into action with the least harm possible. Few understand the importance or possibility of nourishing a more fully-developed condition of well-being as a central dimension of transformational education that builds capacity not only for collegiate success, but also for life achievement and satisfaction. So our colleagues need to learn something about a) the history and significance of well-being in higher education, b) the major definitions and dimensions of well-being in the literature, c) the different arenas of well-being and how they function in relation to one another, and d) methodologies for nourishing well-being. Such an education will help everyone in the community understand how rich and comprehensive the idea well-being is—far more than the health and wellness programs that we frequently think are sufficient for such learning.

## MAKE WELL-BEING MISSION-CENTRAL

Most exhortations about starting something new in colleges and universities rightly emphasize the importance of the support of institutional leaders. What is even more critical for well-being, however, is that it be recognized as a core aspect of the institutional mission, an essential ingredient of the educational purpose of each college and university. Leaders come and go, and the focus on well-being cannot depend on the changing agendas of individual leaders. Rather, it must be clearly embedded in institutional mission statements that are more lasting than individual leaders. Further, the mission must be woven into the daily life of the institution through educational goals and objectives, collaboration of curriculum and co-curriculum, and integration of theory and practice. The achievement of mission centrality requires not only the affirmation of faculty and administration, but also the affirmation of institution trustees, who also must be educated to understand the importance of this aspect of education.

## ANCHOR WELL-BEING IN THE ACADEMIC PROGRAM

Academic learning is at the heart of our educational enterprise, and it engages many critical dimensions of whole-person education. Because it is the one common feature of institutions of higher education, the academic curriculum must contribute in some significant way to well-being in order to ensure that all students, residential and non-residential, can benefit from it. This may be the most difficult challenge of all, for the evolution of higher education has led us to sequester the non-intellectual aspects of education outside the academic program in the co-curriculum. As faculties have become ever more expert in their intellectual disciplines, they have developed what Thorsten Veblen called a "trained incapacity"[2] to address matters of student well-being. When we look closely, however, we will see that many aspects of well-being are directly supported by our academic knowledge, norms, and pedagogies. For example, in addition to their intellectual and civic dimensions, our curricula contribute to developing life meaning and purpose, the capacity for self-guidance, and personal integrity, all important dimensions of personal wholeness that supports well-being.[3] While nourishing well-being in the academic program may require some new pedagogies, such education will make clear that well-being is not just about feeling good but instead involves systematic learning and cumulative development.

## BUILD A CURRICULUM AND PEDAGOGY OF WELL-BEING

Too often we think of personal well-being as a happy by-product of the learning experience, especially in residential colleges. We have not been as intentional or systematic as we might be in designing learning processes that are the most productive in fostering well-being.[4] Unlike most academic learning outcomes, well-being is fundamentally developmental, an ongoing and emergent process of becoming. It is also wholistic, engages multiple dimensions of the person, and draws together experience, reflection, and action. And the social context within which well-being is nurtured is pivotal to its development. More like a process of socialization than a didactic learning program, well-being education requires its own curriculum and pedagogy to be effective. On the academic side, what is required is the integration of well-being into an overall curriculum and the identification of points at which well-being can be nurtured and drawn out in the process of formal learning. In the co-curriculum, however, the challenge is to create more formal curricula rather than to rely on ad hoc and uncertain processes. In both areas, it will be important to develop affirmative, experiential pedagogies as case studies that provide real-life examples, personal coaching about challenging life situations, and engagement with multiple role models that demonstrate what well-being can mean in daily life.

> *More like a process of socialization than a didactic learning program, well-being education requires its own curriculum and pedagogy to be effective*

## EXPLOIT ADVISING AS A KEY POINT OF LEVERAGE

Student advising is a pivotal point at which to mentor students for well-being, but rarely are its possibilities realized. Too often, advising has become merely a bureaucratic process of processing students through a system of requirements. To foster well-being in advising, we must reframe advising as a personalized, educational relationship devoted to student learning and provide the organizational support to make that possible. Colleges can do so in several ways. First, we can develop advising protocols that define how advising can be utilized for productive well-being development. Second, we can require students to produce assessable learning products on well-being as part of the advising process. Third, we can deploy all faculty and professional staff for advising as part of their workloads with sufficient time allocated to foster genuine education. Finally, we can create advising/mentoring partnerships among advisors with different types of experience and expertise to ensure multidimensional mentoring.

## ASSESS LEARNING OUTCOMES RELATED TO WELL-BEING

Many people believe that well-being is not readily assessable because it is a qualitative, developmental process that is rarely complete and not easily measured. But social scientists have developed the tools to measure such qualities and to capture their temporal development. If we are serious about this work, we must utilize those methods to assess well-being just as rigorously and sensitively as we do other learning objectives. In doing so, it will be important to ensure that we focus on the person whose well-being is being developed, not the programs that we create. Because well-being is developmental, its assessment should not be a one-time event; it should be periodic, ongoing, and cumulative over time. Qualitative indicators will naturally take center stage in our assessments, but we should not be timid about employing quantitative measures where appropriate. Perhaps most importantly, we should always utilize such assessment for learning—for the students and for the institution—and not merely to confirm or disconfirm developmental progress. As we do so, we can then also improve our practice and student outcomes.

I am frequently challenged to explain how these concepts are possible at very large institutions, not just at small colleges, how they can be realized in on-line as opposed to face to face learning environments, and how they apply to adult learners who are already well-formed versus traditional college-aged students (18–22 year olds).

The first two challenges betray the misunderstanding that developmental well-being was simply a happy coincidence of small, intimate communities, not a core purpose of higher education in all its manifestations. On the contrary, neither large size nor learning at a distance is in principle an impediment to learning for well-being, particularly because well-being can and should be grounded in the academic curriculum. To be sure, those situations will require some different approaches to ensure that well-being can be effectively integrated into the educational program, but we are seeing that institutions who are purposeful about well-being can build successful programs of substance by following the steps above.

The third challenge betrays the frequent misunderstanding of education for well-being as a simple process of maturation into adulthood, when it is in fact an ongoing part of life at every age. There may be different specific foci of well-being for adult students and rising adults, but the fundamental issues remain the same: everyone is part of an ongoing developmental process, and higher learning can always contribute positively to that development. Indeed, we should count the rich expression of well-being as one of those things that makes what we do count as higher education that takes us above and beyond mere maturation.

We have diminished our educational birthright by abandoning the effort to educate the whole person, not just the mind. While we understand the forces that led to that result, they did not prevent us from nurturing well-being; they just made it easier to neglect it. In effect, we lost our will to champion and sustain this critical aspect of higher education. We now understand what it takes to renew this protean element of our vocation. Not to do so would be to deny an essential part of our reason for being.

NOTES

1. Andrew Delbanco, *College: What it Was, Is, and Should Be* (Princeton, NJ: Princeton University Press 2012), 46.
2. Robert K. Merton, *Social Theory and Social Structure,* enlarged ed. (New York: Free Press, 1968), 197–98.
3. Theodore E. Long, "Evoking Wholeness: To Renew the Ideal of the Educated Person," in *Transforming Undergraduate Education: Theory that Compels and Practices that Succeed,* ed. Donald W. Harward (Lanham, MD: Roman and Littlefield Publishers, 2011), 125–40.
4. Richard M. Hersh et al., "A Well-Rounded Education for a Flat World" (paper presented at the Leadership Coalition President's Symposium, Washington, DC, November, 10, 2008).

# 29
## PROVOCATION

# Why Institutional Commitment to Well-Being Bridges the Academic and Student Affairs Divide

*Kevin Kruger and Stephanie A. Gordon*

THE NEED FOR AND THE BENEFITS OF COLLABORATION between academic and student affairs have been debated and discussed among those in higher education for decades. In 1998, *Powerful Partnerships: A Shared Responsibility for Learning* called for a new collective vision in the academy, one that "require[d] a commitment to and support for action that goes beyond the individual faculty or staff member. It is only by acting in the context of common goals that our accumulated understanding about learning is put to best use."[1] One year later, Robert Hersh echoed this sentiment by stating that a truly rich college experience "takes place at the nexus of profound intellectual and social/emotional development. Most institutions dichotomize the various facets of learning as if our intellectual, emotional and ethical lives were compartmentalized."[2] These themes of dichotomization and compartmentalization are common in critiques of faculty and student affairs.

More recently, Keeling argued for learning that was comprehensive, holistic, and transformative—learning that integrated classroom knowledge with the equally valuable learning experiences that take place beyond the classroom.[3] *Learning Reconsidered* built the case that institutions should be accountable for providing "resources that will enable all educators to meet new expectations about student learning and to contribute effectively and purposefully to achieving students' holistic learning outcomes. Both members of the academic faculty and student affairs educators must be prepared to assess and change their work."[4] Yet despite these consistent calls for greater cooperation, implementation of collaborative partnerships on an institutional level between academic faculty and student affairs educators has been varied.

The need for faculty and student affairs staff to assess and change their work to find new collective learning opportunities for students is the central premise of this essay. Why are there so few excellent examples of this kind of transformative learning? Why do the silos between faculty and student affairs persist when all evidence suggests that a more holistic view of learning is so desperately needed? For more than 15 years, learning and discovery along with preparation for future careers and a meaningful life have been fundamental aspects of the core mission of postsecondary education—these common and basic goals should provide a visible foundation for collaborations between faculty and student affairs.

Considering that one's life is linked together through background, family connections, work, and education and is the result of a culmination of many experiences, the postsecondary environment is just one part of the many pieces that develop individuals into active and engaged citizens in the community. The lives of students, no matter their circumstances, are rich and complex. Given this reality, academic and student affairs educators must recognize that students do not experience college in precisely defined segments with organizational charts; rather, there are many contributing factors to learning on a college campus. The outdated notion that academic affairs and faculty are responsible for classroom learning alone, and student affairs educators are regulated to co-curricular activities can no longer be the justification for a lack of coordination to meet the responsibility of fostering students' well-being.

*The outdated notion that academic affairs and faculty are responsible for classroom learning alone, and student affairs educators are regulated to co-curricular activities can no longer be the justification for a lack of coordination to meet the responsibility of fostering students' well-being*

There are several campus structures, formal and informal, through which faculty, academic affairs administrators, and student affairs educators can contribute to enabling student well-being. One important structure is that of explicit and transparent institutional commitment—a sphere in which there are at least three major ways that successful collaboration can affect student success and well-being. As one example, we share the methodology of behavioral intervention teams that focuses on an individual student who may be struggling to succeed. A second focus pertains to the roles that family, faculty, and student affairs professionals play in addressing mental health and well-being as they relate to student well-being, success, and completion. Finally, we discuss the importance of advising and academic coaching that we consider the responsibility of the entire academic enterprise.

## COMMUNITY ACTION RESPONSE FOR EMERGENCY (CARE) TEAMS OR BEHAVIORAL INTERVENTION TEAMS

Well-being and increased rates of college success and completion will not occur with a singular focus on the curriculum. A coordinated effort must be developed, managed, and executed by all members of the higher education community. Many campuses accomplish this effort through coordinated community action response for emergency (CARE) teams. Institutions have several names for these teams, but the most common is a behavior intervention team (BIT). These teams are unique to each campus, and the development and emphasis may be different depending on the institutional type. A CARE team has two primary objectives: to prevent the oversight of instances of disturbed or disturbing behavior and to connect disparate pieces of information that may indicate a more acute problem.[5]

Taking a broad approach to a community response group allows academic and student affairs administrators to work in partnership to provide an inclusive approach to student support and learning. An important aspect of this kind of team methodology is that it allows the campus to respond to behavioral issues and to issues of engagement and patterns of belonging and self-identity within the community. It is these connections to well-being that are necessary to highlight within a CARE or BIT team. Many times, a CARE or BIT team is solely focused on threat assessment. We advocate for teams that provide relationship building functions across campus that allow for recognition of acute issues within an institution and for a parallel connection to the overall social, economic, and civic purpose of the institution.

## Mental Health: Preventing Stigma as an Institutional Commitment to Well-being

It has been well documented that during the last decade, college counseling centers have seen a significant rise in the number of students who have serious psychological issues.[6] Two-thirds of counseling center directors reported an increase in the numbers of students with severe psychological problems who seek treatment in the counseling center.[7] What is more challenging is that most of the students who experience mental health issues never seek treatment from the counseling center. In fact, only 20% of students who committed suicide in college sought help from the counseling center.[8] The problem is two-fold: there will never be enough counselors to meet the rising mental health needs of college students, and not enough students seek help when they struggle with mental health issues. This is one clear area where faculty and student affairs professionals must find common ground because although it may seem that mental health issues are only managed through therapeutic counseling, the entire institution "has a role in prevention, providing support, and in offering a range of opportunities to enable students to participate in higher education."[9]

This may seem daunting to faculty and staff given the complex nature of the issues on campus today. As of a study published in 2014, members of the most recent entering freshmen class had the lowest, self-rated, emotional health in the last 20 years.[10] The findings from the most recent American College Health Association (ACHA) *National College Health Assessment* underscore the emerging mental health crisis among college students. In 2015, the vast majority (85%) of students reported that they "felt overwhelmed by all they had to do," two-thirds felt sad or lonely, and almost half (48%) reported "feeling things were hopeless."[11] Of even greater concern is that more than one-third of students (34%) "felt so depressed it was difficult to function," and more than half (54%) felt "overwhelming anxiety."[12]

It is critical that institutions engage faculty as partners in supporting the mental health and wellness of their students. Faculty members are in unique positions to identify symptoms of mental health distress well before the problems become severe. In particular, faculty may be trained to observe and note a sudden decline in academic performance; a pattern of dropping classes; consistently missed deadlines; excessive, unexplained absences; severe reactions to a poor grade on a test or paper; or any other out-of-character behavior in the classroom.[13]

*There will never be enough counselors to meet the rising mental health needs of college students, and not enough students seek help when they struggle with mental health issues*

The integration of faculty into the holistic life of the student is essential to an institutional commitment to well-being. However, all faculty will not greet bridging the gap between the academic and student affairs enthusiastically: "Institutional leaders, frontline advisers and faculty members have been led to believe that if college students do well academically—and take advantage of internships and student activities or develop a scholarly relationship with a close faculty mentor—then they will also be happy, healthy and flourishing in higher education and life. That is a false belief that we should not perpetuate."[14] In fact, what may be necessary is a deliberate process to create programs that allow faculty to engage with students around their educational, career, and personal goals and through the development of life-management skills that can increase their capacity to deal with the normal stress and anxiety of college life.

## COACHING AND INTRUSIVE ADVISING

While mental and behavioral health services are a critical component of the institution, the best way for academic and student affairs educators to collaborate is to develop a community that ensures a campus culture and commitment to a learning environment that supports healthy minds and develops resilience in students. The Gallup-Purdue Index Report, *Great Jobs Great Lives,* indicates that students who felt connected to a faculty member or an advisor typically also felt supported by their colleges or universities—a factor that appears to be key to their overall sense of well-being in the future.[15] This report provides evidence that these advising processes are important to building an institutional climate that can increase the overall sense of well-being and ultimate success following graduation.

Through systematized coaching and advising processes, students could take advantage of wrap-around services that will ensure success. What we do know is that coaching, intrusive advising, and one-on-one mentoring significantly increase the likelihood of college completion. For-profit companies, such as InsideTrack, match students to coaches, and through a combination of mixed media technologies and curricula, students receive personalized support to assist them through their first year of college.[16] This customized support is particularly important for low-income, first-generation students since they may not have mentors in their lives who can help them navigate the complexities of the college environment. Additionally, programs such as the City College of New York's Accelerated Study in Associate Programs for low-income students have been shown to double the graduation rates through a multipronged approach of financial support, cohort curriculums, and a comprehensive advisement system.[17]

> *What we do know is that coaching, intrusive advising, and one-on-one mentoring significantly increase the likelihood of college completion*

In addition to coaching, more engaged academic advising may also provide important ways for faculty, academic advisors, and student success staff to collaborate in advising efforts that increase degree progress for students at risk of dropping out. We currently have a national crisis regarding the achievement gap for Black, Hispanic, and low-income students. While many of these students leave school for financial reasons, many also struggle academically without the social capital necessary to find resources and seek help. This is clearly an area in which faculty partnerships can yield significant results. Much of this approach falls into what was originally called *intrusive advising*, a term first used by Robert Glennen in the mid-1970s. Intrusive advising was created because it was documented that students who were struggling academically failed to seek help voluntarily. "The Intrusive Advisement program was based on the philosophy that the university should call students in for advising numerous times during the year instead of the normal once-a-semester meeting between a student and his or her advisor and instead of waiting until the student's academic career is in serious trouble."[18] More recently, the term *proactive advising* has been used to describe the process by which advisors create deliberate interventions to enhance student motivation, facilitate greater involvement and interaction with students, and provide more intensive advising and outreach to students before academic challenges develop.[19]

The challenge then is to identify training and provide opportunities for faculty to utilize proactive advising strategies. Often these strategies will intersect with students' desires to discuss career planning, life purpose, values, and strengths—all potential facets of their senses of well-being.

## AN INSTITUTIONAL COMMITMENT TO COLLABORATION FOR WELL-BEING

Among the significant conversations and provocative offerings in this volume of how we, as educators, contribute to the well-being of students, our essay provides one perspective on how the institutional commitment to well-being can be achieved through partnership and focus. The unique nature of higher education environments, combined with the complexity of students' backgrounds, provide a challenging situation for faculty and student affairs professionals. There is not a universal collaborative model. Students come to our campuses with varied skill sets with which to understand and manage the pressure of the college environment. "Given what it takes to be successful in higher education—and later, in life and work—students have to be *ready to learn*—in a state of physical, psychological, emotional, intellectual, social, and spiritual well-being."[20]

As Baxter Magolda indicates, individual students make meaning from personal experiences, reasoning patterns, and a worldview that helps to influence their cognitive development.[21] It is the responsibility of every higher education educator, no matter his or her status or role on campus, to assist in developing and executing a holistic college student experience. The only way we are going to be successful in postsecondary education is if faculty, academic affairs professionals, and student affairs educators work together to create opportunities for students to engage in the learning process; develop overarching senses of well-being; and become active, productive members of the world following graduation. It is essential, now more than ever, that faculty and student affairs professionals put the evidence we have known for decades into practice.

NOTES

1. American Association for Higher Education, American College Personnel Association, and National Association of Student Personnel Administrators, *Powerful Partnerships A Shared Responsibility for Learning,* June 2, 1998, 1, http://www.myacpa.org/sites/default/files/taskforce_powerful_partnerships_a_shared_responsibility_for_learning.pdf.
2. Richard H. Hersh, "Generating Ideals and Transforming Lives: A Contemporary Case for the Residential Liberal Arts College" in *Distinctively American: The Residential Liberal Arts Colleges*, ed. by Steven Koblick and Stephen Graubard, an augmented version of *Daedalus*. Vol. 128, No. 1, (Winter, 1999), pp. 182.
3. Richard P. Keeling, ed., *Learning Reconsidered: A Campus-Wide Focus on the Student Experience* (Washington, DC: American College Personnel Association and National Association of Student Personnel Administrators, 2004).
4. Ibid, 13.
5. Higher Education Mental Health Alliance, *Balancing Safety and Support on Campus: A Guide for Campus Teams* (New York: Higher Education Mental Health Alliance, 2011), http://www.jedfoundation.org/campus_teams_guide.pdf.
6. Robert P. Gallagher, "Thirty Years of the National Survey of Counseling Center Directors: A Personal Account," *Journal of College Student Psychotherapy* 26 no. 3 (2012): 172–84.

7. David Reetz, Brian Krylowicz, and Brian Mistler, *The Association for University and College Counseling Center Directors Annual Survey,* Reporting Period: September 1, 2013 through August 31, 2014, http://www.aucccd.org/assets/documents/2014%20aucccd%20monograph%20-%20public%20pdf.pdf.

8. Ibid.

9. Nicky Stanley and Jill Manthorpe, eds., *Students' Mental Health Needs: Problems and Responses* (London, UK: Jessica Kingsley Publishers. 2002), 30.

10. Kevin Eagan et al., *The American Freshman: National Norms Fall 2014* (Los Angeles: Higher Education Research Institute, UCLA, 2014).

11. American College Health Association, *American College Health Association-National College Health Assessment II: Reference Group Executive Summary Spring 2015, (Hanover, MD: American College Health Association; 2015),* 13.

12. Ibid.

13. Dan Wilcox, "Working Together to Help Distressed Students on Campus," in *More Than Listening: A Casebook For Using Counseling Skills in Student Affairs Work*, ed. by Ruth Harper and Nona Wilson (Washington, DC: National Association of Student Affairs Administrators, Inc. (NASPA), 2010) , 253–272.

14. Henry G. Brzycki, "Faculty Members Must Play a Role," *Inside Higher Education*, January 5, 2016, https://www.insidehighered.com/views/2016/01/05/helping-faculty-members-help-improve-students-mental-health-essay.

15. Gallup, Inc., *Great Jobs. Great Lives* (Washington, DC: Gallup, Inc., 2014), https://www.luminafoundation.org/files/resources/galluppurdueindex-report-2014.pdf.

16. Eric Bettinger and Rachel Baker, "The Effects of Student Coaching in College: An Evaluation of a Randomized Experiment in Student Mentoring," The National Bureau of Economic Research, 2011, http://www.nber.org/papers/w16881.

17. Susan Scrivener et al., *Doubling Graduation Rates: Three-Year Effects of CUNY's Accelerated Study in Associate Programs (ASAP) for Developmental Education Students, (MDRC: 2015).*

18. Robert E. Glennen and Dan M. Baxley, "Reduction of Attrition through Intrusive Advising," *NASPA Journal* 22, no. 3 (1985): 12.

19. Jennifer Varney, "Proactive (Intrusive) Advising!" *Academic Advising Today*, 35 no. 3 (2012), https://www.nacada.ksu.edu/Resources/Academic-Advising-Today/View-Articles/Proactive-(Intrusive)-Advising!.aspx.

20. Louise A. Douce and Richard P. Keeling, *A Strategic Primer on College Mental Health* (Washington, DC: American Council on Education, 2014), 1.

21. Marcia B. Baxter Magolda, "The Integration of Relational and Impersonal Knowing in Young Adults' Epistemological Development," *Journal of College Student Development* 36, no. 3 (1995): 205–16.

# 30

# Distilling Career Advice
# from the Happiness Literature

*Robert H. Frank*

FOR THE PAST SEVERAL DECADES, social scientists have been examining statistical measures of human well-being in an attempt to identify the conditions that promote satisfying lives. As a long-time spectator of the happiness literature and an occasional contributor to it, my aim in this essay will be to summarize how what we've learned might help people better plan their lives and careers. When I use "you" in what follows, I'll be addressing a young person who's currently trying to decide what to do in life.

In plotting your career, one of the first questions you'll confront is, "How much money will I need to be happy?" Existing studies don't serve up as clear an answer as you might hope, but there are nonetheless useful insights to be gleaned from a careful reading of those studies.

One pattern observed early on was that average income levels in a country tend to rise much more rapidly over time than the corresponding levels of average happiness. Many interpreted that finding to mean that having extra income didn't make people appreciably happier. But that interpretation was quickly challenged by the economist Richard Easterlin, who noted that if we examine the income-happiness relationship in a second way, income seems much more important.[1] Easterlin noted that in studies comparing *groups* of people at different points along the income scale, average happiness levels increased sharply as income increased. But the individual data points were very noisy, meaning that studies of individual happiness and income data didn't show nearly as clear a link between the two. There were plenty of poor people describing themselves as extremely happy, for example, and likewise many rich people describing their lives as miserable. But once income and happiness values were averaged for large groups of people, it became clear that the wealthier groups were much happier, on balance, than those with lower incomes.

Easterlin's explanation was simple and intuitively appealing. He said that the discrepancy between the two ways of looking at the income-happiness relationship stemmed from the fact that relative income differences account for more of the observed variance in happiness than absolute income differences. What matters most, he argued, is a person's percentile position in the income distribution at any moment in time. When average income in a country grows over time, people's respective positions in the income distribution tend to remain stable, which means we shouldn't expect average happiness levels to change much with income growth. But when we look at people at different points along the income scale at a single moment in time, we're by definition comparing the happiness levels of people with different rankings in the income distribution. And when we look at the data that way, people with higher incomes are clearly happier on average than their counterparts with lower incomes.

These findings have become a little less clear in the light of more recent work. The economists Betsey Stevenson and Justin Wolfers, for example, suggest that average happiness levels in a country do tend to rise significantly over time as average income grows.[2] They argue that in earlier studies, authors failed to detect this tendency because there weren't enough data to facilitate accurate comparisons. Scholars continue to debate the validity of these more recent findings.[3]

But even if measured happiness levels did not increase with income growth over time, it would be a mistake to conclude that income growth isn't beneficial. After all, societies with higher incomes tend also to enjoy cleaner air and water, better schools, less noisy environments, safer working conditions, longer life expectancy, and many other obvious benefits.

One way to summarize what we've learned about the income-happiness relationship is to ask how it might inform your choice between two parallel worlds that were alike in all respects except for any differences associated with their different income levels. A clear implication of existing studies is that if you'd occupy the same position in the income distribution in both worlds (say, the 50th percentile), you'd have compelling reasons for choosing the richer world. You'd probably feel at least a little happier in that world, but even if not, you'd be likely to live significantly longer.

What if you faced with a choice between being in the 25th percentile in a high-income society or being in the 75th percentile in a society in which your income would be lower in absolute terms? Here, the answer is less clear. If the income difference were very small, the 75th percentile position would probably be more satisfying. But for sufficiently large income differences, that conclusion could easily flip.

The choice just described closely resembles the actual choices you'll confront when you face several competing job offers. Figure 1 depicts three hypothetical offers, one from a firm with highly talented workers (Firm 1), another from a firm with workers of intermediate talent levels (Firm 2), and a third from a firm whose workers have relatively low talent levels (Firm 3). The dark lines in the diagram show the pay schedules for the three firms, which tell us how much workers with differing productivity levels will be paid. Like the schedules we observe in practice, they are upward-sloping, meaning that the more productive a worker is, the more he or she gets paid. But note that in each case, pay rises less than dollar-for-dollar with increases in productivity. This too is a feature almost universally observed in actual pay schedules.

In this example, I've assumed that your productivity is $180/hr, meaning

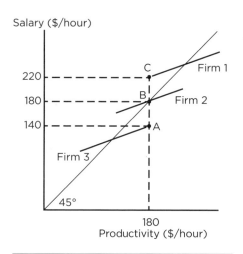

*Figure 1.*

**THE TRADEOFF BETWEEN LOCAL RANK AND PAY.**

*Well-Being and Higher Education*

that if you worked for free, any firm that hired you would enjoy $180/hr in additional net revenue. If you chose to work in Firm 1, you'd occupy the job labeled C, making you the least productive worker in that firm. In that job, your pay would be $220/hr. If you instead chose to work in Firm 2, you'd occupy the position labeled B, placing you in the middle of that firm's productivity distribution, where your pay would be $180/hr. Finally, you could choose to work in Firm 3, where you'd occupy the job labeled A, be paid $140/hr, and be the most productive worker in your firm.

Which job should you choose? If all you care about is money, the job at C in Firm 1 would clearly be your best option. But in choosing that job, you'd also be the least productive worker in the firm, and if that prospect would make you sufficiently uncomfortable, you might want to consider one of the other options. By choosing job B in Firm 2, for example, you'd sacrifice $40/hr in pay but would move up to the middle of the co-worker productivity distribution. Or for an additional $40/hr sacrifice in pay, you could choose Job A in Firm 3 and be the most productive worker in that firm. In short, you face a difficult tradeoff between two things you value: your hourly pay, on the one hand, and your rank among your co-workers on the other.

The upshot is that your best choice among these three options depends on how strongly you feel about these two job dimensions. If you don't care much about your local rank among your co-workers, job C is probably your best option, since the extra pay would be enough to compensate for whatever negative feelings you might have about being the least productive worker. But if you're highly sensitive about interpersonal comparisons, the other extreme option might be best. In that case, the satisfaction you'd derive from being the most talented worker in Firm 3 might be more than enough to compensate for any misgivings you might have about your lower rate of pay. If you fall between these extremes, perhaps job B at Firm 2 would be your best bet.

*One of the most important sources of compensating wage differentials involves how workers feel about their employer's mission*

My point in presenting this example is not to identify one of the options as being better than the others, but rather to emphasize that your choice among jobs merits careful consideration of the many important ways that jobs differ along dimensions other than pay. The economist's theory of compensating wage differentials holds that the more pleasant a job is generally regarded to be, the less employers will have to offer in order to fill it.[4] (Or equivalently, the more unpleasant the job is, the more they'll have to offer.) The specific non-salary dimension highlighted in that example was your local rank among your co-workers. On the plausible assumption that most workers like high rank better than low rank, an employer that offers you the option of high rank can get by with paying you less.[5] Analogous compensating wage differentials have been documented for autonomy, opportunities for learning, workplace safety, and a host of other desirable job characteristics.

One of the most important sources of compensating wage differentials involves how workers feel about their employer's mission. Consider this thought experiment: You have two job offers, one to work for the American Cancer Society writing advertising copy for a campaign to discourage teenagers from smoking, the other for a tobacco company writing ad copy for a campaign to encourage teen smoking. If both positions paid the same and offered otherwise identical working conditions, which would you choose?

Long ago, when I posed this question to a group of Cornell University seniors about to enter the job market, almost 90 percent said they'd pick the American Cancer Society position. And when I asked them to report how much more the tobacco company would have to pay before they'd change their minds, they demanded a salary premium of more than 80 percent on average.[6]

These magnitudes shouldn't surprise you. If you're like most people, when you leave work in the evening, you'd feel better if your day's efforts had made the world better in some way or at least hadn't made it worse. As it turns out, compensating wage differentials for morally satisfying jobs are among the largest of any we observe in practice.

Many job seekers mistakenly focus primarily on the salaries of competing offers. That's a natural error, since salary is not only an important feature of any job, it's also by far the easiest one to observe and compare among jobs. But a central lesson of the happiness literature is that money explains only a small proportion of the observed individual differences in happiness levels. Your efforts to focus on the numerous other job characteristics that people find important will yield big dividends. If an employer is offering what seems like an unexpectedly high salary for someone with your experience and skills, consider the possibility that that she or he may want you to do things that most people would find noxious. In short, when shopping for the right job, be sure to pay careful attention not just to the salary you're offered, but also to the long list of other working conditions you care about.

*A central lesson of the happiness literature is that money explains only a small proportion of the observed individual differences in happiness levels*

In the same vein, I'll note that *Business Week, The U.S. News & World Report*, and other college ratings services might better serve their readers if they too paid closer attention to job characteristics other than salaries. One component of the ranking formulas employed by those services is average graduate starting salaries, which gives schools an incentive to encourage students to pursue high salaries to the exclusion of other goals. We should instead be trying to encourage students to focus on a much broader suite of relevant job characteristics.

Findings from the happiness literature can also be combined with observations about recent labor market trends to gain insight about how better to position yourself to land a job you'll find satisfying. As Charlie Munger, the vice-chairman of Warren Buffett's Berkshire Hathaway, has written, "The safest way to try to get what you want is to try to deserve what you want."[7] But what must you do to deserve the job you want, one whose combination of high salary and attractive working conditions you're most likely to find personally satisfying?

To merit high pay, you have to be able to produce goods or services that buyers value highly. That can happen even if only a few buyers value what you do, if those buyers value it highly enough. But you're more likely to become highly valued if what you do is valued by many buyers. Changes in technology have been making it easier than ever for individuals to serve larger numbers of buyers. But those same changes have also been concentrating demand on a dwindling number of the best performers in every arena.[8] For example, the best federal income tax accountant in a city could once serve only a small number of that city's most important clients, but the author of the best income tax software program can now serve an unlimited number of clients nationwide. That's why the author of the best tax software program earns so much more than the best local accountant used to. One side effect, however, has been to reduce the demand for local accountants. So as technology has extended the reach of the best performers in almost every arena, their income growth has far outpaced that of others.

One implication is that if you want to earn a lot of money, your first priority should be to find something that you can develop deep expertise at doing. In almost every domain, people who get really good at what they do capture a much larger share of total incomes and leave correspondingly smaller shares available for others. Become an expert at something!

That's obviously easier said than done. Those who have studied expert performance estimate that it takes many thousands of hours of difficult practice to develop true expertise at any task.[9] That's why my first response when students ask me for advice about how to succeed is to ask whether there's any activity they've ever engaged in that they found completely absorbing. On reflection, most answer affirmatively. I then suggest that they try to prepare themselves for a career that entails tasks as similar as possible to the activity they named. Even if it's one that doesn't normally lead to high financial rewards, I tell them not to worry. My point is that becoming an expert is so challenging that you're unlikely to expend the effort necessary to do it unless the task is one that you love for its own sake. But if it's a task you love, the process of becoming an expert at it will be highly rewarding quite apart from whether it leads to high pay.

In the happiness literature, "flow" has been identified as one of the most deeply satisfying human psychological states.[10] Flow occurs when you're immersed in an activity to such an extent that you lose track of the passage of time almost completely. If you can land a job that enables you to experience substantial periods of flow, you'll be among the most fortunate people on the planet. What's more, as the years pass, you'll almost surely develop deep expertise at whatever it is you've been doing.

*Flow occurs when you're immersed in an activity to such an extent that you lose track of the passage of time almost completely. If you can land a job that enables you to experience substantial periods of flow, you'll be among the most fortunate people on the planet*

At that point, you may find that your services have become extremely valuable economically, even if not many people in any given location place high value on what you do. Again, that's because technology has been steadily extending the geographic reach of those who are best at what they do. If even a tiny fraction of a sufficiently large set of buyers cares about your service, you may be worth a fortune.

There's of course no guarantee that you'll become best at what you choose to do, or that even if you do you'll find practical ways of extending your reach enough to earn a big paycheck. But if you'll think about your choices carefully, you'll see that the downside risk of my recommended course of action is limited. By choosing to concentrate on a task you love, you'll be able to report truthfully that you enjoy the substantial proportion of your life that you spend at work, which is much more than billions of others can say. And the happiness literature should also reassure you that it's possible to live a very satisfying life indeed even if you don't earn a lot of money.

Bottom line: One of the best ways to spend the extra money you could have earned by taking an unpleasant job is to savor the experience of the more satisfying one you chose instead.

NOTES

1. See Richard Easterlin, "Does Economic Growth Improve the Human Lot?" in *Nations and Households in Economic Growth: Essays in Honor of Moses Abramovitz,* ed. Paul David and Melvin Reder (New York: Academic Press, 1974) and Richard Easterlin, "Will Raising the Incomes of All Increase the Happiness of All?" *Journal of Economic Behavior and Organization* 27 (1995): 35–47.

2. Betsey Stevenson and Justin Wolfers, "Economic Growth and Subjective Well-Being: Reassessing the Easterlin Paradox," NBER Working Paper No. 14282, August 2008.

3. Eric Falkenstein, "Stevenson and Wolfers' Flawed Happiness Research," Falkenblog (blog), July 7, 2013, http://falkenblog.blogspot.com/2013/07/stevenson-and-wolfers-flawed-happiness.html.

4. This venerable theory traces all the way back to Adam Smith, *The Wealth of Nations* (New York: Modern Library, 1937), 100.

5. You may be wondering how Firm 1 can pay you $220/hr if your productivity is only $180/hr. The answer is that high rank, a job characteristic that workers value, could not exist if others were unwilling to accept positions of low rank. The $40/hr premium you get at C compensates you for the negative consequences of your holding a position of low rank, and Firm 1 recovers that premium by paying its top-ranked worker $40/hr less than the value of his productivity. He is willing to accept that pay cut because of the value he places on high rank.

6. Robert H. Frank, *What Price the Moral High Ground* (Princeton: Princeton University Press, 2004), Chapter 5.

7. Charles Munger, "USC Law Commencement Speech," University of Southern California School of Law, Los Angeles, CA, May 13, 2007.

8. Robert H. Frank and Philip J. Cook, *The Winner-Take-All Society* (New York: The Free Press, 1995).

9. K. Anders Ericsson and Jaqui Smith, eds., *Toward a General Theory of Expertise: Prospects and Limits* (New York: Cambridge University Press, 1991).

10. Mihaly Csikszentmihalyi, *Beyond Boredom and Anxiety: Experiencing Flow in Work and Play* (San Francisco: Jossey-Bass, 1975).

PART 4

# The Logic of Change: Why, What, and How?

# 31
## ESSAY

# Institutional Transformation in the Service of Well-Being: A Cross-Cultural Perspective

*Eric D. Lister, MD*

WHAT INSTITUTION IN THE UNITED STATES FITS THE FOLLOWING PROFILE?

- There is heterogeneity among ownership models (private for profit, private not-for profit, governmentally owned) within this institution
- Within its not-for-profit sector, philanthropy is quite important.
- This institution is known, rightly, more for its adherence to tradition than its ability to be nimble.
- In one way or another, this institution touches the vast majority of our citizens.
- Operations are decentralized with significant autonomy at each facility.
- A group of highly compensated but quasi-independent employees are instrumental to success.
- For this particular group of workers, morale and engagement are problematic, more so than in past decades.
- There is a significant power and knowledge gradient between the institution providing service and recipients of service.
- Costs are increasing significantly faster than inflation.
- Despite escalating costs, organizations within this institution feel under-resourced to fulfill their missions.
- Public pressure for value (improved quality, lower cost) is increasing relentlessly.
- In the public arena, questions are being asked about whether the services provided are in fact the services desired or needed by recipients.
- Models are being suggested and in some cases piloted that may radically change the way member organizations conduct their business. Some of these models relate to the use of technology; others relate to mechanisms of payment.
- Access for the poor is problematic; the same can be said of access to service for the socioeconomically compromised

Of course, in a book devoted to higher education, the answer is clear: America's colleges and universities.

But the health care industry also meets each and every one of these qualifications. Across the campus from every college and university in America there is a hospital. Sometimes the hospital is actually on campus, indeed, academic medical centers inhabit both worlds. Always, however, they are no more than a few miles apart. As higher education wrestles with the challenges listed above, it might prove interesting to look across campus and mine the world of health care in search of lessons to be learned.

This volume offers rich and varied perspectives on the concept of well-being. If we are to meaningfully bridge the institutional silos of academe and health care, it will be critical to establish the presence of some similar construct within the medical world.

There are four foci of activity ever-present in serious discussions of the future of health care, which, taken together, bring us very close to the notion of well-being as that term is used in this volume:

- Quality and safety: It often comes as a shock to lay audiences, but in fact American hospitals—for all the miracles of healing practiced on a daily basis—are relatively unsafe places. Mistakes are made. People suffer and die as a result of these mistakes. They happen on a daily basis. As the health care industry has faced this problem, transparency has become a watchword along with the need to reflect soberly on what we do, rather than simply wrap ourselves in the flag of good intentions. The compelling literature on this topic asks caregivers and the institutions in which they work to bring different attitudes and to attend in a different way to self-awareness, self-study, and relentless self-improvement.

- Engagement: With growing clarity, health care leaders appreciate that the culture of the medical environment has a profound effect on not only quality and safety, but also on the human experience of caregivers, patients, and families alike. Some of this attention degrades to a focus on marketing, but in the best of institutions, there is a real understanding that the essence of the healing relationship itself is mediated by the culture of the institutions in which medical care is offered and the attitude displayed by caregivers within these institutions.

- Efforts to marry art and science: The physician and author Abraham Verghese is leading a project at Stanford Medical School to re-immerse young physicians in the art of the physical examination, a ritual that arguably seeks to re-position technology into a role where it supports rather than displaces the sacred encounter between healer and supplicant upon which medicine, at its very best, is based.[1]

- The empowerment of patients and families: Increasingly, medicine is shedding its authoritarian doctor knows best power dynamics for a much more democratic collaboration between those who deliver care and those who receive it by including, involving, and empowering patients and their families to be true partners in the pursuit of health.

None of these currents within medicine translates *exactly* to well-being or its synonyms, such as flourishing, but taken together, they relate closely with their emphasis on breadth, humanism, more lofty and challenging goals, as well as attention to nuance beyond business as usual (doing surgery or providing education).

In both enterprises—higher education and healthcare—we need to distinguish between isolated islands of progressive activity on the one hand and comprehensive, institutional commitment to a restated mission on the other hand. It would be hard to find a campus that does not have *some* department, program, or class where well-being has not been an essential goal for many years. Similarly, every hospital is home to some area of practice that has long embraced collaborative inclusion of patients, deep engagement of providers, nuanced attention to marrying the art and science of medicine. The golden ring, as it were, is *institutional* adoption of such activities to the point that they are embedded not only in formal mission and vision statements, but also in the performance expectations of leaders at every level and the metrics used to define success across the institution.

There may indeed be lessons to be learned from the world of medicine—not because health care has progressed to a degree warranting any awe, but because a constellation of internal and external forces has been relentlessly demanding substantial change for well over a decade. These forces are highly varied. They include self-generated commitment to mission (and the realization that the status quo falls short of truly fulfilling mission), demands from regulators, demands from payers, demands from employers, and competitive threats.

As a consequence of such pressures, hospitals are consolidating at an ever-increasing pace. An entire consulting industry has emerged, offering to help steer major changes. Efforts to date provide us with fertile ground for cross-cultural study.

*Expecting pockets of success or exuberance to spontaneously spark comprehensive, radical, and organization-wide change is naive*

If a rich array of experiments constitutes good news, the relatively slow progression of the field at large is discouraging. We can, however, say from experience that there are three tempting approaches to institutional transformation that are *not* likely to bring the desired and lasting results. Looking first at these methodologies, those committed to change in the world of higher education can at least be warned to avoid what have been, in health care, well-worn paths to disappointment.

RECIPES FOR DISAPPOINTMENT

*The Fantasy of Bottom-up Emergence*
Within most large and complex organizations there already exist positive outliers, departments or service areas that have seemingly spontaneously found ways to defy the norm and exemplify truly inspirational practice. Change agents often hope to catalyze spread from such internal centers of excellence. The same change agents look for internal champions or service areas undergoing upheaval for piloting initiatives in discontinuous change. Both ideas are to be applauded, but expecting pockets of success or exuberance to spontaneously spark comprehensive, radical, and organization-wide change is naive. Inertia, with its many institutional determinants, is simply too powerful a force to be so easily overturned.

*Institution-wide Initiatives Designed to Import Best Practices*
*(The Converse of Our First Example)*
Numerous large health care organizations have experimented with all in attempts at transformation by importing programs that offer a vision of a straight path to a radically different future. Two of the most publicized efforts involve replicating Disney's approach to customer service[2] and Toyota's approach to lean manufacturing.[3] These and other efforts rely upon importing and imposing proven methodologies through changed management practices that often include the indoctrination of thousands of employees and hundreds of management staff.

Successes, unfortunately, are rare and occur only when commitment is sustained over years with relentless intent and major resource investment, as has been the case with the Virginia Mason organization in Seattle. In many instances, the "Iron Law," a term coined by Peter Rossi in 1987, comes into play.[4] Rossi suggests, provocatively, that when one measures efforts directed toward large-scale social change, the results can be predicted to be nil.[5]

*Assigning Responsibility for Institution-wide Change to Some Obvious Party*
*(An Early Adapter, Perhaps, or a Content Expert)*

It is not hard to find passionate advocates for the radical improvement of quality and safety on any hospital campus. Often these men and women have formal assignments within the departments variously titled "Quality," "Quality and Safety," "Risk Management," "Quality Improvement." Who better to task with the job of driving organization-wide change? But it does not work. Why? How could such a commonsensical idea fail and fail repeatedly? The answer lies in a set of mutually-reinforcing barriers:

- Rarely are resources allocated proportional to the desired end state and the magnitude of change necessary to reach that end state.
- While the designated change agents may passionately embrace the vision of a different reality, they rarely have sufficient breath of knowledge to fully grasp the change agenda necessary.
- Nor are they likely to have sufficient cross-departmental experience to understand the barriers to change that exist in other areas of the organization.
- Rarely is the designated change agent imbued with the formal authority to direct the rupture and recreation of established processes.
- Rarely does the designated change agent have enough soft influence or enough time/staff to garner soft influence in order to coax and cajole others into changing.
- The fact that responsibility for change has been delegated to one sub-division of the organization creates tacit permission for other divisions to abjure their own responsibility.

These common paths to failure might suggest that we are doomed to cycles of destruction and re-birth, hoping that whatever Phoenix rises from the ashes is better suited to a more complex future. There is, however, reason for greater optimism because it is possible to identify organizations that have, in fact, differentiated themselves.

By turning away from the previous list of tactics to avoid and looking closely at organizations whose performance is notably superior, we can begin to sketch a conceptual roadmap designed to guide intentional action.

## ATTRIBUTES OF UNIQUELY SUCCESSFUL HEALTH CARE ORGANIZATIONS

*Change is Embraced*

Health care organizations that outperform their peers have made institutional commitments to being in the vanguard of change and innovation. This commitment is clearly expressed by the board, senior leadership, and executives at the departmental level. It involves partnerships with technology innovators (The Palo Alto Medical Foundation, the Ochsner Health System), commitment to redesigning models of care (The Everett Clinic), and investment in understanding the scholarship of change and change management (ThedaCare, Baylor Scott and White).

*The Rationale for Change References Both Inspirational Ideals and Marketplace Imperatives*

Within the stress and strain of today's health care delivery system, starry-eyed idealism and exhortations to do better run a high risk of a flat reception. Similarly, fear-filled admonitions that unless we change, we are lost have been overdone to the point that they sound like the apocryphal Chicken Little who was convinced that "the sky is falling."

What is needed in order to motivate hard-working and beleaguered professionals is a more nuanced message combining a call to the higher purpose of medicine (or education) with a frank, unvarnished picture of the external forces demanding change in the status quo. Accomplishments that exemplify a combination of excellence, service, and innovation are called out for celebration, as across the institution, *everyone* is enjoined—and expected—to engage together in making a new future.

*Admonitions that unless we change, we are lost have been overdone to the point that they sound like the apocryphal Chicken Little who was convinced that "the sky is falling"*

In fact, an inspirational message that re-focuses the entire organization on the higher purpose of medicine—so long as this message is conveyed in terms that do not pretend away real contemporary challenges—is a prerequisite for a truly engaged and deeply committed workforce. Might the same not be true of higher education?

*The Commitment to Superior Performance Includes a Redefinition of Quality and Service*
The Cleveland Clinic, long one of the country's leading health care brands and a worldwide destination for complex cardiac care, recently acknowledged that despite unimpeachable clinical results, it was not meeting the expectations of its patients in terms of their human experience as recipients of care. They acknowledged that they could do better and publicly committed to doing so. They invested resources, energy, and attention to turning this around, and by all objective measures, they have.[6]

*Top-down and Bottom-up Approaches are Balanced and Synchronized*
Institutional commitment articulated in the boardroom and by senior management finds expression in programmatic strategies within each department, in the recruitment of physicians, and in the allocation of funds for innovative programs. These programmatic strategies are supported by pilot initiatives. And successful pilot initiatives are aggressively transformed into the way we do things.

While it is not uncommon to find significant tension between physicians and the organizations in which they practice (cf. university faculties, perhaps), uniquely successful health care enterprises have worked hard to forge common commitments between the board, management, and the physician workforce.

*Screening Providers for Values, Attitude, and Capacity to Advance Overarching Agendas*
In their efforts to recruit young physicians, department chairs of leading health care institutions are committed to focus on the values and attitudes essential to provide coordinated, comprehensive, patient-centered care. They have willingly relinquished the prerogative to recruit with only departmental needs or technical brilliance as criteria. This focus on the ability of new recruits to meet organizational goals rather than simply to meet personal ambitions or departmental goals, while still relatively unusual, is a common denominator of America's great group practices.

Leadership development programs challenge young leaders to develop and pilot innovative programs that bring the organization's values and vision to light. These programs are presented to senior leadership for review, feedback, and funding.

*Leadership Goals at the Departmental or Operating Level Reflect Institutional Priorities*
America's leading health care organizations are committed to partnership between clinicians and operational executives, a model that may not have a natural point of resonance with colleges and universities. Within this spirit of partnership, however, we can describe a willingness to soften the line between professional (physician or professor) and administrative (health care executive or academic chancellors, deans, even departmental administrators) roles. At Baylor Scott and White in Texas, the goals of departments (clinical specialties) and operating units (facilities, etc.) are all linked clearly and explicitly to the organization's commitment to developing a transformative model of care.[7] Departments are expected to collaborate across traditional silos and are rewarded for innovation in care delivery.

These organizations and others like them explicitly repudiate the false logic that attention to culture and softer goals inevitably compromises hard accomplishments.

AT EACH LEVEL OF THE ORGANIZATION
We can take these reproducible features of uniquely successful health care systems and re-cast them into a set of guidelines for each of the following organizational strata:

*In the Boardroom*
Until the recent past, the governing bodies of health care organizations were generally quite passive, focusing on cheerleading and philanthropic activity. Often deferential to both the status of physicians and the expertise of lay executives, the typical board twenty years ago had little to say about strategy, patient-centered care, or quality and safety.

*These organizations and others like them explicitly repudiate the false logic that attention to culture and softer goals inevitably compromises hard accomplishments*

That state of affairs has changed dramatically. In 2006, The Institute for Healthcare Improvement launched the "Boards on Board" initiative designed to educate and mobilize health care boards to demand discontinuous improvement in quality and safety. This initiative began to change the field, and researchers have since demonstrated a clear correlation between board-level attention and organizational performance.[8]

Today's progressive health care board takes a strong role in setting mission-focused strategy, linking both capital spending as well as executive evaluation and compensation to metrics of strategic success. These boards have changed their committee structure to focus not only on the financial health of the organization, but also on the degree to which the organization is aligned with its mission and the level of success that has been attained. Regulatory demands and attention certainly help to focus health care boards and offer a forceful direction that may not exist in higher education, but the best organizations have active boards as well as pointed policies driving patient-centered, integrated, and high quality service, well beyond what is required for regulatory compliance. These boards are leading, and insisting. They are respectful but no longer deferential.

## At the Executive Level

The senior leadership teams of exemplary health care organizations are demanding and focused on change. They appreciate that society cannot sustain current rates of health care inflation, inadequacies and unfairness in access to care, or preventable errors. They are impatient with arguments about how we have always done things and look to drive alignment both within as well as across traditional departments. Jim Leonard, the physician leader of the Carle Foundation, told the press in his home community that his greatest fear concerning the new medical school to be created by his organization and the U. of Illinois was that it would be too traditional, shying away from the opportunity to energize and re-envision what medical education can be.[9]

This activism inevitably abrades the traditional prerogatives of departmental leadership, asserting as it does that alignment toward common purpose and unifying goals is essential. No longer is excellence within some traditional silo sufficient. In order to successfully advance such an agenda, the call of a common mission and shared focus needs to be absolutely clear, along with a convincing description of the advantages to all concerned when synergies are exploited across departments, across schools, and across research, teaching, and service departments. Successful senior leaders hardly sacrifice all their autonomy, but they are selected based on their willingness to appreciate that excellence within traditional boundaries is indeed compatible with being part of a collective that achieves a different level of excellent by virtue of what it does *across* all of its subsidiary domains.

## Departmental or Operating Unit Leadership

Departmental leaders are selected for their ability to advance multiple sets of organizational goals—goals framed in terms of local responsibility as well as goals framed in terms of overarching, institutional commitments. These days, particularly, they are selected and promoted with attention to their ability to manage complex change agendas and to resist the pull of zero sum arguments that they have to win the resource game at the expense of other departments in order to flourish. The complexity of institutional survival and the challenges of new reimbursement models are forcing institutions to find operating unit leaders who can work collaboratively with their colleagues. Long-maintained status hierarchies between specialists and primary care providers are melting away in this environment, as each group appreciates its dependence upon the other.

## At the Clinician Level

Health care enterprises can only be as good as the clinical experts who actually provide care. While physicians get the lion's share of attention, they are hardly the only members of what is increasingly recognized as a team sport. However, they (physicians) enjoy the highest level of autonomy, are traditionally the most hierarchical, and are the most generously compensated.

Despite the fact that clinical care is increasingly recognized as a collaborative endeavor, medical training has retained a dogged focus on individual responsibility and individual prerogatives. Given that we expect physicians to be able to make life and death decisions, often with incomplete data and often in highly stressful situations, an emphasis on autonomy is perhaps understandable.

This traditional value, however, is not great preparation for understanding the concept of interdependence or for collaborative practice. And collaboration is an essential dimension of effective clinical work, particularly in institutions aspiring to the sophistication, safety, and interpersonal sensitivity that stands as our proxy for well-being. Not only is there a *clinical* team operating in every care delivery environment, there also is the need to collaborate with patients and their families, to operate with fiscal restraint, and to understand one's needs and wishes within an organization context often marked by resource constraints.

*The best organizations are intentionally focused on learning how to learn how to exploit what technology offers without allowing it to dehumanize medicine*

Here the best organizations work relentlessly to look beyond technical mastery and beyond dogged commitment to autonomy prerogatives, selecting clinicians instead for attitude and interpersonal skills. These organizations pay close attention to onboarding and organizational acculturation and have very clear behavioral standards. They look for and cultivate an appreciation that interdependence is a fact of life in modern health care and that autonomy should only remain an ascendant value when it is exercised for professional reasons to benefit patients, not when it is exercised for guild reasons, that is, for the caregivers' convenience, ego, or aggrandizement.

*At the Service Delivery Level*

Far from the boardroom, health care is delivered at the bedside, in the clinic, in patients' homes, and in classrooms devoted to education and prevention. Here, in the best of organizations, we see the ways in which values and institutional priorities have survived the risks of dilution inherent in a complex organization. Here is where carefully chosen caregivers present the face of organizational values to their patients.

Connectivity is the issue: connectivity between senior leaders and hands-on caregivers, between the boardroom and the bedside. Technology is both an enabler, as it makes data available, and a threat, as machines threatens to come between care provider and patient. The best organizations are intentionally focused on learning how to learn how to exploit what technology offers without allowing it to dehumanize medicine. A commitment to teamwork and the willingness to include the patient in that team furthers a mutually sustaining connection between the givers and receivers of care. In the best organizations, these issues receive relentless attention.

CREATING AN INTEGRATED FRAMEWORK:
THE HYPOTHETICAL CASE OF XYZ UNIVERSITY

Imagine a medium-sized, successful university whose dean feels passionately that well-being needs to be incorporated as a driving principle across her institution. Over the last few years, she has successfully connected several similarly inclined faculty members with BTtoP grant opportunities. One such pilot was an unqualified success; another was successful although it fell a bit short of expectations.

Why not reach out to a like-minded colleague—the Director of Student Health, who also oversees the Counseling Center, for instance—and ask this individual to spearhead the effort?

While this may seem like an obvious strategy, it risks embodying our third recipe for disappointment. Consider the obstacles:

- As important as the Student Health Center is, can its director be assumed to have the status, relational capitol, formal authority, or moral authority to shape the behavior of dozens of academic chairs and hundreds of faculty member?

- As much as the members of the Health and Counseling Departments know about helping young adults with problems, can we trust that their theoretical knowledge or professional experience is richly informed by the teachings of positive psychology, the scholarship of well-being, and sophisticated theoretical frameworks for adult development? In all likelihood, their training has had more to do with various models of pathophysiology and psychopathology. Their orientation is likely to be toward relieving symptomatology rather than with fostering well-being because *someone* has to help sick or troubled students, and that responsibility will not vanish with an institutional commitment to well-being.

We could make similar arguments against any of a number of other likely candidates for leading change: a religion chair, a social work school, a multidisciplinary program for the humanities, etc.

So what might our dean do? Arguably, she needs to focus relentlessly, systematically, and with calculated intentionality on two foundational activities, which, over time, will create an environment primed for discontinuous change: "establishing a guiding coalition" and articulating the "burning platform" for change.[10]

The coalition she puts together needs to be chosen not simply for its enthusiasm, but also for breadth, reach, political capital, and moral authority. It needs to include individuals with proven business skills, some with the experience of having driven innovation in the past and some who have experience interacting with the university's board. The idea here is not simply to collect the most committed voices but to collect voices that can craft unimpeachable arguments nuanced in such a way as to address local concerns and possess a gravitas that cannot be ignored.

It may take many months to solicit, engage, and convince the right people, and this group cannot simply be allowed to become another committee. To be successful it will have to marry personal passion, local knowledge, relentless focus, and a strategic approach to driving an action agenda.

Hand in glove with the process of recruiting coalition members comes the need to construct the case for change, a case that balances inspiration with an appreciation of the risk involved if attention to well-being remains marginal. These arguments will be necessary in order to recruit members of the guiding coalition and will form a scaffold for the further dissemination of the coalition's recommendations. The relevant arguments will need to be translated into language that reflects the history, values, concerns, tensions, and priorities particular to XYZ University.

A successful guiding coalition will work to refine its proposals and enlarge its sphere of influence in transit to its first goal. That goal involves securing a formal mandate issued jointly from the governing body, president, and faculty senate to return with an action agenda. Inevitably, given the politics of any complex organization, such a mandate will come with constraints and will reflect a host of other implicit or explicit agendas. That cannot be avoided. However, even given political complexities, some level of formal support from all three centers of political power within the institution will create a propitious environment for a real change agenda, one that can be driven simultaneously from the bottom up and the top down—change that can last.

## Conclusions

We are left not with construction blueprints (excessively detailed and prescriptive, a set-up for the Iron Law) but with conceptual sketches drawn from health care, an enterprise similar enough that lessons may indeed translate.

This comparison suggests the need for a program of concerted work on multiple fronts simultaneously. It is, of course, enormously difficult to sustain coordinated efforts across time in the presence of near infinite distractions. It may, however, be far easier than dealing with the consequences of inaction.

And if these lessons from the world of health care are at all useful to those in the world of higher education, think what else might be sparked by serious efforts to share interdisciplinary experience, perspective, and expertise.

---

Notes

1.  Abraham Verghese, "A doctor's touch," filmed July 2011. http://www.ted.com/talks/abraham_verghese_a_doctor_s_touch.

2.  Fred Lee, *If Disney Ran Your Hospital* (Bozeman, MT: Second River Healthcare Press, 2004).

3.  Mark L. Dean, *Lean Healthcare: Deployment and Sustainability* (New York: McGraw-Hill Education, 2013).

4.  Peter Rossi, "The Iron Law of Evaluation and Other Metallic Rules," *Research in Social Problems and Public Policy* 4 (1987): 3–20.

5.  Ibid.

6.  Toby Cosgrove, *The Cleveland Clinic Way: Lessons in Excellence From One of the World's Leading Healthcare Organizations* (New York: McGraw-Hill Education, 2014).

7.  Robert Pryor (President and Chief Medical Officer), personal communication with author.

8.  Ashish Jha and Arnold Epstein, "Hospital Governance and the Quality of Care," *Health Affairs* 29 (2010): 182–7, doi: 10.1377/hlthaff.2009.0297.

9.  James C. Leonard, personal communication with author.

10. John P. Kotter, "Leading Change: Why Transformation Efforts Fail," *Harvard Business Review* (January 2007): 92–107.

32

ESSAY

---

# Reinventing Higher Education
# for the 21st Century

*Peter Leyden*

THE MOMENT HAS COME FOR HIGHER EDUCATION TO REINVENT ITSELF AND HELP CREATE A 21ST-CENTURY CIVILIZATION

I come to this conversation about the future of higher education as an outsider but a very sympathetic one. I've spent the last 20 years rooted in Silicon Valley and the San Francisco Bay Area and have followed the front lip of the digital revolution as it disrupted whole industries and fields. I originally came to San Francisco to work at the early *Wired* magazine, which played an instrumental role in explaining the coming effect of new digital technologies and the internet to broader audiences. *Wired* also played a key role in reinventing how media worked on the nascent World Wide Web. Since the *Wired* days in the 1990s, I have moved through a variety of startups and entrepreneurial ventures and have built a wide network of people who track or are building the next generation of technologies and adapting systems around them. My current company, Reinvent, routinely brings together diverse groups of these kinds of innovators over the new medium of interactive video to work on how to fundamentally reinvent various industries and fields. During the last couple years, I have worked with Georgetown University on two such projects and have been applying what I have learned over the years in Silicon Valley to how to reinvent higher education for the 21st century.

The time truly has come to reinvent higher education. Certainly internal pressures (such as cost increases) are building for a change that those inside the academy can and do frequently lay out. But as an outsider, I see the outside changes that are mounting to the point at which higher education has no choice but to adapt. It is impossible for higher education not to go through a fundamental change when the planet is going through a historical world shift simultaneously on several fronts. People in 50, or 100, or 500 years will look back on the first half of the 21st century as the historic moment when three unprecedented shifts with centuries-long repercussions occurred. First, the world went fully digital. The computerization of everything and the interconnection of everything through the internet will be seen as giving human beings what amounts to a step-change in capabilities. It can be said without much exaggeration that everything can be reorganized for the better (faster, cheaper, more efficient, more productive) around these new technologies. Second, the world went fully global. Previous centuries had at best international systems, but now almost all systems are truly global and working on a planetary scale. Third, the world went fully sustainable—or if not, people may not be around in 500 years to comment. Climate change is such a mind-boggling challenge that it defies comparison with all previous historical challenges. The level of transformation the world must go through in the next 50 years to meet this challenge is, as they say in California, epic.

In this context of profound, historic, world change, how could systems of higher education not change in fundamental ways too? In the short-term, you can see vigorous resistance. Some of this is the typical conservative response of any entrenched institution that faces the unknown. Some of it is because many in academia mistake the early versions of new technologies that have been layered on to higher education as the be-alls and end-alls. Massive open online courses (MOOCs) caused a stir and then were dismissed as not very effective rather than being seen as early the prototypes of what is to come. The more thoughtful concerns are about how to preserve the aspects of higher education that have to do with developing the whole person or fostering well-being, the theme of this book. The application of the early digital technologies to higher education tended to be cruder and lost the nuance of complex interaction traditionally associated with immersive liberal arts education. The early technologies were about creating efficiencies and scale in order to drive down costs, or they were best applied to teaching more technical skills in the fields of science, technology, engineering, and mathematics (STEM).

## HIGHER EDUCATION'S STRATEGIC ADVANTAGES

The march of technology, however, never stops, and many new technologies are maturing that will fit more efficiently with a wider range of higher education applications, particularly those that pertain to the liberal arts and humanities. I have long been a champion of interactive group video, and my company Reinvent has been a pioneer in the field. Only 10 years ago in 2005, YouTube was founded and popularized one-way broadcast video over the internet. This occurred because high bandwidth connections reached the point at which enough businesses and homes in the United States and the Western world were able to move large video files over the internet. We then started to see the inexorable rise of one-on-one interactive video, most notably on Skype. Just several years ago, around 2012, many of the technology giants began investing heavily in interactive group video, which brought together as many as ten people in the same, live, video conversation. Apple expanded its FaceTime, Google created Google Hangouts, and Microsoft bought Skype and expanded the number of individuals who could participate at one time. We also saw an explosion of startups working on these new group video platforms and adapting them initially for business. It's always useful to follow the money in Silicon Valley to get an insight into what's next. This time is no exception. And you can begin to track the data metrics too. In 2005, almost no traffic on the backbone of the Internet carried video. By 2010, half of all traffic on the internet involved huge video files. By 2018 video is projected represent close to 90 percent of all internet traffic. Much of this traffic will be television and movies via Netflix and the like, but much will be interactive video exchanges across America and the world.

*New technology will not necessarily undermine higher education but could super-empower it*

The reason this matters for higher education, and particularly for the liberal arts sector of higher education, is that so much of the value of higher education up until now has been transferred through face-to-face, small group interactions in physical locations on college and university campuses. So much of the higher value work of higher education has been

*Well-Being and Higher Education*

done in a room with one to ten people going deeply into complex conversations that rely heavily on the subtlety of communication through facial expressions and body language and on working on common documents. A one-on-one tutorial, a graduate seminar, or even a faculty committee meeting—everything gets done that way. Now increasingly, those same kinds of interactions can be done reliably, efficiently, and productively over group video. And it's getting better and better each year.

Meanwhile, we are watching an inexorable buildout of the global wireless infrastructure that puts us on track to have pretty much everyone in the world connected to the internet within a decade. Already 75 percent of the people on the planet have mobile phones, and 40 percent are on the internet. We have watched how the buildout works over the last 15 years in the developed world, and we can count on this to take place next: all people, with some exceptions, will soon have mobile phones that can receive at least a voice signal. But once that thin, wireless connection is established, the network can be built out over time to allow basic internet connections to send email, and then soon after that, to make higher bandwidth connections (such as 4G and soon 5G) to move video. So within 10 years, all businesses and all those in higher education can expect everyone on the planet to be capable of connecting with anyone else on the planet over high bandwidth video and all other kinds of collaborative tools.

Seen through this lens, new technology will not necessarily undermine higher education but could super-empower it. The rarified physical environments of academia could open up to the world, and the world could come flowing back to enrich academia. The pace of interactions could greatly accelerate, the scale of reach could ramp up, and the costs could decrease. By no means would the need for physical campuses go away, but they could be greatly augmented to the benefit of all. The super-charging through the high-bandwidth interactive video infrastructure is just one clear way higher education could benefit from the innovative application of new technologies.

There are also many other ways. For example, we're only in the early stages of the Big Data revolution, and a dramatically increasing amount of human activity is now being monitored, captured, and then analyzed. No longer will professors rely primarily on an occasional intuitive insight and a final essay to judge what a student has learned or to understand his or her process for getting there. The professor will have many ways to watch that process and see the critical junctures at which intervention could provide the perfect learning moment. This is not the place to lay out a comprehensive list of new technologies that could positively affect the mission of higher education. My intent is just to point out that one of our three world historical shifts, the world going fully digital, should be understood as actually playing to the strengths of higher education.

The second, historic, world shift—the world going fully global—also plays to academia's strengths. In fact, there are few institutions better positioned to help the world make the transition to a much more highly interconnected, cross-cultural, integrated future. This is particularly true of those fields in the humanities that currently are more undervalued than other practical fields and are most associated with developing the well-being that is the theme of this book. A more interconnected global future needs those with expertise in languages, history, religion, philosophy, and the study of cultures of all sorts. We will more successfully knit the world together with a deeper appreciation and understanding of the humanities. The knowledge and skills that come from the broad range of the humanities are by definition practical in this great human endeavor. They also happen to foster greater individual well-being and help to develop the whole person. But don't lose sight that they are practical too.

It's worth pointing out to American readers that the arrival of an increasingly global era will not diminish the value of American universities and colleges, but rather will increase this value, at least in the first half of this century. American higher education is still a magnet for foreign students and will be for a long time. The more transparent nature of all media and the opening up of these great interactive video conduits will make it easier for people from around the world to take advantage of the gold standard of higher education. That may well change over the decades as the globalization process flattens the historical advantages accrued in the United States and Europe. In the second half of this century, the best students may well migrate to China or another regional powerhouse, but not for now.

The third meta-shift—the move to a fully sustainable world—is an even more perfect fit for higher education. In fact, probably no institution is better positioned to help drive that comprehensive transformation for several reasons. No other institution brings together such a comprehensive range of different disciplines. If ever there was a challenge that calls for a multi-disciplinary response, it is climate change. The creation of truly sustainable systems will touch on nearly every aspect of how humans live and work. The solutions will need to be built on expertise from almost all disciplines, and the ramifications of a shift to sustainability will reverberate through all fields. Academia is also one of the few institutions that maintains a long-term perspective on everything, and its roots go back centuries, even millennia. Unlike frenetic business, it is the one place in society that is optimized for more sober, long-term thinking. Most importantly, higher education is where the best and brightest of the next generations are prepared for their long careers. The real hope for solving the climate crisis and all the associated environmental problems will be the younger generations that are just coming of age in this new century, this new era.

## PREPARING THE NEXT GENERATION FOR THE NEW WORLD

One of the main objectives of the entire higher education game is to help prepare young people for tomorrow's world. Tomorrow's world, the world of the 21st Century, the world in the next several decades—however you want to define it—will be radically different than the 20th century world that shaped and still defines higher education. Almost all the students in college today can expect to live to see the end of the 21st century. We are still in the beginning stages of our understanding of genetics, but our knowledge is on a path of exponential acceleration. The biotechnology industry today is roughly where the digital technology industry was 30 years ago—poised for gangbuster growth. Those in the Millennial Generation, generally considered those aged 18 to 35 today, can almost certainly expect to live 100 years due to scientific and technological advances. The generations after them possibly could live to 120 years, the point most scientists currently think of as the limit of human cellular structure. The bottom line is that we are now literally preparing students for the entire century. And as I have argued above, that century will have at least three unprecedented characteristics that will make how the world works radically different from how the world works today.

The coming all-digital world will have one development with a huge effect: artificial intelligence. Computers are already becoming so advanced that they are starting to be able to do knowledge work that for all previous eras was the exclusive domain of humans. We are seeing how low-level, white collar jobs related to office administration are being shifted to tireless smart machines. And higher-end, white collar jobs that involve legal work and medical analysis are now becoming vulnerable. There is a robust discussion in high tech circles about where the advance of artificial intelligence ends. Could computers become as intelligent as humans in the coming decades? Could they become more intelligent and move beyond human control? Set aside the more extreme speculation about future robot overlords. There is no doubt that the world is heading into a period in which new generations of thinking machines will create massive disruption in industries and fields that previously were immune to such disruption.

How should individuals best prepare for that high-tech world? How should higher education reinvent itself to help those individuals better prepare? In 2015, Georgetown University initiated a project with my company Reinvent to explore some of these themes. We conducted a dozen, in-depth interviews with innovators inside and outside academia to start the project and to get their insights on what was needed. One of them was John Markoff, veteran technology and science reporter for *The New York Times* and author of the new book *Machines of Loving Grace: the Quest for Common Ground between Humans and Robots*.[1] Markoff made a strong case that autonomous artificial intelligence was not on the horizon anytime soon but that widespread disruption from the application of artificial intelligence and advanced robotics was imminent. Some of this, like the arrival of self-driving cars, will have a big effect on jobs such as taxi driver and truck driver. But the applications will rapidly move up the food chain. "I've been traveling the country having a debate with Jerry Kaplan, who wrote *Humans Need Not Apply*. We both have come to the conclusion that one of most valuable things to have in this economy is a liberal arts education," Markoff said. "We're seeing a world where people do different things every two to five years."[2]

*A liberal arts education also fosters the kind of adaptable mindset—the ability to think critically—that always will be needed in any context*

There will be plenty of work for humans to do in the coming decades and throughout the century, but it will be work that humans are best suited to do, not machines. That's one reason why Markoff argued that a versatile liberal arts education, including work in the humanities, will be useful, even practical. The STEM disciplines are actually a more amenable environment for the encroachment of smart machines. The study of the humanities and social sciences is the study of humans, the understanding of which may lie beyond the reach of artificial intelligence for the foreseeable future. A liberal arts education also fosters the kind of adaptable mindset—the ability to think critically—that always will be needed in any context. Dr. Vivienne Ming, a theoretical neuroscientist and technologist working in the field of artificial intelligence, put it this way: "The characteristics that will make people successful are the same things that today are predictors of a successful career, the same things that are predictive of success in children, the same things that have probably been driving human success throughout history. To put it as succinctly as possible, it's about being a problem-solver."[3]

The world for the foreseeable future is not going to run out of problems to solve. And it seems unlikely that machines will be able to acquire the capacity for creative problem solving in the foreseeable future. Tim Kobe, the founder and CEO of the strategic design firm Eight Inc., knows a few things about creative problem solving. Kobe personally worked with Steve Jobs every week for a dozen years, and his firm was responsible for the initial idea and launch of the Apple retail stores. He came to understand how Steve Job's brain worked, and he has since sought to find similar traits in all the positions he fills in his global firm. "Particularly today, there's an emphasis on STEM and the development of the more analytical way of thinking about things, but we haven't seen that in the most successful people," Kobe said. "In the most successful people, we've actually seen an incredible balance in the ability to move between right and left brain capabilities."[4]

From the individual's view, the shrinking world of our increasingly global future will bring its own challenges. A planet of seven billion people is charting towards a crest of at least nine billion, and the vast majority of them have a long way to go to achieve Western standards of living. A big part of the project of the next century will be the inexorable integration of all of the planet's people into a more workable whole. In such a context, people skills will go up in value. And the higher education experience devoted to the humanities and disciplines and focused on understanding or working with people will go up in value as well. Take the example of the study of literature, as explained by Edward Maloney, a professor of English and the Executive Director of The Center for New Designs in Learning and Scholarship at Georgetown: "The idea of getting inside someone else's head and seeing emotional connections and interactions between individuals, even as they're fictionalized, allows you to imagine what it means for you to have those kinds of interactions with someone in the world," Maloney said. "In some ways, it's a way of practicing your sense of empathy."[5] Here's where higher education's timeless goal of fostering well-being in the individual (developing empathy and the like) will gain practicality in a more globalized world.

The meta-challenge of climate change this century should also shape how higher education prepares an individual. Many of the capabilities we have touched on above will be needed here: adaptability to increasingly strange weather patterns and disasters, constant problem solving to scale up new sustainable systems, and empathy for people in other parts of the world who are harder hit and migrating. Other softer skills and knowledge beyond those provided by the hard sciences and engineering will be needed. "You are never going to solve global warming if you don't understand the cultures in which global warming is happening and the cultures of resistance to changing it," said Helen Small, Professor of English Literature at Oxford University and author of *The Value of the Humanities*. "We know what science tells us is required to change the picture, and changing it will come down to changing cultures. And that's the ground in which you really do need humanistically-trained people, people who are equipped with the skills that humanities especially provide to go out there and make a case, and to argue it articulately with language as well as with figures."[6]

The main contribution that higher education can make to the long-term, decades-long battle to turn the tide on climate change will be instilling in coming generations a sense of common purpose, a fundamental belief in the common good. Here we touch on another of the overarching themes of this book: the realization of higher education's greater purpose at the individual level will instill a sense of well-being at the societal level; it is building a bedrock commitment to the common good. It is hard to see how humans will be able to solve the monumental challenge posed by climate change without a level of sacrifice last seen in the great World War in the middle of the last century. This time we must muster such an effort without the fear of an enemy but with the attraction of a common goal. This time we need to be all on the same team working for a common purpose. The world will need help to get there.

## Building a 21st-Century Civilization

If you pull back the historical lens even farther than we have so far, what lies ahead of this century will amount to civilizational change. In 500 years, people will look back on the 21st century the way we do on The Enlightenment. They will see a vast array of changes across almost all fields that were so profoundly different than what came before that they will have to categorize what emerged as a new civilization. The defining features of that civilization will be grounded on our three big shifts and built on an all-digital, computerized foundation. This foundation will be understood as one global system operating on a planetary scale, completely attuned to the limits of the natural environment, and designed to operate sustainably within it. To us today, the three shifts look like nearly impossible challenges that we will never figure out. To people of the future, those shifts will look like inevitable developments that humans obviously had to go through and did.

*The main contribution that higher education can make to the long-term, decades-long battle to turn the tide on climate change will be instilling in coming generations a sense of common purpose, a fundamental belief in the common good*

The last time humans went through a full civilizational change of this magnitude was during the Age of The Enlightenment, which I define as spanning from the scientific revolution of the 17th century through the political upheavals of the 18th century. The sweet spot would be around 1650 to 1750, centered in Europe, and more specifically London and Paris. I expect many in the academic community might debate this proposition, including the temporal boundaries, but hear me out for the purposes of my main argument. It is worth looking back and thinking through the main developments of that era to better understand what lies ahead for us. One could argue that in the space of about 100 years, all the key pieces of modern Western civilization were put into place—constructs that not only the West, but also the whole world still work within today. In science, we invented the scientific method that was the first move towards modernity. In government, we shifted from rule by monarchs to representative democracies. In economics, we created financial capitalism based on stable currencies and reliable banking. In energy, we figured out how to tap into the power of fossil fuels, starting with coal and moving towards oil. In industry, we invented division of labor factory production as the building block for the industrial revolution. In culture, we moved increasingly from religious superstition towards humanism. You get the picture.

The role of universities at that time was absolutely central to what unfolded. Though universities existed before The Enlightenment, their numbers exploded across Europe during the 17th and 18th centuries. An estimated 80 percent of key figures in the scientific revolution were university trained, and half of them held posts in universities to do their work. Isaac Newton was a professor at Cambridge University and was also Master of the Royal Mint—the man charged with figuring out how to create a reliable gold standard for England to jumpstart modern capitalism. Those within higher education at that time were integrally involved in the transformation of the society around them. And why wouldn't they be? Those privileged enough to work within the academy were among those best positioned to help society move through such a complex transition on such a comprehensive range of fronts.

The same holds true today. Those working within higher education are uniquely positioned to operate on the civilizational plane. Unlike those in business, they are not accountable to shareholders pressing for results in three-month quarters. Unlike politicians and government officials, they are not scrutinized at all times by citizens within two-year time horizons. They have the relative luxury to think long-term and to think outside the box without outside pressure, which is the only justification for the continuation of tenure from an outsider's perspective. They have the relative time and freedom in their research to dive deep and to make broad cross connections between disciplines. And they are charged with preparing the next generations to make an impact that stretches even farther into the future.

Today we are facing the same level of deep structural changes in how we work and live that Europeans faced during The Enlightenment. Our scientific understanding of the world is going through fundamental changes. Our core technologies are shifting under our feet. We are just beginning a massive transition to new sources of renewable energies. We have to rethink how we produce almost everything to fit a new sustainable paradigm that leaves much less waste. The way the economy works needs an overhaul in order to better serve everyone, all classes of people, and not only in the developed world but over the whole planet. Capitalism itself may need a fundamental reinvention to deal with its reckless growth and many externalities. And representative democracy itself may need to transition to some new form of democracy that can better serve society and get things done.

If ever there was a time to live up to the full realization of higher education's greater purpose, it is now. We need work on all those fronts by people who are not structurally beholden to outside interests and can act in the interests of the larger society. When we build the new digital, global, sustainable systems that will operate in the 21st century, we want those systems designed first and foremost for the well-being of all individuals and society at large. That should be the foundational starting point for designing any system with civilizational reach.

So higher education faces an incredible opportunity but also must face up to an onerous responsibility. Whichever route motivates you, take it. But for the sake of the broader society and for the welfare of future generations, get going soon. Snap out of the cautious internal bickering about whether or not to change. Drop the incrementalism of what amounts to irrelevant small talk. Step back, look around you, stake stock of what's really happening, and get on with the reinvention of your institutions as the fundamental prerequisite for helping reinvent our world. We've got a 21st-century civilization to build.

*Well-Being and Higher Education*

NOTES

1. John Markoff, *Machines of Loving Grace: the Quest for Common Ground between Humans and Robots* (New York: Ecco Pubishing, 2015).

2. "How to Survive an Explosion of Artificial Intelligence and Increasingly Automated World," *Reinvent*, February 12, 2016, http://reinvent.net/how-to-survive-an-explosion-of-artificial-intelligence-and-an-increasingly-automated-world/. See Jerry Kaplan, *Humans Need Not Apply: A Guide to Wealth and Work in the Age of Artificial Intelligence* (New Haven, CT: Yale University Press, 2015).

3. Vivienne Ming and Peter Leyden, "The Skills Most Predictive of Positive Life Outcomes Are Also Most Robot-Proof," *Reinvent*, November 12, 2015, http://reinvent.net/events/event/skills-most-predictive-of-positive-life-outcomes-also-most-robot-proof/.

4. "How to Survive an Explosion," *Reinvent*.

5. "What Role Can the Humanities Play in Tackling Climate Change?," *Reinvent*, February 8, 2016, http://reinvent.net/what-role-can-the-humanities-play-in-tackling-climate-change/.

6. Ibid.

# 33

# Transforming Learning:
# The LEAP Challenge and
# the Well-Being of Students

*Carol G. Schneider*

WHAT KIND OF COLLEGE LEARNING results in the demonstrable increase in the well-being of students? How do educators help foster that kind of learning? What are the connections between empowering learning and U.S. higher education's traditional privileging of the so-called liberal arts—studies in the humanities, social sciences, sciences, or creative arts? How can liberal learning across these domains of study contribute to a life-enhancing education? And finally, but certainly not least, how do those committed to whole-person, college learning build the capacity and the shared commitment to foster higher learning that is life-enhancing by design?

Over the past fifteen years, the Association of American Colleges and Universities (AAC&U) has probed all these questions. We have done this partly in concert with Bringing Theory to Practice and its far-reaching change initiatives and also in partnership with thousands of campus-based educational leaders and faculty scholars in the United States and beyond who seek to make college learning a force for individual and societal good.

In January 2015, in the context of AAC&U's centennial year, the association brought many lines of inquiry and experimentation together in a bold call to the higher education community to embrace the LEAP Challenge—that is, to expect and prepare every college student (yes, *all* college students!) to complete a significant culminating project, a form of learning we call signature work.[1] That work might be research, an entrepreneurial project, or a mentored internship complete with reflection on learning gained from the experience. It might result in an e-portfolio that illustrates a student's best work on a specific problem or topic, or in a substantial creative product, or in the student's own contribution to an ongoing community-based initiative.[2]

Recognizing the wide variety of ways that students might engage in significant and complex learning, the LEAP Challenge is capacious in its conception of what the student's signature work might be. But it is highly focused in its assertion that the signature work should always be driven by questions that actually matter to the student and that have significance to society as well.

Above all, the LEAP Challenge affirms that signature work should demonstrate the student's capacity to apply learning to complex questions to which the right answer is unknown; the student will use inquiry, evidence, and judgment to build the approach to signature accomplishments. And whatever the project, signature work should include significant writing and guided reflection so that the student's insights are not developed in isolation but rather in dialogue with mentors and often with peers and/or off-campus partners.

In sum, the LEAP Challenge makes visible what AAC&U leaders have come to see as the core of transformative and empowering college learning. Transformative learning is significant learning that addresses substantial questions and topics that matter to the student and that matter in some way to the wider community.

Engaging students in the exploration of significant questions and projects helps them to see that college learning involves much more than just completing a required set of often disconnected courses. When students engage with complex, authentic problems related to issues they actually care about, they bring together the entirety of their learning—knowledge, skills, values, practical intelligence, judgment, and inventiveness—to create needed solutions. They engage, in short, in integrative learning. The challenge is how to make this kind of deep, inquiry-driven, integrative learning a goal and an achievement for all college students, not just for the most fortunate or high-achieving college learners.

THE LEAP CHALLENGE:
SIGNATURE WORK AND STUDENTS' GROWTH IN WELL-BEING
Knowing that signature work and growth in well-being are highly abstract concepts, I want to ground this discussion in some visual portraits of learners, fictional and real, who found new senses of purpose and power—transformative learning—in their college studies. The first portrait comes from a striking moment in the 2015 film *Brooklyn*[3] in which Eilis (played brilliantly by actress Saoirse Rowan) literally glows as she describes with transparent pride and joy what she—an initially hesitant immigrant student—gained from her night school studies at Brooklyn College, specifically, her two-year course of study to qualify as a bookkeeper.

Bookkeeping is probably not what most readers of this volume envision when they think of whole-person learning. Yet Eilis's sense of accomplishment is palpable and contagious. Viewers can see how through her night school program and also through her experiential learning as she struggles to make sense of her immigrant experience in 1950s New York, Eilis becomes a person who can and will choose her own path to a fuller future.

In the film and in the Colm Tóibín novel[4] on which it is based, Eilis eventually uses the learning she acquired from her night school classes at Brooklyn College to give something back to her village in Ireland. The novel describes a final college assignment that requires Eilis to translate accounting rules and financial information into the construction of meaningful board and shareholder reports for a fictional company.[5] When Eilis is called back to Ireland unexpectedly, she uses these bookkeeping skills and her keen sense of ethical responsibility to recast salary records that had fallen into chaos at the firm where her late sister once worked. Eilis becomes, in short, a person with new knowledge and new-found capacity to share her knowledge with others. She has gained practical knowledge and she puts it to use.

Watching a gifted actress bring this moving tale of transformative learning to life on the screen, I was forcefully reminded of another set of similarly glowing faces—this time, the faces of the real-life college students whose educational journeys are the subject of AAC&U's centennial year video, *Liberal Education: America's Promise*.[6] The students featured in this video came from a broad array of institutions: California State University-Fullerton, California State University-Northridge, College of Wooster, LaGuardia Community College, Michigan State University, and Worcester Polytechnic Institute. Selected to illustrate the broad range of possibilities for college-level signature work, these students also exuded pride as they described what they accomplished and contributed through college endeavors: research, entrepreneurial projects, community service abroad, integrative e-portfolios, and the experience of mentoring and tutoring other students.[7]

The backgrounds and projects of these students were all different, but they shared with each other and with the fictional Eilis a palpable glow. Their narratives show us minds at work and whole people fully engaged with their learning journeys. In the midst of meta-morphosis, these diverse college students demonstrated joy, pride, and the sense of new possibility in getting educations and in specific, tangible contexts in which they applied learning to work they cared about.

All of these portraits help us to see not only students who achieved well-being in college, but also students with newfound confidence that they can actually use learning to create value. These portraits show us human beings who have become enthralled with the notion that they now know how to put their knowledge to practical use.

## Positioning the Liberal Arts and Sciences as Catalysts for Transformative Learning

Conventionally, liberal learning has been identified with specific areas of study, the so-called liberal arts and sciences that are usually taken to include the humanities, sciences, social sciences, and the arts. Or liberal learning may be identified with participation in a residential college or university, which at least potentially immerses the student in round-the-clock learning that is academic and communal. Or sometimes liberal learning is described in more abstract terms, such as rigor and excellence, or the development of twenty-first century skills such as analytical inquiry, collaboration, and communication.

The dominant message to be taken from the student portraits, however, is the power and the pride that students develop as they gain proficiency in *applying their learning*, whether to projects, or research, or creative work, or service to others. The real pay-off has come for these students not in what they know, although knowing is clearly a source of joy for many learners, but in what they can do.

Often, liberal arts educators worry about the prevalence of a real-world, practical or applied orientation in the views of many students about what matters most in college. Schooled in Aristotelian or even Platonic precepts, liberal arts educators may describe practical learning as merely applied, which perpetuates the view that while truth-seeking calls into play the full powers of the mind and heart, the application of knowledge involves mainly the rote and the routinized. Indeed, when AAC&U released a statement in 1998 that described liberal learning as (among other qualities) "practical," a very well-known college president and humanist wrote to say she could "never" assent to such an assertion. The concept of practical learning degraded the liberal arts, she assured me scathingly.

It is time to insist that those who privilege analysis over application—or discovery over the uses of discovery—disvalue and perhaps even frustrate the aspects of learning that are most empowering to every-day students, citizens, professionals, and society as a whole. Teaching people how to put complex knowledge to use ought to be a primary and highly valued goal for liberal educators. Ours is a world, after all, in aching need of solutions to problems on every possible front. Knowledge is a crucial key to the creation and deployment of those solutions. It is when we put knowledge to use that most learners reach higher levels of comprehension and understanding. An old Chinese proverb captures with precision the transformative learning that the LEAP Challenge promotes: "Tell me, and I'll forget. Show me, and I may remember. But involve me, and I'll understand."

Applied learning, as envisioned in the LEAP Challenge, involves students in significant questions that require exploration, evidence-gathering, collaboration, engagement with diverse perspectives, and often active experimentation with alternative strategies to create the intended solution or creative work. Involvement becomes an ongoing activity, and new learning becomes a continuous process. Specifically, when students begin to apply their learning to complex problems, they necessarily begin to integrate different aspects of their education: knowledge, skills, values, experience, and active consideration of what works and what does not. An emphasis on applied liberal learning teaches students to connect theory and practice and to use each to build upon and amend the other. When done well, applied learning is generative learning that fosters agility in problem-solving and in creating and testing new possibilities.

Moreover, when students tackle complex problems—whatever the topic—their efforts help them see why a good liberal education necessarily includes meaningful study in multiple disciplines and why it places so much emphasis on their learning with and from people whose backgrounds are very different than their own. The truth is that no complex problem belongs entirely to one academic field or another. When we struggle with a problem, we need multiple perspectives that are disciplinary and societal. Unhappily, as AAC&U leaders have noted for more than a quarter century, the basic concept of study-in-depth in a single field tends to mislead students into believing that learning in their majors is all they need for satisfying futures, when in fact they need multidimensional learning for virtually anything they hope to accomplish.[8]

*Problem-centered learning helps students to viscerally experience the value of broad learning across the liberal arts and sciences*

In scholarship, some of the significant breakthroughs lie at the boundaries of disciplines as researchers borrow insights and methods from multiple fields. In the arts, the creator needs to consider what is being expressed as well as the envisioned experiences and responses of those who will encounter the work of art. When we deal with public questions related to health, education, poverty, climate, sustainability, or political change, we necessarily call on insights, evidence, and strategies from many different contexts: political, cultural, economic, historical, ethical, scientific, psychological, and ethical.

Expecting students to apply their learning to complex problems is, then, a powerful way to help them discover the genuine need for the insights of different academic fields and endeavors and for the insights to be gained from working with diverse partners. Problem-centered learning helps students to viscerally experience the value of broad learning across the liberal arts and sciences. Application, in short, makes integrative liberal learning not only a theoretical possibility, but also a lived and potentially transformative experience.

Moreover, the process of practical problem-solving also helps dissolve the artificially constructed, but often vigorously maintained, divide between the true liberal arts and sciences and the various fields that prepare professionals for their careers: business, health, pharmacy, engineering, education, social work, public administration, and the like. Since the majority of today's college students already major in these fields, many of their signature work questions and projects will almost certainly come straight from the practical side of higher education's dividing walls. But when they begin to tackle significant problems in those fields, students soon discover that they need insights from the arts and sciences to make real progress: societal knowledge, historical knowledge, ethical reasoning, cross-cultural knowledge and competence, and quantitative and communicative capacities. Conversely, students versed in the liberal arts and sciences discover that to put knowledge to use, they need practical insights.

The LEAP Challenge is designed to provide an illuminating answer to the perennial question: *Why do I have to take courses outside my major?* By involving students in complex inquiry projects, the LEAP Challenge allows students to discover for themselves that they need broad learning from all parts of the curriculum to tackle complex questions.

Toward Guided Learning Pathways:
Changing the Way Students Experience College

As a reader, you may well think or object that a single, signature work project is insufficient to prompt the kind of transformative, horizon-expanding, integrative learning that I have linked with an empowering liberal education and with student well-being. As a leader in developing the LEAP Challenge, I completely agree. To prompt the kind of life-enhancing learning the LEAP Challenge envisions, the preparation for signature work needs to begin in the initial phase of college—optimally earlier—and to continue at progressively more challenging levels as students move forward. To execute a significant culminating project, students will need *frequent practice* in inquiry assignments to develop needed proficiencies. They also will need opportunities to explore with mentors and peers the questions that matter to them to identify and develop a project they really want to complete.

In other words, to prepare students to tackle and succeed with complex projects, we need to remap the traditional pathways they follow through college into what educators now call *guided learning pathways* that are carefully designed so that students have many opportunities to engage in problem-centered, cross-disciplinary inquiry and exploration and to receive faculty feedback on their questions, strengths, needs, and evolving proficiency in tackling significant questions. In these guided pathways, students will pursue specialized and broad learning *simultaneously* from the outset of their studies. The pathways will include frequent opportunities for students to integrate insights and skills from different fields of study and from scholarship and practice by working on projects that make integrative learning a valued and visible capacity. The college curriculum will become more deliberately cross-disciplinary and more applied.

Calling on educators to rethink and redesign educational pathways may sound dramatic and radical, but this needed remapping has already begun. Many institutions and departments have redesigned educational programs to foster just this kind of problem-centered, cross-disciplinary, and integrative liberal learning. The purpose of the LEAP Challenge is to publicize and accelerate the pace and inclusiveness of educational change that is already in progress. To put it differently, the LEAP Challenge invites those in higher education to think, talk, and act in new ways about the overall organization of the college curriculum.

Specifically, it asks that higher education breaks free—once and for all—of the now weary and outdated curricular design that was put in place at the turn of the twentieth century.

Popularly termed *breadth/depth,* this now outdated curricular organization was once the very latest thing. In 1909, breadth/depth gained visibility and then traction after Harvard faculty adopted a new curriculum built around distribution requirements in the major areas of knowledge and concentration in a specific discipline.[9] Bread/depth positioned broad or general learning in the first two years of the curriculum and specialized learning in a single field—the concentration or major—as the most advanced and significant form of learning to be completed in the final two years of college.

Like any curriculum reform, breadth/depth was a product of its time and useful to replace an elective model that resulted in too many students taking introductory and comparatively shallow courses. The reform agenda was to foster depth in a particular field, and the major is still viewed as a necessary part of a well-organized education. Conversely, however, the breadth component of the curriculum—the primary locus for students' arts and sciences study—was anything but a success. All too often, breadth devolved into a cafeteria style curriculum in which students were faced with a bewildering array of choices as they selected a hand full of courses to complete their breadth requirements. The result for millions of students was confusion at best and departure from college altogether at worst rather than a coherent and empowering experience of broad college learning.

*Revealingly, Arizona State University President Michael Crow told Politico that he required his own children to take double majors in college, because learning across different disciplines fosters creativity*

Today, however, there is abundant evidence that educators are working to reconceive breadth and depth and especially to create new relations between them. Results of recent surveys conducted by AAC&U indicate that educators see general education or breadth as a top priority for educational change and improvement.[10] Because of the prevalence of the breadth/depth model, many assume that general education reform applies only to the initial years of college. But it has been clear since AAC&U first began to ask questions about general education in 2000 that college leaders are working proactively to extend broad learning across the entire four years of college from cornerstone to capstone. Moreover, educators are linking these changes in general education to study in the major and breaking down the dividing walls that traditionally separate general from specialized learning.

For example, the results of a Hart Research study done for AAC&U in 2015 indicate that 46% of our member institutions include some form of upper level required general education study, which negates the notion that general learning should be completed in the first two years of college.[11] The same research shows that a majority of responding institutions seek to foster integrative learning through closer connections between general education and majors and by promoting the kinds of engaged learning practices—research, internships, senior projects, service—that are envisioned by the LEAP Challenge.[12]

Moreover, students themselves increasingly choose multiple majors or majors and minors to create their own strategies for cross-disciplinary learning in the final two years of college. Revealingly, Arizona State University President Michael Crow told *Politico* that he *required* his own children to take double majors in college, because learning across different disciplines fosters creativity.[13] At Arizona State University, Crow has been a national leader in creating cross-disciplinary schools in which scholars and learners from multiple disciplines work together on intellectual and societal problems.

Many other colleges and universities are taking active steps to foster cross-disciplinary learning and to help students blend academic and experiential learning. For example, my own alma mater, Mount Holyoke College, now requires all students to do field-based internships or mentored research projects. Preparatory courses and advising help students develop their projects, and results are shared with the campus community in a post-project LEAP symposium.

Curriculum reports from Harvard[14] and Stanford[15] recommend that faculty find ways to foster cross-disciplinary and thematic learning, not just learning in a specialized field. William & Mary, one of the nation's oldest institutions, recently revised the general education program to foster inquiry and integration from first to final year in a capstone project:

> *The COLL 400 capstone experience takes place in the major, typically in your senior year. Here you'll draw on the knowledge you've gained from studies in your major, the College Curriculum, and your elective courses to take your own scholarly initiative. You'll be expected to synthesize and apply critical analysis, solve problems in an applied and/or academic setting, create original material or original scholarship, and communicate effectively with audiences. You can complete COLL 400 through upper-level seminars, independent study and research projects, and Honors projects, that are specially designated by departments, programs, or schools. As you complete the COLL 400 capstone experience and your undergraduate career at William and Mary, you should be very well positioned to answer the question: What is a liberal arts education?[16]*

In a similar spirit of fostering integrative liberal learning, many institutions have increased the commitment to field-based or experiential learning. Cornell University and the entire SUNY system announced that *every student* should participate in field-based learning while in college. At Cornell, this learning will have a civic focus. In the SUNY system, the emphasis is on ensuring that students will have internships or other applied learning experiences that help them connect college learning with jobs.

Advanced study is, in short, becoming more cross-disciplinary and more experiential or applied. This trend is by no means limited to elite institutions. SUNY and Arizona State enroll the entire spectrum of U.S. college students, from the most well-prepared to the most struggling. In the community college sector, a robust e-portfolio movement is underway that is specifically designed to help students integrate learning and make their accomplishments visible to themselves, faculty, employers, and their own families.[17] In community colleges, there is also growing movement to design more focused and purposeful guided learning pathways because based on the concept that well-structured curricula work better for the large number of first generation students who enroll in two-year institutions. One result of this movement is that students will be steered to general education courses linked to their majors or at least to their likely career interests (e.g., health studies, technology, etc.) and not to the cafeteria, self-service menu that has bewildered so many college students.[18]

What we see from a national vantage point, in sum, is a curriculum undergoing far-reaching re-invention and redesign. Breadth/depth is being replaced by braided, cross-disciplinary, and hands-on learning, organized in guided learning pathways in which culminating projects play an integrative role. The context has been set for all students to plan for and successfully complete meaningful signature work projects that help them simultaneously explore questions they care about and integrate broad learning, specialized learning, intellectual skills, and application.

However, the pace of change is much too slow; nearly half of all college students are doing culminating work, but that means that more than half of all graduating seniors have not done senior projects of any kind, much less ones that meet the vision outlined in the LEAP Challenge. Moreover, many students have no idea that broad learning is critical to their futures. After hearing me argue the economic importance of broad learning, a student said to me in some consternation, "I am very surprised by what you are saying. I always thought that if I just did whatever I was supposed to in my major, I would have everything I need to succeed in my career." Employers overwhelmingly insist that it takes more than a major to succeed in today's economy.[19] This student and millions of others have no idea that employers seek, value, and reward multidisciplinary learning and not just field-specific learning.

*Students need and deserve a more contemporary understanding of what matters in college and strong guidance to help them develop the ability to put their learning to practical use*

Students need and deserve a more contemporary understanding of what matters in college and strong guidance to help them develop the ability to put their learning to practical use. What can educators do to provide the needed guidance and support? How do we begin to remap our educational pathways so that students prepare for and successfully complete significant applied learning projects?

## HOW EDUCATORS CAN MAKE HANDS-ON LEARNING EXPECTED AND FEASIBLE FOR STUDENTS

Ultimately, all educational change like all politics begins at the local level. Each institution will need to assess its own readiness to make signature work an integral part of its educational expectations and degree requirements. Each will need to empower faculty and staff to work together to develop the educational case for the value of signature work and determine how best to advance that cause in their own institutions.

But the shift toward involving students in inquiry-based learning and integrative, culminating projects is already well advanced nationally. Change-minded leaders on any particular campus can and should use emerging evidence on what works for today's students from their own and other institutions. I offer here a few suggestions about how to develop the case that students' completion of signature work should become a shared institutional commitment and how to move forward in designing guided learning pathways that support students' achievement of meaningful advanced projects.

*1. Take a close look at your departments. Many of them already require students to do some form of culminating work. Learn from their leadership.*

A few national data points show us where we are currently in terms of student participation in culminating projects or signature work. The first is from the National Study of Student Engagement (NSSE). Using a definition of culminating work very similar to AAC&U's

definition of signature work, NSSE reported that 46% of college seniors have done or plan to do some form of culminating work.[20] This is an important finding because it allows us to track where we are nationally in terms of The LEAP Challenge. NSSE reports data by institutional type so institutions can compare themselves against national benchmarks and peers.[21]

In a 2015 Hart Research survey of member provosts, results indicated that only 23% of AAC&U colleges, universities, and community colleges currently require culminating work as an institutional requirement for all students.[22] If we juxtapose the NSSE and AAC&U data sets with one another, they provide two points of useful guidance to campus leaders interested in advancing signature work projects for their own college learners.

First, disciplines and departments rather than institutions have taken the lead in making culminating or capstone experiences requirements for students in particular fields. Second, most campuses likely have numerous examples in which departments have already made culminating work an expected part of the curriculum. Thus the most obvious place to begin work on the LEAP Challenge is with individual departments. Talk with department chairs and faculty about their capstone requirements. Are the projects truly substantial and integrative? Are students succeeding in the work? If so, what features of the curricular pathway helped prepare them? If not, what changes are needed to support stronger achievement? Do faculty members assess the projects (or at least a sample) to ensure that students have developed the intellectual and practical skills needed to accomplish inquiry-centered work? How do departments calibrate faculty roles to enable supervision of the intended student work?

Departments that have been working internally to create more purposeful and integrative learning experiences for their students are natural resources for a reform-minded administration. Build from this circle of experienced internal leaders and engage faculty who have standing in the institution as well as the department. Faculty creativity, talent, and commitment are essential ingredients in the kind of reform the LEAP Challenge envisions.

## 2. Probe student participation in high impact practices.

The LEAP Challenge calls for all students to do integrative signature work that builds on evidence about a set of engaged, *high impact*, learning processes that have a beneficial effect on student persistence in college and their achievement of deeper learning. These high impact practices include first year seminars and first year experiences, topically linked courses or learning communities, course-based service learning, writing intensive courses, undergraduate research, internships and other forms of field-based learning, diversity courses and experiences, global learning experiences, collaborative assignments and projects, and capstone or culminating learning. Researchers convincingly demonstrate that the more students participate in such experiences, the greater their success in college. Success is defined in terms of persistence/graduation and in terms of achieving widely endorsed learning outcomes such as critical thinking, communication skills, and civic development.[23] However, researchers further suggest that second generation students are more likely than first generation students to participate in high impact practices.[24] Even when institutions require specific high impact practices for all students, they usually front load them in the first year, most likely as a strategy to encourage persistence.[25]

A purpose of the LEAP Challenge is to map engaged or high impact learning practices across the entire, expected curriculum from first to final year. An institution that seeks to implement high impact learning practices should determine what students are doing now; disaggregate the findings with equity; and with input from faculty, determine how best to engage students early, often, and at an advanced level in inquiry-centered learning and signature work projects.

These high impact practices and others that engage students in inquiry-based learning are necessary for student success in advanced, integrative projects. Make sure they are built into the required educational pathways in general education and in majors. Culminating assignments undertaken without prior preparation are doomed to failure. Once you understand program and student data on high impact practice, a plan can be developed to implement signature work expectations for all students.

*3. Study national models and exemplars.*
While only one fourth of U. S. institutions currently require all their students to complete culminating work, there is much to be learned from these examples. Some may assume that only elite institutions create such challenging expectations, but that is far from the case. With generous support from the Endeavor Foundation, AAC&U is currently developing case examples from highly diverse colleges and universities that already prioritize integrative learning and that have established degree-level expectations for culminating work that all or most students complete. These colleges and universities include LaGuardia Community College, Salt Lake City Community College, Bard College, Hampshire College, Luther College, Case Western Reserve University, Portland State University, Santa Clara University, Southern Illinois University-Edwardsville, University of Wisconsin, Oshkosh, Wagner College, and Worcester Polytechnic Institute. The thirteenth and final example is a school within a school: the School for New Learning at DePaul University, which for nearly 40 years has required all adult learners to complete senior projects in order to graduate and teaches these students the arts of self-directed inquiry and experiential learning in order to help them succeed with this requirement.

Beyond these case examples, AAC&U already has drawn several dozen U. S. institutions into a LEAP Challenge movement, including include Boston University, Community College of Philadelphia, University of Houston-Downtown, and University of Nevada at Los Angeles. With participants in the LEAP Challenge movement located across the United States, any interested college, university, or community college can readily identify partners for ventures in making significant student projects expected rather than optional.

*4. Enlist employers and civic leaders as partners and champions.*
Knowledgeable faculty need to be centrally involved in mapping the educational pathways through which students practice and prepare to succeed in inquiry-based, integrative projects. They should do so in partnership with student life professionals and advisors whose support is essential if students are to be guided toward the most powerful forms of learning. That said, LEAP Challenge efforts also should enlist champions and partners for students signature work from the institution's larger circle of alumni, employer partners, and civic or policy leaders. Employers have been at the forefront of insisting that colleges should prepare students to succeed in big picture learning *and* real-world applications. Data on employer perspectives consistently demonstrate that employers believe colleges and universities should require applied learning projects and that employers are more likely to hire graduates who have done mentored internships, senior projects, and other forms of hands-on work.[26]

Less research has been done on the perspectives of civic leaders, but at every institution, students work on policy projects, on service learning assignments, and on public questions in other forms. The community leaders who make these assignments possible can be enlisted to leadership circles that help make signature work projects expected and feasible. High profile partners can and should help to herald in a new era cross-disciplinary, integrative, and applied liberal learning, not just for some but for all college learners.

*5. Take full advantage of the digital learning environment and recalibrate faculty roles and rewards to make student work on inquiry projects a priority.*
In releasing the LEAP Challenge, AAC&U recognized that the digital revolution will significantly change the way students learn and that the future will bring new combinations of digitally supported, face-to-face, and blended forms of learning. The question is not whether digital progress will proceed apace, but rather how to use it to help students build the knowledge, skills, and mentored experience to deal successfully with unscripted, open-ended problems. The LEAP Challenge seeks to expand opportunities for faculty to work with students individually and in teams to teach them the arts of inquiry and analysis and to help them use digital tools and virtual communities in their projects.

Mentoring student work is time-consuming and challenging. The question then, is: how can we use digital platforms and cognitive tutorials to free up faculty time from such tasks as lecturing so that time can be reassigned to activities from which students will gain the most long-term value? This is not a simple question, but this is the time to ask and answer it. The digital age is already upon us. Higher education must rally to ensure that it provides more—and more empowering—liberal learning for today's students. Anything less will surely mean a diminished future for everyone.

RECLAIMING THE PUBLIC PURPOSES OF COLLEGE:
THE NEXT FRONTIER FOR STUDENT SIGNATURE WORK
I began this essay by underscoring the transformative power of applied learning and related projects. Students with broad, horizon-expanding educations and who can succeed with signature work projects will be far better prepared for today's economy than students who have pursued shallower, less challenging forms of learning.

That said, we also need to claim, explore, and develop the democratic and global potential of applied learning projects if we are to create a more just, inclusive, and literate society and if we want to sustain our planet for future generations. Students already are enthusiastic leaders in tackling problems, and when they make public service projects part of college learning, they model exactly the kind of engaged citizenry that Benjamin Franklin, Thomas Jefferson, and Abigail Adams envisioned at the founding of this country.

Students who tackle public service signature work projects will develop the skills and experience they need for economic success, but they also will emerge from college better prepared than any generation before them to take responsibility for the future of our democracy—its decency, vitality, and ethic of care for the well-being of others. But how, exactly, can we build new public and policy commitment to the value of liberal education for the greater good of democracy's future? How do we reclaim the concept of liberal learning as a public trust, an investment in society's shared future and reverse the current assumption that a college education primarily provides *private* benefit?

Having worked on the LEAP initiative for nearly a dozen years, I have come to believe that students are the best ambassadors not for an abstract concept of public-spirited, liberal learning, but as living exemplars of minds at work that collaborate across difference to create solutions that we need for our shared future. The LEAP Challenge builds from this insight. Ours is a metrics-minded age. We can count and report how many students take part in high impact educational practices and how many do projects that take a semester or longer to complete. We can and should make promulgation of such reports a national priority.

But every age learns best from its own illustrative stories. When students talk to the public about what they have accomplished in college we see higher learning at its best. They show us why cross-disciplinary, hands-on, and integrative liberal learning is so empowering for everyone's future. We need to ensure that every college graduate has a personal story to tell about a challenging and empowering college learning accomplishment. Forty-six percent of college seniors do culminating work, so we are farther toward that goal than most believe. Heartened by this finding, let's organize to create guided learning pathways to meaningful accomplishment for all college students, not just some of them.

The LEAP Challenge is a work in progress. When everyone sees college as an opportunity to build the capacity to put knowledge to use, students will flourish and democracy will flourish as well. And not least, our society can once again reclaim confidence in learning as the foundation of our liberties and the nation's best investment in a globally shared future.

---

NOTES

1. LEAP is an acronym for Liberal Education and America's Promise, AAC&U's ongoing signature initiative. Launched in 2005, LEAP provides a comprehensive and inclusive framework for quality college learning and reform that includes essential learning outcomes, engaged or high-impact learning practices intended to help students practice and achieve the essential learning outcomes, and assessment strategies that make students' authentic work the primary source of evidence on their achievement of the essential learning outcomes. LEAP encompasses all areas of college study, including career and professional fields. For more information, see www.aacu.org/leap.

2. Ibid.

3. *Brooklyn*, Film. Directed by John Crowley. Los Angeles: Fox Searchlight Pictures, 2015.

4. Colm Tóibín, *Brooklyn* (New York: Scribner, 2010).

5. Ibid, 204.

6. *Liberal Education: America's Promise*. Produced by Paul Stern with editorial assistance from AAC&U Vice President for Policy and Public Engagement, Debra Humphreys. Boston: Vox, Television, Inc., 2015. https://www.aacu.org/centennial/video.

7. Ibid.

8. Project on Liberal Learning, Study-in-Depth, and the Arts and Sciences Major, *Liberal Learning and the Arts and Sciences Major: The Challenge of Connecting Learning* (Washington, DC: AAC&U, 1991); Carol Geary Schneider and Robert Shoenberg, *Contemporary Understandings of Liberal Education* (Washington, DC: AAC&U, 1998); The National Leadership Council for Liberal Education and America's Promise, *College Learning for a New Global Century* (Washington, DC: AAC&U, 2007); The National Task Force on Civic Learning and Democratic Engagement, *A Crucible Moment* (Washington, DC: AAC&U, 2012).

9. While Harvard was not the first university to adopt the concentration or major, its leadership helped spur widespread initiation of the breadth/depth design.

10. Hart Research Associates, *Trends and Emerging Practices in General Education* (Washington, DC: AAC&U, 2009), https://www.aacu.org/sites/default/files/files/LEAP/2009MemberSurvey_Part2.pdf); Hart Research Associates, *Recent Trends in General Education Design, Learning Outcomes, and Teaching Approaches* (Washington, DC: AAC&U, 2015), https://www.aacu.org/sites/default/files/files/LEAP/2015_Survey_Report2_GEtrends.pdf.

11. Ibid.

12. Ibid.

13. Caitlin Emma, "A chat with ASU President Michael Crow," *Politico*, January 5, 2016. http://www.politico.com/tipsheets/morning-education/2016/01/a-chat-with-asu-president-michael-crow -new-year-new-edu-clinton-talks-teachers-in-iowa-campus-protest-politics-212003.

14. Harvard University Faculty of Arts and Sciences, *Report of the Task Force on General Education* (Cambridge, MA: Harvard University, 2007), http://isites.harvard.edu/fs/docs/icb.topic830823.files/Report%20of%20 the%20Taskforce%20on%20General%20Education.pdf; "Essays on General Education in Harvard College," Harvard College Program in General Education, http://www.generaleducation.fas.harvard.edu/icb/icb. do?keyword=k37826&pageid=icb.page331351.

15. The Office of the Vice Provost for Undergraduate Education, Stanford University, *The Study of Undergraduate Education at Stanford University* (Stanford, CA: Stanford University, 2012), http://web.stanford.edu/dept/ undergrad/sues/SUES_Report.pdf.

16. William & Mary University, COLL 400: Capstone, http://www.wm.edu/as/undergraduate/curriculum/ coll/400/index.php, accessed February 8, 2016.

17. Bret Eynon and Randy Bass, *Open and Integrative: Designing Liberal Education for the New Digital Ecosystem,* (Washington, DC: AAC&U, 2016).

18. Thomas R. Bailey, Shanna Smith Jaggars, and Davis Jenkins, *Redesigning America's Community Colleges: A Clearer Path to Student Success* (Cambridge, MA: Harvard University Press, 2015).

19. Hart Research Associates, *Trends and Emerging Practices*, 2009.

20. National Survey of Student Engagement, *Engagement Insights: Survey Findings on the Quality of Undergraduate Education—Annual Results 2015* (Bloomington, IN: Indiana University Center for Postsecondary Research, 2015), http://nsse.indiana.edu/NSSE_2015_Results/pdf/NSSE_2015_Annual_Results.pdf.

21. Unfortunately, we don't have comparable data from the Community College Survey of Student Engagement. It should become a high priority to discover how many two-year students are doing significant projects of various kinds voluntarily or as part of their degree requirements and how many of those projects involve integrative learning across disciplines and between academic and field-based learning. Similarly, since most community college students work, we need more much more evidence on practices that link their projects at work to their studies in college.

22. Hart Research Associates, *Recent Trends*, 2015; AAC&U members are, at the four-year level, a representative sample of U.S. higher education, half public, half private, with strong representation from baccalaureate, masters and research institutions. Eleven percent of the responding sample came from two-year institutions so the trends reported are indicative of developments in the two-year sector as well.

23. George D. Kuh, *High-Impact Educational Practices*, (Washington, DC: AAC&U, 2008); Ashley Finley and Tia McNair, *Assessing Underserved Students' Engagement in High-Impact Practices*, (Washington, DC: AAC&U, 2012); Lynn Swaner and Jayne Brownell, "Outcomes of High-Impact Educational Practices: A Literature Review," *Diversity and Democracy* 12, Spring 2009.

24. George D. Kuh and Ken O'Donnell, *Ensuring Quality & Taking High-Impact Practices to Scale* (Washington, DC: AAC&U, 2013); NSSE 2015.

25. Hart Research Associates, *Bringing Equity and Quality Learning Together: Institutional Priorities for Tracking and Advancing Underserved Students' Success* (Washington, DC: AAC&U, 2015), http://www.aacu.org/ sites/default/files/files/LEAP/2015AACUEquityReport.pdf; Hart Research Associates, *Recent Trends in General Education Design*, 2015.

26. Hart Research Associates, *Falling Short? College Learning and Career Success* (Washington, DC: AAC&U, 2015), https://www.aacu.org/sites/default/files/files/LEAP/2015employerstudentsurvey.pdf; Hart Research Associates, *It Takes More than a Major: Employer Priorities for College Learning and Student Success* (Washington, DC: AAC&U, 2013) http://www.aacu.org/sites/default/files/files/LEAP/2013_EmployerSurvey.pdf.

# 34
## PROVOCATION

# Well-Being, Disintegration and the Rebundling of Higher Education

*Randy Bass*

THE CENTRAL TENSION OF OUR TIME

If you believe in well-being as central to the purposes of higher education, then you likely believe in a fundamentally integrative paradigm for learning. The integrative paradigm that animates the best of higher education (liberal and professional education), implicitly or explicitly assumes the interdependence of knowledge, skills, and the broader dispositions that constitute a way of being in the world, such as openness to learning, empathy, and resilience. In this paradigm, curricular and co-curricular learning is seen as part of an integrated whole to help students develop depth of learning, competence, and a broader sense of purpose. In many ways, the goal of cultivating well-being is fundamental to an integrative stance toward learning and education and, in its broadest meaning, to the principle of development that perhaps is most integrative.

For this reason, the conditions for championing well-being as core to the purposes of higher education are more challenging than ever, as this is a moment at which a counter-force paradigm for learning—the *disintegrative* or *disaggregative*—is rising and dominating. In fact, I would argue that the central tension of our time in education is between an integrative and disintegrative vision of learning. By disintegrative I refer to a whole domain of learning opportunities that has grown out of the digital revolution. This paradigm of learning—motivated by the desire to create new and effective means for making education widely available in flexible forms—focuses on discrete or granular learning experiences often honed around targeted skills and structured knowledge; these modular learning experiences often also have capacities to track and personalize individual learner pathways down to the micro-concept level. Most of the attention focused on the effect of these tools has stressed their potentially disruptive nature and the capacity to *unbundle* higher education, make it more efficient, more accessible, and more relevant for workforce preparation.

The driving idea that universities should be unbundled arises from the promise and potential of the digital revolution to create learning opportunities that are *anytime, anywhere*: personalized, mobile, narrowly focused on specific skills, and aimed at employment. As Anant Agarwal, CEO of EdX puts it, it is time to think about "unbundling" higher education in "time, function and content."[1] The applications of learning that have grown out of this context have emphasized dimensions of education that can be commodified: targeted online learning, granular or modular, driven by algorithms that deliver micro-data on student understanding, often with a diminishing role for faculty with a rising role of automation.

During the last decade, the forces of unbundling and disruption have promoted the narrative that higher education is broken, and the traditional college degree is bloated and overly-bundled. In this narrative, traditional, institutional, higher education is ill-equipped to meet the needs of a new, diverse, and expanding population of students, despite the growing evidence to the contrary, that new majority students have the greatest need for connected (if not bundled) services, especially those that connect academic advisement and student support services with academic engagement.

In the context of the discourse of disruption and unbundling, focusing instead on the tension between the integrative and the disintegrative is a useful repositioning that has important implications, all of which ultimately bear on ways to make well-being a value we can centrally design into the future forms of higher education. This tension is particularly salient because it is a threat that is external and internal in origin. A bad combination has unfolded in recent years in response to the discourse of unbundling higher education. A narrow and commodified vision of learning, layered primarily by interests outside traditional institutions, has been layered on top of what is too often a narrowly academic and siloed vision of learning inside institutions.

*We are layering technologies that are particularly good at granular implementation on top of structures that are all too atomized. This combination has many potentially negative consequences*

Essentially, we are layering technologies that are particularly good at granular implementation on top of structures that are all too atomized. This combination has many potentially negative consequences, especially as institutions of higher education respond to pressures related to declining funding and rising demands for accountability by adapting and integrating these tools. This is not to disparage the importance of these innovations. Most of these tools have the potential to improve student learning and success, but when digital tools are looked to as solutions to learning outcomes and cost and completion challenges, they risk misuse if the underlying conceptions of learning are focused on narrow academic aims, and the structures into which they are being integrated are overly segmented.

Most narratives about the future of higher education are being written and articulated by commercial interests rooted in the educational technology industry (most with intellectual roots in the field of artificial intelligence). In these narratives, the future of learning is highly personalized but particulate and granular, targeted at specific skills and narrowly defined skill sets. To be sure, these narratives are focused on a version of human capacity and development in which education, powered by adaptive systems, tracks and responds to the knowledge, skills, and learning histories of learners themselves. There is great potential in these tools. Some of that potential has already been demonstrated and applied in some of the better practices. But this is only one version of learning, a relatively narrow one at that. This is the version of learning that has shaped narratives about the future of higher education. Making a similar critique, George Siemens noted about educational technologies, "Instead of improving teaching and learning, today's technology re-writes teaching and learning to function according to a very narrow spectrum of single, decontextualized skills."[2]

To focus on the integrative-disintegrative tension is to shift away from the sole focus on the digital as the driver of disaggregation. That is, this is not a narrative of the future that is inevitably written by digital technologies themselves. The hazard of disintegration arising out of the new digital context lays in the paradigm of learning that engages these technologies. Naturally, the disruptive, for-profit innovators operate in this disintegrative space, but so might traditional institutions with less than coherent curricula or non-integrated services that leave important disconnections between aspects of the institutions that are separately responsible for supporting students. The risk is even greater when traditional institutions adapt education technologies in search of scale, efficiency, and the reduction of instructional costs.

One way to come at that this challenge is through what I consider the *most* important design question of our moment for education: what would liberal education look like if we were inventing it at this moment in history? If we know what we know about what we value about learning, the digital ecosystem, and the challenges ahead, what would liberal education look like? Such a design question enables us to imagine what it would look like to put whole person learning and well-being at the center. For well-being to find a place at the center of higher education, for all students, digital technologies will have to play a role. Nothing intrinsic in this new digital ecosystem makes it necessarily disintegrative. Many aspects of the new digital environment could support an integrative paradigm. We are reshaping our world with them in the ways we create and sustain communities, build networks, create and share expressions, and document our lives. Higher education and liberal education both arise out of a rich tradition that values the power of connective acts of learning and meaning-making; the digital ecosystem itself is deeply structured by the power of connection to resources, knowledge, and communities. This is especially urgent for the so-called new majority of students who deserve a whole person education as much as anyone: the 98% who are not in liberal arts colleges or elite research universities, the more than 50% who are in community colleges.

In order for us to shape the future of higher education, we have to fashion a narrative that reimagines this integrative vision as something with deep roots in the liberal educa-tion tradition and as something responsive and native to the emerging digital ecosystem in which we live. Writing a future that puts well-being at the heart of higher education means finding the intrinsic synergies between the holistic roots of liberal education and the connective and relational capacities of the digital ecosystem.

Rebundling and Well-being

A framework that puts the disintegrative capacities of the new digital ecosystem in the service of an integrative vision is what I call *rebundling*. Every institution of higher education will go through some version of rebundling during the next decade or more. This process will look different for each different kind of institution (community colleges, comprehensive publics, liberal arts colleges, research-intensives, etc.), and individual institutions, as an act of strategic differentiation, will develop a particular version of rebundling.

Rebundling could involve ways both to make certain dimensions of education and earning a degree more flexible and personalized, more connected and integrative. It could allow institutions greater diversity in the kinds of credentials and pathways they offer as well as a new context for coherence and continuity. Most importantly, rebundling offers the possibility for institutions to make strategic choices, even tradeoffs, to deploy certain resources for automated support systems or customized learning in a larger context of integration. If we assume the increased unbundling of time, function, and content—both

*Figure 1.*

## REBUNDLING: TOWARD A NEW SYNTHESIS IN HIGHER EDUCATION

**Disintegrative (unbundled):**

Design of discrete or granular learning experiences

Elementary and discrete compentency-based learning

Learning decoupled from formal boundaries

Analytics that track narrow or micro learning

**Integrative (bundled, holistic, coherent):**

Curricular & co-curricular conceived as part of a whole

Knowledge, skills & dispositions

Connections & integration

Design of learning experience for whole person development

**Disintegrative in service to the integrative**

inside and outside legacy institutions—then what will hold the pieces together? By what design principles and with what models do we integrate the best of the larger ecosystem and the best of what we know about the long-developed value of higher education and liberal education?

The principles that should drive rebundling need to be rooted in well-being; in this way we can imagine shifting from the whole bundle to the whole person as the principle at the core of an integrative paradigm. What are the ways that rebundling—marshalling the disintegrative in the service of the integrative—could serve the cause of well-being? Here are a few questions we might ask ourselves among many possible:

- What are the most important driving principles for writing a narrative of the future of higher education? In what ways have we put student empowerment and agency at the center?
- Are the primary drivers for making use of digital technologies student agency beyond graduation or are they merely targeted at narrow skills to drive towards completion?
- How are we taking advantage of new learning analytics capabilities? Are they enabling typically disconnected institutions to share data on student performance across silos? Are we making the use of analytics as transparent to students as to faculty and the institution? Are we teaching students how to read and act on the data of their learning?
- Can we make use of new tools and environments to help students chart their own pathways?
- What are the larger purposes that are framing institutional decisions for implementing digital systems to track student performance and success? Are such systems parts of a larger integrative conversation?

Ultimately the goal of rebundling is to create an environment that makes it ever more possible to achieve "integration from the inside out," rethinking how nearly every learning experience can be designed in what Georgetown's Heidi Elmendorf described as, "the white space of possibility that sits at the intersection of knowledge of a domain, knowledge of the world and knowledge of the self."[3] In order to make this shift, however, we first have to recognize what the greatest threat is to the broader purposes and outcomes of higher education. As long as we reify the tension between digital upstart disrupters and traditional higher education we will miss the greatest pattern unfolding in the landscape. However, if we recognize that the greatest threat is the domination of a disintegrative paradigm, then it becomes much easier to see the potential in all innovations to serve a democratic and integrative ideal.

NOTES

1. Anant Agarwal, "Unbundled: Reimagining Higher Education," the blog, February 8, 2014, http://www.huffingtonpost.com/anant-agarwal/unbundled-reimagining-higher-education_b_4414048.html.
2. George Siemens, "Adios Ed. Tech. Hola Something Else," E-learnspace blog, September 9, 2015, http://www.elearnspace.org/blog/2015/09/09/adios-ed-tech-hola-something-else/.
3. Heidi Elmendorf, personal communication with the author.

# CONTRIBUTORS

**Alexander Astin** is the Allan M. Cartter Distinguished Professor of Higher Education Emeritus at UCLA and the author of *Are You Smart Enough? How Colleges' Obsession with Smartness Shortchanges Students* (Stylus, 2016).

**Jerzy Axer** is Dean of the Faculty of "Artes Liberales" at the University of Warsaw (Poland) and founder of the Collegium "Artes Liberales" (University of Warsaw).

**Randy Bass** is Vice Provost for Education and Professor of English at Georgetown University, where he leads the Designing the Future(s) initiative and the Red House incubator for curricular transformation. For 13 years he was the Founding Executive Director of Georgetown's Center for New Designs in Learning and Scholarship (CNDLS).

**John Bronsteen** is professor of law at Loyola University Chicago and author of *Happiness and the Law*.

**Sara E. Dahill-Brown** is an assistant professor of politics and international affairs at Wake Forest University.

**Heidi G. Elmendorf** is an associate professor in the Biology Department and the Director of Science Education Outreach at Georgetown University.

**Robert H. Frank** is a professor of economics at Cornell University and the author, most recently, of *Success and Luck: Good Fortune and the Myth of Meritocracy* (Princeton University Press, 2016).

**Henry Giroux** is the University Professor for Scholarship in the Public Interest at McMaster University in Canada.

**Todd Gitlin** is the author of 16 books, including *The Sixties: Years of Hope, Days of Rage*, and *Occupy Nation: The Roots, the Spirit*, and the *Promise of Occupy Wall Street*. He teaches Communications, Journalism, American Studies, and Contemporary Western Civilization at Columbia University.

**Stephanie A. Gordon** serves as the vice president for professional development at NASPA. Since joining the association in 2003, she has published and presented nationally on the development of student affairs and programs on student learning, persistence, and success.

**Dr. Amanda Hyberger** is the Director of the Quality Enhancement Plan and a Professor of Music at Chattanooga State Community College.

**Eranda Jayawickreme** is an assistant professor of psychology at Wake Forest University.

**Kazi Joshua** serves as the Vice President of Diversity and Inclusion at Whitman college and teaches in the "encounters" program (first year required interdisciplinary course) at Whitman.

**Corey Keyes** is the Winship Distinguished Research Professor and Professor of Sociology at Emory University.

**Julie J. Kidd** has served as President of The Endeavor Foundation, formerly Christian A. Johnson Endeavor Foundation, since 1978.

**Kevin Kruger** draws on more than 30 years of experience in higher education and currently serves as NASPA's first executive-level President. He has published and presented nationally on leadership development, using technology in student affairs, international education, change management, and trends in higher education.

**Peter Leyden** is Founder and CEO of Reinvent, a new media startup that connects top innovators in video conversations to help solve complex challenges. He is a longtime Silicon Valley innovator and entrepreneur, as well as an author and frequent speaker about how new technologies and big trends are shaping the future.

**Eric Lister**, Managing Director of Ki Associates, is a physician and organizational consultant whose work is focused on governance and leadership.

**Theodore Long** is president emeritus of Elizabethtown College in Pennsylvania and a senior consultant with the Association of Governing Boards.

**Nance Lucas** is executive director of the Center for the Advancement of Well-Being at George Mason University and Associate Professor of Leadership Studies at the School of Integrative Studies, where she served as a former dean.

**Jonathan M. Metzl** is the Director of the Center for Medicine, Health, and Society, and the Frederick B. Rentschler II Professor of Sociology and Medicine, Health, and Society, at Vanderbilt University in Nashville, Tennessee.

Elizabeth Minnich served as dean at Barnard College and at Union Graduate School, where she was also Core Professor. She is presently a Senior Scholar with the Association of American Colleges & Universities and teaches moral philosophy at Queens University.

Brian Murphy is the president of De Anza College and the co-founder of The Democracy Commitment.

Elsa M. Núñez is the President of Eastern Connecticut State University.

James O. Pawelski is Director of Education and Senior Scholar in the Positive Psychology Center at the University of Pennsylvania.

Mona Taylor Phillips, PhD., is Professor and Chair of the Department of Sociology and Anthropology at Spelman College in Atlanta, Georgia. She also coordinates Spelman's First Year Seminars (Interdisciplinary Big Questions Colloquia–IBQC), as well as the Ida B. Wells-Barnett Distinguished Speakers and Performance Series.

Sally Pingree is President of the S. Engelhard Center and co-founder of the Bringing Theory to Practice project.

Joan B. Riley is an associate professor in the human science and nursing departments and Assistant Dean for Educational Innovation at the School of Nursing & Health Studies at Georgetown University. She also serves as a senior scholar in the Center for New Designs in Learning and Scholarship (CNDLS).

Amalia Rodas is a student administrative assistant for the First-Year Experience Program and a graduate student in Public Administration at California State University, Chico.

Paul Rogers is a Senior Scholar for the Center for the Advancement of Well Being and the Associate Chair of English at George Mason University.

Carol D. Ryff is Hilldale Professor of Psychology at the University of Wisconsin-Madison where she also directs the Institute on Aging. She is Principal Investigator of MIDUS (Midlife in the U.S.), a national longitudinal study of aging. Her scientific research focuses on well-being—the factors that influence it and how it matters for health.

Carol Schneider is president emerita of the Association of American Colleges and Universities,

an organization she headed from 1998 until mid-2016. While president, she launched Liberal Education and America's Promise, or LEAP, a broad-based national and international movement to help all college students achieve the broad aims and outcomes of quality liberal learning, and to connect big-picture liberal learning with students' career and civic interests.

David Schoem is Director of the Michigan Community Scholars Program and a faculty member in the Department of Sociology at the University of Michigan. His books include *Teaching the Whole Student, College Knowledge: 101 Tips, Engaging the Whole of Service-Learning, Diversity, and Learning Communities, Intergroup Dialogue, and Multicultural Teaching.*

Laurie Schreiner is Professor and Chair of the Department of Higher Education at Azusa Pacific University in southern California.

Barry Schwartz retired in 2016 after 45 years as a professor of psychology at Swarthmore College. Among his books are *The Paradox of Choice, Practical Wisdom, and Why We Work.*

David Scobey is a Visiting Scholar at The National Forum On Higher Education For the Public Good, School of Education, University of Michigan-Ann Arbor. He previously served as Executive Dean of The New School For Public Engagement, The New School, in New York City.

Tricia Seifert is associate professor in the Adult & Higher Education program at Montana State University. She examines the relationships between organizational structures and cultures and measures of student success.

Andrew Seligsohn is president of Campus Compact, a coalition of 1100 colleges and universities pursuing the public purposes of higher education.

William M. Sullivan is senior scholar at the New American Colleges and Universities and formerly senior scholar at the Carnegie Foundation for the Advancement of Teaching.

John Silvanus Wilson, Jr. is president of Morehouse College and a member of the Board of Overseers at Harvard University.

Thia Wolf is director of the First-Year Experience Program and professor of English at California State University–Chico.

*Bringing Theory to Practice (BTtoP) is an independent project in partnership with the Association of American Colleges and Universities. It is supported by the S. Engelhard Center (whose major contributors include the Charles Engelhard Foundation and the Endeavor Foundation, in addition to other foundations and individuals).*

BTtoP encourages colleges and universities to assert their core purposes as educational institutions not only to advance learning and discovery, but also to advance both the potential and well-being of each student as a whole person and education as a public good that sustains a civic society.

BTtoP supports campus-based initiatives that demonstrate how uses of engaged forms of learning that actively involve students, both within and beyond the classroom, can contribute directly to their cognitive, emotional, and civic development. The work of the project is conducted primarily through sponsored research, conferences, grants to colleges and universities of all types, and publications—notably including *Transforming Undergraduate Education: Theory that Compels and Practices that Succeed,* edited by Donald W. Harward (2012), and the *Civic Series Monographs*, with general series editor Barry Checkoway (2013).

BTtoP provides a rare source of intellectual and practical assistance to all institutional constituencies that are seeking to make or strengthen the changes needed to realize their missions of learning and discovery, and that are working to create campus cultures for learning that recognize the necessary connections among higher learning, students well-being, and civic engagement.

Information about current grant opportunities, project publications, and forthcoming conferences is available online at **www.BTtoP.org**.